TANS, TERROR AND TROUBLES

To Ger, Patsy, Jane and Gary Power

First published in 2001 by
Mercier Press
5 French Church St Cork
E.mail: books@mercier.ie

16 Hume Street Dublin 2
Tel: (01) 661 5299; Fax: (01) 661 8583
E.mail: books@marino.ie

Trade enquiries to CMD Distribution
55A Spruce Avenue
Stillorgan Industrial Park
Blackrock County Dublin
Tel: (01) 294 2556; Fax: (01) 294 2564
E.mail: cmd@columba.ie

© T. Ryle Dwyer 2001

ISBN 1 85635 353 2

10 9 8 7 6 5 4 3 2

A CIP record for this title is available
from the British Library

Cover design by Penhouse Design
Printed in Ireland by ColourBooks,
Baldoyle Industrial Estate, Dublin 13

Tans, Terror and Troubles

Kerry's Real Fighting Story, 1913–1923

T. Ryle Dwyer

Mercier Press

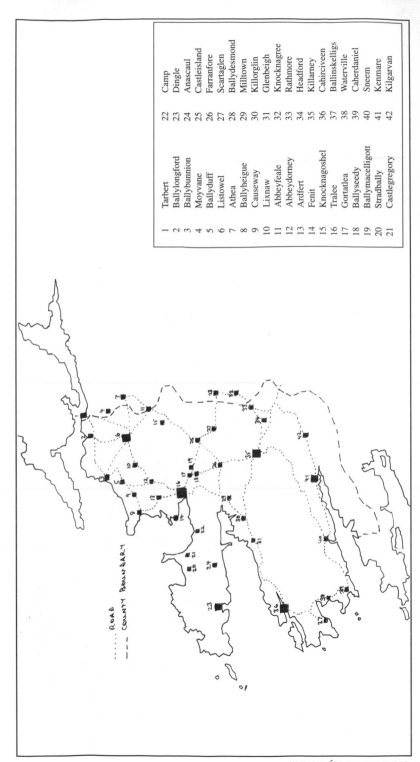

1	Tarbert	22	Camp
2	Ballylongford	23	Dingle
3	Ballybunnion	24	Anascaul
4	Moyvane	25	Castleisland
5	Ballyduff	26	Farranfore
6	Listowel	27	Scartaglen
7	Athea	28	Ballydesmond
8	Ballyheigue	29	Milltown
9	Causeway	30	Killorglin
10	Lixnaw	31	Glenbeigh
11	Abbeyfeale	32	Knocknagree
12	Abbeydorney	33	Rathmore
13	Ardfert	34	Headford
14	Fenit	35	Killarney
15	Knocknagoshel	36	Cahirciveen
16	Tralee	37	Ballinskelligs
17	Gortatlea	38	Waterville
18	Ballyseedy	39	Caherdaniel
19	Ballymacelligott	40	Sneem
20	Stradbally	41	Kenmare
21	Castlegregory	42	Kilgarvan

Map of places mentioned in the text

Ordnance Survey Ireland

CONTENTS

PREFACE   7

CHRONOLOGY   13

1 'WITH RIFLES WE CAN DEMAND'   33

2 'THE SUN IS RISING FOR IRELAND'   42

3 'THE WILDEST EXERCISE IN THE HISTORY OF EUROPE' 57

4 'A NICE WAY TO TREAT AN ENGLISH TRAVELLER'   73

5 'TREATED AS PRISONERS OF WAR'   91

6 'I DIE IN A GOOD CAUSE'   114

7 'WE HAD THE BARRACKS CAPTURED'   126

8 'KERRY IS NOW THE ONE BRIGHT SPOT'   141

9 'WHAT DID I DO?'   157

10 'AN ATTACK OF MAUSERITIS'   172

11 'TOO HOT FOR KERRY NO. 1'   185

12 'WE ARE GOING TO HAVE SPORT NOW'   208

13 'SCENES OF THE WILDEST PANIC'   228

14 'HE DROVE THE PEOPLE CRAZY'   254

15 'BEST PLACE TO SHOOT O'SULLIVAN'   266

16 'TO HELL WITH SURRENDER!'   281

17 'UP KERRY!'   298

18 'THE LAST MAN IN THE WORLD I'D SUSPECT'   323

19 'WADE THROUGH IRISH BLOOD'   340

20 'THE ORDINARY CITIZEN DID NOT COUNT'   353

21 'DIFFICULT TO SURPRISE OR SHOCK US'   366

BIBLIOGRAPHY   379

INDEX   383

PREFACE

'Kerry's entire record in the Black and Tan struggle consisted in shooting an unfortunate soldier the day of the Truce,' General Owen (later Eoin) O'Duffy told a public gathering in Bandon, County Cork, on 15 October 1933. O'Duffy had been a senior member of the IRA during the War of Independence and rose to be chief of staff of the Free State army during the ensuing Civil War, when the worst atrocities took place in Kerry.

O'Duffy must have known that his statement was absurd. Two weeks previously, his visit to Tralee had provoked a riot, during which he was hit on the head with a hammer. In a sense, he must still have been suffering from the effects of that blow when he let off steam in Bandon, because there was no substance to his remarks, as this book will clearly demonstrate.

What actually happened in Kerry has been the subject of a confusion that was undoubtedly coloured by the personalities and events of the Civil War. Many young men joined the IRA during the period following the Truce in July 1921. Having taken no part in the War of Independence, they were rather derisively known as 'Trucileers'. 'This was a pejorative term applied in particular to those who joined in parts of the country where little activity was evident during the War of Independence,' according to Risteárd Mulcahy, the son of the commander-in-chief of the Free State forces. 'Two counties stand out in particular,' Mulcahy continued. 'Kerry and Wexford caused the chief of staff a lot of frustration because of incompetent leadership and inactivity during the War of Independence. Both counties were to be the scene of some of the more vicious atrocities during the Civil War.'

There is no doubt about the viciousness of the atrocities in Kerry during the Civil War, nor that a case can be made for suggesting that Kerry was at times afflicted by a lack of proper leadership during the period as a whole. Nonetheless, it was ridiculous of Mulcahy to suggest that little or nothing happened in Kerry during the War of Independence.

The introduction of a new history curriculum in schools some years ago sparked renewed interest in local history. There are many gaps to be filled in the great jigsaw puzzle that comprises our history. This book seeks to fill a gap in providing a broad view of events in Kerry and putting them in their national context during the decade from the founding of the Irish Volunteers in November 1913 to the ending of the Civil War in May 1923.

Some of the earliest operations of the Anglo-Irish conflict took place in Kerry, or involved people from that county. The guns for the planned national uprising of 1916 were supposed to be landed in Kerry, and it was there that Roger Casement was arrested on Good Friday 1916.

Although Éamon de Valera has been frequently described as the last commandant to surrender during the Easter Rising, and the only one to survive the subsequent executions of 1916, neither of these statements is true. A Kerryman, Thomas Ashe, also survived and he was, in fact, the last commandant to surrender. He was also arguably the most successful commandant, because he was the only one to achieve his objective before surrendering, under the orders of Pádraig Pearse.

De Valera and Ashe were tried on the same day and were both sentenced to death, but the resentment caused by the earlier executions prompted the British to commute their sentences to life in prison. They were released together a little over a year later in the general amnesty of June 1917.

As president of the Supreme Council of the Irish Republican Brotherhood, which was still secretly trying to direct the national movement from behind the scenes, Ashe was quite content to leave the apparent leadership of the movement to de Valera, an academic with a reputation as a moderate. But Ashe enjoyed freedom for only a couple of months before he was arrested again in August 1917 for making a seditious speech. He went on hunger strike to protest his conditions of imprisonment and died as a result of injuries received during forced feeding. The brief oration at his graveside was delivered by Michael Collins, who was shortly to become one of the driving forces of the movement.

Collins had admired Ashe greatly and he then looked to another Kerryman, Ashe's good friend Austin Stack, who was also arrested and jailed in August 1917. While Stack was in prison, Collins engaged in revealing correspondence with him. Collins thought so highly of Stack that he visited him in Strangeways Jail in Manchester and personally supervised preparations for Stack's escape in October 1919. Stack was then appointed deputy chief of staff of the Irish Volunteers – or the Irish Republican Army, as the organisation would shortly be known – but the friendship between him and Collins soon turned into a bitter enmity that would foreshadow the Civil War.

The Soloheadbeg County Tipperary ambush in January 1919 is traditionally seen as the start of the War of Independence, but an earlier raid for arms took place in Gortatlea, County Kerry. Two Volunteers were killed in a shoot-out during that raid, which was arguably the first act of the War of Independence. A few weeks later, the Volunteers sought revenge by ambushing two of the policemen involved in the Gortatlea shoot-out.

The role that Kerry played in the subsequent struggle has been greatly underplayed. At the height of the War of Independence, Tralee was one of the most terrorised towns in all of Europe. For nine days in November 1920, Crown forces shut down the town. Shops, factories and schools were not allowed to open, and publication of the two local newspapers was suspended. Those few people who ventured out were in danger of being killed in the streets by Crown forces.

A visiting French journalist described Tralee as more terrorised than any town that he had seen in France during the First World War. What was happening in Tralee at the time made front-page news on the other side of the Atlantic in newspapers like the *New York Times* and the *Montreal Gazette* on several different days. Amid the international publicity, questions were asked in the House of Commons about the conduct of Crown forces during their siege of the town.

The following week, a visiting camera crew filmed what appeared to be an IRA ambush in Ballymacelligott, a few miles from Tralee. This was supposedly the first time that such footage had been filmed, but the camera crew later falsified the footage by embellishing it with further incidents staged in Dalkey, County Dublin. In the process, a distinctive Dalkey landmark was caught on film, with the result that what was variously called the Battle of Ballymacelligott or the Battle of Tralee was dismissed as a total fabrication. It was possibly due to this confusion that Dorothy Macardle dismissed the whole siege of Tralee in less than a sentence in her mammoth book on the period, *The Irish Republic*.

There was plenty of action in Kerry during the War of Independence; the bitterest incidents of all occurred there during the Civil War. Therein may lie the real explanation as to why the picture of Kerry during this period became so distorted: the conflict was so bitter in the county that many of those who were most deeply involved in it refused to talk about the events afterwards.

Tom McEllistrim arguably played as important a role in the War of Independence as Dan Breen or Tom Barry, but he never wrote a book about his exploits, nor was he prepared to talk about them publicly. The raid on the Gortatlea RIC barracks in April 1918, for instance, preceded the Soloheadbeg ambush by more than eight months. Even though McEllistrim sat in the Dáil for over forty years, he apparently never mentioned this period in Leinster House. It was best left to history, as far as he and his companions, like Tim Kennedy, Johnny O'Connor and Stephen Fuller, were concerned.

Dreadful deeds were committed on all sides, and the survivors were more interested in getting on with their lives than perpetuating the memories of the horrors that were committed during the Civil War – a war in which the best of friends often became the deadliest of enemies. Recalling those times inevitably brought back extremely painful memories, so the key figures in the conflict left the talking to those who had had only a peripheral involvement in it; the latter were all too often windbags and soapbox politicians.

The only attempt to chronicle what happened in Kerry during the War of Independence was *Kerry's Fighting Story*, published by the *Kerryman* in 1947. This book stitched together some published articles along with contemporary accounts that had appeared in the *Kerryman*, but the conflict was not one that lent itself to newspaper reporting. Merely reprinting the contemporary material, with little of the information that subsequently became available, meant that the book was out of date from the outset. It did not even touch on the period of the Civil War that was fought out with particular ferocity in Kerry.

Some of those who were most involved refused to talk about what had happened. They realised that it was necessary to get on with life and leave the past to history. There was, in effect, a conspiracy of silence, but the people involved were acting out of the best of motives. They were forgiving, even if they could never quite forget.

I would like to acknowledge the help of the staff of Kerry County Library, especially Michael Costello, the *Irish Examiner,* particularly Pat Moloney and Declan Ryan, the Archives of University College Dublin and the National Library of Ireland. In addition, I would like to acknowledge the help of Tadhg and Pat Kennedy, the late Tom McEllistrim Jr, Martin Moore, Donal O'Sullivan, Mike Healy, Kathleen Fitzgerald, Gordon Revington, Tommy O'Connor, Kevin Coleman, Brian Sheehy, Tommy Sweeney and Des Fitzgerald.

TRD
Tralee, 2001

CHRONOLOGY

1913

25 Nov   Irish Volunteers formed at the Rotunda, Dublin

10 Dec   Meeting to establish Irish Volunteers in Tralee

1914

18 Jan   Irish Volunteers formed in Cahirciveen

20 Mar   Curragh mutiny

5 Apr   Irish Volunteers inaugurated in Castleisland

1 May   Volunteers corps formed in Currans

16 May   Volunteers corps formed in Ballymacelligott

30 May   Volunteers corps formed in Knocknagoshel

31 May   Volunteers corps formed in Killorglin

6 Jun   Volunteers corps formed in Ventry

7 Jun   Volunteers corps formed in Scartaglin

8 Jun   Volunteers corps formed in Keel

13 Jun   Volunteers corps formed in Lixnaw

14 Jun   Parade of Volunteers in Tralee

28 Jun   Pádraig Pearse inspects Volunteers in Ardfert;
         Ballybunion Volunteers formed at Doon

5 Jul   Volunteers corps formed in Foylemore

25 Jul   Volunteers corps formed in Glenbeigh

26 Jul   Howth gun-running

29 Jul   Volunteer Oireachtas in Killarney

20 Sep   John Redmond's speech at Woodenbridge, County
         Wicklow, calling on IVF to fight on the Continent

24 Sep   Eoin MacNeill calls on IVF to reject Redmond's
         appeal

13 Oct   Tralee Volunteers vote to support MacNeill

18 Oct	National Volunteers corps formed in Tralee
19 Oct	Cahirciveen Volunteers side with MacNeill; Volunteers reorganised in Abbeydorney
21 Nov	County convention of IVF
22 Nov	IVF gather to commemorate Manchester Martyrs
28 Nov	Roger Casement assures MacNeill that he has 'convincing assurances of help'

1915

6 Feb	National Volunteers provide big send-off for John Fitzgerald
23 May	MacNeill reviews Volunteers at Killarney
1 Aug	Volunteers parade in Tralee to mark O'Donovan Rossa's funeral
22 Nov	Jack McGaley sentenced to three months in jail under the Defence of the Realm Act

1916

26 Feb	Pádraig Pearse meets Irish Volunteers in Tralee
9 Apr	The *Aud* leaves Lubeck en route to Ireland without wireless
14 Apr	Germans told not to land arms until Easter Sunday
15 Apr	Franz von Papen sends telegram to Berlin about arms
18 Apr	US Secret Service seizes message and passes it to Britain
20 Apr	The *Aud* arrives in Tralee Bay
21 Apr	Casement arrested near Banna Strand; Austin Stack arrested in Tralee; drownings at Ballykissane Pier; Dr Michael Shanahan and Father Ryan visit Casement
22 Apr	The *Aud* scuttled in Cork; Bailey arrested in Abbey dorney; MacNeill calls off rising
23 Apr	Word reaches Tralee that rising has been called off; Casement interrogated in London; IRB reorganises rising

24 Apr	Easter Rising begins in Dublin
28 Apr	The O'Rahilly of Ballylongford, M. Mulvihill of Lixnaw, P. Shortis of Ballybunion and Patrick O'Connor of Rathmore killed in Dublin
30 Apr	Thomas Ashe is last commandant to surrender
5 May	Tralee Urban District Council condemns Easter Rising
12 May	Prime Minister Herbert H. Asquith arrives in Dublin
8 May	Ashe tried by military court; sentenced to death; sentence commuted to life in prison
19 May	Nineteen Kerry prisoners moved from Tralee to Dublin
23 May	Prisoners deported to England, where they are interned
29 May	Two constables shot in Firies
6 Jul	Twenty-nine Kerry prisoners denounce prison conditions
9 Jul	MPs M. J. Flavin and T. O'Sullivan visit Kerry prisoners
20 Jul	Fifteen Kerry prisoners released from Frongoch
1 Aug	Dick Fitzgerald of Killarney and M. J. Moriarty of Dingle released from Frongoch
3 Aug	Casement executed
13 Sep	John F. O'Shea of Portmagee arrested for writing a seditious article in the *Gaelic-American*
22 Dec	Remaining Kerry internees released from Frongoch

1917

18 Jun	All Volunteer prisoners freed in general amnesty
20 Jun	Tumultuous welcome in Kerry for prisoners
11 Jul	Volunteer Daniel Scanlon killed in Ballybunion
31 Jul	Dublin Castle bans the wearing of unauthorised uniforms
8 Aug	Ashe speaks at meeting to organise new Sinn Féin in Tralee

18 Sep	Volunteer prisoners demand prisoner-of-war status
25 Sep	Ashe dies while on hunger strike
25 Oct	Stack elected honorary secretary of Sinn Féin
29 Oct	P. J. Cahill and five other Volunteers arrested in Tralee
29 Nov	Eight hunger strikers from Kerry released from Dundalk Jail under the Cat and Mouse Act
15 Dec	Serjeant A.M. Sullivan KC prosecutes six Ballybunion men for causing the July riot in which Scanlon was killed

1918

25 Feb	Volunteer show of strength in Listowel
23 Mar	Michael O'Brien shot and wounded in Ratoo
30 Mar	T. Russell of Dingle killed
13 Apr	Raid on Gortatlea barracks for arms; two Volunteers killed
17 Apr	'Monster' rally against conscription in Tralee
14 Jun	Sergeant Boyle and Constable Fallon ambushed in Tralee
5 Jul	All public gatherings banned in Ireland
27 Nov	MP Tom O'Donnell withdraws from election contest
18 Dec	RIC Sergeant Patrick Maloney shot and wounded in Anascaul

1919

21 Jan	Dáil Éireann established; Soloheadbeg ambush in Tipperary
6 Feb	Éamon de Valera escapes from Lincoln Jail
24 Jun	RIC ambushed and disarmed near Camp
17 Jul	New headstone blown up in Killovarnogue
25 Oct	Stack escapes from Strangeways Prison
2 Nov	Detective Sergeant Wharton of Killarney shot in Dublin
30 Nov	Detective Sergeant Barton of Ballymacelligott shot in Dublin

24 Dec   Constable Maurice Keogh of Limerick accidentally shot by a colleague during a fracas in Killarney between soldiers and civilians

1920

3 Jan   Constable Clarke shot in Ballylongford

9 Jan   Serjeant Sullivan attacked in Tralee

13 Feb   Volunteer John Heapley, 19, shot in Ballylongford by RIC

19 Feb   Camp RIC barracks attacked; Sergeant McDonagh and Constables Fagan and Dunphy wounded

8 Mar   Three RIC men disarmed at Ballyronan, near Ballyheigue

10 Mar   RIC Detective Sergeant George Neazer shot dead in Rathkeale

12 Mar   Ballybunion Barracks attacked

16 Mar   Courthouse caretaker C. Kelly, 40, shot dead in Caherdaniel

25 Mar   Gortatlea police hut attacked and burned; Constables Hegarty, Kelly and Shea wounded; jury acquits four men of having attacked Serjeant Sullivan

30 Mar   Constable Flaherty of Cloghane wounded in Killiney; Constable Jeremiah Donovan of Killarney wounded in Durrus, County Cork; Constables Flaherty, Lavelle and Darlington overpowered and deprived of weapons at Stradbally, near Castlegregory

31 Mar   Scartaglin RIC barracks attacked by IRA

2 Apr   RIC patrol disarmed at Causeway

3 Apr   Abandoned RIC barracks burned down in Ardfert, Ballyheigue, Ardea, Lauragh, Templenoe, Mulgrave, Headford and Beaufort; in Tralee, customs house and offices of tax collectors raided and sacked

4 Apr   Vacant RIC barracks burned down in Ballinaskelligs;

	RIC accused of breaking windows in Tralee; RIC barracks vacated at Newtownsandes (now Moyvane)
5 Apr	Vacant barracks burned at Newtownsandes
6 Apr	Vacant RIC barracks in Cordal and Scartaglin destroyed
9 Apr	Constable Daniel McCarthy, 27, of Waterville shot dead near Newport, County Tipperary
10 Apr	Father William Ferris, CC, threatened with death in Tralee
17 Apr	Constable Martin Clifford killed at Bradley's Cross, near Waterville
18 Apr	Dingle Courthouse burned down
21 Apr	Constable Patrick Foley, 25, of Anascaul kidnapped near his home
23 Apr	Constable Foley's body found with 26 bullet wounds at Deelis
25 Apr	RIC Sergeant Cornelius Crean, 48, of Anascaul killed in Ballinspittle
27 Apr	Three RIC men held up in Anascaul; Constable Macpherson wounded
30 Apr	Military supplies burned in Dingle rail yard
3 May	RIC Sergeant Francis J. McKenna, RIC, shot dead near Listowel; two colleagues wounded
4 May	RIC break windows in Tralee
6 May	Father Curtayne, CC, Ballybunion threatened with death
7 May	D. J. O'Sullivan, chairman of Tralee Urban District Council, released from Wormwood Scrubs after fourteen days on hunger strike
8 May	W. Mullins, Tralee; Mortimer O'Connor, O'Dorney; and P. O'Shea released from Wormwood Scrubs after twenty-one days on hunger strike
10 May	Dan Healy, Tralee, and Alexander O'Donnell, Castlegregory, released from Wormwood Scrubs on hunger

	strike; RIC Sgt Garvey, 47, from near Killarney, shot dead in Cork city; RIC Constable William Brick, 32, from Tralee killed by IRA in Timoleague, County Cork
13 May	Bogus Republican collection in Listowel
14 May	Four cannons taken from Ross Castle by IRA
15 May	Vacant RIC Barracks at Lixnaw burned
16 May	Five men sentenced to death in Listowel unless they return money obtained in bogus Republican collection
17 May	Vacant RIC Hut burned at Lisselton
23 May	Brandon Coast Guard station burned down
25 May	Ballyheigue Coast Guard station burned down
26 May	Attack on Black-and-Tan contingent at Glenbeigh
28 May	Liam Scully of Glencar killed in attack on Killmallock RIC Barracks
31 May	Soldier shot accidentally in Dingle Coastguard station
1 Jun	Soldier killed in Dingle shooting accident
2 Jun	IRA attack Fenit RIC barracks; Sergeant Murphy and Constable O'Regan wounded
3 Jun	G.B.F. Smyth appointed Divisional Commissioner of RIC for Munster
5 Jun	Newtownsandes Barracks burned
5 Jun	Military patrol attacked near Newtownsandes
5 Jun	Plan to burn Brosna RIC barracks foiled by military who arrested six Volunteers
9 Jun	Fenit Coastguard station attacked; ex-soldier Richard Johnson of Munster Fusiliers tarred near Tralee
11 Jun	Army petrol consignment seized in Tralee
17 Jun	Constable Patrick J. McKenna, 34, of County Kerry drowned in County Monaghan
18 Jun	Brosna barracks attacked
19 Jun	Army heading for Brosna attacked near Castleisland
19 Jun	RIC mutiny in Listowel

28 Jun	RIC Constable Rael wounded near his home in Ardfert
11 Jul	IRA attack on Rathmore barracks, killing Constable Alexander Will, 24, from Forfar, Scotland
11 Jul	IRA attack RIC barracks in Farranfore, possibly as a diversion for Rathmore attack
13 Jul	Constable Michael Lenihan, 34, of Cork and George Constable Roche, 32, of County Clare, killed in ambush while returning to Dingle from Cloghane; District Inspector Michael Fallon wounded
16 Jul	Constables Cooney and Clear wounded in Glencar ambush; train staff in Tralee refuse to take train with military to Dingle
18 Jul	RIC Divisional Commissioner G. B. F. Smyth shot dead in Cork city
20 Jul	Surprise attack from Train in Tralee
26 Jul	Two RIC constables wounded in Lixnaw
2 Aug	Cloghane RIC barracks burned
13 Aug	Two RIC wounded in IRA attack between Abbeydorney and Tralee
14 Aug	Military stores burned at railway yard in Tralee
14 Aug	Police set fire to printing works of *Kerry News*, *Kerry Weekly Reporter* and *Killarney Echo* in Russell Street, Tralee
18 Aug	Military escort disarmed near Anascaul
19 Aug	Paddy Kennedy of Anascaul killed
21 Aug	RIC Sgt Daniel Maunsell, 49, of Ballyheigue, shot dead in Inchigeela, County Cork
21 Aug	RIC Constable John O'Hanlon of Kerry, 33, killed in Kilrush
28 Aug	Raids for shotguns in Cahirciveen
1 Sept	Attack on Cashenpier Coastguard Station
11 Sep	James Murphy tarred at Golf Links in Tralee

12 Sep   Lixnaw creamery raid by RIC

13 Sep   Mail robbed from train at Gortatlea

14 Sep   RIC Constables Prior, Lavelle and Holmes wounded while returning to Causeway from Tralee

15 Sep   Mail robbed from train at Headford

15 Sep   Two RIC disarmed on a train at Morley's Bridge

17 Sep   Mail robbed from train at Caragh Bridge

17 Oct   Tralee shot up by Black and Tans

18 Oct   O'Dorney creamery burned by Black and Tans; vacated RIC barracks at Anabeg, near Lixnaw, burned out by IRA; Sinn Féin hall at Finuge burned by Black and Tans; military stores at Tralee Railway Station raided by IRA

23 Oct   Black and Tans burn Lixnaw creamery

30 Oct   Constable Timothy Horan, 40, of Kerry, killed in Castledaly, near Loughrea, County Galway

31 Oct   Terence MacSwiney's funeral; Constable William Madden, 20, from Newcastle West, killed and Constables Robert Gorbey, 23, of Newport West, County Tipperary, fatally wounded in Abbeydorney; attack on Ballyduff police station: one killed, two wounded; Constable George Morgan, 23, of County Mayo, wounded; two military police wounded in Green Street, Dingle; Constables Herbert Evans, 22, of Belfast, and Albert Caseley, 24, of Kent, killed at Hillville, near Killorglin; Constables Patrick Waters, 24, of Galway, and Ernest Bright, 34, of London, killed in Tralee; Constable Dl McCarthy shot through knee in Gas Terrace, Tralee; Sailor Bert S. Woodward shot through lung at Moyderwell, Tralee

1 Nov   Creamery and seven homes burned by Tans in Abbeydorney area; John Houlihan killed near Ballyduff; Black and Tans burn buildings in Killorglin and shoot

W. M. O'Sullivan; shots fired as people coming from Mass in Tralee; Volunteers Cantillon and Brosnan killed in Ardfert; John Conway killed in Tralee; foreign journalists visit Tralee; Constables James J. Coughlan and William Muir kidnapped in Ballylongford

2 Nov   Volunteer Tommy Wall shot dead in Tralee

4 Nov   Greenwood asked about threat to Hugh Martin in Tralee

5 Nov   Ardfert Creamery sacked by Black and Tans; M. Maguire of Ardfert killed; seven civilians reported killed in Causeway; Tralee news on front page of *Montreal Gazette* and *New York Times*

6 Nov   Black and Tans threaten Central News reporter in Tralee; T. Archer killed in Kilflynn; Constable Robert Gorbey, 23, dies in Cork of wounds received in Ballyduff; report from Tralee on front page of *Montreal Gazette*

8 Nov   Hugh Martin in House of Commons; M. Brosnan killed in Castleisland; J. Cantillon killed in Ardfert; report from Tralee on front page of *Montreal Gazette* and *New York Times*

9 Nov   Lloyd George says he has 'murder by the throat'; two Black and Tan constables killed at Ballybrack

10 Nov   Siege of Tralee lifted; Frank Hoffman killed by Black and Tans at Farmer's Bridge

11 Nov   Constable Whippen shot and wounded in Castleisland

12 Nov   Ballymacelligott Creamery sacked and press ambushed; J. Herlihy and J. McMahon of Ballymacelligott killed

13 Nov   Constable Patrick Mackessy, 35, of County Kerry, killed at Inch Cross, Glen of Aherlow, County Wicklow

17 Nov   RIC Sergeant James O'Donoghue, 46, of Cahirciveen, killed in Cork city

22 Nov	Eddie Carmody killed in Ballylongford
26 Nov	Soldier shot and wounded outside library, Castleisland
2 Dec	Uniformed men smash windows in Killarney
6 Dec	IRA ambush foiled at Beaufort Bridge
20 Dec	Bishop Coughlan of Cork excommunicates anyone who organised an ambush
24 Dec	Andrew Moynihan of Rathmore killed by Auxiliaries
25 Dec	John Leen and M. Reidy killed in Ballymacelligott
26 Dec	J. Hickey of Knocknagoshel killed
27 Dec	Constable W. Muir, 27, of Edinburgh, comitted suicide in Ballylongford; J. Hackett of Ballylongford killed

1921

1 Jan	J. Lawlor, clerical student, killed in Listowel
11 Jan	Auxiliaries round up men in Tralee
20 Jan	District Inspector Tobias O'Sullivan shot in Listowel
23 Jan	Round-up in Ballymacelligott; Constable Timothy Keane, 32, of Kerry, killed in Tipperary
26 Jan	Cadet Charles Englesden killed accidentally in Listowel
28 Jan	Divisional Commander Philip A. Holmes and Constable Thomas Moyles, 21, of Mayo killed at Toureengarriv, seven miles from Castleisland; Volunteer Bob Browne killed in Fealsbridge
31 Jan	Shops in Ballydesmond burned in reprisal
1 Feb	Cornelius Murphy, Rathmore, executed in Cork Jail
4 Feb	Bridget Walpole, 57, of Ballyea goes missing; Jerh Galvin of Listowel dies after being press-ganged to work on roads
5 Feb	Bridget Walpole found shot dead
6 Feb	Joseph Taylor of Glencar arrested by RIC and later shot

7 Feb	Sergeant and RIC constable wounded by Auxiliaries in Tralee
9 Feb	Constable Molahy wounded in Abbeydorney
10 Feb	Eleven houses burned in Abbeydorney in reprisal; horses seized around Tralee for cavalry search of Dingle peninsula
14 Feb	Round-up in Dingle peninsula begins
19 Feb	M. R. McElligott of Listowel killed
21 Feb	Young men press-ganged in Dingle to work on roads
22 Feb	RIC Constables George H. Howlett, 22, of Middlesbrough, and Wills shot dead in Ballylongford; Constable Banks fired on prematurely and ambush aborted in Ballybunion; some twenty houses burned in Ballybunion in reprisal
24 Feb	RIC boarding train ambushed at Liselton
26 Feb	Cycle party ambushed near Conor Pass
27 Feb	Joseph Taylor shot dead in custody in Glencar
1 Mar	General Strickland visits Tralee on tour of inspection; Thomas Cotter shot outside his Carraclough home as a spy; Martin Daly shot as supposed spy in Inchirumer, near Farranfore
3 Mar	Round-up of men in Tralee
5 Mar	Brigadier General Hanway Cummins killed in Clonbanin ambush; British soldier shot and wounded in Castleisland
6 Mar	Constable throws grenade after assault in Tralee
7 Mar	James Kennelly of Liselton, 65, shot dead by RIC for 'refusing to stop'
8 Mar	Causeway RIC barracks attacked. Three constables wounded. Constable Smith receives shotgun wounds to chest and arm, Constable Wallace receives shotgun wound to hand and thigh, and Constable Beverage is knocked into a fire by a bomb blast

9 Mar	RIC Head Constable of Killorglin escapes ambush outside his home
12 Mar	Cadet Walter Falkiner, 31, of Middlesex, killed in train ambush near Tubrid railway station
13 Mar	Seven-man RIC patrol ambushed in Killorglin, no injuries reported
15 Mar	Constable John Grant of Inverness, Scotland, shot dead near Abbeydorney, where he was stationed; his body was taken to the home of a Mrs Kelleher who then died of fright
17 Mar	Attack on RIC barracks in Farranfore: decoy
21 Mar	Headford ambush, biggest ambush of its kind in Ireland, Allman and Bailey killed on IRA side, heavy British military casualties, two civilians killed; Tans throw small bomb on street in Tralee, three civilians injured
22 Mar	Lispole ambush: M. Fitzgerald of Minard and Thomas Hawley of Tralee killed
23 Mar	T. M. Ashe of Lispole killed
25 Mar	Sardy O'Sullivan shot as spy by IRA near Kenmare
26 Mar	St John Parish Church raked by gunfire in Tralee; Liam 'Sonny' McCarthy of Lixnaw killed in custody by Black and Tans in Tralee
2 Apr	RIC barracks attacked in Farranfore at 12.30 pm: Constables S. Fallon of Nobber, County Meath, and a constable from Donegal injured
2 Apr	RIC barracks attacked in Castleisland at 11.30 pm
6 Apr	John 'Boxer' O'Mahony killed as a spy by IRA, Tralee
7 Apr	Kilmorna ambush, near Listowel; Volunteer Galvin killed
9 Apr	Daniel O'Driscoll shot dead by Auxiliaries at Liscahane, near Ardfert; John O'Sullivan wounded
11 Apr	Newtownsandes incident

14 Apr	Sir Arthur Vicars killed by IRA at Kilmorna
15 Apr	Major J. A. Mackinnon killed in Tralee ambush; military order that no hearings be held on criminal damage alleged against Crown forces
15 Apr	Twelve houses burned by Auxiliaries in Ballymacelligott in reprisal
15 Apr	John Reidy shot dead in Ballymacelligott
19 Apr	Tralee sacked by Crown forces
19 Apr	Head constable of Castleisland ambushed on train at Gortatlea, but uninjured
21 Apr	Denny O'Loughlin, 48, shot by IRA in Tralee; Patrick Bell, 25, cattle dealer from Lusk, fatally wounded by Black and Tans in Tralee
25 Apr	Police patrol ambushed in Ardfert; no casualties
26 Apr	Military ambushed in Glenbeigh; three wounded
27 Apr	Four Listowel businesses destroyed in reprisal for killing of A. Vicars
27 Apr	Military announce that reprisals will be carried out against selected individuals in future
28 Apr	Michael Sullivan kidnapped by IRA in Knocknagree
30 Apr	Patrick Molloy shot dead near Headford
1 May	Denis Touhy, ex-RIC, killed after being arrested by Crown forces in Kenmare
4 May	Old Tom O'Sullivan shot as spy by IRA and body used to lure RIC and Black and Tans into trap at Bog Road, Rathmore; eight constables killed: Sergeant Thomas McCormack, 35, of County Roscommon; and Constables Walter Browne, 29, of Middlesex; William E. Clapp, 21, of Hampshire; Robert Dyne, 21 of Sussex; Alfred Hillyer, 19, of London; and James Phelan, 33, of County Limerick
6 May	Troops arrive by train to burn four houses in reprisal in Kenmare

8 May   Head Constable William K. Storey, 47, killed in Castleisland and Sergeant Butler fatally wounded

8 May   Four constables ambushed in Farranfore; Constable Stockton wounded in shoulder

9 May   Three farmhouses – homes of Humphrey Murphy of Currow, John Walsh of Dromore, and Cornelius Daly of Knockanes – burned in reprisal and John Shanahan shot by Black and Tans as he tried to flee from Daly's house

12 May   IRA Volunteers Patrick Dalton, Jeremiah Lyons and Patrick Walsh killed at Knockanure, near Listowel

14 May   Head Constable Francis Benson shot dead in Tralee; RIC patrol ambushed in Cahirciveen, one constable wounded

14 May   Rathmore Barracks attacked

15 May   Sergeant in Royal Fusiliers shot and wounded in Kenmare; all men in Cahirciveen rounded up; Constable Thomas Gallivan of Guhard, Ballylongford, reported missing in Nenagh, County Tipperary; Constable John Kearney, 35, of Kerry, killed in Ballyturin House, County Galway

16 May   RIC party ambushed and Constable Kilgannon seriously wounded in Cahirciveen; young Bridie Connell seriously wounded in crossfire

17 May   District Inspector Frank Lancaster, 31, of Surrey, wounded in Ballymalis; Constable Charles F. Mead, 36, of Middlesex, shot at Ballyseedy and buried in Ballyfinane, where his body was found on 29 September 1926; four businesses destroyed in Tralee in reprisal

19 May   T. O'Sullivan of Rathmore killed

23 May   Constable Michael Dennehy, 27, of Cahirciveen goes missing in Frenchpark, County Roscommon; large reinforcement of Auxiliaries and British soldiers arrive

in Cahirciveen and commandeer Carnegie Hall and other premises; four houses burned in reprisal; homes of Bartholomew Sheehan, Jeremiah O'Connell, Joseph Brennan, Jeremiah O'Riardan demolished by bombs

25 May Question asked in House of Commons about fate of Denis Touhy, who vanished while in military custody at the start of the month

26 May John Sheehan shot dead four miles from Listowel; J. Shanahan of Coilbwee killed

27 May Ballyheigue Castle burned by IRA

30 May W. O'Brien of Rathmore killed

1 Jun Five RIC killed in ambush near Castlemaine: District Inspector Michael F. McCaughey, 29, of County Down; Sergeant James Colleary, 45, of County Sligo; and Constables Joseph Cooney, 25, of County Roscommon, John S. McCormack, 20, of County Leitrim, and John Quirk, 33, of County Cork; Volunteer Jerry Myles of Tralee seriously wounded

3 June IRA train ambush fails near Castleisland; John 'Cousy' Fitzgerald kidnapped in Tralee

5 June Fitzgerald shot as a spy by IRA at Ballybeggan, Tralee

9 June Train ambushed near Ballybrac; one soldier killed

14 Jun District Inspector Scully of Castleisland and three colleagues injured by a road mine at Ballydwyer; two Royal Marines injured in an ambush near Kenmare; James Keane, retired RIC, shot as a spy near Listowel

22 Jun Police convoy ambushed near Farranfore

26 Jun P. McCarthy killed in Killarney

10 Jul Eve-of-truce shootout in Castleisland; nine killed, including T. Fleming of Castleisland; J. Flynn of Ballymacelligott and R. Shanahan of Castleisand; two Black and Tans shot and wounded in Tarbert

11 Jul Two Royal Fusiliers shot in Killarney

14–21 Jul	President de Valera in London for talks with Lloyd George
11 Oct	Anglo-Irish Conference begins in London
13 Nov	Constables Sydney House, 20, of England, and Constable Cruttenden injured in Brosna
6 Dec	Anglo-Irish Treaty signed in London
12 Dec	Sergeant John Maher, 24, of County Carlow, killed and Constable Gallagher wounded in Ballybunion
14 Dec	Treaty debate begins in Dáil
19 Dec	Austin Stack seconds de Valera opposition to Treaty
23 Dec	Dáil debate adjourns for Christmas
26 Dec	IRA reviewed by Stack in Tralee

1922

3 Jan	Dáil debate resumes
7 Jan	Dáil approves Treaty by 64 votes to 57
10 Jan	De Valera defeated in presidential election
11 Jan	Arthur Griffith elected president
20 Jan	Percy Henefin fatally wounded
2 Feb	Constable Charles F. Ednie, 25, of Edinburgh, killed in Killarney
15 Mar	De Valera launches new party, Cumann na Poblachta
19 Mar	De Valera holds rally in Killarney
20 Mar	De Valera holds rally in Tralee
26 Mar	Anti-Treaty IRA set up own executive in Dublin
7 Apr	Unfounded reports of two RIC men killed and others wounded in Tralee
13 Apr	Republicans seize Four Courts
14 Apr	De Valera says 'majority have no right to do wrong'
22 Apr	Collins holds rally in Killarney
23 Apr	Collins holds rally in Tralee
20 May	Collins and de Valera agree election pact

14 Jun	Collins appears to repudiate election pact
16 Jun	Pro-Treaty candidates win overwhelming majority of Dáil seats
18 Jun	Republicans split over war plans
26 Jun	General J. J. O'Connell kidnapped
28 Jun	National Army attacks Four Courts; anti-Treaty IRA reunited under Liam Lynch's leadership
30 Jun	IRA in Four Courts surrender
2 Jul	IRA Volunteer Thomas Flynn killed near Tralee
5 Jul	Republican forces surrender in Dublin
31 Jul	Members of the Dublin Guard embark for Kerry
2 Aug	Army lands at Fenit and seizes Tralee; Volunteer John O'Sullivan, 25, killed at Kinfenora, near Fenit
3 Aug	Army lands at Tarbert and seizes Ballylongford and Listowel
7 Aug	Collins attends Mass for eleven soldiers killed in Kerry
11 Aug	Army lands at Kenmare
12 Aug	Collins learns in Tralee of President Griffith's death
22 Aug	Collins killed at Béal na mBláth
27 Aug	Prisoner Sean Moriarty shot and left for dead by troops in Tralee
9 Sep	IRA retake Kenmare; Tom Scarteen O'Connor killed
24 Sep	IRA attack on Killorglin
25 Sep	Body of Jack Galvin found, the day after his arrest
27 Sep	Volunteer Herbert Murphy killed while in custody
10 Oct	Catholic hierarchy denounces Republican resistance
15 Oct	Emergency Powers granted to Free State Army by Dáil; military courts set up; unauthorised possession of firearms becomes a capital offence
25 Oct	Republicans set up Emergency Government
30 Oct	John Lawlor's body found in Ballyheigue
13 Nov	Constable Albert Cruttenden of Kent injured in Brosna

17 Nov	Four IRA men executed in Dublin
24 Nov	Erskine Childers executed for possession of a gun
30 Nov	Three more IRA men executed in Dublin
1 Dec	IRA announces that members of Dáil liable to be shot
6 Dec	Irish Free State formally established
7 Dec	Sean Hales and Pádraic Ó Máille shot in Dublin
8 Dec	Four leading IRA men executed in Dublin in reprisal; William Harrington (IRA) killed in Tralee
10 Dec	Sean McGarry's young son dies in IRA fire
19 Dec	Four IRA men sentenced to death in Tralee; seven IRA men executed in Dublin

1923

16 Jan	Volunteer Eugene Fitzgerald killed in custody in Ardfert
20 Jan	Four men executed in Tralee: James Daly, John Clifford, Michael Brosnan and James Hanlon
23 Jan	Volunteer Daniel Daly, engine driver, killed in Tralee
20 Feb	Stephen Fuller arrested in a dugout near Lixnaw
6 Mar	Five Free State soldiers killed by trap mine in Knocknagoshel
7 Mar	Eight IRA prisoners massacred at Ballyseedy: John Daly, Patrick Buckley, Patrick Hartnett, James Walsh, George O'Shea, T. Twomey, T. O'Connor and Michael O'Connell
7 Mar	Four IRA prisoners massacred at Countess Bridge, Killarney: Jeremiah O'Donoghue, Daniel O'Donoghue, Stephen Buckley and Tim Murphy
8 Mar	Volunteer James Taylor killed at Ballyseedy
11 Mar	Captain Frank O'Grady (IRA) killed after being taken prisoner in Killarney
12 Mar	Five IRA prisoners shot in legs and then blown up near Cahirciveen

12 Mar	Jeremiah Casey of Beaufort killed while in custody
14 Mar	Three IRA men from Kerry executed in Drombee, County Donegal: Charlie Daly of Tralee and Tim O'Sullivan and Daniel Enright, both of Listowel
15 Mar	John Kevins (IRA) killed in Beaufort
21 Mar	Army ordered to bury prisoners killed while in custody
22 Mar	James Walsh of Currow arrested
24 Mar	De Valera proposes that IRA stops fighting
27 Mar	Body of James Walsh of Currow found
29 Mar	Body of Jack Fleming of Tralee found, after his arrest the previous day
6 Apr	Free State soldiers attack IRA billeted in Derry na Feena; George Nagle killed
14 Apr	Austin Stack captured
18 Apr	Timothy 'Aero' Lyons killed by Free State soldiers
24 Apr	Daniel Murphy killed while in custody by Free State soldiers
25 Apr	Three IRA executed in Tralee: Edward Greaney, Reginald Hathaway and James McInerney
27 Apr	IRA ceasefire comes into effect at noon
2 May	Two men executed in Ennis
24 May	IRA ordered to dump arms
29 May	Volunteer Jeremiah O'Leary killed in custody in Castleisland

1

'WITH RIFLES WE CAN DEMAND'

As early as 1912 the unionists in the north-east had established the Ulster Volunteer Force and begun importing arms in order to resist the introduction of Home Rule in Ireland. It was not until late the following year – on 25 November 1913 – that Irish nationalists responded by establishing the Irish Volunteers at the Rotunda, Dublin.

The first company of the Irish Volunteers to be established in Kerry was set up in Killarney in a building at the back of Upper High Street, where a local group met frequently to promote the revival of the Irish language. The tutor was Pádraig Ó Siochfhradha, who went under the pseudonym 'An Seabhac'. At the end of a Gaelic League class, a military drill was held and section commanders appointed. They were An Seabhac, Michael Spillane, Michael John Sullivan, Seán O'Casey, Pat Horgan and Tadhg Horgan. Jim Counihan, a post office official, was appointed secretary, and William D. F. O'Sullivan treasurer.

After each parade, the Volunteers sent out organisers to the smaller communities nearby, in Ballyhar, Fossa, Listry, Beaufort, Glenflesk, Firies and other parts of east Kerry. These organisers – people like T. Lyne, C. Fleming, J. Mangan, P. Courtney, J. Hill and J. O'Shea – were called 'missionaries', which reflected the kind of religious fervour they brought to their task.

Matthew McMahon, a young law clerk from Tralee, had witnessed the inaugural parade of the Irish Volunteers while in Dublin with some friends. Afterwards he spoke to the organisers, and obtained some Volunteer membership cards, which he showed to Tom Slattery, an elected member of Tralee Urban District Council. McMahon and Slattery gathered a group of Tralee men in the Irish Club at 2 High Street to discuss the establishment of the Irish Volunteers. The group – which included the club chairman and local curate, Father Charlie Brennan, as well as Austin Stack, a law clerk and prominent member of the Irish Republican Brotherhood – decided to call a public meeting at the County Hall, Tralee, on 10 December 1913.

Slattery presided at the subsequent meeting, which attracted an enthusiastic attendance. A committee was set up representing all of the local parties, clubs and societies. Diarmuid Crean, secretary of the County Board of the Gaelic Athletic Association, was delegated to contact Volunteer Headquarters in Dublin. Crean proposed Slattery to take charge of the whole thing, but Slattery insisted on 'a younger man' being given this job.

The Volunteers were organised on the same basis as the GAA. The delegates selected by each club to the annual county convention of the GAA usually doubled up as the representative of the local Volunteer company.

Austin Stack – or Augustine Mary Moore Stack, to give him his full name – quickly came to the fore among the Irish Volunteers in Tralee. He was the first secretary of the John Mitchel's Football Club, and he was secretary of the Kerry County Board of the GAA from 1904 to 1908. At the time, he played on the club team that won eight consecutive county championships, and he captained the Kerry team that won the all-Ireland football final of 1904. In 1908 he was sworn into the Irish Republican Brotherhood by Cathal Brugha and he quickly became the hub of the movement in Kerry.

As one of eight children, Stack had seen some difficult times. There was never much money at home, as his father, Moore

Stack, was overly fond of the drink. Austin's biographer, Father J. Anthony Gaughan, noted that when Moore Stack was jailed for his Fenian activities in late 1866, he sang like the proverbial canary. He provided the authorities with details of the Fenian movement and requested somebody to help jog his memory so that he could give further details. Although he was distrusted by his colleagues, who suspected him of betraying information even before he began to talk, he emerged after his jail term as a kind of hero in extreme nationalist circles. Austin Stack was therefore thought of as the son of a Fenian patriot.

Diarmuid Crean corresponded with 'The O'Rahilly', a native of Ballylongford and one of the leaders of the movement in Dublin. A follow-up meeting in Tralee, presided over by local newspaper proprietor Maurice P. Ryle, decided to divide the town into four companies. Company A covered the people from areas that came into town via Boherbee, Company B covered those who used Strand Street, and Company C covered the centre of town, while those who used Rock Street were assigned to Company D.

An executive was appointed and meetings were held in the Hibernian Hall, then the headquarters of the Tralee John Mitchel's football club. Father Brennan and Diarmuid Crean became trustees and the Munster and Leinster Bank was made treasurers of the organisation. Parades took place regularly to the Sports Field (now the Austin Stack Park). During bad weather, the Picturedrome was used for close-order drill and lectures. The Volunteers were drilled and instructed by Edward Leen and John Purtill, both ex-soldiers of the British army. The skating rink at the Basin became the local headquarters for the Volunteers, who spread rapidly throughout the county.

A company was established in Listowel in early January 1914 at a meeting convened by Edward J. Gleeson at the old technical school in Market Street. On the following Sunday, the newly formed company, led by Gleeson and Jack McKenna, marched from the courthouse to Finuge and home by Market Street.

Over 300 men from the Cahirciveen district assembled in Daniel Golden's Market Hall for the formation of the local branch of the Irish Volunteers on the night of 18 January 1914. Ernest Blythe and Desmond Fitzgerald, who was living in Cuan, Ventry, organised branches of the Volunteer movement in west Kerry, and Tralee sent delegates to Dingle to help. A company of Volunteers was set up in Rathmore the following month. Reverend Canon Hayes, PP, and David O'Sullivan were active in the formation of a corps of about 120 men in Ballylongford. John Moran was the first chairman of this group, and Roger Mulvihill was later appointed honorary secretary.

The number of Volunteers swelled following the infamous Curragh Mutiny of 20 March 1914, when officers based at the Curragh indicated that their unionist sympathies were so strong that they would not resist the efforts of the Ulster Volunteers to block Home Rule. All of nationalist Ireland seemed to rally behind the Irish Volunteers. John Redmond, the leader of the Irish Parliamentary Party, gave his enthusiastic support to the organisation, on being allowed to nominate a majority of the committee. 'No man worth the name of Irishman should remain outside the ranks of the Volunteers,' declared Tom O'Donnell, the Member of Parliament for West Kerry.

On 5 April 1914 the Irish Volunteers were inaugurated in Castleisland, following a public meeting which was addressed from the balcony of the Crown Hotel. Amongst those on the platform were M. P. McElligott, W. H. O'Connor, T. T. O'Connor, John Geaney and eighty-two-year-old Jeremiah Kelliher, who walked about seven miles to the meeting, which was addressed by Diarmuid Crean.

A company was also established in Ballymacelligott in April with the induction of more than fifty men into the new corps at the local Hibernian Hall. Further companies were set up the following month in Currans, Knocknagoshel, Killorglin and Brosna, where the parish priest, Canon Arthur Murphy, was elected president of the local corps. The Dingle Volunteers were first organised at a public meeting presided over by John Curran of Main Street and addressed by Desmond Fitzgerald, the father of the future Taoiseach Garret Fitzgerald. Seventy-five recruits were enrolled.

In June 1914 companies were formed in Ventry, Scartaglin, Keel, Lixnaw, Ballybunion and Waterville. A mass parade of some 2,000 Volunteers was held in Tralee on Sunday 14 June 1914. They mobilised at the Town Hall, across the road from the Dominican Church, and marched to the market, under the command of Instructor Edward Leen. The parade was headed by the Strand Street and Boherbee bands. There were large contingents from Ballymacelligott, Castleisland, Dingle, Knock-nagoshel, Brosna, Currans, Cordal, Ventry and Ardfert. Bands accompanied most of the contingents, and the march past was watched by an enthusiastic crowd lining the streets.

The parade was reviewed by Captain Talbot Crosbie of Ardfert, who addressed the men afterwards, along with the chaplain to the corps, Father Charlie Brennan. A fortnight later, on Sunday 28 June, there was a smaller parade of the Tralee and Ardfert Volunteers, who were inspected by the national organiser from Dublin, Pádraig Pearse.

That same day the new corps was established in Ballybunion. Some 150 men gathered after 11 o'clock Mass at Doon. They were drilled by J. Summers of Lixnaw, and they then paraded through Ballybunion behind the Listowel Temperance Band. J. Boland, an elected member of the County Council, presided over a meeting. The speakers included County Councillor Thomas Keane, Professor P. Breen of St Michael's College, Listowel, and William O'Sullivan of Ballybunion.

Seán MacDermott, another of the IRB leaders, visited Kerry during the summer of 1914 to address the Volunteers in Tralee. 'Nationalism as known to Tone and Emmet is almost dead in the country and a spurious substitute, as taught by the Irish Parliamentary Party, exists,' he told the gathering. 'The generation now growing old is the most decadent generation nationally since the Norman invasion, and the Irish patriotic spirit will die forever unless a blood sacrifice is made in the next few years. The part of nationality left is the result of the sacrifice of the Manchester Martyrs nearly half a century ago, and it will be necessary for some of us to offer ourselves as martyrs if nothing better can be done to preserve the Irish national spirit and hand it down unsullied to further generations.'

Eamonn O'Connor of Nelson Street (now Ashe Street) succeeded Diarmuid Crean as secretary to the Volunteers, after Crean emigrated to South Africa. Father Brennan also left Tralee, transferred to Millstreet. As he departed, the Strand Street Band led some 200 Volunteers to the railway station, where they presented him with a Mauser rifle, along with a packed bandolier and haversack. The presentation was indicative of the close ties that frequently existed at that time between the local clergy and the more strident nationalist elements. Father Brennan was succeeded by Father Joe Breen as treasurer of the Volunteers.

'Training and arming are the essentials of the movement,' local MP Tom O'Donnell declared. 'With rifles we can demand; without them we must supplicate.' The British government banned the importation of arms into Ireland following the establishment of the Irish Volunteers, even though nothing had been done to prevent the Ulster Volunteers from arming. This was resented, as it was seen as further evidence of a unionist bias on the part of the British.

The Defence of Ireland Fund had been launched to help

finance the arming of the Irish Volunteers. While Volunteers were expected to pay for their own equipment, Roger Casement and a number of Irish people in Britain raised money for Erskine Childers and Darrel Figgis to purchase 1,500 Mauser rifles and 49,000 rounds of ammunition in Hamburg. The material was then landed at Howth and Kilcool, County Wicklow.

The arms and ammunition were handed over to the Irish Volunteers at Howth on 26 July 1914, while the police and a detachment of the King's Own Scottish Borderers looked on helplessly. When a crowd at Bachelor's Walk, Dublin, taunted them later that day, the Scottish Borderers opened fire, killing four people and wounding thirty-eight others, all unarmed civilians.

News of the landing of arms provided a great morale-boost to the Volunteers. On 29 July Austin Stack led almost 500 Volunteers from Tralee district to an enthusiastic county muster in Killarney, on the occasion of the 1914 Oireachtas. It was a week of music, song, dance and parades, against the background of an industrial exhibition and the glitter of a great cultural and political resurgence. Thousands of people descended on Killarney. There were thirty bands from places as far away as Athlone, Dublin and Waterford, as well as from the neighbouring counties of Cork and Limerick.

Members of the Killarney company were the focus of much attention, as they were the only fully armed unit. The slouch-hatted Killarney boys had rifles with fixed bayonets. Here was a real eye-opener. The Kalem Film Company had recently been shooting an Irish film around Killarney. Rifles and bayonets were part of the 'wardrobe' and some of the Killarney Volunteers were members of the cast. The American producer was therefore quite content to leave the guns after the filming.

There was an important muster of Volunteers in Dingle on Sunday 6 September 1914. Some 200 men from Cahirciveen and

Valentia districts, under Commander O'Connor, crossed Dingle Bay in motor trawlers, and they were received at the quay by units from Dingle, Lispole, Ballyferriter and Dunquin. Headed by the Cahirciveen band, the combined forces paraded the streets of Dingle.

The parade halted in the Mall and gathered around Ernest Blythe while he addressed them. Hitherto, he said, many Volunteers had looked on drilling as a form of recreation, but it was in fact part of forming an army to fight for the national freedom of Ireland. They would not fight to hold Ireland for England, he said, but to win Ireland for the Irish people. Although it had been suggested that they would fight the Germans – if they came to Ireland – this would depend on the Germans' aims. If they came to subjugate the island, they would be resisted, Blythe said, but if they intended to liberate Ireland from English rule the Volunteers would flock to their standard. Blythe urged the Volunteers to continue their preparations energetically, because they might soon see the establishment of a free and independent Irish republic: it was within the bounds of possibility that Germany's fleet would acquit itself as well as her army was doing.

Seaghán Óg Mac Murchadha Caomhánach spoke to the gathering in Irish. He suggested that it was pointless if they only came to parade and applaud instead of being prepared to stand in the fighting line. He urged them to get guns. The man with a cow should sell it to buy a gun for his son, he said. The lying, venal press had been assuring people that the Germans were being beaten on land and sea, but the reality was that they were almost at the gates of Paris. England was in trouble, and he reminded the crowd of the old maxim that 'England's difficulty is Ireland's opportunity'.

But that opportunity was being wasted, because political leaders like John Redmond, John Dillon, William O'Brien and

Tom O'Donnell, the local member, were acting as recruiting agents for the British army, he said. There would be eternal shame upon Irishmen who raised a finger to assist the oppressor of their country, as well as eternal shame upon those who were not willing to shed their blood for the freedom of Ireland.

Initially Redmond had promised merely that the Volunteers would defend Ireland so that the Crown forces stationed on the island could be used elsewhere, but then in a speech at Woodenbridge, County Wicklow, on 20 September 1914, he suggested that the Volunteers should not only defend Ireland but also go 'wherever the firing line extends in defence of the right of freedom and of religion in this war.'

Shortly afterwards, Redmond was joined by Prime Minister Herbert H. Asquith at the Mansion House in Dublin, at a rally calling for recruits for the British army. The idea of allowing the Volunteers to be absorbed by this army was too much for Eoin MacNeill and the others who had set up the Volunteers in 1913. MacNeill announced on 24 September that the separatist members of the Volunteer executive rejected Redmond's suggestion, and this provoked a split. Within a month, only about 13,000 of the 180,000 Volunteers remained loyal to MacNeill and the provisional committee. The main body of men called themselves the Irish National Volunteers, while supporters of the breakaway Provisional Committee managed to retain the name 'Irish Volunteers', though they briefly called their movement Fianna Fáil.

2

—

'The Sun Is Rising for Ireland'

In Kerry the first major public reaction to Redmond's speech promising the use of the Irish Volunteers to hold Ireland for the British Empire took place during a Volunteer concert at the Carnegie Hall in Killorglin on 27 September 1914. Tom O'Donnell, the MP for West Kerry, appeared on the stage and urged the audience to stand by the Empire in her hour of need. He was interrupted by a young woman, Una MacCollum, who accused O'Donnell of betraying his country and pointed out that the aim of the Volunteers was not to hold this country for Britain but to strike for freedom at the first favourable opportunity. That opportunity was close at hand, she added. Bedlam broke out in the hall before she had finished speaking, and it was apparent that opinion was fairly evenly divided for and against the Redmondites.

O'Donnell moved quickly to establish his authority over the Killorglin Volunteers. On 2 October a meeting of the local executive unanimously passed a resolution congratulating Redmond and the Irish Parliamentary Party for having the Home Rule Bill placed on the statue-book and tendering them 'our unstinted support in the proposed reorganisation of the National Volunteers'.

O'Donnell was from Killiney, near Castlegregory, where his mother still lived, but he had been living for many years in Killorglin, where he was the driving force behind the Volunteers, who had been established in the town back in May. In the early days of the 'split' he had helped to retain a significant measure of support among the Volunteers for the Redmondites.

Some 70,000 Irishmen volunteered for service in the first year of the war, which was more than the total number who volunteered during the remaining three years of the conflict. The largest number of recruits came from Ulster, and Leinster provided more the half of the remainder. Comparatively few recruits were attracted by the enlistment drives in Munster, and this was especially true in Kerry, despite the fact that the man most associated with the recruiting drive – Lord Kitchener, the Minister for War – had been born and raised in Kerry.

Tom O'Donnell and Michael J. Flavin, the MP for North Kerry, initially canvassed enthusiastically for recruits, while Timothy M. O'Sullivan, the Member for East Kerry, never showed any real interest in recruiting. The Kerry South MP, John Pius Boland – best remembered as Ireland's first Olympic gold medallist, having won two golds in tennis at the 1896 Olympic Game in Athens – spent most of his time in London, where he was whip of the Irish Parliamentary Party. The attempts by the Redmondites to have the Volunteers fight for the British Empire were initially supported by many votes of confidence, but there were comparatively few recruits in Kerry.

Once a Provisional Government executive was established in Dublin under the leadership of Eoin MacNeill, a meeting was called for the evening of Tuesday 13 October 1914 at the Rink in Tralee so that the Volunteers could decide whether to follow MacNeill or Redmond. At the outset of the meeting, the chairman, Father Joe Breen, asked all who were not Volunteers to leave the hall. This was directly mainly at Tom O'Donnell, the MP for West Kerry (which included Tralee). He was not a member of the corps and had come to the meeting uninvited. He attempted to address the Volunteers on behalf of Redmond.

'But the men were in no mood to tolerate this nonsense or

any evasion of the point, and he was requested to leave the premises,' according to the *Kerryman*. 'He demurred, and for a few minutes things looked threatening. Only the stern sense of discipline of the corps saved him from being bodily thrown out of the hall.' A Volunteer placed a miniature Union Jack on the back of O'Donnell's coat without his knowledge, and as he moved about the hall his flag provoked considerable amusement.

After O'Donnell had left the hall, Father Breen spoke of intrigues against the Volunteers and advised them to continue their drilling and to perfect themselves in the use of their rifles, until such time as they would be called upon to fight for the cause for which their fathers had shed their blood and given their lives. They had been formed to guard the rights and liberties common to all Irishmen, and they should stick to that, he told them.

The question before the meeting, according to M. J. O'Connor, was whether they would stand by the men of Dublin who had the courage to found the Volunteers, or by those others who were seeking control of the organisation for party purposes, having sneered at and done their best to kill the movement when it was first founded. It was a question of standing for Ireland or the Empire. They had to decide whether to remain true to the true ideals of Irish nationality or, by embracing imperialism and accepting the leadership of England's recruiting sergeants, to turn their backs on the principles of those who had died for Ireland. Every man had the right to vote as he thought fit, O'Connor declared.

A large majority of those present voted for the Irish Volunteers to adopt a neutral stance in relation to the First World War. The chairman then asked those who wished to remain true to the original Provisional Committee to move to one side of the room and those who wished to support John Redmond to move to the other side.

Only about twenty men expressed their support of the Redmondites. It was assumed that most of them probably felt compelled to vote as they did to protect their jobs. The main employers in the town were unionist-owned businesses like Latchford's, McCowen's and Revington's, while the larger Catholic businesses, like Kelliher's and Slattery's, were owned by staunch supporters of Redmond.

The vast majority of the more than 300 Volunteers at the Rink on that October evening expressed support for the founders of the Irish Volunteers by moving to the side of the hall where Eamonn O'Connor and Dan Finn held aloft a green flag. Those who chose to support Redmond then withdrew from the hall, leaving behind a Union flag that had been derisively flung at them. After the meeting, the secretary, Eamonn O'Connor despatched a telegram to Eoin MacNeill which stated: 'Tralee Battalion stands firm for the old Constitution and the old Committee.'

Tralee delegates were appointed to a national convention of Irish Volunteers which was held at the Abbey Theatre, Dublin, on 25 October. A Company was represented by Matt McMahon, B Company by Joe Melinn, C Company by Eamonn O'Connor and D Company by M. J. O'Connor. Austin Stack also attended as the Kerry delegate to the General Council of Irish Volunteers. He became the mainspring of the movement in Kerry, particularly in Tralee, where he was assisted by his friend Paddy J. Cahill, who had been a teammate of his on the Kerry side that won the 1904 all-Ireland football title in Cork on 1 July 1906. Cahill had attended Tralee Christian Brothers' School before going on to secondary school at Blackrock College, County Dublin, which he attended while Éamon de Valera was a boarder at the school. After school, Cahill became secretary of St John Donovan's & Sons, but he resigned in protest over its policy of supplying British troops.

Tom O'Donnell retreated to lick his wounds following his treatment at the Volunteer meeting at Tralee. 'As far as west Kerry is concerned, the party versus MacNeill has long ago been decided,' O'Donnell wrote to his colleague John Dillon. 'There was no constituency in Ireland where the poison of the Gaelic League was more extensively sown than West Kerry,' O'Donnell went on. He noted that what happened in Tralee had 'been grossly exaggerated and misrepresented'. There were strong feelings amongst '*some* of the young men', but he complained that this had been 'carefully fostered by Father Brennan and later by Father Breen' in the absence of O'Donnell in London. The priests had convinced people that Redmond and company were really opposed to the Volunteers and had taken control of them only when the movement became popular. 'I am holding a meeting in Town Hall, Tralee, on Wednesday next and all the district round is strong with the Irish party,' O'Donnell continued.

Dillon recognised that the Irish Parliamentary Party was in trouble. 'The MacNeill crowd have poisoned the country with the story that we have entered into some secret bargain with Kitchener and the government to turn the Volunteers into soldiers, whether they are willing or not,' Dillon wrote to O'Donnell on 18 October.

The forthcoming meeting, to which O'Donnell had referred in his letter, was held on 21 October 1914. It was a well-organised response to the Sinn Féin elements. Volunteers under the command of M. Walsh gathered at the Dingle Railway Station and O'Donnell had some seventy-five rifles distributed to them. They marched through the town to the County Hall, where the reviewing platform was dominated by local businessmen who controlled the Urban District Council. Two members of Parliament, Tom O'Donnell and Michael J. Flavin, were present, along with Councillors Jeremiah M. Slattery, Tom Dennehy, James Bailey and J. O'Rourke, as well as other prominent businessmen, like Maurice Kelliher, T. J. Liston, Maurice P. Ryle, F. B. Slattery and Dr. Bryan McMahon Coffey.

Jeremiah Slattery, the chairman of the council, presided at the meeting. He declared that everyone who had the commercial interests of the country at heart were present. Maurice Kelliher, chairman of the Harbour Board, proposed the resolution:

> That we, people of Tralee, desire to express our unbounded confidence in Mr Redmond's policy with regard to the Volunteers, and we hereby form a branch of the National Volunteers in Tralee who will be true to his leadership and under the control of the national committee which he has formed.

Kelliher warned that the country was dependent on the British navy for protection. 'If we had not a navy we might live on to the first of March, but we would be in queer street for many months after,' he warned. The resolution – which was seconded by Maurice P. Ryle, editor of the *Kerry Sentinel* – was carried unanimously.

Tom O'Donnell complained about those who criticised Britain's role in the war. 'For those men to attack England for defending the small nations, it is most contemptible and cowardly,' he reportedly said. 'What did those men expect? Was it to tear down the British Empire and establish an Irish Republic? Was that what they wanted? Then he would say they should be sent to Killarney.' By this he meant the psychiatric hospital in Killarney.

Maurice Ryle provided enthusiastic press support for the Irish Parliamentary Party and the National Volunteers in the *Kerry Sentinel*, while the *Kerryman* supported Sinn Féin and the Irish Volunteers. Ryle courageously continued his support of the nationalist line, but he was ploughing a lonely furrow, as the *Sentinel* folded, along with the two other papers that he started: the *Kerry Advocate* and the *Kerry People*. One of his granddaughters was the international singing star Dusty Springfield. Although some 550 men initially joined the National Volunteers in Tralee, that number had dwindled to 150 by 25 November 1915.

The Volunteers in Cahirciveen met in the Carnegie Hall on 19 October 1914 to decide whether to follow Eoin MacNeill or affiliate with the Redmondites. Captain Michael J. Healy presided, and the speakers included Joseph Brennan, William Drummy, Denis J. O'Connell, Edward Moriarty, John Reidy and James J. O'Shea. O'Shea proposed that the Corps remain faithful to the original committee; this was carried by thirty-seven votes to twenty-seven.

The minority refused to accept the decision. They held a separate meeting the following Sunday night in the same hall. Eugene J. Ring protested against the split, but the gathering was not interested in his views. The National Volunteers were established with sixty-three inaugural members. Even though the Volunteers in Cahirciveen had split, they remained on cordial terms and frequently marched together afterwards.

While the vast majority of Volunteers around the country voted to support Redmondites, most of those in Kerry went the other way. About 80 per cent of the volunteers in Dingle remained loyal to MacNeill, while Ballyferriter and Bally-macelligott were unanimous in their support for him, and Cordal voted by sixty-eight to two in his favor. In Listowel, following a visit by Ernest Blythe, the Volunteers voted by 139 to 7 to accept the leadership of Eoin MacNeill.

On Sunday 8 November 1914, almost 1,000 Volunteers converged on Castleisland, where W. H. O'Connor was appointed chairman and D. J. Griffin, secretary. Those in attendance included Tom Slattery and Austin Stack from Tralee, and Desmond Fitzgerald from the Provisional Committee in Dublin.

Eighty-two men enrolled when the Volunteers reformed in Abbeydorney on 21 November 1914. Austin Stack was present here, and again at Brosna, where he and Dan O'Mahony of Castleisland assisted as D. Guiney exhorted the fifty young men of Brosna to remain faithful to the Irish Volunteers.

On 3 February 1915, at a special meeting of the National Volunteers, a presentation was made to John Fitzgerald to mark the fact that he was the twentieth member of the National Volunteers 'to go to the front'. That only twenty had gone by then in what had been the most intensive period of recruitment so far was an indication of just how marginalised the National Volunteers had become. Tom O'Donnell turned out at the railway station with the National Volunteers in full uniform, along with a detachment of the RIC under Head Constable Kearney, to see Fitzgerald off.

O'Donnell was by this time the only Member of Parliament actively recruiting for the British army in Kerry. While his activities were lauded in the unionist *Kerry Evening Post* and in Maurice Ryle's newspaper, they were generally resented by the public, especially when Sinn Féin began to highlight the fact that he was recruiting others to fight but was not prepared to go himself. The businessmen on the platforms with him were usually too old to serve, but O'Donnell was a relatively young man. In fact, he was ten years younger than Willie Redmond and Stephen Gwynn, fellow Members of Parliament who volunteered to fight in France. Despite the taunts of critics, O'Donnell continued to speak from recruiting platforms throughout 1915, but it was a largely forlorn effort.

The two Volunteer corps in Cahirciveen got together with a combined force of about 500 men for a St Patrick's Day parade in 1915. The unarmed National Volunteers headed the parade to the West End, and the Irish Volunteers, all of whom were armed with rifles, led the procession on the return journey. They paraded together again on 25 July 1915, when they celebrated the anniversary of the Howth gun-running.

While the Volunteers drilled, the parades provided the big occasions. Hence there was no shortage of such parades, just as there was no shortage of historical events, whether recent or distant, to commemorate. The Irish Volunteers paraded regularly in honour of W. P. Allen, M. Larkin and Michael O'Brien, the famous Manchester Martyrs, who had been executed forty-eight years earlier. Over 500 Volunteers from Tralee, Ballymacelligott, Abbeydorney and Listellick marched from the Rink in Tralee behind the Tralee Pipers' Band, through the town centre to the Sports Field, where they were reviewed and addressed by Pádraig Pearse, who exhorted each Volunteer to play his part in ensuring the success of the movement.

A similar parade was held in Castleisland on Sunday 21 November 1915. The procession was led by the Currans band and a party of torch-bearers. Banners with inscriptions like 'Remember the Manchester Martyrs', 'Remember '98' and 'Thou Art Not Conquered Yet, Dear Land' were carried in the parade, which marched through Castleisland, from the Volunteer Drill Hall to the graveyard about a mile away.

There was an animated spectacle on the streets of Cahirciveen on 28 November, when the massed Irish and National Volunteers of Iveragh mobilised to honour the Manchester Martyrs. Shortly afterwards, a sensation was created in town when Thomas Moore of Listowel and Jeremiah Sullivan of Cahirciveen, two young students in the Atlantic Wireless College, were expelled for participating in the commemoration. The order of expulsion was issued by the Postmaster General. Members of the Irish Volunteers also lost their jobs. Such actions did not break up the movement, as intended, but strengthened it. Although the police began to interfere with the Irish Volunteers under the Defence of the Realm Act, the work of organisation went ahead steadily.

Companies were formed in Blennerville, Ballyroe, Farmers' Bridge, Fenit and Oakpark.

By the end of 1915 it seemed that Tom O'Donnell had been virtually disowned in his native west Kerry. When he attempted to hold a recruiting meeting in Dingle on 14 December, for instance, no man from the district would join him on the platform. In the course of his speech, he complained that Ernest Blythe and Desmond Fitzgerald had been paid by the Germans to lead the people astray.

The Volunteers in Killarney went with the Redmondites but the numbers in the company quickly diminished, and on 7 May 1915 they held a meeting at the Volunteer Hall in High Street to reorganise in favour of MacNeill. Speakers who urged the company to affiliate with the Irish Volunteers included Michael Spillane, Michael J. O'Connor of Tralee, Dick Fitzgerald of Killarney and Ernest Blythe. Fitzgerald asked those in favour of affiliating with the Irish Volunteers to move to the right side of the hall. There was then a cheer as every man present went to that side.

Michael Spillane was elected captain of the company. Michael J. O'Sullivan was elected first lieutenant and Dick Fitzgerald second lieutenant, with N. F. O'Donoghue honorary treasurer and Sean C. O'Casey honorary secretary. Eleven new members were enrolled and the proceedings closed with the singing of 'A Nation Once Again'.

The Volunteers gathered under the command of Austin Stack at the old cricket field in Killarney on 23 May 1915, when they were reviewed by Eoin MacNeill. Tralee sent a detachment of 300 armed men, while others came from as far away as Ballyferriter, Cahirciveen and Listowel. 'We have no fear,' MacNeill told the gathering. 'We have no doubt that the sun is rising for Ireland.'

Sir Morgan O'Connell, the senior magistrate in Kerry, purported to be a staunch Redmondite but exhibited strong loyalist tendencies. He tried to disrupt the plans for the gathering.

'If you will have all special trains to Killarney tomorrow cancelled without previous notice,' he telegraphed the Lord Lieutenant, 'meeting will be an absolute failure.' Nothing was done to stop the trains, and O'Connell never received even an acknowledgment that his message had been received. From then on, he later said, 'Sinn Féinism spread like a fire on a mountain. Arms and ammunition found their way into the county, and as a result recruiting for the army became a farce.'

All of the other Kerry MPs shied away from recruiting meetings, but Tom O'Donnell continued to hold them, even though the response was discouraging. The local recruiting agents used some choice language about those who declined to rally to the Union Jack. According to people like RIC District Inspector Frederick Britten, Tralee was full of dodgers, shirkers and slackers, but critics were quick to note that none of the well-paid, loud-mouthed imperialists, nor their pals, were rushing to join the colours.

At a rally organised by the Tralee Trades and Labour Council at the '98 Memorial in Denny Street in December 1915, William T. Partridge told the crowd that the District Inspector should be called 'Great Britten' because of his lofty police rank. He added that it was incongruous for Britten, an Englishman, to insult the locals as shirkers while effectively shirking his own duty at the front.

Following a summer of inactivity, the desperate circumstances to which Redmond's National Volunteers were reduced in Kerry were illustrated by a circular issued by the organisation on 17 September 1915:

To Each Member of the Committee:

Dear Sir,
A meeting of the Committee of National Volunteers, at which you are requested to attend, will be held at the

Hall, Edward Street, on tonight, Friday, at 8.30 o'clock.

This committee consists of twelve members, and no more than two or three have attended the meeting summoned during the past six months, though circulars have been sent to each member and notice of meeting published in the press.

For the past seven or eight months the usual weekly contribution of two pence has not been paid by the Tralee Volunteers, as they have not attended for drill purposes, with the result that there is no fund to meet the demand for rent and expenses. Under the circumstances, the occupation of the Drill Hall for any further period cannot be expected unless something is done by the leaders and public men to reorganise the movement and enlist the support of the public.

Mr Redmond is expected to visit Kerry next month to attend the Convention and review the Volunteers, and if nothing is done in the meantime he will be disappointed at the apathy existing towards the Movement in Kerry.

Yours faithfully, Hon Secretary, Tralee Battalion

Attempts were made to persuade John Redmond to review what was left of the National Volunteers in October 1915, but he declined. His refusal was depicted by the *Kerryman* as recognition that Kerry was an area hostile to the National Volunteers.

In late 1915 the Royal Irish Constabulary made determined efforts to disrupt the Irish Volunteers. There were many arrests under the Defence of the Realm Act; one of the first men sentenced was Jack McGaley. On 22 November 1915, the Tralee Petty Sessions Court sentenced him to three months' imprisonment for the crime of wishing the damnation of the English king to a British soldier at Tralee Races. At Listowel

Petty Sessions, Edward J. Gleeson was sentenced to four months' imprisonment for making a speech in the AOH Hall in Duagh on 21 November 1915 that was considered likely to be prejudicial to recruiting and cause disaffection to the king. Ernest Blythe, who had been banned from entering Dingle since early 1915, revisited the town on 5 February 1916. He was met by the Dingle Volunteers, all of whom were armed, and was escorted by them through the streets. In his address he advised the Volunteers to train conscientiously and to be prepared for the great struggle which lay ahead.

Tom O'Donnell continued his futile recruiting efforts until early 1916. The National Volunteers made a good show in Dingle, when they paraded in uniform on St Patrick's Day, 1916. They were reviewed by Tom O'Donnell, who was accompanied on this occasion by the Marquis MacSweeney of Mashanaglass, the Inspector General of the Redmondite Volunteers.

Although the recruiting agents stressed that Home Rule had already been passed, the *Kerryman* remained sceptical:

> In those times, when we are occasionally inclined to feel fatigued by being reminded to an undue and tiresome extent that Home Rule is on the statute-book, that 'no power on earth' can remove it therefrom and that it will display traces of animation immediately the war ceases, it is good by way of variety to find that there is another side to the picture. Dull uniformity is impossibly monotonous. Hence, it is refreshing to learn from the English and Tory *Morning Post* that 'there is no such bargain' as that Irish self-government will take effect after the war. In effect it says: 'We are inclined to agree with the Bishop of Limerick that the Home Rule Bill may never come into operation.' The war, it transpires, has 'so clearly proved the advantages of unity of government' that there is 'likely

to be a change of sentiment on this question in both countries after the war.' Now for you! What has anyone to say about broken treaties and 'scraps of paper' after this? And the Irish, we discover, are fighting 'not because of any hope of Home Rule, but because they are British subjects and loyal to their king and country.' Set down this declaration, beside the dope handed the public by Redmond and Devlin and Dillon, not forgetting our own Tom O'Donnell – and meditate! There is no need, or, indeed, room for any comment.

An indication of Killarney's resistance to the recruiting efforts of the British army was apparent in a letter to the London *Times* by Sir Morgan O'Connell:

Mr Redmond has issued a further appeal to the manhood of Ireland to do its duty and fill up the reserves of our gallant Irish regiments. I fear that this appeal will fall on very deaf ears in this county of Kerry. Recruiting in this county, with a population of some 165,000, is dead. The open and avowed pro-German anti-recruiting Sinn Féin element has been allowed to spread and spread until every village in Kerry is rotten with it. In May last I warned the Lord Lieutenant that if meetings openly anti-recruiting in their objects were allowed to be held, trouble would surely follow. The reply to that reads: 'If any breach of the Defence of the Realm Regulations occurs, it will be dealt with by a competent military authority.' On February 4 a recruiting meeting was being held in Killarney. A Sinn Féin mob headed by a band marched up and down through this meeting with the usual accompaniment of booing and yelling. This riotous mob was led by one of the Justices of the Peace for Killarney.

C. Percy, JP, an honorary recruiting worker, later stated that Killarney was the first place where he found Sinn Féin operating against recruiting. He could not get a chairman to preside over the meeting there and had tried the Member of the Parliament, the chairman of the Town Commissioners and the administrator. Sir Morgan O'Connell explained that a recruiting drive would be counter-productive, because it would only galvanise the opposition, and this would kill the little existing recruitment.

Recruitment received a further setback in Killorglin in March 1916, when a batch of Belgian refugees passed through the town on their way to Glenbeigh. Amongst the Belgians were some young men who, to all appearances, were well fitted for service at the front. The editor of the *Kerryman* noted that those Belgians were drifting from the theatre of war, while the Redmondite policy was to replace them with fighting Irishmen who scarcely knew what the war was about, beyond what they had heard of the party prattle about the defence of small nations.

The Irish Volunteers were not opposed to the war on the Continent because they were afraid of a fight. They preferred to fight at home for Irish independence. Members of the IRB were quietly organising the Irish Volunteers to stage a rebellion.

The possibility of landing arms in Kenmare Bay was explored by the Killarney Volunteers but this came to nothing. Instead, Mick Spillane and a colleague went to Dublin with £200 to purchase fifty-two Martini Lee Enfield rifles, two magazine Lee Enfield rifles, 1,700 rounds of .303 ammunition, ten revolvers and 500 rounds of revolver ammunition. They purchased the arms and ammunition in a Herbert Park house owned by The O'Rahilly. The 'arsenal' was consigned to Killarney as cutlery and was delivered safely. The Killarney Volunteers were therefore ready to take part in the projected rebellion.

3

'THE WILDEST EXERCISE
IN THE HISTORY OF EUROPE'

Sir Roger Casement was an unlikely Irish nationalist. Born in Kingstown (now Dun Laoghaire), County Dublin, in 1864, he was reared a Protestant in County Antrim and went on to distinguish himself in the British consular service by exposing the inhuman exploitation of the natives by commercial interests in the Belgian Congo and the Amazon basin. He was knighted for his work in 1911, but he was so disillusioned at the way the natives were mistreated that he grew to detest colonialism. Even though officials of the British Foreign Office lauded his work, he realised that they had no real time for the natives.

Casement had come to despise the likes of Arthur J. Balfour, who had been Chief Secretary to Ireland in the time of Charles Stuart Parnell, when he had earned the sobriquet 'Bloody Balfour'. Balfour served as Prime Minister for a short time and was one of the most influential voices on foreign-policy matters. 'The cur is incapable of any honest or straightforward act of human sympathy,' Casement wrote. 'They make me sick, these paltry English statesmen with their opportunistic souls and grocers' minds.'

He retired from the consular service and in 1913 returned to Ireland, where he was a founder member of the Irish Volunteers. He also helped raise money that was used in Hamburg to buy the guns landed at Howth in July 1914. At the time of the Howth gun-running, Casement was in the United

States raising funds. He immediately made contact with John Devoy, one of the leaders of the IRB's sister organisation, Clan na nGael. Devoy was an old Fenian who had emigrated to the United States and become the proprietor and editor of the *Gaelic American* newspaper. Once the First World War began, Devoy and Casement shared the conviction that England's difficulty would be Ireland's opportunity.

Devoy made contact with the German ambassador to the United States, Count Bernstorff, and the military attaché at the embassy, Franz von Papen, to inform them that Irish nationalists intended 'to use the opportunity presented by the war to make an effort to overthrow English rule in Ireland and set up an independent government.' But they did not have adequate arms or trained officers to achieve this, and they wanted Germany to support them.

Casement went to Germany in October 1914 with the aim of recruiting an Irish brigade among Irishmen who were being held as prisoners of war. He hoped to persuade the Germans to equip his brigade and provide additional men to strike a blow at Britain. Initially he was delighted with his reception in Berlin. 'I am entirely assured of the goodwill of the government towards our country, and beg you to proclaim it far and wide,' Casement wrote to Eoin MacNeill. 'They will do all in their power to help us to win national freedom.'

Initially it was hoped to stage a rebellion in September 1915 but it gradually became apparent to Casement that the Germans would provide only a limited number of guns. They had no intention of sending an expeditionary force to fight for Irish freedom. They actually suspected that Casement might be a British agent, and they could hardly have been impressed with his efforts to raise an Irish brigade among the prisoners of war. His initial attempt to recruit among those captured at Mons was pathetic. Most of these Irishmen had been in the British army for at least ten years, and were not likely to desert their colleagues at Casement's behest. He managed to recruit only fifty-three men from among all the POWs, and many of these were poorly trained, having joined up as part of the wave of enthusiastic recruitment at the start of the war.

Casement was in very poor health. He wanted an American officer to lead the men, but the United States was gradually moving towards war with Germany and, as a result, John Devoy was unable to find any suitable American officer ready to undertake the task. He therefore appealed to Tom Clarke, the driving force behind the IRB in Dublin. Clarke asked Robert Monteith to lead the force. Monteith was a veteran of the Boer War and a founder member of the Irish Volunteers. He was also one of the organisation's initial instructors. After the Redmondite split, he had been dismissed from his job with the Ordnance Survey and he was ordered to stay out of Dublin under the Defence of the Realm Act, even though he had a wife and children in the city. He moved to Limerick, where he acted as a full-time organiser for Volunteers for some ten months. During that period he visited Tralee.

Monteith agreed to go to Germany to help with the formation of the Irish Brigade there. He packed up his family and emigrated to the United States, where, with the help of Clan na nGael, he was smuggled on board a ship to Scandinavia. He eventually met up with Casement in Munich on 24 October 1915, and he was put in charge of the Irish Brigade. Casement had been ill and Monteith was appalled by his condition.

'SRC [Sir Roger Casement] is not well,' Monteith noted in his diary on 6 November. 'I do not think he is mentally fit and I am afraid to ask him to see a doctor.' Two weeks later, he feared that Casement was suicidal. 'I am seriously afraid he contemplates self-destruction,' Monteith wrote on 24 November. By then, of course, Monteith had also found out at first hand how difficult it was to recruit among the Irishmen in the prison camps. 'A lot of them are absolutely impossible,' he wrote. Most of the Irish soldiers were hostile to those who joined the Irish Brigade.

It was in October 1915 that Pádraig Pearse first told Austin Stack that there were plans to stage a rebellion. He was in Tralee at the time to appoint Stack brigadier of the Irish Volunteers. During a subsequent visit in February 1916, Pearse told Stack, Alfred W. Cotton and Father Joe Breen that the whole thing was timed to begin on Easter Sunday. He explained that arrangements had been made with the Germans to send arms and explosives to Tralee Bay. The local volunteers were to receive and distribute the arms among volunteers from Kerry, Cork, Clare, Limerick and Galway. Cotton was assigned to formulate a plan.

Cotton had joined the IRB while still a teenager. In 1912 he was appointed an organiser by the IRB. He was active in the Gaelic League and the Freedom Club, and he helped to establish the Sligo Battalion of the Irish Volunteers and became its honorary secretary while working as a civil servant in Sligo.

In June 1914, Cotton was transferred to Kerry. While working in the labour exchange, he was appointed captain of the Tralee Volunteer Cycle Corps. He was dismissed from the civil service as a result of his Volunteer activities in early 1915. He then became the full-time Volunteer instructor and organiser for County Kerry, with the rank of vice-commandant of the Tralee Battalion and brigade adjutant.

According to Cotton's plan, the Volunteers were to arrange for a pilot to be ready and on the lookout for the arranged signals from the arms ship so as to meet her and bring her in to Fenit Pier. The plan envisaged the seizure of the post office by the Volunteers in order to control telephone and telegraphic communications.

'They would seize and hold the railway station and have the

goods train ready to proceed to Fenit,' Cotton explained. 'Members of the RIC on duty or outside their barracks would be captured. Those in the barracks would, if possible, be enticed outside and a party of Volunteers conveniently passing would rush the barracks, capture and disarm the police, and take possession of any arms and ammunition found in the barracks. If this action was impossible, or failed, Volunteers would take suitable positions covering all exits from the barracks and force the police to surrender, if necessary destroying the barracks either by fire or with explosives. Similar action would be taken to deal with the small force of British troops in Ballymullen Barracks. All roads leading from the town would be closed, to prevent any British adherents from carrying information to Cork or Limerick. Local Volunteers in each area throughout the county would, where necessary, take similar action to capture or destroy all RIC barracks, especially those in such places as Listowel, Castleisland, and Killarney. Posters announcing the proclamation of the Republic would be posted up throughout the area; Citizens' Committees and special police would be formed in the towns to prevent disorder and cooperate with the Volunteer authorities. Having thus established full control in the area, the way would be clear for the reception and distribution of the arms.'

Some of the German weapons were then to be distributed to the Kerry and Cork Volunteers and the remainder were to be sent by train towards Limerick for distribution amongst the Volunteers in the West, according to Cotton. 'In a general way, the position would be that the Cork Volunteers would move out to Macroom and link up with the Kerry Brigade, which would be in touch with the Volunteers from Clare, Limerick and Galway. They would ultimately hold positions in a line running roughly down the Shannon through Limerick and east Kerry to Macroom.'

The rebellion would begin with the proclamation of the Republic in Dublin. The Volunteers would seize strategic buildings in the city, while colleagues in the surrounding counties would move against British forces and attempt to relieve the pressure on the Dublin men. 'It was essential to preserve absolute secrecy up to the last minute,' Cotton continued. 'Only the very minimum of information considered necessary was to be given to the men selected for any special work, and these were to be carefully selected for their particular job.'

Cotton began preparing for the arms landing by holding some weekend camps in the Banna area, which was quite near Fenit. 'These camps were just weekend holiday camps attended by a few unemployed Volunteers, who would go out on Friday or Saturday morning, and members of the Cycle Corps going out from Tralee on Saturday evening or Sunday morning,' Cotton recalled. 'The time was mainly spent in bathing, playing games and generally enjoying themselves. The Volunteers carried arms but there was little display of military activity.'

The RIC were curious at first but they got used to the camps and took little notice of them. 'As these camps had ceased to interest the RIC, I intended that on Good Friday a small but effective armed force of Volunteers would be encamped there to deal with any emergency which might arise and to have men on the spot when the arms ship arrived,' Cotton explained. 'But unfortunately this intention was not carried out, for while on a visit to Belfast in March 1916, I was served with an order under the Defence of the Realm Act forbidding me to return to the counties of Cork and Kerry and confining me strictly to the city of Belfast.'

Cotton said that he planned to ignore the exclusion order but Seán MacDermott was afraid that his presence would endanger the arms landing and Cotton was told to return to Belfast and sever all connections with Kerry until the rising took place. 'I was unaware of what was happening in Kerry but I was confident that the Volunteers would be ready when the time came,' Cotton went on. 'I thought of what would have happened had a party of Volunteers been in camp close by when the ship arrived and if Casement and his comrades had found our men ready to give immediate assistance when they came ashore. However, there was no weekend camp and I remember that MacDermott did not like the idea of that camp. He seemed to think it would be dangerous. I was quite confident that it would not arouse any suspicions. I don't think he was satisfied, and orders may have been given to cancel any such arrangement.'

Cotton was later told that Seán Fitzgibbon, a staff captain of the Volunteers in Dublin, was sent to give final details about the arms landing to Commandants Con Colivet in Limerick, and Stack in Tralee. There were about 1,000 British troops in Limerick, so the Limerick Volunteers would move out to north Kerry. Men from Clare would cross the Shannon and combine with local forces to seize Listowel. These Volunteers would take the RIC barracks and disarm the police; they would also occupy the railway station. It was planned that Volunteers from Tralee would arrive with some of the arms landed at Fenit and the train would proceed with the Clare men to join the Volunteers from Limerick. After settling the details with Stack, Fitzgibbon returned to Limerick on the Wednesday night to check with Colivet and arrange some details at that end.

Casement learned from Monteith that a definite date had been set for the rebellion. The Germans had informed only Monteith that Devoy had requested the arms for the rebellion and they were ready to comply with the request. Casement's growing disillusionment with the Germans intensified with the realisation that they had not trusted him with the information that they had given to Monteith.

Devoy was informed that the Germans would send a ship to Tralee Bay with 20,000 rifles, ten machine-guns, ammunition and explosives. They wanted to send Casement with the guns, along with some fifty members of his brigade, but he rejected this, as he believed it would mean certain death for the men. 'I am in this a passive agent, powerless to act according to my judgement, and with a course of action forced upon me that I wholly deprecate,' he wrote to a friend in the German Foreign Office on 30 March 1916. 'I am being used as a tool for purposes of which I disapprove, by pressure that I am powerless to combat, since I am practically a prisoner.'

Casement persuaded the Germans to send him ahead to prepare for the landing of the arms, which were to be put ashore at Fenit Pier on some evening between 20 and 23 April 1916. The Germans asked for an 'Irish pilot boat to await the trawlers at dusk, north of the Island of Inishtooskert, at the entrance of Tralee Bay, and show two green lights close to each other at short intervals. Please wire whether the necessary arrangements in Ireland can be made secretly through Devoy. Success can only be assured by the most vigorous efforts.'

On 6 April 1916 Joseph Mary Plunkett informed Casement by telegram from Berne, Switzerland, that the rebellion would begin on Easter Sunday, and that the German arms should therefore arrive in Tralee Bay not later than dawn of Easter Saturday. He also suggested that a German submarine would be needed in Dublin Bay, and that it was imperative that German officers be provided for the Irish Volunteers.

Believing that the rebellion was doomed unless the Germans provided more help, Casement decided to try to stop it. He attempted to warn Plunkett that the Germans were sending little more than a token arms shipment to Ireland. He had been looking for ten times as many rifles as were supplied. Moreover, the Germans would supply neither officers nor submarines. His message to Plunkett was never delivered.

Casement was so desperate that he recruited a couple of Irish-Americans to go to London to tell Prime Minister Herbert

Asquith and Foreign Secretary Sir Edward Grey what was going on. Although the two Irish-Americans initially agreed to undertake the mission, they then changed their minds.

Meanwhile, the Germans went ahead with their gun-running plans. Captain Karl Spindler was selected to command the *Libau*, a 1,400-ton vessel formerly known as *Castro* which had been seized from the British. Spindler selected a crew of young, unmarried men for the dangerous mission. He relished the challenge, even though he still did not know the details of the operation. 'I reckoned myself, at that moment, the luckiest man on earth,' he explained.

He was called to Berlin, where he was given his mission. The German navy would manoeuvre off the east coast of England, in order to divert attention from the west coast of Ireland. The *Libau* sailed on 9 April, supposedly carrying a cargo of timber. The crew dressed in Norwegian uniforms and some newspapers and magazines from Norway were strewn about the ship. The men also carried letters and photographs of supposed girlfriends in Norway, and all the tinned food was of Norwegian origin.

Additional equipment aboard would enable Captain Spindler to change the nationality of the ship to German or British, if desired, but she did not carry a wireless. The ship looked like any ordinary tramp, her sides daubed with red lead. The name *Libau* was effaced at sea and the name *Aud-Norge* painted on the sides in large letters. Huge Norwegian flags were hoisted, and *Aud Bergen* was conspicuously painted on the deck.

The first real danger lay along the Norwegian coast, where the British navy was enforcing a blockade. Neutral vessels had been ordered to sail within a ten-mile limit of Scandinavia in order to facilitate examination, but Spindler decided to run well outside the limit, hoping that the British fleet would be concentrated around the coast. His calculations proved correct, and the *Aud* sailed on without incident. She passed in sight of several warships but none interfered with her.

Meanwhile, Casement had prevailed upon the German High Command to send a submarine, in which he proposed to travel with Captain Robert Monteith and Sergeant Julian Beverley, whose real name was Daniel Bailey. Bailey was a Dubliner who had served in the Royal Irish Rifles and was working as a porter at London's Paddington Station when the war broke out. As he was in the reserves at the time, he was called up and sent to France as part of the First Expeditionary Force. He was taken prisoner by the Germans in September 1914. At the time he had the rank of private but he was made a sergeant when he joined the Irish Brigade in Germany.

While the submarine was meant for Casement to get home to take part in the rebellion, some of the Germans were convinced that he wished to stop the rising. They were still prepared to go to extraordinary lengths to facilitate him in order to get rid of him, because they considered him a nuisance. 'I am now driven – I can use no other word – to embark on what I believe to be the wildest exercise in the history of Europe,' Monteith wrote. 'It is a deliberate, cold-blooded attempt to get rid of Sir Roger Casement and myself, under the pretence of helping our country.'

They set sail on *U-20* on 12 April, but it developed problems and had to return to port after two days, and they transferred to *U-19*. The trip to Ireland took a further five days and the *Aud* was already in Tralee Bay when they arrived.

Spindler and his crew made ready the steam winches and unloading tackle on 20 April. Hatches were uncovered, slings were put in position and case-openers were left to hand. If, on the other hand, the ship was attacked at sea, the British would never get the *Aud*'s cargo, because explosives and incendiaries were already placed in position to scuttle the ship.

The German naval ensign was lying handy, and the crew

changed into the uniform of their country. Captain Spindler then informed the majority of them, for the first time, of their real destination and detail. He also warned them that their uniforms might not save them from being summarily shot in the event of failure. Spindler steered into the bay, but there was no sign of any Irish pilot boat. The 200-foot masts of the British wireless station loomed up in relief on Kerry Head, guarded by guns pointing seaward. Soon they came near Inistooskert, but there was still no sign of a pilot boat.

Austin Stack was supposed to make arrangements to meet the *Aud* but he was told not to expect it until 23 April, Easter Sunday. Two or three weeks before Easter, he contacted Pat O'Shea of Castlegregory.

'I received a message from Austin to call upon him the first day I happened to be in town,' O'Shea wrote. 'I met him in the office of the late Dr O'Connell a few days after that. He told me of the rising that had been planned, and that one small vessel would shortly leave a German port, laden with arms and ammunition for the Irish Volunteers. Austin asked me to make the necessary arrangements for procuring a pilot. He stated quite definitely that the gun-runners would be off Inistooskert on the night of Easter Sunday or the morning of Easter Monday, but not before.

'As the ship was to arrive in the night, or at dawn, we were to look for a green light on her bridge,' O'Shea continued. 'The answering signal was to be two green lights on the pilot boat. It was our intention to board the vessel, accompanied by Mort O'Leary and Maurice Flynn, both of Maharees.'

Around the same time as he contacted O'Shea, Stack informed Cahill about the plans for the rebellions and he sent him to Dublin to get the green lamps. 'I got two boat lamps from Seán McDermott for use in the pilot boat that was to meet the *Aud,*' Cahill recalled. 'The lamps had green glass on the outside.

They were kept in the Volunteer Hall at the Rink and were to be taken on Sunday afternoon, or early on Monday morning, to the Maharees, Castlegregory, where the pilot resided. Two green lights close together were to be shown from the pilot boat.'

'The time of the arrival of the *Aud* was given me quite definitely by Austin; it was the night of Easter Sunday, or the morning of Easter Monday, when Fenit Pier and the Great Southern Railways were to be seized and the arms landed and distributed,' Pat O'Shea recalled. Mort O'Leary, who was to pilot the *Aud* to Fenit Pier, was informed of this task only on Holy Thursday, by Tadhg Brosnan, the captain of the Castlegregory Volunteers.

'I was to go up to him on Saturday afternoon, when he would give me all particulars,' O'Leary explained. 'That evening when I went home I saw a two-masted boat about a mile north-east of Inistooskert but, having no information and not expecting any boat until Sunday night, I took no notice of her.'

There was confusion over the arrangements because the leaders in Dublin had changed the date for the arrival of the *Aud*. Philomena Plunkett, a sister of one of the leading Volunteers, was sent to New York with the message: 'Arms must not be landed before the night of Easter Sunday, 23 April. This is vital. Smuggling impossible.'

Philomena Plunkett had arrived in New York on 14 April. Devoy immediately passed on her message to von Papen, who forwarded it to Berlin by wireless on 15 April, but the *Aud* was already on its way to Ireland and it had no radio. Hence its crew was unaware that it was not expected until Easter Sunday.

Thereafter everything seemed to go wrong. The events were a catalogue of disasters and blunders, from the Irish perspective. On Tuesday 18 April, the United States Secret Service raided the office of the German consul in New York and discovered the message from Ireland. They promptly passed it on to the British.

London and Berlin therefore knew that the Irish were expecting the arms ship on 23 April, but Spindler did not know that the date had been changed, because the *Aud* had no radio and it had set sail for Ireland six days before the vital message reached Berlin.

The Irish leaders were also unaware that the *Aud* had no radio. Long before Spindler put into Tralee Bay, Joseph Plunkett had been vainly endeavouring to make contact with the ship using a home-made apparatus at Larkfield House, Kimmage. On Holy Thursday, Con Collins arrived in Tralee from Dublin. His mission was to establish a wireless station in the home of John O'Donnell in Ballyard, Tralee. The transmitter was to be stolen in Cahirciveen the following day by a group sent from Dublin.

While the *Aud* was waiting in Tralee Bay, Casement, along with Monteith and Bailey, arrived on the submarine in the early hours of Good Friday. They went ashore at Banna beach. Their small boat had capsized near the shore; they all got wet but had no change of clothes. Of course there was nobody to meet them, because nobody knew they were coming. Their boat and the footprints in the sand were seen by John McCarthy, who went to pray at what was considered a holy well at 2 o'clock on that Good Friday morning. It was really a chance encounter, as McCarthy later testified that he had never prayed there before and did not even know the name of the well. He had gone at that early hour to ensure that other people did not see him praying. At around 4.30 am, Casement, Monteith and Bailey were seen by Mary Gorman, a servant girl, as they passed the farmhouse in which she worked. She mentioned to a farmhand, Tom Madden, who was having breakfast at the time, that she had seen them.

Casement had gone to Germany to arrange help for a rebellion, but he returned to Ireland in the hope of calling the whole thing off, because he realised the rebellion was doomed militarily. He intended to arrive before the *Aud* but the submarine in which he set out from Germany developed engine trouble and he lost valuable time getting a second submarine. While they were at sea, the situation was further complicated by a recurrence of his malaria. He was now too sick to walk the six miles to Tralee, so he went into hiding in a rath called a 'fairy fort' locally, while Monteith and Bailey went ahead to arrange transportation for him.

'When I landed in Ireland that morning,' Casement later explained, 'I was happy for the first time in over a year. Although I knew that this fate awaited me, I was, for one brief spell, happy and smiling once more. I cannot tell you what I felt. The sand hills were full of skylarks rising in the dawn – the first I had heard for years. This was the first sound I heard as I waded through the breakers, and they were rising all the time to the old rath at Currahane . . . and all around were primroses and wild violets and the singing of skylarks in the air, and I was back in Ireland again.'

Meanwhile, the *Aud* was cruising slowly between Fenit and Kerry Head, giving the agreed signals and hoping to be met, but there was no response from the shore. Through the night, the crew continued to flash their light at intervals but they got no response. At one point Spindler steered to a distance of one hundred yards from the pier. The signal was again given. Again, there was no response. Close to the headland, the *Aud* moved to the shelter of Inishtooskert and dropped anchor.

At daybreak, the lookout shouted: 'Steamer on the starboard bow – the pilot steamer!' The crew's delight was short-lived, however, for as the supposed pilot boat approached, the ensign of the British navy could be seen clearly flying on the ship's mast. Those on the *Aud* were again dressed for the part, ready to the last to bluff their way through as Norwegians. His Majesty's warship, *Shatter II*, drew alongside.

'Where are you from?' the ruddy-faced commanding officer

asked. 'Hullo! Where are you from?' he bellowed again, having received no answer from the *Aud*'s mate. Again he received no reply, and he exploded: 'God damn you, man! I asked you where are you from?'

'Good morning,' the *Aud's* mate shouted.

'Hell and damnation!' blurted the Englishman. 'I don't want your civilities, I want to know where you came from.'

Without more ado, the captain and six men boarded the tramp and, after an inspection, they were satisfied as to its Norwegian nationality. The captain accepted a good cigar from Spindler, but refused a cup of coffee. His ruddy face, however, did not lie, and he said 'yes' to a good glass of malt. And, after having said 'yes' many times, the *Shatter*'s commander becomes loquacious. It was only a couple of weeks since he had been sent from Aberdeen to intercept a German steamer bound for Tralee with a cargo of arms, he told Spindler. 'The damned Germans want to join the Irish in bringing about a revolution. Look around,' he said, 'the whole bay is bristling with guns. Nothing can get in.' And, wishing Spindler 'safe voyage', he departed, albeit very unsteady on the legs.

Captain Spindler scanned the newspapers that the Englishman had given him. He read of the arrest of prominent Sinn Féiners. An Irish pilot had also been taken into custody. To Captain Spindler, that explained everything.

Still, he did not give up hope, but waited for a sign from the shore. The men, meanwhile, were overhauling the engines. Near noon, a more modern warship than *Shatter II* was observed altering her course at a distance of about nine miles and speeding towards the *Aud*. Captain Spindler decided to make a run for it. It looked as if the arms ship was now suspect, as signals flashed in all directions around the bay. The *Shatter II* again came into view. Spindler decided to ram her and make sure that they both went down together.

To his amazement, however, the warship made way and signalled: 'Bon voyage'. The second warship continued to give chase and, after a short exchange between this warship and the officers of *Shatter II*, both British ships gave chase. But the *Aud*, which was making fifteen knots, out-distanced the chasing ships. With Spindler well out into the Atlantic, the pursuers turned for port.

4

—

'A NICE WAY TO TREAT AN ENGLISH TRAVELLER'

After Monteith and Bailey parted company with Casement at McKenna's Fort, near Banna, they set out for Tralee. They reached the town at about 7 o'clock on the morning of Good Friday. There were few people on the streets at that hour, and all the shops were still closed. Neither knew anybody in the town, nor even the name of the commander of the local Volunteers. Their only hope was to meet someone wearing the tricolour, or to find some shop displaying revolutionary emblems.

Eventually, they saw posters advertising the *Irish Volunteer* and *Workers' Republic* outside a hairdresser's salon owned by George Spicer. Spicer informed them that he owned both the newsagent's and the hairdresser's shops. Assuming that they needed a shave, he told them that his son would be down in a minute to shave them. Whilst awaiting Spicer's son, they stood at the shop counter, looking over the various papers displayed.

'You sell the right sort of papers,' Monteith remarked, taking up the *Irish Volunteer* and *Honesty*.

'Oh yes, sir,' Spicer replied, 'I sell all sorts.'

It was evident that Monteith had made him suspicious by his remark, and further attempts to open up conversation failed. Time was flying, so Monteith decided to hazard all on a chance.

'Look here, I am in a hole,' he declared, 'and have to trust you as an Irishman to help me out. I must see the commander of the local Volunteer Corps at once. Can you give me his name and address?'

Spicer seemed puzzled, and his manner showed that he did not trust Monteith. That was only to be expected, as every stranger was regarded with suspicion, especially if he asked questions. Spicer asked why they should have come to him for information. Before Monteith could answer, Spicer's daughter Hanna, who, unseen, had been listening to the conversation, came into the shop. She too was suspicious of Monteith.

'Don't give these people any information, father,' she said.

'I don't blame you for doubting me, madam, but please let me explain,' Monteith said to her. 'I have a message for the commander of the Tralee Volunteers. This message is so urgent that we had to swim to get here.'

Drawing to her attention his wet clothes, Monteith went on: 'You need not give me the commander's name or address: I merely want word conveyed to him that a man named Murray has arrived with a very urgent message – a message which must be acted upon at once.'

Hanna Spicer sent her brother to Austin Stack, who had never heard of a man named Murray connected with the revolutionary movement. He replied that he would be down in an hour. Monteith said his message was too urgent for such delay, and sent the girl back to stress the immediate nature of his business. While they were waiting for Stack, Spicer's son took Monteith and Bailey to a nearby house, where a lady served them with tea, bread, butter and eggs. It was the first food they had tasted for over twenty four hours – and their first square meal since leaving Germany.

When they had finished eating, Monteith and Bailey returned to Spicer's shop, but Austin Stack had not yet arrived. There was nothing to do but wait. Hanna Spicer invited them into her sitting room and tried to make them comfortable. She brought them two complete sets of underclothes, and a pair of trousers for Monteith. She provided Bailey with a suit of clothes, in addition to a cap, which fitted him splendidly. Someone also gave Bailey a mackintosh; the clothes appeared to make a new man of him. The two men changed and warmed themselves in front of a glowing fire.

Monteith fell asleep in his chair and George Spicer then took him upstairs and made him comfortable on a sofa. Monteith had difficulty walking, owing to an injury to his foot that he had sustained when attempting to scuttle the small boat in which they had landed at Banna. The foot had become so swollen that he could not get it into his boot. His right hand was also badly injured. While Monteith rested on the sofa, some men whom he did not know came in, but Hanna Spicer vouched for them. They chatted until Stack's arrival.

Stack was accompanied by Con Collins, who recognised Monteith at once. The others then left the room while Monteith talked to Stack and Collins. 'Monteith told me what purported to be the view of Sir Roger Casement with regard to the rising,' Stack later wrote. 'The attempt would be pure madness at the moment.' Casement was therefore anxious to 'transmit a message to headquarters to try to stop the rising.'

Stack insisted on speaking to Casement himself. A man was sent to procure a motor car in order to go to Casement's assistance. As they waited for the car, Monteith told of the nature of the munitions which the German government had sent: 20,000 rifles with bayonets and ammunition, ten machine-guns, ammunition for the Howth rifles, and a supply of explosives and incendiary bombs. He also informed them that field guns or crews were not coming, nor were the officers asked for in the despatch to Berlin, and that the arms had no escort. In his book *Casement's Last Adventure*, Monteith stated that he then asked Stack why the pilot boat had not appeared, and that Stack replied that, as far as his instructions went, the ship was not due until Sunday night. Mossy Moriarty arrived in a motor car, and

Monteith directed Bailey to go with Stack and Collins as a guide to Casement's hiding place. Hanna Spicer accompanied them in order to give the appearance of a pleasure trip. They were trying to locate Casement in order to get him safely away to Dublin. Unfortunately, Bailey did not know the area, and it was some time before they realised that Casement was hiding in Carraghane, near Banna. But by then the police were already searching the area. John McCarthy, who had first spotted the boat, returned to the scene at dawn with a neighbour, Pat O'Driscoll. There he found three revolvers, and a tin box containing some 900 rounds of ammunition. They arrived to find McCarthy's daughter playing with a revolver on the sand.

McCarthy reported the find to the police when he went to the creamery that morning. It was largely by chance that the RIC learned that people had been seen coming from the strand. When he told Tom Madden in Ardfert later that morning about finding the collapsible boat, Madden blurted out that Mary Gorman had seen three men coming from the area before dawn. His remarks was overheard by RIC Sergeant John Thomas Hearn and Constable Bernard O'Reilly of Ardfert. They had already gone to see the boat, and they now collected a loaded carbine each and returned to the area to look for the three men.

When Stack and company reached the Banna area, they were stopped and questioned by Sergeant Daniel Crowley of Bally-heigue, and Stack decided to leave. He took off in the car in the direction of Ballyheigue, with Crowley tailing them on his bicycle. A policeman on a bicycle tailing a motor car certainly added a rather farcical touch to events. But the car was not the fastest and, on the unpaved roads of the time, the sergeant was able to keep them in sight.

At 1.20 pm Constable O'Reilly spotted Casement hiding in the bushes in McKenna's Fort, overlooking the beach at Currahane. 'He had his face from me,' O'Reilly later testified.

'I went close to him, and covered him with my carbine.'

When Casement turned, the constable was obviously jumpy. 'If you move a hand or a foot, I'll shoot,' he warned.

'That's a nice way to treat an English traveller,' Casement said.

'Have a care, now.'

'I'm not armed,' Casement said.

'What are you doing here?'

'I was out fishing and got lost in the fog.'

O'Reilly blew his whistle to call Sergeant Hearn, who took up the questioning.

'Am I bound to answer you?' Casement asked.

'I can ask you any question I like,' Hearn replied, 'and, if you don't answer, I can arrest you under the Defence of the Realm Regulations. What is your name?'

'Roger Morten.'

'Where do you live?'

'The Savoy, Denham, Buckinghamshire.'

'Your occupation?'

'I am an author.'

'Give the name of some book your have written?'

'*The Life of St Brendan.*' This was a particularly nice touch, because St Brendan was believed to have founded a monastery a few miles from the scene.

'What port did you arrive at in Ireland?'

'Dublin.'

'When?'

'At eight this morning.'

'Have you a passport or any papers which will identify you?'

'No.'

If Casement had only arrived in Dublin at 8 o'clock that morning, it would have been virtually impossible for him to get to where he was, and especially to have time to get lost in the early-morning fog. If that had not been enough to arouse the sergeant's suspicion, the legs of Casement's trousers were wet and his shoes were sandy. Hearn therefore decided to take him in for questioning.

Casement was too weak to walk very far, so they got a twelve-year-old boy – Martin 'Mort' Collins, who happened to be coming along the road in a pony and trap – to take them to Ardfert. On the way, they stopped to have Mary Gorman identify Casement as one of the three men that she had seen that morning.

While Collins was at the police station in Ardfert, young Collins arrived with some torn pieces of paper. He had noticed Casement drop them behind his back before getting into the trap. The boy said nothing at the time but he went back to retrieve them afterwards. They were a code that Monteith had given to Casement.

Hearn formally charged Casement. 'In the name of His Majesty King George V,' he said, 'I arrest you on a charge of illegally bringing arms into the country, contrary to the Defence of the Realm Act.' Sometime between 3 and 4 o'clock that afternoon, Casement was taken to Tralee in a sidecar by two policeman.

Meanwhile Stack and the others had returned to Tralee. Con Collins went to visit friends, while Stack set off for a meeting at the Rink at which plans were to be finalised for Sunday. The meeting was attended by Michael Doyle, Daniel Healy, Joe Melinn, Michael J. O'Connor and Dan O'Mahony. The meeting had already begun when Cahill arrived. Most of those present still knew nothing of the plans for the rising on Sunday.

By this time, Casement had already been transferred to Tralee. Casement was ill and Head Constable John Kearney sent a sergeant to get Dr Mikey Shanahan to treat him. Casement identified himself and asked the doctor to get word to the local

Republicans. Shanahan assumed the man wished to be rescued, even though he never actually mentioned this; a rescue would have been comparatively easy to achieve, as the front door was open. The place was virtually undefended and half a dozen men with revolvers would have had no problem taking Casement, in Shanahan's opinion.

Kearney realised that he had Casement in custody. Among the things found on the prisoner was a German railway ticket that was a little over a week old. Before Shanahan left the barracks, Kearney showed him a newspaper picture of Casement; Kearney placed some paper over the beard and commented that it looked like the prisoner. Shanahan loyally dissented.

Some weeks later, in notes for his lawyer, Serjeant Alexander M. Sullivan, Casement mentioned that he had been well treated by Kearney. 'The chief constable of Tralee was very friendly to me,' he wrote. 'I said a lot of things to him during the night.' Casement was actually planning to commit suicide and he wanted somebody to know how he felt: 'I was bent on taking the poison I had, and wanted this friendly man to tell my friends.'

Although many of the Volunteers were hostile to members of the RIC as agents of the Crown, most of the policemen considered themselves Irish. Many proved invaluable to the Republican forces in the ensuing struggle. Indeed, they were to be the backbone of the intelligence organisation established by Michael Collins, and Head Constable Kearney was to be one of his agents. When Kearney showed the doctor the picture of Casement, he was not looking for information but was giving Shanahan a subtle warning that the police realised that they had captured Casement and that the Volunteers had better act quickly.

The doctor called on the prominent Volunteers, but they refused to accept that the prisoner was Casement. They said he was a Norwegian sailor. The doctor told them what he thought of them 'in very plain language'. Later they told the doctor that they did know it was Casement, but they felt their hands were tied because Pearse had insisted during his recent visit that there should be no trouble in Tralee before the arms were landed at Fenit on Sunday evening.

Cahill stated afterwards that he had wished to rescue Casement, but Stack refused, in view of Pearse's instructions. At a hastily convened meeting of the local Volunteer executive, Stack explained that a rising was planned for Sunday and nothing was supposed to happen before it began. He added, according to Cahill, that 'it was absolutely certain at this time that the police did not know Casement, who could casually be rescued on Sunday.'

Stack 'was being exceedingly naive in thinking this state of ignorance would continue until Sunday and that the prisoner would be detained in Tralee until then,' according to his biographer, Father J. Anthony Gaughan. In fact, Stack's assumption was utterly absurd in the light of the head constable's remarks to Shanahan.

After deciding not to attempt to rescue Casement, Stack made an extraordinary decision. He decided to go to the RIC barracks, because he was told that Con Collins had been arrested and wished to speak to him. Cahill warned him not to go: 'I told him he would not be allowed out if he went there. I took his revolver and about a hundred rounds of ammunition from him and he looked through his papers and said he had nothing of importance on him.'

Cahill asked if the Volunteers should try to rescue him, if he was held by the RIC.

'No,' Stack replied, but he advised Cahill to take somebody into his confidence in case he was arrested too.

Although Stack said that he had no papers of importance on him, he later wrote to his brother Nicholas that he was carrying 'a large number of letters, i.e. fully twenty or thirty letters, I imagine.' These included correspondence from James Connolly, Bulmer Hobson and Pádraig Pearse. The Hobson letter included a circular from Eoin MacNeill urging the Volunteers to resist forcefully any attempt by the Crown authorities to suppress or disarm the Irish Volunteers. One must ask why Stack went to the barracks and why was he was carrying such letters. With things obviously going badly wrong, did he want to be arrested? Once he entered the barracks, he *was* arrested, and he did not get out again for over a year.

'The leadership of the Kerry Volunteers,' William Brennan-Whitmore wrote, 'deserves the severest censure.' Nobody seemed ready to take charge of the situation. Stack was blindly following instructions from Dublin, and Cahill apparently did not wish to take responsibility for doing anything.

Kearney sent for a priest for Casement around 9 o'clock that night. Father Frank Ryan OP arrived from the nearby Dominican Church. Casement explained who he was and asked the priest to get a message to the Volunteers. 'Tell them I am a prisoner,' he said, 'and that the rebellion will be a dismal, hopeless failure, as the help they expect will not arrive.'

Father Ryan was taken aback. He had come on a spiritual mission and had no desire to get involved in this kind of politics.

'Do what I ask,' Casement pleaded, 'and you will bring God's blessing on the country and on everyone concerned.'

'After deep and mature reflection,' Father Ryan said, he realised 'that it would be the best thing, not alone for the police but also for the Volunteers and the country, that I should convey the message to the Volunteers and thereby be the means through which bloodshed and suffering might be avoided. I saw the leader of the Volunteers in Tralee and gave him the message.'

By then, Stack was already in police custody and Father Ryan conveyed the message to Cahill, who sent word to Dublin via two different messengers: Billy Mullins of Moyderwell, a brigade quartermaster of the Irish Volunteers, and William T. Partridge of the Citizen Army. Partridge was one of James Connolly's ablest organisers. He had been sent to Tralee to arrange for the local transport workers to help in discharging the German boat on its arrival in Fenit. The Tralee engine drivers and fishermen were to meet Austin Stack on Sunday morning and receive definite instructions about trains from Tralee to take arms to Cork and Limerick.

Mullins and Partridge took separate routes. One went via the Mallow line and the other travelled through Limerick. Despite earlier accounts that they carried written messages, Mullins was quite clear that Cahill's message was a short, verbal one: 'The only help Germany could give was the boatload of arms – small and big.'

Meanwhile, another part of the drama was being played out near Killorglin. The men who were to set up the radio station in Ballyard, Tralee, were on their way to Valentia to steal the radio. On Friday night, two drivers from Limerick, Sam Windrim and Tom McInerney, were asked to pick up five men coming from Dublin by train and drive them to Cahirciveen, where they were to steal a radio transmitter. They met the men at the road junction heading for Killorglin about a quarter of a mile from the cathedral in Killarney. The five included a couple of Kerrymen – Con Keating and Denis Daly of Cahirciveen. The others were Charles Monahan of Belfast, Colm O'Loughlin of Dublin and Donal Sheehan of Templeglantine, County Limerick.

'We were then to proceed in the two cars via Killorglin to Cahirciveen, force an entrance to the Wireless College there as quickly as possible, remove the necessary equipment in the cars and take it to a point on the Castlemaine–Tralee road where a party of Tralee Volunteers was to take it over,' Denny Daly explained afterwards. 'It was estimated that we would be able to complete the mission and hand over the wireless equipment to the Tralee men before daylight on Easter Saturday morning.'

Daly and O'Loughlin went with Windrim, while the others followed on in the second car with McInerney, who lost sight of the tail lights of the first car and had to ask directions at the bridge in Killorglin. 'Turn to the right and follow the main road,' he was told.

Instead of following the main road around a bend a few hundred yards further on, however, McInerney drove straight on along the road which led to Ballykissane Pier. He did not realise his mistake until it was too late. Even when they reached the pier, he thought it was a bridge over the River Laune. It was only when the car began to bump over the rough paving stones at the head of the pier and the water suddenly appeared before him that he jammed on the brakes and brought the car to a standstill on the very edge of the pier, with the front wheels already over the edge. McInerney shouted a warning to his three companions and jumped from the car as it toppled into the water.

Timothy O'Sullivan and his family had just recited the family rosary when they heard the car passing. Realising the danger posed by the unprotected pier, O'Sullivan went out to see what was happening. When he saw no car, he immediately assumed the worst. He rushed to the pier and held a lighted candle aloft. Almost immediately, from the water McInerney let out a cry for help.

McInerney reached the strand to the west of the pier in a state of near-exhaustion. He was helped to O'Sullivan's house, but there was no sign of the other three men: Monahan, Sheehan and Keating. McInerney told the police, who arrived at the scene, that he had been hired to drive the men to Cahirciveen and did not know the purpose of their trip. The car was later dragged from the water but it was some days before all three bodies were recovered from the estuary. According to Daly, 'the main purpose of our mission was to enable wireless contact to be made with the *Aud'*. Thus their mission was doomed from the outset because the *Aud* had no radio and, anyway, it had arrived at – and fled from – the scene earlier that day. It was intercepted off the south-west coast by the British warship *Bluebell*, which was ordered to follow it into Queenstown (now Cobh).

The whole saga of the radio had been a disastrous affair from start to finish. Con Collins, who had been sent to organise the Tralee end of the project, had been arrested, while Con Keating, the radio technician, had been drowned, along with two of the colleagues who were to help him steal the radio. What happened at Ballykissane was a tragic accident; it was a debacle that had no real bearing on the other debacles taking place elsewhere in Kerry.

Mullins and Partridge continued their separate journeys to Dublin. Their two trains joined up at Limerick Junction, so they arrived in Dublin at 4 o'clock on Easter Saturday morning. They made their way on different sides of the Liffey to Liberty Hall. On reaching the building, both men were admitted, but they did not meet the leaders for another five hours.

'No matter what has happened, the original plan will stand,' Mullins was told by Pearse, who was sitting at a table with the five other signatories of the Proclamation.

'What are your plans now, Willie?' Pearse asked.

'I thought I was free, having my job done,' replied Mullins.

'What is the first train you can get back to Tralee?'

'Three o'clock at Kingsbridge.'

'You'd better get that train, as you'd be more useful in your own unit,' Pearse told him.

The rebellion was really the brainchild of a clique within the IRB, and the Irish Volunteers were merely being used by them. Eoin MacNeill, the chief of staff, found out about the plans and threatened to call the whole thing off, but he was persuaded to go along with it when Pearse said that the authorities planned to arrest the leadership of the Volunteers so that they could then introduce conscription. He also assured MacNeill that German help was coming.

Casement was walked through Tralee to the railway station under a strong RIC guard and was put in a private carriage on the 10.30 am train to Dublin. He was escorted by Sergeant James Butler of the RIC. When the train stopped in Killarney, the local head constable looked into the carriage.

'Did you hear what happened to the two lads at Puck?' the head constable asked.

'No,' Butler replied.

'They ran into the tide and were drowned.'

This was a reference to the incident at Ballykissane Pier some hours earlier. Casement, assuming that the man was referring to Monteith and Bailey, reportedly broke down. 'I am sorry for those two men – they were good Irish men,' he said to Butler. 'It was on my account that they came over here.'

Meanwhile, the *Aud* was trying to stall for time. The *Bluebell* ordered Captain Spindler to go faster, but he responded that he was having engine trouble and was able to make only five knots an hour. Spindler inspected the explosives and incendiaries. The German naval ensign was ready. Spindler donned his uniform and arrangements were made to scuttle the boat.

He gave the signal. The German ensign was run up. There was a muffled explosion. The *Aud* shuddered from stem to stern. The crew took to the boats. Now they were rowing hard to get clear. The *Bluebell* fired once. A white flag was raised in the lifeboat. The *Bluebell* did not fire again. The ammunition was exploding on the *Aud*, as she belched smoke and flames. The tramp rose perpendicularly and then sank.

Monteith had spent Friday night in an upstairs room of the

Ancient Order of Hibernians building in Tralee. He had heard of the arrest of Stack and Collins and learned on Saturday that Tralee was swarming with police and that they were still arriving on all sorts of conveyances: motor cars, jaunting cars, traps, bicycles – and on foot. Two trainloads of troops had arrived in Tralee during the night, and details patrolled the town regularly.

On Saturday the *Kerry Evening Post* reported the sensational arrest of 'a stranger of unknown nationality' not far from where a collapsible boat was found between Banna and Barrow. 'A rumour is around that he is not less a personage than Sir Roger Casement,' the report added. 'The captured man was taken under a strong armed escort to Dublin by the 10.30 train this morning.'

There was an even more extraordinary report in the Dublin *Evening Mail* the same day. It was a short interview with Father Ryan, who gave details of his interview with Casement at the police barracks in Tralee the previous night. He quoted Casement as warning that the rebellion would be 'a dismal, hopeless failure' because the expected help was not coming. The interview continued in an intriguing fashion, as Father Ryan said: 'I saw the leader of the Volunteers and gave him the message, and he informed the head constable of the steps he had taken and his reasons for doing so.' Although this could mean that the leader of the Volunteers had informed the head constable, it seems more likely that Father Ryan was stating that Casement had told Kearney.

By the time the *Evening Mail* was on the streets, the RIC in Tralee certainly knew about Casement's mission, because Bailey had been arrested near Abbeydorney on Saturday, and he immediately offered to talk, in return for immunity. He obviously had enough information for the local sergeant, a man by the name of Restrick, to conclude that they had something out of the ordinary on their hands, because he called Tralee, and

District Inspector Frederick S. Britten came out to interview Bailey personally at about 4 o'clock that Saturday afternoon. Bailey then told him about the planned rising and the arms ship that was supposed to land at Fenit.

With the plans for the rebellion unravelling, Eoin MacNeill, the head of the Irish Volunteers, issued orders cancelling all operations for that weekend. In the circumstances, not to have done so would have been extremely foolhardy. He sent out messengers to various centres, with the order to call off all manoeuvres for the weekend; also he inserted an advertisement to this effect in the *Sunday Independent*.

At about 10 o'clock on Saturday night, Monteith was brought to the Rink in Tralee, where a group of twelve or fourteen armed men were on guard. Paddy Cahill was there at the headquarters. 'Now that Stack has been arrested, you will take command tomorrow,' Cahill told Monteith.

Monteith pointed out that he would be at a great disadvantage as commander of the Tralee men whom he did not know. Moreover, he knew nothing about the plans of the leaders in Dublin and had no topographical knowledge of Tralee and its surroundings. But Cahill explained that he did not feel qualified to command, because he had only acted as secretary to the battalion and had no military experience whatsoever.

After further discussion, Monteith decided to take command. His first action as commander was to meet the other officers and talk matters over. 'They were splendid fellows, spoiling for a fight, but they had not much training,' he recollected later in his book *Casement's Last Adventure*.

Monteith began to map out a general plan of operations for Sunday and, having inquired what plans had already been made for the fight, was told that Stack had made them all but that none of his subordinates knew anything about them. They had a general idea of taking military barracks, police stations, telegraph offices and railway stations. This completed, they were to run a special train to Fenit and unload the arms ship, after which they were to dispatch arms and ammunition to Killarney, Limerick and Galway. His officers estimated that Monteith would have about 300 men under his command, of whom about 200 would have firearms. As there were 500 military personnel in the barracks at that stage, and about 200 fully armed police officers, all on the alert, in and about the town, it was obvious that a full day's work lay ahead.

Having obtained this information, Monteith asked for a pilot boat to be sent to the arms ship. All the men were to be ordered to stand ready for instant action. It soon transpired that these things could not be done, as all boatmen were watched and no boats could get out beyond the British patrols. Furthermore, it was declared impossible to get the men together that night. Monteith asked for a map of Tralee and district but none of the officers had one. Eventually a map was found, but it was useless. The military situation was desperate, as untrained and half-armed boys had little hope of success against regular infantry who were greatly superior to them in terms of numbers and armaments.

At 7 o'clock on Easter Sunday morning, Monteith despatched scouts to Fenit to report on the arms ship, to Ardfert, and to Tralee, where they were to patrol the town. One, who had a motor car, was despatched to Killarney with orders to get in touch with the commander of the Volunteers there and to find out his plan of operations. Owing to subsequent events, Monteith received no reply and never saw the messenger again.

Soon afterwards, Mullins arrived back from Dublin with word that they should go ahead with the original plans. Monteith derived some comfort from the fact that Volunteer Headquarters in Dublin knew exactly how they stood with regard to the German aid.

At 8.30 am, two scouts arrived from Dingle, reporting that the Dingle contingent was on the march and would probably arrive at about 11 am. Monteith then gave orders that, if there was any money in the local Volunteer funds, it should be spent at once to provide a good meal for the Dingle men. At about the same time, the women of the Cumann na mBan arrived at the Rink and bustled about, providing breakfasts.

The Dingle men came in on schedule; they were over one hundred strong, footsore, weary and hungry, having marched all the way, with the expectation of a hard fight at the end of their journey. They were immediately attended to by the women, and after a meal most of them stretched themselves on benches or on the hard floor and were soon asleep.

While the Dingle men were eating, some forty soldiers from the Ballymacelligott Company arrived. Smaller parties came from other districts until, eventually, Monteith had about 320 men under his command. About 200 of these had a variety of guns – different makes of rifles, double- and single-barrel shotguns, and revolvers. A few even had rifles equipped with bayonets. Eighty per cent of the men were young and athletic, while the other 20 per cent were either boys or elderly men. The boys marched proudly, without so much as a walking stick to defend themselves with.

Rain had been falling steadily since 11 o'clock, and this increased to a downpour around noon. Lieutenant Patrick Whelan of the Limerick City Regiment of the Irish Volunteers arrived at the Rink shortly afterwards. Monteith knew him personally. Whelan reported that he had been sent to inform the commander in Tralee that all operations for Easter Sunday had been cancelled. He said that The O'Rahilly had personally brought the order from Dublin. Whelan had then been despatched to Tralee, while The O'Rahilly went on to Cork with the countermanding order. Monteith subsequently handed back command of the Volunteers to Vice-Commandant P. J. Cahill and determined to leave town, as the police had been looking for him.

In order to show some reason for the mobilisation of the Volunteers, the men drilled in a nearby field. At 5 o'clock in the afternoon, they returned to the Rink, where they were fed by Cumann na mBan. After dark, Monteith marched out of town with the Ballymacelligott Corps, who provided him with an overcoat, a uniform cap, a bandolier and an old hammerless double-barrel shotgun which had been used for drilling purposes. Monteith fell into the ranks of the Ballymacelligott men, only two of whom, in addition to the commander, were aware of his presence and identity. These two men were placed one on either side of him.

As they marched out of the Rink, opposite which a bright gas lamp burned, the men were subjected to the scrutiny of police on each side, but Monteith passed unnoticed. As the Ballymacelligott men marched through the town, they were accompanied by the Strand Street Band and a company of Tralee Volunteers. At one point in the town, they were jeered and ridiculed by 'separationist' women: those whose husbands were fighting on the Continent in the British army.

On arrival at Ballymacelligott, the corps started to break up and go to their homes. Every few hundred yards, one or more dropped out of the ranks, until Monteith was left with just two men: Lieutenant John Byrne and Volunteer Tom McEllistrim. Lieutenant Byrne's wife was waiting for him, although she did not really expect him back that night. As Monteith wrote subsequently in his book *Casement's Last Adventure:* 'Women the world over have a fashion of awaiting the return of the men to the household, even when they have a foreboding that they might not return.' Mrs Byrne served a splendid supper, and Monteith was then taken to Tommy McEllistrim's house until a safer location for him could be found.

5

'TREATED AS PRISONERS OF WAR'

Although Eoin MacNeill called off the Easter Rising after he learned of the arrest of Casement and the scuttling of the *Aud*, the IRB leaders and James Connolly made preparations to stage the rising in Dublin the following day. This caught the British authorities by surprise – which was understandable, because the whole thing was so hastily reorganised that most of the Volunteers were also taken unawares. As a result, the rebellion was largely confined to Dublin.

Some Kerry people, such as The O'Rahilly of Ballylongford, played a role in the rising in Dublin. It was he who sent word to Kerry calling off the whole rebellion, but on learning, upon his return from the south, that Pádraig Pearse and the others were going ahead with the operation the following day, he joined them. He fought in the rebel headquarters in the General Post Office and was shot dead in the Moore Street area shortly after evacuating the GPO. Another Kerryman, Patrick Shortis from Ballybunion, was killed around the same time in the same area. He had been active in the Irish Volunteers in London; like Michael Collins, he had come to Dublin in January 1916 following the introduction of conscription in Britain.

Thomas Ashe, who was born at Kinard, near Dingle, on 12 January 1885, was arguably the most successful commandant of the rebellion, because he achieved his objective and was the last one to surrender. He had been teaching in County Dublin for some years and had been an enthusiastic member of the Gaelic

League and the IRB, as well as being a founder member of the Irish Volunteers. He was one of the IRB members of the Gaelic League that the League's president, Douglas Hyde, had tried to purge in the summer of 1913. After failing to oust them, Hyde soon retired from the organisation which he had founded; he complained that it had become too politicised.

With some sixty or seventy men under his command, Ashe was assigned to disrupt Crown communications around north County Dublin. He adopted guerrilla tactics, disrupting railway lines and raiding police barracks in Swords, Donabate and Ashbourne, County Meath. His men won a major victory in Ashbourne, where they disarmed a much larger force, capturing a sizeable number of arms and some twenty police vehicles. One of those who distinguished himself under Ashe's command was Richard Mulcahy, who would later serve as chief of staff of the Irish Volunteers – or the Irish Republican Army, as the force would soon become known.

Many of Ashe's men wished to continue the fight after they received the surrender order signed by Pádraig Pearse, but Ashe argued that, as soldiers, they should obey orders. It was a measure of their success that it was not until the Sunday evening, more than twenty-four hours after the collapse of the rebellion, that the British were able to accept Ashe's surrender.

Ashe and Éamon de Valera were court-martialled by the British army on 8 May 1916. Both were sentenced to death, but the sentences were promptly commuted to penal servitude for life. The two men were then deported to serve their sentences in England.

While the rebellion was unfolding around Dublin, there was general confusion among the Irish Volunteers in the remainder of the country. At midday on Tuesday 25 April, Monteith heard the first news of the rising. Tommy McEllistrim returned from a visit to Tralee with word that a meeting would be held to decide on the advisability of staging a rebellion in the town. He said Cahill had told him that, if they decided to fight, Monteith would have to take command.

Monteith said that he would rather not take command but that he would march with the Ballymacelligott Corps and give all possible assistance. He stated that he could command the Ballymacelligott men and help the Tralee vice-commandant by making a flank or rear attack on whatever party he might engage, or, alternatively, that he could carry out such other action as Vice-Commandant Cahill might order.

There was a considerable quantity of cartridges in McEllistrim's home, but they were only partially filled. They were capped and charged with powder but not filled with shot. These cartridges were for the single-loader shotguns of the Ballymacelligott Corps. McEllistrim had the necessary wads and shot, as well as a machine for filling them. He informed Monteith that an additional 500 cartridges were being filled in a shop in a nearby village. Monteith instructed him to go at once to get those cartridges and distribute them to his company, and then find out the decision of the Tralee Volunteer Council. McEllistrim returned, dejected, with the news that the council had decided that the Volunteers would not turn out.

Following inquiries the next day about a stranger in Ballymacelligott, the captain of the company and Lieutenant Byrne brought Monteith further on, to the house of Arthur Lenihan. Here Monteith remained until the following Saturday, when news came that Lenihan's house was possibly about to be searched. That afternoon, Monteith moved to the home of Seán Tadhg Lenihan, an old recluse who lived in Glenaneenta, where the next day Arthur Lenihan came to him with news of the surrender in Dublin.

Shortly afterwards, Father O'Flaherty of Brosna helped Monteith get out of Kerry. He picked him up in a motor car at Glenaneenta and gave him a clerical disguise. He then drove Monteith to Limerick, where the Jesuits harboured him for some time. In mid-November Monteith went to Cork City and got a boat to Liverpool, from where he made his way to the United States, working his passage as a fireman on a ship.

Meanwhile, Austin Stack and Con Collins were taken to Spike Island on Easter Saturday night. They were immediately brought to one of the dungeons there and, by lantern light, stripped and thoroughly searched by soldiers. Then they were left in complete darkness and without their clothes.

During the days which followed, the prisoners were subjected to various indignities. At no time were they permitted light or ventilation, nor were they even allowed to talk to each other. After some days, they made contact with each other and decided to fight for better treatment. Collins opened the campaign by demanding the attention of the prison doctor. For the next several days, he repeated this demand. The officer in charge noted the request but did not respond to it. Eventually, one morning the exasperated Collins threw his breakfast into the face of the officer. The doctor turned up immediately after this incident. Ten days later, Stack and Collins were transferred to Richmond Barracks in Dublin.

At the first meeting of Kerry County Council following the rebellion, John Baily of Tralee proposed a resolution deploring 'the criminal folly in Dublin'. The council chairman, J. T. O'Connor, refused to entertain the resolution. Not enough notice had been given for it to be passed other than unanimously, and there was no chance of that. After Baily left the meeting, a resolution calling for the release of Volunteers who had been arrested in the Castlegregory area was passed unanimously.

Later the same day, at a meeting of Tralee Urban District Council, Timothy Slattery proposed a resolution condemning the Easter Rising:

That we deplore with horror the outbreak in Dublin, which brings the blush of shame to every honest Irishman. We have every confidence in John Redmond and the Irish Parliamentary Party by constitutional means bringing Ireland into the full possession of her rights; that we tender to the Lord Mayor and citizens of Dublin our sympathy at the destruction of life and property.

John Baily seconded the resolution. Tom Dennehy, who questioned the need for the resolution, noted that the county council had refused to consider a similar proposal.

'We will never follow that body either in administration or politics,' Slattery replied. 'Don't mention them to this council.'

'They are called the superior body,' Dennehy argued.

'I called them the other way,' Slattery replied. The majority obviously agreed with him, because the resolution was adopted.

Although people who expressed doubts about the Easter Rising later ran the risk of being branded revisionists, it is worth noting that the response to the rising in some quarters in Kerry at the time was certainly less than supportive. The Bishop of Kerry, Dr John Mangan, for instance, roundly condemned the rebels from the pulpit in Killarney. He said that he was filled 'with feelings of dismay and horror' at their actions. 'The situation that has been so unexpectedly created demands that I, as the spokesman of the Catholics of this diocese, should give public expression to their strong disapprobation of the action of some misguided men, who, if they had their way, would plunge this country into all the horror of civil war,' he said. He went on to denounce Casement as 'a traitor to his country'.

Prominent Sinn Féiners were arrested around the county. 'I am sorry I have come to arrest you,' Head Constable John A. Kearney said when he arrived at M. J. O'Connor's Tralee home on 8 May 1916. O'Connor was taken to the RIC station and charged with 'being engaged in a conspiracy to land German arms in this country'. After being formally charged, he was escorted by an RIC sergeant and three constables on foot through the green and to the county jail in Ballymullen, on the other side of the town. Joe Melinn, who had just been arrested on the same charge, was with him.

On the way, they were greeted by people with 'warm handshakes and hearty good wishes', according to O'Connor. At the jail, they joined Sam Ruttle, Thady Brosnan – the captain of the Castlegregory company of the Volunteers – and a number of Brosnan's men. Tom McInerney of Limerick, the survivor of the car accident at Ballykissane, was also there. He was dressed in a RIC sergeant's uniform that was much too big for him; he had been given the uniform to wear instead of his wet clothes.

'I am here for being alive,' he would tell officials who asked why he had been arrested. 'If I were drowned with the three passengers, I would not be here and there would be no charge against me.'

Detachments of infantry and police halted opposite each house in which arrests were to be effected. Those taken into custody included J. O'Donnell, P. J. Cahill, Thomas Slattery, P. J. Hogan, T. J. McCarthy, Ed Barry, Michael Doyle, Dan Healy, Dan Finn, William Farmer, J. P. O'Donnell, William Mullins, Tim O'Sullivan, Joseph O'Brien, Florence Walsh, Joseph Vale, William Drummy and Maurice Griffin of the *Kerryman*. A number of Traleemen were already in custody: Thomas McMahon, Patrick Landers, Servelus Jones, Austin Stack, Alfred Cotton, Joe Melinn and John Dunne.

Other Kerrymen were arrested around the county: Dan O'Mahony, David J. Griffin, Michael Reidy, William McSweeney and Thomas Fitzgerald, all of Castleisland; John Byrne, Tommy McEllistrim and Thomas O'Connor of Ballymacelligott; Brian O'Connor of Gortglass; T. T. O'Connor of Cordal; Brian

O'Connor of Scartaglin; Henry Spring of Firies; Michael O'Connor and the brothers Michael and James Moriarty of Dingle; James Counihan of Anascaul; Tadhg Brosnan, Michael Duhig, Abel Mahony, Michael McKenna, James Kennedy and Daniel O'Shea of Castlegregory; J. Goodwin and Frank Goodwin of the Maharees; Timothy Ring of Cahirciveen; John Francis O'Shea of Portmagee; Tom O'Donoghue of Renard; Maurice O'Connor of Farranfore; Mortimer O'Connor of O'Dorney; James Sugrue of Listowel; and Mick Spillane, Michael John Sullivan, Patrick O'Shea, Willie Horgan and Dick Fitzgerald of Killarney.

Nineteen Kerry prisoners were transferred from Kerry County Jail to Richmond Barracks, Dublin, for spells of between three days and six weeks. While M. J. O'Connor was there, Prime Minister Herbert H. Asquith came to assess the situation in Dublin for himself, on 12 May. Asquith talked to some of those being held at Richmond Barracks. 'They were mostly from remote areas of the country and none had taken any part in the Dublin rising,' Asquith wrote to his wife.

The prime minister instructed the military to comb out the prisoners properly and only send to England those against whom there was a real case. Tadhg Brosnan of Castlegregory was convicted and sentenced to twenty years in jail, but the remainder of the Volunteers from Castlegregory were allowed to go home. While there, they were well supplied with food – in marked contrast to their poor diet while they had been held in Tralee.

On 23 May the nineteen men were marched from Richmond Barracks through the city, to the North Wall, where they boarded the steamship *Slieve Bloom*. They were all huddled together in the part of the ship usually reserved for cattle. The night was rough and the journey to Holyhead unpleasant.

The men reached Wakefield Prison at about 8.30 the following morning. They were allocated to different portions of the detention prison, which at the time was one of the largest in England. Other Volunteers from Kerry were interned at Stafford Military Detention Centre and Knutsford.

Few of them could have known in advance what solitary confinement would be like. Initially they were confined to their cells for twenty-three hours a day. At first, they had nothing to read, smoking was strictly prohibited and they were not allowed to speak during the exercise hour. No shaving was permitted, and the men grew long beards and developed matted hair. After some days, the prisoners were allowed to speak at exercise, and they could also smoke. They were not permitted to use knives and forks, however, and had to eat their food with their hands as best they could.

After rounding up the most active Volunteers, the RIC tried to gather as many guns as possible around Kerry. On Saturday 29 May, two policemen, Constables Cleary and McLoughlin, began following Jim Riordan as he walked from Farranfore to his home in Firies. Riordan, who was carrying a revolver at the time, turned on the two RIC men. He claimed that they went for their guns and that he shot and wounded both of them. The RIC raided the Riordan farm and mistreated Jim's father, but Jim went on the run and managed to emigrate to the United States.

The trial of Austin Stack and Con Collins did not begin until 16 June. They were charged with conspiring to bring about a rebellion and harbouring Monteith and Bailey, whom they knew were engaged in the illegal importation of arms. Stack furnished a written statement to the court stating that he had always been a believer in the right of Ireland to self-government and was prepared to support it by means similar to those which had been adopted in Ulster against Home Rule. He did not know Monteith or Bailey before meeting them: they might have come from Timbuktu, as far as he knew, he said. Both Stack and Collins were sentenced to life in prison.

Casement went on trial in London during the last week in June; the trial lasted only four days. Several Kerry witnesses testified. Michael Hussey stated that he had seen a red light flashing from a boat in Tralee Bay on the eve of Good Friday. It was the *Aud* trying to make contact with a pilot to guide the boat. John McCarthy testified about finding the boat. There was a ludicrous exchange as he was questioned about his daughter finding the pistol.

'How old is your daughter?' the prosecutor asked.

'What?' McCarthy demanded, in his thick Kerry accent.

'How old is your daughter?' the prosecutor asked again, but this time distinctly and deliberately.

'Ah,' McCarthy sighed, as if suddenly understanding the question. 'About a hundred yards,' he replied, as the court dissolved in laughter.

Mary Gorman testified about seeing three men pass in the early hours of Good Friday, and Martin Collins told of finding the code discarded by Casement. Constable Reilly and Sergeant Hearn testified about arresting the accused, and District Inspector Britten told of finding a German railway ticket in the pocket of Casement's coat.

The jury deliberated for less than an hour before finding Casement guilty of treason, and the Lord Chief Justice then pronounced the death penalty. A public campaign for clemency followed. Despite the initial condemnation of the Easter Rising, public opinion in Ireland was aghast at the prospect of executions, and there were strong calls for Casement's sentence to be commuted. An appeal was drawn up by Sir Arthur Conan Doyle, the creator of Sherlock Holmes. Those who signed it included the writers Arnold Bennett, G. K. Chesterton and John Galsworthy. It was an election year in the United States, and President Woodrow Wilson came under strong pressure from Irish-Americans to intervene on Casement's behalf, especially after a resolution was introduced in the United States Senate and William Randolph Hearst threw the support of his chain of newspapers behind the campaign. George Bernard Shaw advocated that Casement should be treated as a prisoner of war rather than a traitor.

It was ironic that Casement had been sentenced to death for treasonous conduct in trying to organise German help for the rebellion, because it was his arrest by the Crown authorities which had prevented him from trying to call off the rising. In order to undermine the calls for clemency, the British started a whispering camapign against him. Some selected journalists were shown extracts from an infamous diary which included references to Casement's involvement in homosexual activities. Among those shown excerpts from this diary were Walter H. Page, the US ambassador to Britain. When he mentioned having seen the diary, Prime Minister Herbert Asquith was delighted: 'Excellent!' Asquith said. 'You need not be particular about keeping it to yourself.'

A smear campaign ensued, suggesting that Casement was a moral degenerate for whom decent people should have no compassion. This spreading of rumours was a travesty of justice, because in the end it became unclear whether Casement was really executed for treason or for homosexuality, which was not a capital offence even then.

'Only those who have heard just the merest whisper of what is in the infamous diary that has come into the possession of the police can say whether it is right that Roger Casement should be spared,' one English newspaper declared. 'His life as outlined by himself has been one continuous immersion in the depths of depravity, and which may well explain how his sense of loyalty became dethroned and rendered him a willing and pliant tool in the hands of the enemies of this country. That diary cries out to reason and justice against any tampering with the sentence of the court; it should destroy the last flimsy foundation of the sentimental plea that a rebel dead is a greater danger than a rebel alive.'

The *Kerry Evening Post* reprinted that contemptible article immediately after Casement's execution, thereby essentially endorsing its content. But then, the *Kerry Evening Post* was clearly out of touch with the people it supposedly served. Having survived and even thrived since 1774, it folded within a year of the rebellion. Few in Ireland lamented the passing of the newspaper, but Casement became a martyr.

While Casement was on trial at the Old Bailey, some 1,800 untried Irish prisoners were moved to an internment camp at Frongoch, near Barra in north Wales. About forty Kerrymen were interned. They included Mortimer O'Connor of O'Dorney; John Byrne, Tom McEllistrim and Thomas O'Connor of Ballymacelligott; Denis Daly, Mortimer O'Connell and Thomas O'Donoghue of Cahirciveen; Batt O'Connor of Brosna; Dan O'Mahony of Castleisland; Dermot Corkery, Thomas Fitzgerald and James and Michael Moriarty of Dingle; Henry Spring of Firies; J. O'Callaghan of Kenmare; Dick Fitzgerald, Willie Horgan, Pat O'Shea, M. J. O'Sullivan and Michael Spillane of Killarney; John Francis O'Shea of Portmagee; Con Murphy of Rathmore; P. J. Cahill, E. J. Barry, Michael Doyle, Bill Farmer, Dan Healy, P. J. Hogan, John Horan, Michael Knightly, Thomas J. McCarthy, Joe Melinn, Billy Mullins, M. J. O'Connor, Jack O'Reilly, Tom Slattery and James Wall of Tralee; and Tim Ring of Valentia Island.

The camp, which had recently housed German prisoners of war, was divided into two barbed-wire compounds, which were separated by a road. The north camp consisted of a series of thirty-five wooden huts which were sixty feet long, sixteen feet wide and only ten feet high in the centre. They had little room to spare, with thirty internees crammed into each one.

It was a particularly wet summer and the grass pathways between the huts quickly turned into a mass of slippery mud. The huts were cold and draughty even during the summer; this gave rise to anxiety among the men as to what conditions would be like later in the year.

The south camp contained a disused distillery, in which an abandoned granary building had been converted into five large dormitories, with between 150 and 250 beds in each. The beds consisted of three boards on a frame, four inches off the floor; each man had two blankets. The nine-foot-high ceiling contributed to the claustrophobic atmosphere in the large rooms, in which the men were confined at night. Long before the morning, the air would become quite foul, no doubt aggravated by the renowned flatulent qualities of the men's daily diet of beans.

To make matters worse, the place had been infested with rats ever since it was a granary. 'Had a most exciting experience myself the other night,' Michael Collins explained in one letter. 'Woke up to find a rat between my blankets. Didn't catch the blighter either.'

The internees were given the control and management of the camp within the bounds of the barbed wire. Some readily adapted themselves to the conditions and made the most of their internment. Between lock-up at 7.30 and lights-out at 8.45, they were free to read or play cards. 'They were listening all the time to talk and plans about the continuance of the war as soon as we got home,' according to Batt O'Connor. Many of the men had their own musical instruments, and they frequently staged concerts and sing-songs.

In the morning the men rose at 6.15. After breakfast, about a quarter of them were assigned to various fatigue groups to clear out fireplaces, sweep buildings, take out rubbish, prepare meals, tend vegetable gardens and so on. Those not on fatigue duty would normally go to a playing field until 11 o'clock, when all the internees gathered for inspection. The commandant, accompanied by internee officers, inspected everything. The blankets on the bunks had to be folded precisely and placed on the bed boards so that they were in a straight line from one end of the room to the other, and sometimes the commandant used his stick to determine whether the line between two beds was exactly straight.

The camp commandant, Colonel F. A. Heygate-Lambert, whom the internees nicknamed 'Buckshot', was a cranky, fussy individual with a lisp who was always looking for something to complain about. 'It's hard to imagine anything in the shape of a man being more like a tyrannical old woman than the commandant in charge of this place,' Michael Collins complained. 'The practice of confining to cells for trivial things is a thing which the commandant glories in.'

'Conditions are not quite so rosy as sometimes painted,' Tom Slattery wrote home, 'but being treated as prisoners of war, the liberty given is a boon.'

Following morning inspection, the men were free to do much as they pleased within the camp. They played football, engaged in athletic contests and set up classes to teach Irish, French, German, Spanish, shorthand, telegraphy and various military skills. They drilled regularly and held military lectures, using manuals smuggled into the camp.

The men also arranged intercounty football games. The Kerry internees had some fine footballers to choose from. Dick Fitzgerald had won five all-Ireland medals with Kerry and had twice captained the team to success – in 1913 and 1914 – and Paddy Cahill had played on one of the successful teams. In the same issue of the *Kerryman* in which it was reported that Kerry had beaten Louth by a point in Frongoch, there was an article stating that Kerry would not be contesting the all-Ireland championship in either senior or junior football. There was no explanation for this, but one could not have been blamed for concluding that, with so many young men in jail, the county could not field a proper representative team. In fact, it was later explained that the county board of the GAA was acting for financial reasons.

Some of the Kerrymen, including Mike Knightly of Tralee, Denis Daly of Cahirciveen and Batt O'Connor of Brosna, had been living in Dublin and had taken part in the rebellion, but most had not. The latter group had a real sense of grievance, and this was quickly recognised by the Irish public, with the result that some of the Irish Members of Parliament vied with each other to represent the interests of the men at Frongoch.

Listowel Rural Council passed a resolution calling on the Crown authorities 'to release or bring to trial at once Kerrymen arrested in connection with the recent rebellion.' This resolution specifically referred to two of the Traleemen – Tom Slattery, who had a shop in Rock Street, and Thomas J. McCarthy, an engineer from Edward Street – as individuals of 'unblemished character and high social standing'.

Michael J. Flavin, the MP for North Kerry, announced that he was going to visit Frongoch and would also try to get permission to see Austin Stack at Dartmoor, where he hoped to give Stack some books that he had requested. 'We must say,' the *Kerryman* remarked, 'that the Member for North Kerry is doing all in his power for the release of the Kerry prisoners still in custody.'

The *Kerryman* was particularly enthusiastic in its support for the prisoners. Maurice Griffin, a co-founder of the newspaper, and its managing director, had spent time in Wakefield Prison. Tom Nolan, the other co-founder of the *Kerryman*, and its editor, became president of the Irish Volunteers Dependants' Fund. Not surprisingly, this organisation's fund-raising efforts received enormous coverage in the *Kerryman*, which published long lists of names of people who donated as little as a shilling to the cause. Other prominent members of the fund-raising committee were the joint treasurers, solicitor J. D. O'Donnell and Dr Mikey Shanahan, and the joint honorary secretaries, D. J. Browne and Timothy P. Kennedy of Anascaul. We will hear much more of Kennedy – who was Kerry County Council's accountant later.

Frongoch proved to be a veritable training camp for the Volunteers. They might never have organised themselves so efficiently had the British not made the mistake of interning them together. 'They [the Volunteers] could not have come to a better school,' Batt O'Connor of Brosna wrote. 'They were thrown entirely into the company of men to whom national freedom and the old Irish traditions were the highest things in life.'

People from the camp were later to be found in the forefront of Irish life throughout much of the next half-century, especially in the army and police, as well as in the political arena, with future Cabinet ministers, including Richard Mulcahy, Seán T. O'Kelly, Oscar Traynor, Tom Derrig, Jim Ryan and Gerry Boland, among their number.

Hitherto, the movement had largely consisted of disparate local groups, but for six months these groups were afforded the opportunity of making broader contacts and cementing friendships under ideal conditions, and thereby forging a cohesive discipline. At Frongoch, the Volunteers learned the efficacy of propaganda by waging a successful campaign to protest against their conditions as well as their actual incarceration.

'In one part of the camp, 250 Irish prisoners sleep together in one room,' the *Irish Independent* complained, 'and there are no arrangements for the celebration of Mass and the hearing of Confessions in one section of the camp.' Within a week, the local chaplain informed the press that 'the authorities now allow me to celebrate Mass in each camp.' Nonetheless, the physical conditions at Frongoch remained dreadful. 'Is it not a fact that this camp at Frongoch was condemned by the Americans who inspected it when it was used for the detention of German prisoners of war?' the *Irish Independent* asked. 'Yet it is being used for the internment of Irishmen.'

Following pressure from Members of Parliament and others, the British government set up a five-man advisory committee to recommend what to do with those who had not been formally tried. All of the men were, in turn, brought before the committee in London.

On 5 July the *Irish Independent* reported that Mike Flavin, the MP for North Kerry, and his colleague Tom O'Donnell, the MP for West Kerry, were trying to secure the release of the Kerry Volunteers. O'Donnell had long been a hate figure among the Volunteers as a result of his recruiting efforts for the British forces. The internees reacted with outrage to the news that he was trying to help them.

'As far as I know, not one of the Kerry Volunteers had asked Mr O'Donnell to use his influence to secure release from the camp,' Paddy Cahill wrote to the *Kerryman*. He added that they would 'remain indefinitely at Frongoch rather than have their freedom attributed to' Tom O'Donnell. This was signed by all but two of the Kerry contingent; the two exceptions were Tom Slattery and T. J. McCarthy, both from Tralee.

Later that week, twenty of the Kerrymen were taken to London and held overnight at Wormwood Scrubs, where they appeared before the official advisory commitee. After arriving, Billy Mullins was visited by O'Donnell. They knew each other, but Mullins pretended not to recognise him.

'Mullins, how are you?' O'Donnell asked.

'I'm grand, doctor,' Mullins replied.

'I'm not a doctor. Don't you know me? I'm Tom O'Donnell, MP for West Kerry!'

'You are not my MP. We don't believe in you any more,' Mullins told him.

Flavin, who had a business in Rock Street, Tralee, did not make the mistake of introducing himself as MP for North Kerry. When he approached Paddy Cahill, he simply said he was Mike Flavin from Rock Street. The internees were glad to meet anybody from home.

Next day, Flavin and T. O'Sullivan, the MP for East Kerry, attended the advisory-committee hearings and testified to the character of the men, but O'Donnell was notable by his absence. However, he did appear on behalf of Slattery and McCarthy, the two who had not signed Cahill's letter to the *Kerryman*. They had possibly had representations made to him beforehand, and that may explain why they did not sign the letter which emphasised that none of them had asked O'Donnell to use his influence on their behalf.

The appearance of each of the internees before the advisory committee was brief, lasting 'anything from one to five, or at most ten, minutes,' according to M. J. O'Connor. After the standard questions about the man's name, address, age, occupation and marital status were put, a few questions were asked about where he had been during Easter week, and the man was then shown out.

Next day the men returned to Frongoch by train. As they were waiting at Paddington Station, Flavin came up to Dan Healy of Tralee and gave him tobacco, sandwiches and newspapers.

'I suppose you won't eat the sandwiches, as they were made in the House of Commons,' Flavin added, apologetically.

'We're so hungry we'd eat not only the sandwiches but the Speaker himself, if you brought him,' Healy replied, much to the amusement of his colleagues.

One of the newspapers that Healy was handed was the latest edition of the *Kerryman*, which contained Paddy Cahill's letter of protest. This letter was highlighted by being offset in a box in double spacing, spread over columns at the top of a page.

Almost half of the Kerry inmates were released on 21 July. They included Cahill, Hogan, McCarthy, Barry, Farmer, Mullins, Doyle, Wall and Slattery, as well as the two Moriartys from Dingle, Spring from Firies, Byrne and McEllistrim from Ballymacelligott and O'Connor from Cordal. Two weeks later, the Killarney contingent – Fitzgerald, Sullivan, Horgan and O'Shea – were released.

Even though the GAA County Board had decided not to contest the football championship any further, what was described as 'a sort of a Kerry senior team' lined out against Mayo in the all-Ireland semi-final in Ennis on 6 August, according to the *Killarney Echo*. Fitzgerald, who had been released from Frongoch just four days earlier, lined out as captain of the Kerry team. 'It was worth being in Frongoch and other parts to come out and be welcomed as Dick was,' the *Killarney Echo* added. 'At the entrance of the teams, the Kerry captain received a great ovation.'

'Our senior team, or what could be collected together of it, had to meet Mayo, God help us,' the match report continued. The game had been preceded by the all-Ireland junior football semi-final, in which Kerry defeated Mayo, but so many of the senior team failed to show up that six of the juniors were drafted into the senior team, which proceeded to lose by just two points. One of the stars of the Kerry side that day was Humphrey 'Free' Murphy, who will figure more prominently in the story later on.

By mid-August, over 600 men had been released, and there were just over a dozen Kerrymen remaining. It was decided to shut the north camp and transfer everyone to the south camp, leaving the former as a punishment centre. On 17 August the inmates were told that they were interned and that the order would stay in force. The men concluded that they were unlikely to be released in the near future, so they settled down, held sports events and staged weekly concerts, usually on Sunday evenings.

If the Crown officials thought that those released were going to be grateful and desist from their separatist activities, they were to be sorely disappointed. On 22 September M. J. Moriarty of Dingle, Dick Fitzgerald of Killarney, Timothy Ring of Cahirciveen and John Francis O'Shea of Portmagee arrived back at the camp. They had been arrested under the Defence of the Realm Act. No charges were brought against them, though O'Shea was told that he had been arrested for writing a seditious article in the *Gaelic-American* newspaper.

'It doesn't look as if we're going home when they send back Fitzgerald and Moriarty' was a common refrain among the inmates. Others claimed that the Kerry crowd had sent Fitzgerald and Moriarty back so that Kerry would win the football in the camp.

By then there had been a number of incidents within the camp, and an ongoing war of wits was being fought out between the guards and the inmates. On 3 September Hugh Thornton, one of the internees, was informed that, because he had been living in Britain at the outbreak of the war, he was being conscripted into the British army. About sixty internees fell into the same category.

When the authorities came looking for Thornton two days later, however, he refused to identify himself. The guards could not recognise him. The camp adjutant ordered that the roll be called, in order to have the internees line up in numerical order. Later, when the camp authorities tried to identify others by the same method, around 300 of the men refused to answer. This was to protect the so-called 'conscriptables', who included Michael Collins. Even those who answered did so with the agreement of the others, in order to keep communications open with the outside.

The men naturally took delight in upsetting the guards. One morning while a count was being conducted, an internee started coughing, and the officer in charge shouted at him to stop, whereupon all the internees began coughing. Some of the guards would become frustrated when the men were slow to identify themselves on routine matters. 'For Christ's sake,' one exasperated guard exclaimed, 'answer to the name you go by, if you don't know your real name!'

Conscription applied only to those who had been living in Britain at the outbreak of war, so none of the Kerrymen were liable to be conscripted. Another aspect of the test of wits was the refusal by internees on fatigue duty to clear rubbish from the huts of guards on 9 September 1916. That work had previously been contracted to an outside company, but the camp commandant decided to save money by using internees. When they baulked at this, he ordered as a punishment that those who refused to carry out the assigned duties should be sent to the north camp and deprived of letters, newspapers, smoking material and visits. Each day thereafter, eight more men would be transferred after they refused to do the work.

The inmates had managed to smuggle out detailed reports of the refuse strike to Alfie Byrne of Dublin Corporation, who proceeded to publicise the whole affair at a meeting on 4 October. They also smuggled details of the strike to Tim Healy, a rebel nationalist Member of Parliament, who raised the matter in the House of Commons. As a result, the refuse strike received extensive coverage, especially in the Irish-American press.

The camp authorities relented on 21 October. That day, about a dozen Kerrymen were summoned to the visiting room. It was only when they got there that they learned that their visitor was Mike Flavin, the MP for North Kerry. He told them that he had been to Portland Prison with Nicholas Stack to see the latter's brother, Austin Stack. Flavin complained that he had not been allowed to observe conditions in Frongoch.

'I gave him an account of our conditions and treatment, which I said was given not as a complaint but as a statement of facts, as we did not wish to make complaints to him,' M. J. O'Connor recalled. 'He interjected a few remarks and I then politely asked him whether he came in his private capacity or as a Member of Parliament. He flared up at this and lost his temper and said he should not be asked that question. I said we were pleased to see him as a Kerryman but we wanted to make things clear.

'Dan Healy said he might as well tell him that the men in the camp did not want any help from the Irish Parliamentary Party; in fact, the majority blamed the party for their internment,' O'Connor continued. Others followed in a similar vein. Dan O'Mahony of Castleisland said: 'It would be far more humane for the British government to have had us shot after we had been arrested and had finished our punishment than to be dragging us from prison to prison and tormenting and ill-treating us in a most disgraceful manner.'

Flavin regained his composure and asked if he could do anything for the men. 'We told him quite clearly and plainly that all we wished him to do was that he might tell our friends that we were as well as could be expected under the circumstances,' O'Connor noted. 'We then shook hands with him.'

The men took umbrage when the *Freeman's Journal* reported that 'the complaints they had to make were concerned with want of variety in food and the fact that the bread supply was occasionally bad.' At no point in the report was Flavin actually quoted, but they resented the idea that any member of the Irish Party would use their situation at Frongoch to gain publicity for himself.

The Kerrymen in the camp decided unanimously that, as Dan Healy put it, they would 'give Flavin a touch of what we gave Tom O'Donnell'. A letter was prepared to three different newspapers, emphasising that the information given to Flavin 'concerning the conditions in the camp was given not as complaints, but as a mere statement of facts.' They went on to stress that 'before departing we emphatically told him we did not want the intercession of the Irish Party on our behalf, either in Parliament or elsewhere.' The letter was signed by all thirteen Kerrymen who were then in the camp. The censor refused to allow it to leave the camp, but it was smuggled out by a departing prisoner and duly published.

In early November the camp authorities tricked one of the conscriptables, Fintan Murphy, into identifying himself by announcing that he should pick up a package. They also tried to single out Michael Murphy by saying he was to be released as his wife was ill, but that ruse failed because he was not married. The commandant then tried to find him by using the same tactic that had been used to uncover Thornton, but this time 342 men refused to answer to their names. As a punishment, they were moved back to the south camp and their privileges were withdrawn. They protested by going on hunger strike, but that did not last even two days before the authorities relented and returned the men to the other camp. Further efforts were made to uncover Michael Murphy but the others backed up the conscriptables in order to protect him. The camp authorities soon tired of the hunt.

The internees had become more trouble than they were worth, and the British seized on the Christmas season as an excuse to release them, on 22 December. 'The journey home was a long and tedious one,' according to M. J. O'Connor, 'but the anticipation and delight of getting back once more after months of weary exile, and at such a time as Christmas too, made up for all.'

The other sentenced prisoners, like Thomas Ashe and Austin Stack, remained in their British jails, but only for another six months, even though they had been given life sentences.

6

'I DIE IN A GOOD CAUSE'

The two years following the 1916 Rising were marked by an amazing spread of the Sinn Féin movement and by intensive training and reorganisation among the Irish Volunteers. The Volunteers were not officially connected to either Sinn Féin or the secret IRB. Sinn Féin proper, as it evolved under Arthur Griffith, could be termed the right wing of the independence movement, while the IRB formed its left wing.

One of those freed from Frongoch was Michael Collins, who began reorganising the IRB. He managed to establish secret communications with Thomas Ashe by means of visitors smuggling messages into the jail. In the wake of the executions of the IRB's recognised leaders, Ashe was now considered the head of the organisation.

In April 1917 Collins devised a plan to nominate one of the IRB prisoners in Lewes Jail, Joe McGuinness of Longford, as a candidate for a forthcoming by-election. The plan was to dramatise the issue of the prisoners by asking the people to elect McGuinness as a means of demonstrating public support for the release of all the prisoners who had taken part in the rebellion.

Ashe, who was considered among the Irish prisoners to be the deputy leader to Éamon de Valera, was amenable to the plan, but he was overruled by his colleagues. De Valera and some of the others feared that, if McGuinness was defeated, the movement would be set back too much, but the young, headstrong Collins would not be deterred.

'If you only knew of the long fights I've had with A.G. [Griffith] and some of his pals before I could gain the present point,' Collins wrote to Ashe. He had only with difficulty persuaded Sinn Féin not to put up a candidate, in order to avoid splitting the separatist vote. Although Griffith had played no part in the Easter Rising, the rebellion was widely identified in the public mind with his party, because Sinn Féin had been in the vanguard of the separatist movement for more than a decade.

A stubborn, opinionated and determined politician, Griffith was unselfishly dedicated to the separatist cause. He wanted full independence for Ireland, but he was not a Republican. Instead, he advocated an Anglo-Irish dual monarchy on Austro-Hungarian lines, believing that Irish independence could be achieved by non-violent means. Hence he agreed not to put up a Sinn Féin candidate against McGuinness in order that the release of all the remaining prisoners who had taken part in the rebellion could be made an election issue.

'Never allow yourselves to be beaten,' de Valera argued. 'Having started a fight, see that you win. Act then with caution. Carefully size up the consequences of a projected action. If you feel that *in the long run* you can be beaten, then *don't begin.*' He persuaded McGuinness to decline the invitation to stand in the by-election.

But Collins would not stand for such timidity. Ignoring his instructions from Lewes Jail, he had McGuinness nominated anyway – much to the annoyance of IRB prisoners like Seán McGarry and Con Collins, who had sided with de Valera against Ashe on the issue.

'You can tell Con Collins, Seán McGarry and any other highbrows, that I have been getting all their scathing messages and am not a little annoyed, or at least was, but one gets so used to being called bad names and being misunderstood,' Collins wrote to Ashe. The Big Fellow's judgement was vindicated when

McGuinness was elected on the slogan: 'Put Him In to Get Him Out'.

McGuinness's victory, announced on 16 May 1917, helped increase pressure on the Lloyd George government to release the remaining prisoners. Although de Valera had been slow to appreciate the changes in Ireland during his absence, he was a better judge of the international political scene. After the United States entered the war in April 1917 with the avowed aim of making the world 'safe for democracy', American pressure on the British was increased to force them to do something about the Irish question. Lloyd George announced plans for a convention in which people representing all shades of Irish opinion would be charged with drawing up a constitution for Ireland. Astutely perceiving that the British government might try to curry favour with public opinion by making a magnanimous gesture, the remaining Irish prisoners initiated a prison protest strike in order to deprive the British of any credit that the prime minister might hope to gain from releasing them.

The prisoners were led by the three surviving commandants from the rebellion: de Valera, Ashe and Thomas Hunter. The protest strike began on 28 May at the insistence of Ashe, while de Valera and Hunter wished to postpone it. Exaggerated accounts of what was happening in the prison were published in the Irish newspapers, and a public meeting was called in Dublin for 10 June 1917 to 'protest against the treatment of the men in Lewes Jail'. Although the meeting was banned by the military authorities, a crowd of some 2,000 to 3,000 gathered in Beresford Place in the early evening. They were addressed by Cathal Brugha, a veteran of the rebellion. He was arrested by Inspector John Mills of the Dublin Metropolitan Police, and a riot ensued in which the inspector was mortally wounded when hit by a hurley. Against such a backdrop, the British received little credit for their generosity when they released the prisoners later that week. It seemed that Lloyd George was simply trying to make a virtue out of necessity.

All the remaining prisoners were freed on 18 June 1917, having spent about fourteen months in jail. One of their first acts on their release was to draw up a formal appeal to President Wilson and the American Congress. This appeal was signed by twenty-four of the released prisoners, including Thomas Ashe, Austin Stack and Fionán Lynch, as well as the London-born Desmond Fitzgerald, who had spent much of his time in the Dingle area.

The men were accorded a tumultuous reception on their return home on Wednesday 20 June 1917. The ex-prisoners from north Kerry, west Kerry and Tralee were met at Killarney railway station by Dr Michael Lawlor, Jack Lawlor, P. J. Quinlan and others, who brought them by motor car to Tralee. At Ballycarthy Cross there was a great muster of Volunteers and of the general public to welcome them home. Jack McKenna from Listowel, chairman of the county council, and Morty O'Sullivan from Abbeydorney led the north Kerry contingent, while the Castleisland men were under the command of W. H. O'Connor and Con Browne.

O'Connor and Browne, Volunteers of the cyclist corps, led the huge procession into Tralee, where bonfires blazed a welcome and Republican flags were flying from most buildings. In many private houses there was a display of lighted candles in the upstairs front windows.

The event provided some of the most extraordinary and enthusiastic scenes ever witnessed in Tralee. On their arrival at the outskirts of the town, the prisoners were taken from the motor cars of their friends and, amidst wild cheering, were borne shoulder-high, first through the streets and then to their homes. The welcome was marred only by some bottles thrown by the wives of soldiers serving at the front. The homecoming of the prisoners was actually filmed and shown to enthusiastic audiences at the old County Hall a few weeks later.

Fionán Lynch was accompanied on his triumphant return to Cahirciveen by his brother, a curate in Glenbeigh, and by Miss MacCollum and Floss O'Doherty. At Killorglin, Glenbeigh, Mountain Stage, Kells and other stations along the line, enthusiastic crowds were assembled to welcome him home. At Kells he was greeted by Mrs Pearse, mother of Pádraig and Willie Pearse, who had been executed after the Easter Rising.

The biggest welcome awaited Lynch in his native Cahirciveen, which was thronged with Volunteers, Cumann na mBan and members of the general public, eager to honour him. Jerome Riordan was in charge of a party of 200 horsemen. The Volunteers on foot were commanded by Denis Daly and Mort O'Connell, while the Cumann na mBan were led by Mrs Jeremiah O'Connell. When Mrs Pearse and Lynch came to the window of Riordan's house to address the crowd, there was great enthusiasm, and Mrs Pearse seemed greatly moved. It was little over a year since her two sons had been executed in disgrace for their part in the Easter Rising, but now the country was rallying to the Volunteers' cause.

At Lispole, Kinard and Dingle, bonfires blazed and huge crowds assembled to welcome home Thomas Ashe and the other west Kerry prisoners, who were accompanied by Austin Stack of Tralee.

The remainder of the summer became a hectic round of speaking engagements. There were suggestions that Ashe should stand for election in East Clare, where a by-election had been called to fill the Westminster seat vacated by Willie Redmond following his death at the front. Ashe stepped aside for de Valera, however. This was in line with the IRB's policy of allowing academic moderates like MacNeill and de Valera to front the movement, while the IRB controlled things in the background.

De Valera was duly elected, and Sinn Féin supporters celebrated throughout the country. Across the Shannon in Ballybunion, people began marching up and down the main street, carrying Republican flags and shouting, 'Up Valera' at about 10 o'clock at night. 'There was no band, but a drum enlivened the proceedings,' according to the *Kerryman*. 'The whole town was illuminated, and there were rejoicings on all sides. The cheering crowd was composed largely of women, and the men who were in the procession had neither sticks nor hurleys.'

Around midnight, somebody threw a stone and it broke a pane in one of the windows of the RIC barracks. With that, the RIC fired more than a dozen shots. It was assumed that these were just warning shots, but one hit and mortally wounded a young Volunteer, Dan Scanlon, who was only a spectator: he had been leaning against the wall of Jim Clarke's house across the street.

At the subsequent inquest into Scanlon's death, Miss May Mason testified that she had seen Constable James F. Lyons, at a first-floor window, aim his rife and fire at Scanlon, who collapsed. 'Boys, come and take me up,' Scanlon reportedly cried. 'I'm wounded.' He died in hospital a few hours later. The jury returned a verdict of 'wilful murder' against Constable Lyons and his sergeant, as the officer in charge of the firing party in the barracks. Mike Flavin raised the issue in parliament. He asked the Chief Secretary for Ireland, Henry E. Duke, what actions the authorities were going to take.

'The evidence, so far as I know,' Duke replied, 'is that an armed party fired shots into the police barracks, with the result that there was the narrowest possible escape from murder of members of the police and their families.' This response would be symptomatic of the future willingness of the authorities to excuse the overreaction of the police, justifiying their behaviour on the grounds that they had thought they were under attack, or that they had shot somebody who was trying to escape. Lyons was never forced to answer the charges, but six young men were charged with rioting that night: Maurice Beasley, James O'Sullivan, Patrick Mulvihill, James Breen and John Stack, all from Ballybunion, and John Houlihan, from outside the town. They were prosecuted by Serjeant Sullivan, the man who had defended Casement, but the court refused to convict them.

De Valera's victory was followed shortly afterwards by the election of W. T. Cosgrave in a Kilkenny by-election. In between, the British used the Defence of the Realm Act to proscribe the wearing of uniforms in public, or the carrying of weapons. On 8 August 1917 Thomas Ashe spoke at a meeting of the Kerry Organising Committee of Sinn Féin in the Sports Field, Tralee. J. D. O'Connell presided; the other speakers included Stack and Frank Fahy. The same speakers addressed a massive gathering at McKenna's Fort near Banna three days later, to mark the anniversary of Casement's execution. Some 12,000 people thronged the area; there were Volunteer contingents and their bands, Cumann na mBan and members of the general public from every town and village in the county.

Ashe was so busy with speaking engagements that he spent only two days at home in Kinard before setting off around the country. He stayed for a while in the Longford area, where he was courting Maud Kiernan, one of four daughters who were helping their brother Larry to run the family hotel, the Greville Arms in Granard. At the time, young Michael Collins fancied her sister Helen, while Harry Boland was seeing another sister, Kitty.

In late August Ashe was arrested and charged with having made a seditious speech in Ballinalee, County Longford, where Collins had shared the platform with him. Collins visited Ashe while the latter was in custody at the Curragh and attended his court martial a fortnight later. 'The whole business was extremely entertaining

– almost as good as a "Gilbert and Sullivan skit trial by jury",' Collins wrote to Ashe's sister Nora immediately afterwards. 'The president of the court was obviously biased against Tom and, although the charge is very trivial and the witnesses contradicted each other, it is quite likely that Tom will be sentenced.'

Ashe was duly convicted on the evidence of two policemen's recollection of his speech. He was sentenced to two years' imprisonment with hard labour. Fourteen others, including his friend Austin Stack, were also convicted, on similar charges.

More than a few among his friends and fellow inmates regarded Ashe's conviction as foreshadowing his doom. They demanded prisoner-of-war status for Ashe and, when this was refused, broke up the furniture in their cells. Ashe was deprived of his bed, bedding and boots, and they protested by going on hunger strike. The authorities decided to feed the protesters forcibly, a process whereby a tube was forcibly inserted in the subject's nose, down through his throat and into his stomach; the food was then poured into the tube. On the fourth day of the hunger strike, 25 September 1917, Ashe suffered internal injuries during a forced feeding and died shortly after being moved to the Mater Hospital.

'If I die, I die in a good cause,' Ashe told the Lord Mayor of Dublin as he lay dying. As a schoolteacher, he used to express the hope that his pupils would one day get the chance to fight for Ireland. 'I hope I will get the privilege myself – to fight and die for Ireland,' he once said.

Ashe's tragic death had a tremendous impact on the country, causing deep resentment and providing an even greater boost to Republican recruitment than the executions following the Easter Rising had done. His body lay in state in the City Hall in Dublin, dressed in the uniform of the Volunteers. Austin Stack would probably have delivered the funeral oration but he was in jail, so the task fell to Michael Collins.

'I grieve perhaps as no one else grieves,' Collins wrote at the time. Dressed in the uniform of a vice-commandant, he delivered the graveside address after the last post was sounded and ceremonial shots were fired over the coffin. The oration was stirring in its simplicity. 'Nothing additional remains to be said,' Collins stated. 'That volley which we have just heard is the only speech which it is proper to make over the grave of a dead Fenian.'

The cruel circumstances of Ashe's death resulted in an inquest that was destined to become historic. 'They have added another blood-spot to the Irish Calvary,' said T. M. Healy, addressing the coroner's jury. 'They have added bloody footprints on the road on which Irish martyrs have trodden. Have they gained by it? No. Other nations – not merely our own – will read with horror, and will set to the account to which properly it should belong, this terrible story of the death of Thomas Ashe. Other nations will read of it; and when they read it in time long yet to come, they will be enheartened, and perhaps in their distress consoled, by the story of the uncomplaining martyrdom of this humble schoolmaster.'

On 8 October Collins went back to speak in Ballinalee. 'In the circumstances,' he wrote, 'I came out on the strong side'. He delivered the main speech, in which he denounced the local police for lying at Ashe's court martial. 'Thomas Ashe is not dead,' he added. 'His spirit is still with us.'

The Republican prisoners in Mountjoy Jail had won – for the time being, at least – the concessions that Ashe had sought. 'I need no assurance that you and all our other friends throughout the country are delighted at our success in receiving better treatment,' Stack wrote from the prison the next day. 'All's well now – with the terrible exception of Ashe's loss – and we are in enjoyment of the treatment which we demanded for ourselves and for our fellow countrymen.'

The IRB had no recognised leader following Ashe's death, so the organisation threw its full support behind de Valera when the various separatist organisations unified under the Sinn Féin banner on 25 October 1917. De Valera was the obvious choice because he had been a member of the IRB and was not closely associated with any of the other political organisations. In addition, his role as one of only two surviving commandants of the Easter Rising made him a symbol for Republican militants.

The three main contenders for the leadership of the party were Count Plunkett, de Valera and Arthur Griffith, the existing president of Sinn Féin. A few days before the Sinn Féin Ard Fheis was due to begin, de Valera prevailed upon Griffith to propose him for the presidency. With that, Plunkett withdrew, and de Valera was unanimously elected. In his absence, Austin Stack was elected joint honorary secretary, with Darrell Figgis, while Fionán Lynch was elected to the twenty-four-strong executive, which included Michael Collins and Ernest Blythe, the man who had done so much to organise the Volunteers in the Dingle area.

There was a great deal of excitement in Tralee on 29 October when Paddy Cahill, Dan Healy, Jack McGaley and Billy Mullins were arrested for illegal drilling, along with the brothers John and Tom Foley of Rock Street. A crowd gathered and followed them to the RIC barracks and later to the railway station: the men were to be being transported under escort to Cork. The crowd, which was largely made up of women, was not allowed into the station. They booed and heckled the police throughout. Afterwards the police baton-charged the protesters.

Other Volunteers who were arrested around the same time included Timothy (Tadhg) Brosnan and Maurice Beasley of Ballybunion. They, and the Tralee contingent, were tried by court martial in Cork. Thomas Foley was convicted of participating in movements of a military nature and wearing a uniform of a military character whilst in charge of an advance party of eighteen which formed part of a parade of 640 men. He was sentenced to eighteen months in jail, one year of which was remitted. Jack McGaley, Dan Healy, and Billy Mullins all received similar sentences. Paddy Cahill, who marched at the head of that parade in uniform, was sentenced to two years' imprisonment, one of which was remitted. Tadhg Brosnan of Castlegregory, who was convicted of taking part in military movements in his home town on 12 October, was sentenced to eighteen months in jail, one year of which was remitted. All the prisoners refused to recognise the court. Evidence was given against the Tralee prisoners by Sergeant Thomas O'Rourke, Acting Sergeant Francis J. McKenna and Constables George Neazer and Michael Quinlan. Sergeant James Regan and Constable Michael Brophy gave evidence against Brosnan.

Paddy Cahill and Thomas Foley were sent to Cork Jail and the others to Dundalk. All went on hunger strike and were released shortly afterwards. The Crown authorities subsequently adopted what was known as the Cat and Mouse Act; under the terms of this act, those who went on hunger strike were released after a certain period and then rearrested when they had recovered from the effects of the hunger strike.

Early in 1918, Ned Horan of Tralee was arrested in Listowel and the Foley brothers were rearrested in Tralee. All three went on hunger strike and were released again soon afterwards. In March a young Dingle man, Tom Russell, died as a result of bayonet wounds received as the army dispersed a gathering at Carrigaholt, County Clare.

At around this time, the Volunteers were organised to strike back. In November 1917 they had established a twenty-six-man executive, which appointed a smaller 'resident executive' to oversee the day-to-day running of the Volunteers. Cathal Brugha was put in charge of the executive, but things were still disorganised, so it was decided to set up a headquarters staff. Seven of the most prominent members of the resident executive met in Dublin to select a chief of staff in March 1918. The choice was between Michael Collins and Dick Mulcahy, who had been Thomas Ashe's deputy during the Easter Rising.

Even those closest to Collins were 'wary of entrusting him with anything like complete control', according to Mulcahy. They clearly had doubts about his volatile temperament, and they looked to Mulcahy instead. 'We agreed among ourselves that I would become chief of staff,' Mulcahy wrote. He was a very different character from Collins but the two men got on very well together. Austin Stack was chosen as deputy chief of staff, despite the fact that he was in jail. This was a tribute to his standing within the movement. Much of the adminstrative work relating to the Volunteers was delegated to Collins as adjutant general.

Support for the newly united Sinn Féin was particularly strong in Kerry. Nonetheless, the party suffered a series of setbacks elsewhere, losing the first three by-elections of 1918 to the Irish Parliamentary Party; Sinn Féin's failure to capture a seat in Waterford was a particular disappointment. In April 1918, however, Lloyd George's government delivered a mortal blow to the Irish Parliamentary Party by introducing legislation to extend the Conscription Act to Ireland.

7

—

'We Had the Barracks Captured'

The Irish Parliamentary Party withdrew from the House of Commons in protest at the British government's introduction of legislation to authorise conscription in Ireland, and all shades of nationalist opinion formed a solid front to resist the measure. Sinn Féin and Irish Parliamentary Party leaders addressed protest meetings from joint platforms, but it was Sinn Féin which really developed and expanded under this grave menace.

All sides prepared to resist conscription by force, if necessary, but nowhere was the determination to resist more apparent than in Kerry, where what was arguably the first military operation of the War of Independence occurred, in April 1918. A group of Irish Volunteers raided the Royal Irish Constabulary barracks in Gortatlea, a railway junction between Tralee and Castleisland. The attack on two policemen at Soloheadbeg, County Tipperary, nine months later is usually cited as the opening shots of that conflict. This attack occurred on the same day that Dáil Éireann was established and, from the historical standpoint, it had the added advantage that one of the participants wrote a first-hand account of what happened. Dan Breen exhibited no false modesty in calling his memoirs *My Fight for Irish Freedom*. This book provided a graphic account of his own and his companions' exploits on that day.

In a way, it was appropriate that the first shots should have been fired in Kerry, even if the outcome was another fiasco, seeing that the first act of the drama of 1916 was played out in

Kerry too. Tom McEllistrim was one of those who was to have helped with the distribution of the German arms that were supposed to have been landed at Fenit on Easter Sunday 1916. He was arrested in the nationwide round-up following the Easter Rising and was transported to Britain, where he spent four months in Wakefield Prison and Wormwood Scrubs before being interned at Frongoch.

'After our release from prison, the Ballymacelligott Company of the Irish Volunteers was again organised and I was elected captain of the company,' McEllistrim related. He was a young man, itching for action.

Over the years, many misconceptions have developed about the struggle for Irish independence. It was not – as has often been supposed – the executions following the Easter Rising that drove the Irish people into the arms of Sinn Féin, but the introduction of the bill to establish compulsory military service in Ireland in April 1918. This provoked outrage throughout the island. As the anger reached its height, on 10 April 1918, seven members of the Ballymacelligott Company of the Irish Volunteers – John Cronin, Maurice Carmody, Maurice Reidy, John Browne, Richard Laide, John Flynn and Tom McEllistrim – decided to arm themselves properly to resist conscription by raiding the RIC barracks at Gortatlea for weapons.

Their plan was to hit the barracks on Saturday night, 13 April, while two of the four RIC men stationed there were out on a routine patrol. John Flynn was placed on guard at the railway station near the barracks, while McEllistrim and the other five waited on the railway line about sixty yards away. Flynn was to bring them word when two policemen went out on patrol. Cronin, Carmody and Browne were armed with shotguns, Reidy and Laide had batons and McEllistrim had a revolver. They all wore masks, as they were well known to the RIC men.

While waiting at the station, Flynn got into conversation

with a local man and, as the two RIC men left the barracks, he saw an opportunity to establish an alibi for himself. He accompanied his new friend home and then came back to tell those waiting that Sergeant Martin Boyle and Constable Patrick Fallon had left on patrol. What he did not know, however, was that they had only gone a matter of yards to the railway station, where they were awaiting the arrival of the Cork–Tralee train.

As the train pulled into the station at about 10.25, McEllistrim and his five colleagues walked up to the door of the barrack in single file. 'I was first, Cronin next, the others followed,' McEllistrim related. 'When I reached the barracks door, I lifted the latch, believing the door would not be locked, as we had information that the door was seldom locked at that hour.' But this time it *was* locked, so he had to knock.

'Who is there?' Constable John Considine asked.

'It is me,' replied McEllistrim.

'Who are you?'

'It is me, come on and open!' McEllistrim persisted in a friendly tone.

Considine opened the door and McEllistrim dashed past him and made for Constable Michael Denning inside the barracks kitchen, while the others overpowered the startled Considine at the door.

Denning tried to make a run for it. 'When he saw me enter with mask and gun, he made a dash for the inner room. He had no gun on him,' McEllistrim explained. 'I pushed the door open and we got a body-hold of each other in the room, which was now in complete darkness, as the door had closed behind us. In the struggle that followed, we both fell to the ground.'

Cronin came to McEllistrim's assistance. 'When he pressed the point of his double-barrelled gun on Constable Denning's chest, there was no further resistance by him,' McEllistrim noted.

Denning was uninjured, but Considine was bleeding, as he

Volunteer parade in Dingle in 1914

Tralee Volunteer leaders at the Sports Field, Tralee, in 1915. Front row, from left: Dan Healy, Austin Stack and Alfred Cotton. Middle: Michael Doyle, Frank Roche, Danny Mullins and Eddie Barry. Back: Joe Melinn, Ned Lynch and Mick Fleming.

On the tower of the submarine of the *U-20*. Those pictured include Robert Monteith (second from left, with mcustache) Private Daniel Bailey (third from left) and Roger Casement (fifth from left).

Witnesses at Roger Casement's trial for treason. They include Mary Gorman (front row, fourth from right), young Jack Collins (front row, third from right), Mossy Moriarty and Jack McCarthy.

Tommy O'Connor

Austin Stack

Fionán Lynch

Head Constable John A. Kearney

Dick Fitzgerald

Stephen Buckley, killed by the Free State army at Countess Bridge, Killarney

John Joe Sheehy's brother, Lance Corporal Jimmy Sheehy, killed in the Battle of the Somme in September 1916

Kerry's Eye

Former Volunteer prisoners taken in Yorkshire. Front: Billy Mullins. Middle row, from left: Michael Moriarty of Dingle and Michael Colivet of Limerick. Back: Joe Melinn of Tralee, Seamus McInerney of Limerick – the driver at Ballykissane – and M. J. O'Connor of Tralee.

Thomas Ashe's funeral at Glasnevin, Dublin.
Michael Collins can be seen waiting for the coffin behind the Celtic cross.

Kerryman

had received what McEllistrim described as 'a few baton strokes' at the front door. 'We had the barracks captured in less than three minutes and our two RIC prisoners were placed standing face to the wall with their hands up,' McEllistrim related. 'Cronin and I proceeded to collect the arms in the barrack room and had taken two rifles off a rack and placed them on the table when a shot rang out.'

Sergeant Boyle and Constable Fallon had noticed the Volunteers heading for the barracks door and had watched the whole thing from the railway station. They were both armed – Fallon with a carbine and Boyle with a pistol. They quietly approached the open door of the barracks and could see what was going on inside. They said they could hear Considine pleading for his life. 'Lads, don't kill me,' he cried.

The sergeants said that at that point one of the raiders spotted them at the front door. 'The police are outside,' one of the Volunteers shouted. 'Fire.' The two policemen outside contended that they were shot at first and that they had merely returned fire by shooting, without aiming, into the crowded kitchen. But Tom McEllistrim stated that the two RIC began shooting and that he and his companions were caught completely by surprise.

'I rushed to the kitchen and saw Browne, who had been doing guard with a shotgun over the prisoners, reel and fall flat on the floor,' McEllistrim related. 'In less than a minute the barracks floor was covered with blood. Browne was shot through the temple and the bullet came right out at the back of his head. Richard Laide was also wounded.

'We now found ourselves in a serious situation. We knew that the bullet which hit Browne had come from the outside and we quickly decided that we would have to fight our way out of the barracks, not knowing what we had to meet on the outside.

'We thought at first that we had been surrounded, that

perhaps our planned attack had been given away. Perhaps police or military had arrived at the station [on the train from Cork].' They could only guess.

'Will we shoot those two prisoners before leaving?' one of the men asked.

'How can we shoot them with their hands up?' McEllistrim replied.

'We lifted up Browne, carrying himself and his gun through the door, firing two shots as we went into the darkness,' the author continued. 'There was no response from outside until we were lifting Browne's body over the railing which surrounded the barracks, then another volley of fire came in our direction. We were compelled to leave Browne's body where it was and rush for shelter.'

Laide was taken to a nearby house and then to hospital in Tralee, while Browne lay dying on the spot where he had been left. He never really had a chance of survival, because of the nature of his wound. The police in the hut could hear him moaning, but they were afraid this was an attempt to lure them into a trap. After about half an hour, they finally brought him into the barracks and called a doctor.

By then it was too late. John Browne was dead. The doctor upbraided the police for not bothering to call a priest, as the victim was obviously a Catholic, seeing that he had rosary beads around his neck.

When people came to take Browne's body away, Constable Fallon, who was from Strabane, County Tyrone, was very dismissive. 'You can wrap the green flag round him,' he is reputed to have remarked. Richard Laide died the following afternoon of peritonitis as a result of his wounds. 'That ended our first attempted attack on Gortatlea Barracks,' McEllistrim concluded.

A 'monster' public meeting was held in Tralee on the evening of 17 April. The meeting was preceded by a parade from the county hall to the meeting site in the Square. The meeting, which represented all shades of nationalist opinion, had been called by the Catholic Bishop of Kerry, Charles O'Sullivan, but he was not able to attend, as he had been summoned to a conference of bishops in Maynooth. Nevertheless he left a message, denouncing the conscription legislation, that was read to the meeting. 'The action of all English parliamentary parties during the passage of this bill is signal proof of their callous indifference to considerations of justice and prudence where Ireland is concerned,' he wrote. 'Self-respect, self-reliance and trust in God must be our motto.'

The message was read by a local curate, Father Lyne, who presided at the public meeting. 'England has not changed, but the veil of cant and hypocrisy in which the England of a few years ago veiled her soul and her heart has been cast aside,' he said.

'Up de Valera!' somebody shouted.

'Yes,' said Father Lyne. 'Up de Valera!'

Sinn Féin had been the most vocal opponent of conscription. The bill had been passed at Westminster over the stringent objections of the Irish Parliamentary Party, which walked out in protest. This was tantamount to endorsing the abstentionist policy being pursued by Sinn Féin. The parliamentary party had failed and now the people were looking to the Republicans to save the country from the scourge of conscription. At any rate, there was no doubt that Father Lyne was looking to Sinn Féin with his cry of 'Up de Valera!'

The Lord Mayor of Dublin, Lawrence O'Neill, convened the famous Mansion House Conference, bringing the various parties together in the the face of the national danger on 18 April 1918. Éamon de Valera and Arthur Griffith represented Sinn Féin, John Dillon and Joseph Devlin attended on behalf of the Irish

Parliamentary Party, and William O'Brien, Tom Johnson and Michael Egan represented Labour. Also present were the disaffected parliamentary party member Tim Healy, and William O'Brien of the All for Ireland League.

The conference agreed an anti-conscription pledge: 'Denying the right of the British government to enforce compulsory conscription in this country, we pledge ourselves solemnly to one another to resist conscription by the most effective means at our disposal.'

The conference also unanimously passed the following declaration:

> Taking our stand on Ireland's separate and distinct nationhood and affirming the principle of liberty that the governments of nations derive their just powers from the consent of the governed, we deny the right of the British government or any external authority to impose compulsory military service on Ireland against the clearly expressed will of the Irish people. The passing of the Conscription Bill by the British House of Commons must be regarded as a declaration of war on the Irish nation. The alternative to accepting it as such is to surrender our liberty and to acknowledge ourselves slaves. It is in direct violation of the rights of small nationalities to self-determination, which even the Prime Minister of England – now preparing to employ naked militarism and force his act upon Ireland – himself officially announced as an essential condition for peace at the Peace Congress. The attempt to enforce it will be an unwarrantable aggression, which we call upon all Irishmen to resist by the most effective means at their disposal.

Éamon de Valera was responsible for drafting both the pledge and the declaration. At his instigation, members of the conference also met Irish bishops, who, following a meeting in Maynooth, issued this manifesto :

An attempt is being made to force conscription on Ireland against the will of the Irish nation and in defiance of the protests of its leaders. In view especially of the historic relations between the two countries from the very beginning up to this moment, we consider that conscription forced in this way upon Ireland is an oppressive and inhuman law, which the Irish people have a right to resist by every means that is consonant with the law of God. We wish to remind our people that there is a higher power which controls the affairs of men. They have in their hands the means of conciliating that power by strict adherence to the divine law and by more earnest attention to their religious duties and by fervent and persevering prayer. In order to secure the aid of the Holy Mother of God who shielded our people in the days of their greatest trials, we have already sanctioned a National Novena in honour of Our Lady of Lourdes, commencing on the third of May, to secure general and domestic peace. We also exhort the heads of families to have the Rosary recited every evening with the intention of protecting the spiritual and temporal welfare of our beloved country and bringing us safe through this crisis of unparalleled gravity.

The bishops' manifesto was signed by Michael Cardinal Logue, Chairman; Robert Browne, Bishop of Cloyne, Secretary; Patrick Foley, Bishop of Kildare and Leighlin, Secretary pro tem. The country was in a state of considerable unease. The vast majority of Irish people appeared to believe that England had no moral right to force conscription on Ireland. In the face of the united resolve of the Irish people to resist conscription, Lloyd George's Cabinet decided to postpone implementation of the measure.

Meetings to protest against conscription were held throughout Kerry. The Sinn Féin Clubs became the rallying centres for resistance. People who had previously shied away from Sinn Féin now turned to it. The contemptuous way in which the British had overridden the objections of the Irish Parliamentary Party undermined the Redmondites, who were henceforth a spent force.

The British reorganised the Dublin Castle executive. The Viceroy, Lord Wimborne, was replaced by Lord French, who, on taking over, declared that he would soon name the date on which young men would have to report for conscription in the various districts. 'If they do not come,' he said, 'we will fetch them.'

If the British had pushed ahead with conscription, they would have had to confront the determined resistance of all nationalist Ireland, which would have required more troops to control than they were ever like to conscript, especially with the Catholic hierarchy virtually sanctifying resistance to the measure.

In the midst of the conscription crisis, the British discovered the so-called 'German Plot'. The Germans had landed an Irish prisoner of war on the west coast to contact Sinn Féin leaders, but he was apprehended before he succeeded. The British used this as a pretext to round up seventy-eight of the better-known Sinn Féin leaders, including Éamon de Valera, Arthur Griffith and William T. Cosgrave. The Sinn Féin leaders were warned of their impending arrest by Michael Collins, who had been establishing his intelligence network, but they decided to allow themselves to be taken, believing that their arrest would solidify support for their party. But Collins refused to allow himself to be taken. He was determined to continue his work of reorganising the Irish Volunteers with greater intensity than ever. If the aim of the round-up was to eliminate the obstacle that Sinn Féin posed to conscription, the move failed.

No evidence has ever been produced to suggest that Sinn Féin leaders were engaged in any plot with the Germans in 1918. As a result, people quickly assumed that the plot was either a bogus excuse to arrest the leaders or merely a figment of the hysterical imagination of the British Cabinet. No doubt the Germans would have liked to involve the Irish in another struggle with the British at the time, but the Irish were no longer looking to Germany, because the Germans had shown so little interest in helping in 1916.

The conscription crisis became enmeshed with land agitation in the first week of May when the High Court in Dublin issued an order for contempt of court against fourteen men from the Listowel area. Acting on behalf of the Sinn Féin Food Committee, the men had been involved in ploughing what was known as Lord Listowel's front and back lawn on 25 February 1918. That day, Irish Volunteers from nearby areas marched into Listowel, armed with hurleys and led by bands, with ploughs and horses bringing up the rear. They joined with the Listowel Company of Irish Volunteers and, led by Commandant James Sugrue and Patrick Landers, marched to Lord Listowel's estate office in Feale View.

They had already demanded access to some of Listowel's lands for plots for the townspeople, but Lord Listowel's agent, M. Hill, refused permission for this on the grounds that he did not have instructions from his employer. 'As everybody knows that Hill is Lord Listowel,' declared Jack McKenna, 'keys or no keys, we are determined to enter the fields and plough them up whatever the cost.' The Volunteers then broke open one of the gates leading into the back lawn near the national schoolhouse and also the main gate at Danaher's Lodge leading into the front lawn.

A large force of police under County Inspector Heard and District Inspector Molloy, along with a company of British soldiers from Tralee, had placed three machine-guns in strategic position covering the entrances to the lands. D. J. Flavin and the two graziers to whom the lands had been let – John Keane and James Kenny, both of Church Street – approached the inspector in charge. They explained that they had surrendered their rights to the Sinn Féin Food Committee legally through a solicitor, and they produced the transfer documents.

'As far as I can see, this is a dispute between Lord Listowel and these two gentlemen who hold the land as graziers and I don't see that the military have any right to interfere, as he has his remedy in the courts,' the officer in charge explained as he withdrew his men and returned to Tralee.

Having successfully completed their day's tillage, the ploughmen and Volunteers returned to town and marched to Upper William Street. There Jack McKenna addressed them from the balcony of the Temperance Hall, claiming a great victory for the people of the town, for whom the Volunteers had procured and tilled the land to supply food. This was seen as one of the movement's great early victories in Listowel.

But the Earl of Listowel then secured a court order against people trespassing on the lands and ploughing them up. The injunction was posted on the gates of the lands and copies were served on the known leaders of the agitation. The locks of the gates were smashed and the people again entered the lands. On 23 May a large force of police was drafted into Listowel to arrest fourteen men, who were taken to Cork to serve a month in jail. They were the chairman of the Urban District Council, Thomas Walsh, and Councillors Dr Micg323hael O'Connor, D. J. Flavin and James Lynch, along wth T. D. O'Sullivan, R. M. Danaher, Thomas Murphy, Michael Mulally, Patrick Sharry, Edward Murphy, William Lawlor, E. J. Gleeson and Morgan Sheehy.

Jack McKenna was also on the list but he was already in prison, serving twelve months for concealing arms, contrary to the Defence of the Realm Act.

There was great excitement in Listowel on 23 June 1918, when the thirteen townsmen arrived home to a hero's welcome after serving their prison sentences in Cork Jail. A large crowd turned out at the railway station for the homecoming. They cheered the released prisoners enthusiastically and carried them shoulder-high to a waggonette on which were hoisted a couple of Republican tricolours. They were then driven in triumph through the streets, headed by the Listowel Brass Band and followed by a huge procession, with people carrying banners.

They first walked to the Square, then turned up Church Street and went down Forge Lane and then Charles Street. They stopped opposite the Temperance Hall, from where T. J. Walsh, as chairman of the council, addressed the gathering. There were cheers for Jack McKenna, who was still in Belfast Jail, and then the people dispersed to their homes.

While the men were in jail, the controversial land had been sold. The Sinn Féin committee then bought the lands from the purchaser for the same price he had paid for it. The front lawn was divided amongst twenty people, each of whom had the right to graze one cow in perpetuity, and the back lawn was divided amongst twenty-eight poor people for tillage purposes.

Meanwhile there was a dramatic sequel to the Gortatlea raid when McEllistrim and Cronin sought to avenge the deaths of Browne and Laide. Although the two policemen responsible for the killings were transferred out of Kerry, McEllistrim learned that they would be in Tralee on 14 June 1918 to give evidence in a court case. The five surviving Volunteers from the Gortatlea raid met on the eve of the court hearing.

'It was arranged that John Cronin and I would go to Tralee the following morning to shoot Boyle and Fallon,' McEllistrim wrote. 'We selected a reliable Volunteer, Dan Stack, to take two shotguns for us to Tralee. The shotguns were to be taken by him in a donkey cart, concealed in a large sack. Stack was to sit in his donkey cart in front of the main entrance to Tralee Railway Station. It was our intention to shoot Boyle and Fallon coming off the morning train from Cork.'

'Cronin and I arranged to cycle separately to Tralee on the morning of the fourteenth and had arranged to meet at Ballybeggan Racecourse gate,' McEllistrim added. This was not far from Tralee Railway Station, but as McEllistrim waited for Cronin, Moss Carmody arrived to inform him that Boyle and Fallon had been seen in Tralee the previous night.

'We will shoot them coming out of the courthouse at lunch hour,' McEllistrim suggested. 'What about it?'

'By God, Mac, I could never do it.'

'All right, go out and send in Cronin and tell him I will meet him at the back of Tom Harty's licensed premises near the entrance to the Market.'

McEllistrim continued: 'I cycled to Tralee Railway Station, where I found faithful Stack right in front of the station – quite at ease – sitting in his donkey cart with his shotguns. I told him quietly our plan had to be changed and to bring his car and guns to the back of Tom Harty's.' Cronin arrived at about 11.30 am.

'We took our two shotguns, concealed in the sack, into Harty's and got into a small snug where we were in full view of the main street, as Harty's premises opened into the main street,' McEllistrim wrote. 'The snug was most suitable for our purposes. It was right opposite the bar, with the door opening inwards, and the door, when opened, served the purposes of concealing our guns from those in the bar. No one in Harty's premises at the time knew us.'

Dan Stack was told to go to the courthouse and report back when Boyle and Fallon had left. The pub was on the only direct route between the courthouse and the RIC barracks, so they waited confidently. 'We knew that Boyle and Fallon would have to pass that way,' he explained. They drank a few minerals in order not to arouse suspicion.

'The two ladies in the bar came across chatting with us and, in fact, came into our snug, but did not see the loaded shotguns behind the door,' McEllistrim relates. It was a busy day in Tralee and, with the court in session, there was a great deal of police activity.

At five past one, Stack put his head into the snug. 'Coming down the other side of the street: Boyle and Fallon,' he said.

'We snatched our guns and moved quickly to the door,' McEllistrim explained. 'We could now see Boyle and Fallon, in uniform, going down the other side of the street. There were scores of people passing to and fro.

'I was leading and, as I dashed through the door, I collided with someone, slipped and fell on one knee. When I got to my feet, Cronin was by my side and we dashed together across the street. There was great excitement and shouting and, when we got halfway across the street, Boyle and Fallon heard someone shout, "Look out!"

'They turned in our direction and saw us facing them with two shotguns. They first attempted to draw their guns. We lifted our guns to fire. We were not ten yards from them. As we did, they flung themselves backwards into a somewhat sitting position on the flags. We took aim and fired.' Fallon turned instinctively and was hit in the back around the shoulder, while Boyle was missed altogether.

'Cronin and I dropped our shotguns in the middle of the street and dashed again for Harty's front entrance, out through the shop to the back, where we jumped on our bicycles and got clear away.'

Moss Carmody was not so lucky. He had declined to take part in the attack, but he was arrested anyway that day, along with another totally innocent man named Robert Browne. Both were charged with the shooting of Fallon and the attempted shooting of Boyle, but the charges against Browne were quickly dropped.

Questions were asked in the House of Commons at Westminster about attempts to bribe witnesses to testify against Carmody but the Crown's case collapsed anyway. The charges were dropped and Carmody was freed after spending some six weeks in jail awaiting trial.

By then Fallon had recovered completely. The buckshot used had particularly large pellets and these were easily removed from his shoulder. He was awarded £30 for his personal injuries and was promoted to the rank of sergeant, while Boyle was made head constable.

8

―

'KERRY IS NOW THE ONE BRIGHT SPOT'

During June 1918 Austin Stack led another campaign for political status for Republican prisoners at Crumlin Road jail in Belfast, where their behaviour attracted crowds on the nearby streets. After three nights of protest, the warders came in to remove the prisoners from their cells. 'The whole ninety-five prisoners began to smash up everything in their cells and to barricade the doors,' Stack wrote to his brother Nicholas on 7 July 1918. 'A large force of police was brought in and there never was such tumult in any jail. Mountjoy "wasn't in it". Some of our fellows battered down and through their doors and came out to fight. Conversely, the warders and police were breaking into other men's "apartments" and playing on the occupants with fire hoses, to flood them out if they could not drown the prisoners themselves. The windows were smashed to pieces – not alone the glass but the iron frames as well – in all cases, and a goodly number of the men burrowed through the walls into their neighbours'. Tables, stools, bed boards were broken into smithereens.' The authorities had regained control by about one o'clock the following morning.

'The men were left in handcuffs all night,' Stack continued. 'They had to sleep, or try to, with hands ironed behind backs. It was torture. This was Thursday night, the twenty-sixth of June. On Friday we were – about seventy-five of us – brought before visiting justices and told that our "privileges" were taken from us – that we were ordinary criminals thenceforth. We defied them of course. We remained in irons all day Friday. Had to take meals thus, but in most cases the cuffs were removed to the front on that day. On Saturday morning we attended Mass. A lot got irons off and we smashed them "carefully". Re-enter police – about a hundred. Handcuffed again and removed to bare cells in C Wing. Later brought before "Justices" and condemned to No. 1 diet (bread and water).

'Sunday morning all went to Communion in handcuffs. After "dinner" on Sunday handcuffs removed without request on our part. Again smashed windows and the fun began in real earnest. There was music in Belfast, I tell you. To make a long story short, we sang and shouted all the time, particularly from 7 o'clock each night until 12 or 1 o'clock, so that "in the stillness" the sweet and soft sounds floated over the best part of a half-mile radius. The respectable Orange inhabitants could not sleep. I am told and I am further informed that the governor and justices were deluged with requests to "abate the nuisance". Really, Sinn Féiners have lungs – and voices – some of them. (Think it better to qualify the latter, as you might be inclined to say "Liar".)

'On Wednesday last we were told we could have our "privileges" restored if we gave an undertaking to be good boys for the future. Of course we refused to "undertake". The racket went on all the week, and on Saturday evening, after ten days' fight, our rights were restored unconditionally.

'It was a great win, and we are all in the best of form, even those who got "bashings" – which were not very serious. I was not damaged in any way. I was one of the first removed before the police arrived and the governor was present. The handcuffs and diet did us no injury either. It was worth anything to go through the thing. The final scene was splendid. I lined up the men in military formation.'

The governor of the prison, his deputy, and the visiting

justice, an Orangeman, spoke to the men. Addressing the Republican prisoners, the visiting justice complained about their outrageous conduct when the prison authorities had been treating them 'with leniency, kindness and mercy', as he put it. As the official party was moving off, Stack addressed the justice. 'I asked him to hold his place to listen to a word on behalf of the men,' Stack writes. 'I was choking with anger but said something to this effect: "That we did not expect or want or believe we were getting either leniency, mercy or kindness from Dublin Castle, that we had never got anything from them save by fighting for it, and that we expected to have to fight them again and were prepared to do so." I added that I believed his assertion as to leniency to be quite on a par with England's claim that she was fighting in the present war on behalf of small nationality. At this, our fellows broke into a terrific cheer and you could hardly see the visiting justice and his companions, they ran away so fast.'

On 5 July 1918 the British government banned all public gatherings, including political rallies and even football matches, unless a police permit was issued for them. Sinn Féin set about defying the ban. The GAA held football and hurling matches throughout the country in open defiance of the prohibition on 4 August and again on Assumption Thursday, eleven days later. In all, Sinn Féin held some 1,800 public rallies throughout the country in mass defiance of the government.

Much of the resistance was organised by Michael Collins, who was rapidly establishing himself as the driving force not just in the Volunteers but within the whole Republican movement. The best insight into the thinking of Collins around this time can be gleaned from his correspondence with Austin Stack.

Stack had been close to Ashe, his fellow Kerryman, and this probably prompted Collins to hold Stack in extremely high regard – a feeling which could only have been increased by Stack's effective leadership in Crumlin Road Jail. They could hardly have known each other very well at the time, because Collins had been in England for the decade prior to 1916 and Stack was in jail for much of the time thereafter. Yet Collins wrote to Stack in effusive terms, informing him of happenings on the outside and seeking his advice.

'I was very glad to get your letter, especially the personal note, which I appreciated,' Collins wrote to him on 29 August 1918. 'Without insincerity, I can say that I do appreciate it more from yourself than from anyone I know.' He did not normally express himself so openly: his remarks in this instance clearly indicated the profound respect he had for Stack.

The two men had probably met through Thomas Ashe. Stack was in jail when Ashe died and it was Collins who was therefore selected to deliver the oration at Ashe's funeral in September 1917. Collins had a number of strong connections with Kerry people. Batt O'Connor of Brosna, who worked as a master carpenter in Dublin, was one of the Big Fellow's most trusted friends. O'Connor constructed hidden cupboards for him in the walls of his offices, where he could hide his most secret documents. Collins sometimes had important meetings in O'Connor's home, which was one of his safe houses.

Following his release from Frongoch, Collins moved into the Munster Private Hotel, which was also known as Grianán na nGaedhal. Located at 44 Mountjoy Street, near Broadstone Railway Station, it was owned by Miss Myra T. McCarthy, a native of Waterville, County Kerry. It was a popular digs for students and young businessmen from Munster, especially those active in the Gaelic League.

Various pioneers of the Gaelic League stayed regularly at the Munster Hotel while in Dublin. These included Fionán MacCollum of Killorglin, who was a Chief Organiser of the Gaelic League; An Seabhac; Peadar Ó hAnnrachán of Cork; Cormac Ó Cadhlaigh, the future Professor of Modern Irish at

University College Dublin; and Father John Lynch and his brother Fionán, who were nephews of Myra McCarthy. Other early guests were Cathal Brugha, Gearóid O'Sullivan and Con Keating. Brugha served as president of the Gaelic League's Keating Branch – the branch popular among Munstermen in Dublin.

Gearóid O'Sullivan and Fionán Lynch had become good friends as students in St Patrick's Teacher Training College in Drumcondra. They joined the Irish Volunteers on the night the organisation was founded, in November 1913. As a result of the friendship formed within the Gaelic League, Number 44 became a centre of activity for the Irish Volunteers. Piaras Beaslaí, who lived across the street, was a frequent visitor, as were Seán MacDermott and Con Collins, who were then in digs on the North Circular Road. The men often played bridge at Number 44.

At the time, MacDermott was running *Irish Freedom*, the organ of the IRB, to which people like Beaslaí and P. S. O'Hegarty frequently contributed. Fionán Lynch, Sullivan and Con Collins often helped with the production and circulation of the issues.

During the week before the Rising, some of the leaders feared arrest, so they stayed elsewhere in the city, with armed Volunteers to protect them. Seán McDermott moved into 44 Mountjoy Street; it was there that the plans to steal the radio in Cahirciveen were made. MacDermott stayed there until Easter Sunday.

On Easter Saturday morning – between 4 and 5 am – those staying at Number 44 were alarmed by a heavy knock on the hall door. The Volunteers feared it might be a raid by the British, but it was Seán Connolly with a dispatch for MacDermott informing him of the arrest of Roger Casement in Kerry. Next evening the Dublin Metropolitan Police called to the Munster Hotel to inquire about Con Keating. This was the first that his comrades heard about the tragic accident at Ballykissane Pier. In view of that accident, the various Volunteers staying in the building decided to spend the eve of the Rising elsewhere. Seán MacDermott and Gearóid O'Sullivan went to stay at Fleming's Hotel. Fionán Lynch went with Diarmuid O'Hegarty to his 'digs' in St. Peter's Road and Floss O'Doherty stayed with Michael Collins in his digs at Rathdown Road.

Gearóid O'Sullivan fought in the General Post Office as part of Seán MacDermott's staff. Fionán Lynch was captain of the company that fought in the area adjoining the Four Courts, along with Mort O'Connell and Floss O'Doherty. O'Doherty escaped following the surrender, made his way back to Number 44 and resumed his teaching job, as if he had not been involved in the Rising. Gearóid O'Sullivan and Mort O'Connell were deported and subsequently interned in Frongoch, while Fionán Lynch was sentenced to death, but the sentence was commuted to ten years' penal servitude. Following their release, the Munster Hotel became a popular haunt and Collins stayed there until December 1919, when he had to move after the police raided the building looking for him. Thereafter, however, he was a regular visitor as Myra McCarthy continued to do his laundry.

While Collins was staying at the Munster Hotel, the letters that he wrote to Stack in jail were some of the most revealing that he wrote to anyone: he frequently unburdened himself to Stack. Collins had been elected to replace Pádraig Pearse as national organiser of the Irish Volunteers and his letters to Stack often gave details of events or provided his assessment of individuals.

As a member of the Sinn Féin executive, Collins concentrated on organisational matters within the Volunteers and was largely contemptuous of politicians. Sinn Féin executive meetings were poorly attended, and the discussions 'lacked any great force,' according to him. He was particularly critical of Sinn Féin Vice-

President Father Michael O'Flanagan for associating with Crown officials.

'Things have been happening in SF [Sinn Féin] circles that are somewhat calculated to upset one,' Collins wrote to Stack on 21 August 1918. 'Certain well-known personages in the movement – officers, in fact – have been hobnobbing with people like Jas. O'Connor [the Lord Justice of Appeal in Ireland].'

Collins was determined 'to unearth and destroy any attempt at compromise.' With the various leaders still in jail since the round-up during the conscription crisis, he felt that Sinn Féin 'lacks direction at the present moment. The men who ought to be directing things are too lax and spend little or no time at Number 6.' This was a reference to the party headquarters at 6 Harcourt Street, Dublin. 'In the meantime,' he concluded, 'I am giving you the tip that all is not as well as it might be.'

Collins was deeply involved with the publication of *An t-Óglach*, to which he contributed 'Notes on Organisation'. It was through his contact with Stack that Collins secured an article written by Ernest Blythe, who had done so much to organise the Irish Volunteers in the Dingle area.

'We must recognise,' Blythe wrote, 'that anyone, civilian or soldier, who assists directly or by convenience in the crime against us, merits no more consideration than a wild beast, and should be killed without mercy or hesitation as opportunity offers.' Collins was so impressed with Blythe's writing that he asked Stack to try to get more of the same kind of stuff. 'Do get Earnán to repeat those articles if you possibly can,' he wrote.

As early as 22 August 1918 the political correspondent of the *Daily Chronicle* of London noted that there was a real danger that the Irish Parliamentary Party would be wiped out by Sinn Féin. 'The prospect of a clean sweep of the constitutional nationalists by the irreconcilables must be faced.' Sinn Féin was agitating at every possible opportunity. The public unease over the possible introduction of conscription continued, as the British refused to abandon it. The threat hung over the Irish people like a kind of sword of Damocles, fuelling unease and boosting the political fortunes of Sinn Féin, which was credited with having compelled the British to postpone the implemention of conscription.

Political activists were being arrested continuously throughout the country, and Kerry was no exception. Dan McCarthy, chief organiser for the movement, was arrested in September at Milltown, where he had been on the run for some weeks. One of the more far-reaching consequence of the arrests was the vacuum that these left at the top of the movement. With relative moderates like de Valera, Griffith, and MacNeill in jail, militants like Michael Collins and Cathal Brugha became more influential than ever.

Collins gained effective control over both the IRB and Sinn Féin. He became 'the real master' of the Sinn Féin executive, according to Darrell Figgis, who described him as 'a man of ruthless purpose and furious energy, knowing clearly what he wanted and prepared to trample down everybody to get it.'

Anxious regarding the moderate stance taken by some members of the movement, Collins was worried that the war might end before the Volunteers had another opportunity to exploit Britain's difficulties. Hence the peace efforts on the Continent made him uneasy. 'Generally speaking, I'm not very impressed,' he wrote to Stack on 7 October 1918. 'It must come some time, though, and one of the greatest signs is the newspaper offensive waged by the British press for some time back. It's very hard to form an opinion that one could stand up to, as we only get such garbled versions.'

If the war should end, it would be necessary to re-evaluate the whole situation, he wrote. 'We can go into the wilderness again and maybe be better prepared for the next clash.' There was no doubt in his mind that there would be another clash. It was just a matter of when – and that would depend on Irish considerations. 'The only thing that concerns us is this country,' he emphasised. 'I wish to God there were more of the people out whom one could discuss things with and in whom confidence could be reposed.'

The armistice ending the Great War came into effect the following month, on 11 November. There were several days of celebrations in Dublin, marred by some very ugly incidents on the second night that were probably prompted more by drink than patriotism. Collins seemed to take a vicarious delight in writing about attacks made on soldiers. 'As a result of various encounters there were 125 cases of wounded soldiers treated at Dublin hospitals that night', he wrote to Stack. 'Before morning three soldiers and one officer had ceased to need any attention and one other died the following day. A policeman too was in a precarious condition up to a few days ago, when I ceased to take any further interest in him. He was unlikely to recover.' This was Collins at his least attractive.

While in Frongoch, he had asked that those who had taken part in the Easter Rising should be judged by what they attempted rather than what they achieved, yet he was unwilling to judge the soldiers who had fought in the Great War by the same standard. Those who had answered Redmond's call to battle had undoubtedly believed they were acting in Ireland's best interest. Some 200,000 Irishmen fought, most voluntarily, and some 50,000 lost their lives. Against these figures, the number of Irishmen who fought or died in the War of Independence pales into relative insignificance.

The curious thing about the people that Collins wrote to Stack as having been killed during the armistice celebrations was that the newspapers did not report any deaths, but Collins explained that somebody from the *Irish Independent* gave him the story. The newspaper had tried to report the details, but they were 'absolutely struck out by censor'.

The war veterans, scoffed at by Sinn Féin, were shamelessly betrayed by Lloyd George and his government, who were prepared to sacrifice almost everything for short-term political gain. The wily Welshman sought to exploit public emotions by calling a general election and campaigning on a promise to squeeze Germany until the pips squeaked. In the process, he and his ilk helped generate the conditions in which Adolf Hitler and the Nazis would later thrive. Britain would pay dearly for the selfish, calculating policies of Lloyd George. Indeed, she would come perilously close to losing all in the summer of 1940.

With so many Sinn Féin leaders in jail, it fell to Collins and his colleagues Harry Boland and Diarmuid O'Hegarty to arrange for the selection of Sinn Féin candidates when the general election was called in November 1918. They suggested the names of the various candidates who were then nominated at local level. As the architect of the McGuinness election in 1917, Collins followed the same practice of putting as many of the jailed leaders as possible up for election, on the basis of the successful slogan: 'Put Him In to Get Him Out'. Austin Stack, Fionán Lynch and James Crowley, three of the Sinn Féin candidates nominated for seats in Kerry, were in jail at the time of their nominations, while the fourth, Piaras Beaslaí, was on the run.

Austin Stack was also selected by the South Tipperary Sinn Féin executive to be their parliamentary candidate. As his name was being selected, police entered the room where the executive meeting was in progress and demanded to know what business was being transacted. When the policemen refused to leave, the Sinn Féiners withdrew and resumed their meeting in a wood about half a mile outside Cahir, where they chose Stack. The West Kerry Sinn Féin executive, while expressing their appreciation of the compliment paid to Stack by the south Tipperary men, pointed out that they could not part with him, as he was urgently needed at home.

J. D. O'Connell, Solicitor, presided over the West Kerry Sinn Féin executive meeting, which nominated Stack. Other members who attended were Diarmuid Crean, J. P. O'Donnell, Tom Slattery, M. E. Mangan, J. Conroy, as well as Tom Dennehy of Tralee, Tadhg Brosnan of Castlegregory, J. E. O'Shea of Milltown, Dr McDonnell and 'An Seabhac'.

Such was the extent of the backstage management of the party's campaign that many of the candidates did not even know they had been nominated until the prison authorities informed them that they had been elected to Parliament. The whole election process was a necessary propaganda exercise in which Collins played a very active – though he would have had colleagues believe it was a reluctant – part. 'Damn these elections!' Collins exclaimed in a letter to Stack in the midst of the election campaign. He indicated that he would have preferred to have been able to devote more time to preparations to spring Stack from Belfast Jail, where he was leading another protest.

John Doran of Loughinisland, County Down, was being court-martialled for shooting at a policeman. Stack demanded that he should be treated as a political prisoner, but the governor of Crumlin Road Jail argued that it was a military matter, even though Doran was being held in the remand section of the prison. After attending Mass one Saturday in November, Doran raced past the guards to join the political prisoners. He was given food and a mattress and locked into the attic of the prison with a colleague by the inmates.

When it came to the count, the men shuffled so effectively that the prison guards came up with the total complement, even though the two were hiding in the attic. The prison authorities eventually relented. 'I will give my word of honour that no attempt will be made to recapture Doran without I giving you twelve hours' notice,' the governor promised Stack.

Three of the four sitting Kerry MPs – Timothy M. O'Sullivan in East Kerry, Michael J. Flavin in North Kerry and John Pius Boland in South Kerry – did not stand for re-election. In West Kerry, which included Tralee, Tom O'Donnell initially indicated that he would stand for election. There was an ugly incident in Anascaul on 27 November 1918, when Constable Michael Ryan tried to remove a Sinn Féin poster from the open window of the home and place of business of John Walsh, a local carpenter who did a good trade in mending the wheels of carts for farmers.

Tomás Walsh, one of the sons in the house, caught the constable's arm, and a fracas ensued. RIC reinforcements arrived and, as they tried to take Tomás Walsh away, his brother, Patrick, created a commotion. 'Don't leave him go, boys,' Patrick shouted to neighbours. In the mêlée, his mother was knocked to the ground. Walsh and his two sons were subsequently arrested and charged with assault and obstruction.

That same day, Tom O'Donnell informed a meeting of his supporters in Tralee that he was withdrawing, leaving the way open for Stack to be elected unopposed. 'I offered myself for re-election in order to give the people an opportunity to express their views in one of the most momentous crises that has ever occurred in our country,' O'Donnell explained. 'I think the Sinn Féin policy, devoid of reason and sanity, has ruined and will further ruin my country. It has embittered and united opposition to our claims for freedom, both in Ireland and abroad. It advocates a policy in which no honest or sane man believes and it pushes its programme by methods which are the very antithesis of liberty. My friends, in spite of noisy shouting there are yet thousands of sane, decent Irishmen who will save our country in the near future. It has been agreed that in view of the state of the register, packed with boys and girls, we will not engage in the contest at present, and with that decision I most heartily agree. A whirlwind of political insanity is passing over the country; promises are made which can never be realised and there are appeals to prejudice to embitter feelings and distort men's vision. The storm will pass, leaving the stable, honest Irishman untouched after it has scattered the froth and the chaff. With confidence I await that time and most earnestly appeal to my friends throughout west Kerry to bear themselves as men in what is only a temporary and very short-lived period of confusion.'

'I see that Tom O'D [O'Donnell] is gone now,' Collins wrote to Stack next day. 'Kerry is now the one bright spot.' All four Sinn Féin nominees were elected unopposed: Austin Stack in West Kerry, James Crowley in North Kerry, Piaras Beaslaí in East Kerry and Fionán Lynch in South Kerry. All of them were in jail at the time, as were many other Sinn Féin activists. The Irish Parliamentary Party had ducked a contest. 'Glory be to our own Kerry – north, south, east and west – a clean sheet!' the *Kerryman* exclaimed.

There were scenes of great enthusiasm in centres like Tralee, Killarney, Listowel, Dingle, Caherciveen and Castleisland. At four o'clock on the afternoon of the election, David Roche, solicitor, declared Piaras Beaslaí elected as parliamentary representative for East Kerry. Supporters of the victorious candidates marched behind a couple of bands from the courthouse through the town to the market cross, where a meeting chaired by Father Finucane was addressed by Tim O'Shea, Dick Fitzgerald and Henry Spring.

In Listowel following the announcement of James Crowley's election in North Kerry, the Volunteers there paraded through the town behind a brass band. Addresses were then delivered from the window of the Sinn Féin election headquarters, popularly known as 'Liberty Hall'. Supporters were congratulated on their notable victory by Crowley's election agent, Daniel J. Browne.

Sinn Féin swept most of the country, winning seventy-three

seats, against twenty-six for the Unionist Party and only six for the once-powerful Irish Parliamentary Party. The total vote for Sinn Féin came to 47.7 per cent, but this figure was undoubtedly distorted by the fact that so many of the party's candidates were returned unopposed in areas like County Kerry, where the party's support was strongest. There was no doubt that Sinn Féin could claim a clear mandate for its platform to establish an Irish republic with its own sovereign assembly.

There was a sequel in Kerry. John Walsh and his two sons were taken to Cork for trial, over the election-poster fracas. RIC Sergeant Patrick J. Moloney testified at the trial on 17 December, but on his return to Anascaul that night he was attacked. Tim Kennedy, the director of intelligence of the Volunteer organisation in Kerry, happened to arrive home on the same train.

'On coming out on the platform, I was told by a young lad named John O'Shea that the sergeant was to be shot,' Kennedy recalled. 'I ran from the station towards the village and just as I reached my own house I saw a chap on one knee put up a shotgun and fire at the sergeant.' Moloney was wearing a heavy greatcoat over his uniform and the clothing absorbed most of the shot. He suffered little more than shock and some shallow pellet wounds to the backside.

RIC District Inspector Tom Walsh of Dingle headed the investigation. Tim Kennedy's family home was searched by the RIC. Walsh found a military-training manual and some compromising documents belonging to Tim, but he just pocketed them. His eldest daughter was about to marry Dr Paddy Moriarty, a first cousin of the Kennedys. Some years later, she gave Tim Kennedy the material that her father had lifted and kept to himself.

Several local people were arrested, including Tim Kennedy's brother, Paddy, and John 'The Hawk' O'Connor, who was staying at their home. Three first cousins of the Kennedy brothers – Patrick T. Kennedy, Patrick J. Kennedy and his brother John J. Kennedy of Curticurrane, were also arrested. The actual assailant was Patrick Kennedy of Coumduffmore, near Anascaul. The RIC obviously had information that they were looking for a Kennedy, but Walsh was not really looking for anybody. Indeed, he may have been responsible for muddying the waters by arresting so many Kennedys when there was only one assailant.

The frustration of the RIC at being unable to apprehend anyone for the attack on Sergeant Moloney was compounded when Walsh and his two sons were acquitted of the charges that had given rise to the court case in the first place. District Inspector Tom Walsh came under suspicion, and he was transferred to Cork shortly afterwards – much to the disappointment of Tim Kennedy. He was 'very sympathetic in a difficult time in 1919,' Tim noted. 'I have no doubt but I would have succeeded in getting him on our side, as he was one of our own people.'

Unfortunately the whole thing had a tragic sequel. Tim Kennedy's brother, Paddy, was later shot dead by a British soldier after he had been wrongly pointed out as Sergeant Moloney's assailant, but that story will be covered later.

Just after Christmas there was trouble in Crumlin Road Jail over indignities to which visitors were being subjected. Stack demanded reform, but the prison governor replied that he had his orders. Stack therefore announced that he would exercise no further restraint on the men. This amounted to encouraging them to revolt. The prisoners protested by going on the roof of the laundry and the warders' quarters. They hoisted a large tricolour on the chimney. A hostile loyalist mob gathered on the Crumlin Road and began stoning the jail. While the prisoners on the roof sang Republican songs like 'The Soldier's Song', the crowd in the street replied with Orange and loyalist songs like 'Dolly's Brae' and 'Rule Britannia'.

A young priest tried to persuade the prisoners to call off their protest before soldiers and RIC were introduced to regain control of the prison. 'Father,' Stack said to him, 'if they are coming to attack us, we will fight them.' The Republicans fortified themselves on an upper floor and dismantled the stairs. Some eighty men were sent onto the roof to smash it. Stack ordered that all their food be collected and stored. Men came forward with the contents of their Christmas parcels. On the night of 28 December, the results of the general election were officially announced. The prisoners began celebrating the Sinn Féin victory during a three-day siege of the jail.

The Bishop of Down and Conor and future Cardinal Joseph MacRory was brought in to negotiate a settlement, but Stack raised the stakes. He demanded that the Republican prisoners be moved to an internment camp and treated as prisoners of war. This was to strengthen rebel claims to be heard at the post-war peace conference. The prisoners were given to believe that Dublin Castle agreed to these demands, but then once they gave up their protest, the promised reforms were not implemented. Some of the men were kept in handcuffs for up to a month. This dispute simmered throughout the early months of the new year.

9

―

'What Did I Do?'

In 1919, when the Volunteers reorganised, Kerry was divided into three brigades. Kerry No. 1 Brigade extended from Glenbeigh to Tarbert and included all the Dingle peninsula. The brigade was divided into seven battalions, with Paddy J. Cahill as the brigadier and Joe Melinn as his deputy. Denis O'Sullivan was adjutant and Billy Mullins was the brigade quartermaster.

The 1st Battalion was centred on Tralee, under the command of Dan Healy, with Mick Doyle as deputy leader, Michael Fleming as adjutant and Paddy Barry as quartermaster. The 2nd Battalion was based in Dingle, under the command of An Seabhac, with Michael Moriarty as his deputy, while the 3rd Battalion was in the Castlegregory area, under the command of Tadhg Brosnan. The 4th Battalion was in Listowel, under the command of P. Landers, while the 5th was in Ardfert, with Tom Clifford in charge. The 6th Battalion was in Killorglin, under F. Doherty, and B. O'Grady was the officer commanding the 7th Battalion, headquartered in Lixnaw.

Kerry No. 2 Brigade consisted of five battalions in the east and south of the county. Dan O'Mahony of Castleisland was the officer commanding, with Denis Dennehy as his deputy, while R. Devane was brigade adjutant and Humphrey Murphy the quartermaster. The 1st Battalion was drawn from the Castleisland area under Tom O'Connor, while the 2nd Battalion was based in Firies under P. Riordan. The 3rd Battalion was in Killarney, with M. Spillane in charge. M. J. Sullivan was his deputy, Pat

O'Shea the adjutant, and Jim Coffey the quartermaster. The 4th Battalion was in Rathmore under H. Sullivan, while John Joe Rice was the officer commanding the 5th Battalion in Kenmare.

Kerry No. 3 Brigade was based in the south-west of the county, in the Iveragh peninsula. J. O'Riordan was the officer commanding, with Denis Daly of Cahirciveen as his deputy. The brigade consisted of a number of local companies in Cahirciveen, Killoe, Ballycarbery, Filemore, Glen, Balinskelligs, Waterville, Mastergeeha, Portmagee, Caherdaniel, Valentia, Loher and Bahoo.

Tim Kennedy was appointed director of intelligence for No. 1 Brigade, covering the northern half of the county. He reported directly to Michael Collins, with whom he had already become quite friendly since first meeting him during a holiday in Ballybunion in 1913. At that time, Collins had been with his mentor, Sam Maguire.

Kennedy shared a passion for the Irish language with the RIC's Special Crimes Sergeant, Thomas O'Rourke. He was the main man in the barracks dealing with political crimes and political intelligence. As a result of their friendship, O'Rourke indicated how RIC intelligence was gathered, by explaining how they kept a constant watch on all national organisations, placed their own representatives within the IRB and had their own civilian sources of information from members of the Masonic Lodges.

Kennedy began to build up an intelligence network in Kerry in much the same way as Collins was doing in Dublin. Kennedy recruited a variety of people as sources of information. Austin Stack introduced him to Tom Dillon, the chief clerk at Tralee General Post Office. Dillon explained ways of getting hold of letters and telegrams to local British forces. With his help, Kennedy explained, 'I gradually made the acquaintance of every member of the staff and roped them into my organisation singly and had no difficulty in getting what I wanted.' Jack Sullivan, a former soldier, was good at spotting military and police communications. The chief postal sorter was another ex-serviceman who proved invaluable. Miss Margaret Pendy, who was in charge of the telephone exchange, used to listen in on calls and report anything of importance to Kennedy.

Members of Na Fianna were placed in the post office as telegram boys. One of them, Congs Griffin, was caught by Ned Myers, the chief telegraphist, while copying a coded telegram. Griffin was promptly dismissed. The Republicans retaliated by threatening Myers that they would forget what he had done only if he supplied them with copies of coded messages for the RIC. 'We frightened the life out of him and he became as enthusiastic as ourselves,' Kennedy noted.

Of course, the coded telegrams were of no use without a means of breaking the codes, and Kennedy developed his friendship with Sergeant O'Rourke, who realised that his friend was probably involved in intelligence work. He told Kennedy that he was anxious to channel information to the Republican leadership. 'I hadn't such experience of intelligence at the time and I was scared to have much to do with the RIC,' Kennedy explained. He therefore consulted Michael Collins, who advised him to seize the opportunity to ask O'Rourke to furnish a copy of the key to the RIC code.

'I asked him for the key,' Kennedy added, 'and he delivered it to myself. I sent it to Mick Collins and henceforth I was able to supply it to headquarters every month and after each change where the RIC suspected we had got it. Mick told me afterwards that it was the first time he was able to procure the key regularly and it laid the foundation of the elaborate scheme of intelligence in the post offices.'

On the day that Dáil Éireann was formally established in Dublin – 21 January 1919 – some Volunteers ambushed a couple of RIC men escorting a consignment of explosives to a mine. The attack, which took place at Soloheadbeg, County Tipperary, is usually considered to mark the start of the War of Independence. The ambush, in which the two policemen were killed, was a purely local action, which was actually resented by many of the leaders in Dublin because it drew some attention away from the formation of Dáil Éireann.

Michael Collins was blamed for the Soloheadbeg attack, but he was not even in the country at the time. He was in England finalising arrangement for Éamon de Valera's escape from Lincoln Jail. De Valera made his successful break on the evening of 6 February. The driver of the getaway taxi was Paddy O'Donoghue, a Kerryman.

Collins had helped de Valera to escape in the confident belief that the latter would lead a renewed struggle against the British. 'As for us on the outside,' Collins wrote to Stack the following week, 'all ordinary, peaceful means are ended and we shall be taking the only alternative actions in a short while now.' He was planning to provoke a war with the British. He had already conceived of a broad plan to undermine Dublin Castle. This would be done initially by destroying the regime's intelligence system, which was dependent on the police and detectives reporting on political matters. Eliminating them would have the effect of disabling the Dublin Castle set-up.

'To paralyse the British machine, it was necessary to strike at individuals,' Collins later explained. 'Without her spies, England was helpless. It was only by means of their accumulated and accumulating knowledge that the British machine could operate.' If those people were eliminated, Dublin Castle would be virtually deaf and blind. 'Without their police throughout the country, how could they find the men they wanted?' he asked. Of course Collins realised that the British would retaliate, but if they did not have proper intelligence, they would do so blindly and in the process hit innocent Irish people, thus driving the people into the arms of the Republicans.

A determined, opinionated young man, Collins was capable of making fast decisions with all the confidence of youth, but his determination was combined with an arrogance that frequently made him intolerant of the views of others. He had acquired the nickname 'the Big Fellow' not because he was a big man but because he was always considered to have a swelled head or an exaggerated sense of his own importance. Even close colleagues distrusted his judgement. As a result they backed the election of Richard Mulcahy as IRA chief of staff in 1918.

Aware of the opposition to himself, Collins initially looked to de Valera to lead a renewed struggle, but the Long Fellow had other ideas. In view of President Woodrow Wilson's eloquent pronouncements about the rights of small nations – for which Americans had supposedly gone to war in 1917 – de Valera thought Ireland's best chance of success lay in enlisting American help. He therefore decided to go to America in an attempt to secure that country's support, but before leaving he undermined the Big Fellow's plans to provoke an early confrontation with the British by ensuring that the more moderate elements had control of the standing committee of Sinn Fein.

'It is very bad,' Collins wrote to Stack. 'The chief actor was very firm on the withdrawal, as indeed was Cathal [Brugha]. I used my influence the other way, and was in a practical minority of one. It may be that all arguments were sound, but it seems to me that they have put up a challenge which strikes at the fundamentals of our policy and our attitude.'

Following his election as Príomh Aire (Prime Minister) of Dáil Éireann in April, de Valera was anxious to secure international recognition for Ireland rather than resorting to a military confrontation. He advocated a policy of ostracising the police and their families as servants of a foreign power. The

Clerk of the Dáil drafted an outline of what 'social ostracisation' entailed. The police 'must receive no social recognition from the people; that no intercourse, except such as is absolutely necessary on business, is permitted with them; that they should not be saluted nor spoken to in the streets or elsewhere, nor their salutes returned; that they should not be invited to nor received in private houses as friends or guests; that they be debarred from participation in games, sports, dances and all social functions conducted by the people; that intermarriage with them be discouraged; that, in a word, the police should be treated as persons who, having been adjudged guilty of treason to their country, are regarded as unworthy to enjoy any of the privileges or comforts which arise from cordial relations with the public.'

'Volunteers shall have no intercourse with the RIC, and shall stimulate and support in every way the boycott of this force ordered by the Dáil,' IRA headquarters ordered. 'Those persons who associate with the RIC should be subjected to the same boycott, and the fact of their associations with and toleration of this infamous force shall be kept public in every possible way. Definite lists of such persons in the area of his command shall be prepared and retained by each company, battalion and brigade commander.'

Many shopkeepers refused to serve members of the RIC, but police officers retaliated by simply taking whatever they wished and suggesting that the bill be sent to the local police barracks. Although the boycott of the police seems drastic, de Valera was trying to keep the hardliners in check while at the same time imposing democratic restraints on the militants. At a special Sinn Féin Ard Fheis on 8 April 1919, he secured approval for the party's standing committee to have a veto over government action. If a minister decided that Irish people should no longer pay income tax to the Crown, for example, he said that the proposal would need the approval of the committee.

The example he gave was particularly significant, because, as Minister for Finance, Collins had been advocating that the Irish people should be obliged to pay their taxes to the Dáil, not the Crown government. Now, however, the more moderate leadership of Sinn Féin was being given a virtual veto over Collins.

'The policy now seems to be to squeeze out anyone who is tainted with strong fighting ideas, or should I say the utility of fighting,' Collins wrote to Stack on 17 May 1919. Describing the party's executive as 'a standing committee of malcontents,' he complained that they were 'inclined to be ever less militant and more political and theoretical.'

'We have too many of the bargaining type already,' he grumbled in another letter the next day. 'I am not sure that our movement – or part of it, at any rate – is alive to the developing situation.'

With the moderates in control, Collins considered himself 'only an onlooker' at the executive-committee meetings. When Harry Boland went to the United States to make preparations for de Valera's forthcoming tour, the party replaced him as national secretary with Hannah Sheehy-Skeffington, the wife of a pacifist murdered during the Easter Rising. Collins was appalled. He felt that there was a lot of hostility towards him.

There were 'rumours, whisperings, suggestions of differences between certain people,' he informed Stack. All of this he described as 'rather pitiful and disheartening'. It belied the national unity of which de Valera boasted and tended towards confusion about the best way of achieving the national aims, he believed. 'At the moment,' Collins exclaimed, 'I'm awfully fed up.'

'Things are not going very smoothly,' he wrote three weeks later. 'All sorts of miserable little undercurrents are working and the effect is anything but good.'

Charles P. Crane was an Englishman who had joined the

RIC in 1879 and had served in Kerry and Donegal before his appointment as a resident magistrate. During the First World War he was seconded for service in the British army, but when he returned to Kerry he found that conditions had greatly altered. 'What a change one found on all sides,' he wrote. 'The old Ireland of previous days seemed to have disappeared. The beauty of the hills alone remained as a memory of past times. A sulky, anti-British spirit prevails all over the country.'

He believed in law and order and initially thought that progress was being made. 'Illegal drilling has been reduced to small dimensions by the resident magistrates, who, under the provisions of the Prevention of Crimes Act, were enabled to try offenders and sentence them, when necessary to various terms of imprisonment in lieu of finding sureties for future good behaviour,' Crane wrote. 'As far as my district was concerned, this enforcement of the law had an excellent effect, and after a few months the illegal drilling ceased in various localities where it had been rampant.'

Collins began to get his own way after de Valera went to the United States in June 1919. But Kerry was again doing its own thing. Sergeant Bernard Oates and Constable J. J. O'Connell were attacked and disarmed near their RIC station in Camp on the night of 24 June 1919. They were returning on bicycles from patrol duty in Aughacasla at about ten o'clock.

The constable had a loaded rifle attached to his bicycle and a quantity of ammunition in his pouch. The sergeant was unarmed. As the police approached Fitzgerald's house at Meenascarthy, they were surprised by six or seven armed men, who rushed through a gateway and knocked them off their bicycles. The men promptly seized the constable's rifle and ammunition, but Oates grappled with a couple of the assailants. One of them had a revolver and fired at him from three or four feet. According to Oates, the bullet pierced his tunic but was deflected by a buckle on his braces. The Volunteers smashed the bicycles of the two RIC men, before retreating in the direction of Aughacasla.

Following the attack, Michael Spillane, Timothy Spillane, John Butler, Michael Flynn, Michael Maunsell, Martin Griffin, John Farrell, Tom Crean, Denis Sugrue and Michael Griffin were arrested and brought to Tralee police barracks. Sergeant Oates identified Michael and Timothy Spillane, and Flynn, as having been in the attacking party, while Constable O'Connell identified Maunsell and Griffin. The resident magistrate, Edward M. Wynne, then discharged the other five. Timothy Spillane was subsequently sentenced to three years in jail for his part in the attack, while Michael Spillane and Michael Flynn each got eighteen months with hard labour. Michael Maunsell received a fifteen-month sentence and Michael Griffin got nine months, both with hard labour.

On the night of 17 July 1919, Volunteers in Cahirciveen blew up a monument that had recently been erected in the family burial ground at Killovarnogue cemetery to Captain James Roche, a local man who had been killed in France during the First World War.

Piaras Beaslaí, the Dáil representative for East Kerry, had been arrested in March by Detective Sergeant Patrick Smith for making a seditious speech. Some incriminating documents were found on Beaslaí. Although Smith was warned not to produce these documents in court, he ignored the warning and Beaslaí was sentenced to two years in jail, instead of the two months he might otherwise have expected.

Collins was authorised by Chief of Staff Richard Mulcahy and Defence Minister Cathal Brugha to eliminate Smith, and the famous 'Squad' was set up to kill him. Smith was shot and mortally wounded outside his Drumcondra home on the night of 30 July 1919.

He lingered for five weeks before finally succumbing to his wounds on 11 September 1919. Dublin Castle reacted to the killing by banning Sinn Féin; this played directly into the hands of Collins by undermining the Sinn Féin moderates. The checks that de Valera had placed on the militants were wiped out by the banning of the political wing of the movement, which prompted one leading British civil servant, Sir Warren Fisher, to conclude that the Castle regime, was 'almost woodenly stupid and quite devoid of imagination'.

Sinn Féin headquarters were raided on 12 September, the same day the party was banned. Collins reacted by having one of the detectives involved in the raid killed that night in the street. Things were deteriorating so rapidly that in September the RIC were issued with rockets, Very pistols, shotguns and hand grenades for their own protection. Members of the force were seen carrying hand grenades in Cahirciveen shortly afterwards.

In the following weeks, Collins turned his mind in earnest to springing Stack from jail. He had been planning to do this for more than a year, first from Dundalk Jail and then from Belfast Jail, but each time Stack was moved before arrangements could be finalised. Now he was in Strangeways Jail in Manchester.

Collins actually visited Stack in prison to discuss plans for the escape, which was finally set for 25 October 1919. Some twenty men were posted outside the jail, under Rory O'Connor. A rope ladder was thrown over the wall and a diversion created while the prisoners in the yard scaled the wall. Piaras Beaslaí had escaped from Mountjoy in March using this technique, but he had been recaptured by Detective Sergeants Smith and Wharton. Beaslaí was involved again in Strangeways as he, Stack and four others managed to escape. They were taken to safe houses in the Manchester and Liverpool area. It was a measure of how highly Collins thought of Stack that he even went back to England to arrange for Stack's return to Dublin.

On the eve of their return, Detective Sergeant Wharton, from Killarney, was shot and seriously wounded by a member of the Squad as he walked near St Stephen's Green. Although he survived, his injuries forced him to resign from the police, but he was luckier than his fellow Kerryman, Detective Sergeant Johnny Barton of Ballymacelligott. Barton was investigating the Wharton shooting and was shot dead in the street near the detective division's headquarters in New Brunswick Street (now Pearse Street), Dublin, at the height of the evening rush hour on 30 November 1920.

'What did I do?' Barton moaned repeatedly as he lay dying. He had been in the detective division for only two months. In eyes of Collins, he had committed the unforgivable sin of trying to find Wharton's assailants.

By this stage, Collins had become the most wanted man in the country. There was never formally a price on his head, but there were rewards totalling £50,000 for the arrest and convictions of those responsible for the murders of the detectives that his Squad had eliminated. The British were looking for Collins but they had no idea where to find him. In November 1919 they received an offer of help from a resident of the Munster Hotel, Timothy A. Quinlisk.

Quinlisk had joined Casement's brigade in Germany as a prisoner of war. On the first anniversary of the armistice – 11 November 1919 – he wrote to the under-secretary at Dublin Castle, offering to furnish information on Collins. 'I was the man who assisted Casement in Germany and, since coming home, I have been connected with Sinn Féin,' he wrote. 'I have decided to tell all I know of that organisation and my information would be of use to the authorities. The scoundrel Michael Collins has treated me scurvily and I now am going to wash my hands of the whole business.'

He was invited for questioning to the headquarters of the

Dublin Metropolitan Police. That was a major mistake, however, because Collins had Ned Broy, one of his own most trusted agents, inside the building. Broy typed up Quinlisk's statement and made an extra carbon copy for Collins. But Quinlisk had taken the precaution of telling Collins that he had gone to the DMP merely to get a passport so he could emigrate to the United States. He said the police had put pressure on him, including offering him money, to inform on Collins. He told Collins that he merely pretended to go along with them.

Collins was not in the Munster Hotel when the DMP raided it some days later. He moved and spent much of the next nineteen months moving about, never staying in any one place for very long. He continued to keep clothes at Number 44, and Myra McCarthy continued to do his laundry, but the Munster Hotel was marked thereafter and raided regularly in the coming months. Quinlisk was subsequently shot as a spy by the IRA in Cork.

Stack had meanwhile become Minister for Home Affairs with responsibility for developing the Republican courts and police system. He had already been appointed deputy chief of staff of the IRA, but he never really functioned in that position. There had been a suggestion that Stack would return to Kerry and set himself up there, but Collins wanted him in Dublin. 'My own idea would be that you'd be indispensable in Dublin and I don't think any consideration would change my mind in this regard,' he wrote to Stack. He was obviously looking forward to fruitful cooperation between them but things turned out differently, because Stack was a poor administrator. He shirked difficult decisions, and he later admitted he was out of his depth as Minister for Home Affairs, never mind that he was also deputy chief of staff of the IRA.

'Stack told me how unfitted he was for the job of Minister of Home Affairs,' his friend Tim Kennedy later recalled. 'He hadn't either the education or the ability, he felt. He was a very humble man and he had no illusions about his own abilities.' Collins was impatient at Stack's failings.

Things were already changing dramatically in Ireland. Faced with the killing of the most active detectives, Lord French, the Lord Lieutenant, set up a three-man committee to consider what to do about the deteriorating intelligence situation. The three men were the acting inspector general of the RIC, the assistant under-secretary at Dublin Castle and a resident magistrate named Alan Bell. They suggested infiltrating the Republican movement with spies in order to assassinate selected leaders.

It seemed like a race as to whether Collins would get his enemies first, or they would get him. Collins ordered that French should be assassinated. He was part of an ambush gang one night, but that had to be called off when French took another route to his official residence in the Phoenix Park. On 19 December the IRA did catch up with him near the Phoenix Park, but French escaped unscathed.

RIC constable Maurice Keogh, a native of Killmallock, was not so lucky the following week. He was shot and fatally wounded in Killarney on Christmas Eve, but his death had as much to do with drink as with the deteriorating political climate. Some soldiers had created a ruckus after they were refused more drink at Casey's bar. Keogh was one of six constables who went to investigate.

'We met some soldiers who had arguments,' Keogh told District Inspector Riordan afterwards. They then went to Bohereail laneway. 'I heard a stone fall there,' Keogh continued. 'We went into the archway. I heard four shots. The first shot struck me.' He indicated that the shot came from the other end of the lane.

Keogh was a big, strong man. He walked back to the

barracks, despite his wound. He was then hospitalised, but he developed septic peritonitis. He then changed his story and said that a colleague had shot him.

'Father Harris told me I am dying,' he said to Riordan on 30 December. 'I know well it was Constable Egan hit me.' Egan had obviously been drinking, though one of his colleagues was not prepared to say he was 'very drunk,' but he was obviously considered a danger, because they disarmed him even before they realised that he had shot Keogh. 'When I said some days before that shots were fired up the lane,' Keogh told Riordan in a deathbed confession, 'I wanted to save Constable Egan.' Keogh died the following day, the victim of a tragic accident. It was a bad end to the year.

The new year was only a few days old when Constable Clarke was shot dead in Ballylongford. He had been in town paying bills. At about 7 o'clock on the Saturday evening, 3 January 1920, somebody ambushed him with a shotgun from behind a wall. He was hit in the shoulder and neck from about eight to ten yards' range, and suffered in the region of 150 pellet wounds. The attack was undertaken simply to seize his gun.

The celebrations ending the Christmas season got particularly rowdy in Waterville at the bar of the Butler Arms Hotel, which was packed with around 250 people on the night of 6 January 1920. The RIC was called and Constables Holland and Kenny arrested one Michael O'Shea for making trouble but they were surrounded by an angry crowd and compelled to free O'Shea. Sergeant Benson and Constable Hamilton arrived to give them back up. There was clearly a strong Republican element in the crowded hotel bar, because there were chants of 'Wrap the Green Flag Round Me, Boys', 'Up Knocklong', 'Solohead', 'Up Tipperary' and 'To Hell with the Police'.

Somebody threw a full bottle of stout at Constable Hamilton and he was cut in the eye when the bottle smashed off the wall beside him. Benson ordered him to fire warning shots; people scattered but then quickly returned.

'Come on, boys, there are only four of them,' somebody shouted. But Benson ordered Kenny to shoot and again the crowd backed off. Just two people, Thomas Fenton and Maurice Fitzgerald, were arrested, and they were charged with unlawful assembly.

10

'AN ATTACK OF MAUSERITIS'

Business, politics and religion were inexorably becoming mixed up in the national struggle. During the second week of January there was a sensational development in Tralee, where Serjeant Alexander M. Sullivan, KC, the lawyer who defended Roger Casement, was involved in a shooting incident. He had been in town in connection with a compensation case for malicious damage. The dispute – between Ballymacelligott Cooperative Creamery and a private creamery in Kilquane, Ballymacelligott, owned by Jeremiah M. Slattery of Tralee – had been going on for some years.

The parish priest in Ballymacelligott, Father Timothy Trant, involved himself in the case by taking a strong stand on the side of the cooperative creamery as a means of advancing the interests of the farmers in order to promote the prosperity of their parish. 'This is a matter of such vital importance that even the young people of the parish should take it up in a whole-hearted fashion and with all the fire and enthusiasm of youth,' he said.

The cooperative creamery in Ballymacelligott was taken to court for unfair business practices and lost a judgement, but that was overturned by the High Court, only to be reinstated on appeal by the House of Lords. Then the boys of 'Ballymac' took the law into their own hands and bombed Slattery's creamery in Kilquane on the night of 25 September 1919. Afterwards a notice was posted on the church gate, explaining that the bombing had been in reaction to the decision of the House of Lords.

'To the people of Ballymacelligott,' the notice began. 'Be it known to you that the crippling of the machinery at Kilquane was done for no mean motive but for the prosperity of the parish.' The message concluded that 'there is a higher tribunal than the House of Lords, and that tribunal decided that Slattery's creamery no longer exists. No man in future must convey milk to Slattery's creamery. This is the last warning, so take it. Explosives at hand.'

On his way to the creamery shortly afterwards, Laurence Keane was stopped on his horse and cart 'by an undisguised ruffian named Leen, a well-known criminal, who ordered the man off the car and shot the horse opposite a cooperative creamery in broad daylight, in the presence of a number of people, and in the holy parish of Ballymacelligott this scoundrel enjoyed immunity,' according to Sullivan.

'Shame on the county where such a thing could occur,' he added. 'It was a disgrace to civilisation.' He went on to note that between 30 September and 13 October 1919 a series of threatening letters were sent by the self-styled 'Buckshot Brigade' to anyone using Slattery's creamery.

Garret McElligott was stopped by armed men who shot holes in his tankards, while Martin Reidy, Michael Leen and James Daly had their horses stolen. William Hill was stopped, and his milk was spilled, while Timothy Bailey's home was fired into, and 'an old man named Herlihy had his whiskers cut off, and mud forced down his throat by a gang of ruffians, the worst that could be found in the lowest English slums.'

In the face of such intimidation, the creamery naturally lost business and Slattery sued for malicious damage. He was represented by a local solicitor, Edmond B. Slattery, who secured the services of Serjeant Sullivan as senior counsel. In presenting the case, Sullivan was particularly critical of the role of the parish priest. Sullivan clearly believed that some bishops, like the late

Dr O'Dwyer of Limerick and Fogarty of Killaloe, were failing in their Christian duty because they essentially supported Sinn Féin. Sullivan was especially critical of Father Timothy Trant, the local parish priest, for essentially encouraging what he depicted as 'this shameful and disgraceful condition of paganism in his parish'.

That evening, Friday 9 January 1920, Sullivan was dining with Edmond Slattery in the latter's home at Clounalour when there was a knock on the door. Slattery answered and was accosted by seven or eight armed men. Sullivan came to his assistance and grappled with one of the gunmen. In the ensuing mêlée, some five to seven shots were fired and Sullivan suffered a flash wound to his left eyebrow. Slattery slipped on the tiled floor and was kicked repeatedly while he was down. Nobody was seriously injured, though Slattery's wife collapsed in a faint.

The Dean of Kerry, Monsignor David O'Leary, who noted that the only explanation he could find for the wanton attack was some insulting remarks that Sullivan had made about Father Trant in court, denounced the incident from the pulpit. He said that, even if those remarks had not been calculated to serve any useful purpose, they did not excuse the outrageous behaviour of those who perpetrated the incident.

Serjeant Sullivan was far from happy with the attitude of the Catholic hierarchy. 'There will be no peace in Ireland until the bishops preach Christianity as applied to private as well as to political and public life,' he declared in response to the attack. This prompted a stinging attack from the *Irish Catholic*, which suggested that he should change his menu, as 'roast bishop and deviled priest are not wholesome as a steady diet.'

People were quick to suggest that the incident had nothing to do with the political situation, but eleven Volunteers from Ballymacelligott were arrested and charged with the attack. They included John Leen, Maurice Carmody and Cornelius Sullivan, who were reportedly identified by Serjeant Sullivan. As Sullivan left Tralee on the Cork train, there were reports that he had been shot at. What actually happened was that a lamp broke loose on the train and banged off a window in the carriage in which Sullivan was travelling, breaking a window.

Meanwhile, the British had stepped up their efforts to get Collins. One of the first men they used to infiltrate the Republicans was an agent of the Secret Intelligence Service, John Charles Byrne. He made contact in Britain with Thomas J. McElligott, a former RIC man from Duagh, County Kerry.

McElligott had joined the force as a nineteen-year-old in 1907. While stationed in Trim, County Meath, he was promoted to sergeant and established the Irish branch of the National Union of Police and Prison Officers. He became its chairman in 1918. He had strong Republican views and, using the pen name 'Pro Patria', opposed conscription and supported Sinn Féin. He resigned from the RIC on 22 May 1919 in protest against his transfer to County Mayo because of his activities in the police union. Collins, who had been making great use of disaffected policemen within his intelligence network, quickly recruited McElligott, who went to Britain to try to stir up union trouble within the British police.

Byrne, who was trying to infiltrate the Sinn Féin movement using the alias Jameson, made contact with McElligott and came to Dublin with an offer to procure arms for the IRA. He managed to meet both Collins and Richard Mulcahy. A further meeting was arranged with Collins at Batt O'Connor's home.

By this stage, Detective Inspector W. C. Forbes Redmond had been brought from Belfast as assistant commissioner to reorganise G division of the DMP. Informed that Jameson had already met Collins, Redmond foolishly ridiculed the police for having been unable to find Collins when he had somebody who could come over from England and meet him within a fortnight.

Collins was actually at Batt O'Connor's place when Redmond set out with a raiding party on 16 January 1920, but before they reached the house, two of the Big Fellow's men left the building and a lookout mistakenly thought that Collins had departed, so the raid was called off. One of the men Redmond had brought on that raid – James McNamara – was a spy for Collins, and realised that the latter had a very narrow escape.

Four days later, Redmond was to pay for the mistake with his life. He was shot dead by the Squad outside his hotel. Little over three weeks later, on 18 February, Quinlisk was lured into a trap and shot dead in Cork; Byrne (alias Jameson) was taken out and shot on 2 March 1920. The British Cabinet was informed that Byrne had been one of its best agents.

In Kerry, attacks on the RIC were stepped up. Camp barracks were attacked at 1 o'clock in the morning on 19 February 1920. The attackers reportedly used an assortment of weapons, while Sergeant MacDonagh and six constables inside retaliated with hand grenades and rifle fire. The telegraph lines in the area had been cut and the roads leading to Camp were blocked with felled trees. An extra barricade had been constructed at Anna, near Blennerville, to delay any reinforcements being sent to the police from Tralee.

The attackers managed to blow out a wall of the barracks but the police refused to surrender, and after an assault lasting about an hour, the attackers withdrew. The only apparent casualty was Sergeant MacDonagh, who received a bullet wound to his cheek.

By this time, the whole British system of law and order was coming apart. People were ignoring the Crown courts in the more remote areas of south Kerry, according to the local resident magistrate, Charles P. Crane. 'I arrived to dispense justice, and having taken my seat on the bench in solitude, a young man walked into court with his cap on and smoking a cigarette,' he wrote. 'I ordered him out, but on looking around I saw no one to carry out my orders! The police were not present, and all I could do was to order the fellow out.' The man eventually complied, leaving Crane on his own. 'I could do no more than adjourn.'

Then his driver quit. 'My man, whom I had taught to drive, came to the conclusion, "for his wife's sake", that he could not bear the danger of driving with me,' Crane wrote. 'He had what the local doctor called an attack of mauseritis.'

The policy of jailing people for illegal drilling and then jailing them again if they did not provide sureties of good conduct was breaking down under the strain of events. 'On the last occasion on which it was my duty to deal with one of these cases, the defendants adopted the usual method of defying the court, asserting that they were "soldiers of the Irish Republic", and behaving with studied insolence,' Crane wrote. When the accused refused to provide sureties, he sentenced them to further terms of imprisonment. 'The courthouse was crowded with sympathisers, and ringing cheers greeted the ebullition of insolence on the part of the defendants,' he continued. 'An escort of soldiers and constabulary took them to the train en route to Cork Jail and left the streets of Killarney without a policeman. Driving along in my car on my way from the court, I was surrounded by a savage, booing mob, some of whom shook their fists in my face, shouting, "You will be dead in six months."

'Never before as a magistrate had I such an experience,' he added. 'It was significant of the fact that respect for the law was fast disappearing.' Crane packed up himself in March 1920 and returned to England.

The IRA's policy was simply to disrupt the British administration in every way possible. The attacks were purely opportunistic, rather than systematic.

A three-man RIC patrol was held up and forced to surrender its arms at Ballyronan, near Ballyheigue, on 8 March. They were then let go. But the men who attacked Sergeant George Neazer a couple of days later were not looking for his weapon. They intended to kill him. He was shot dead while dining at the Hibernian Hotel in Rathkeale.

'Georgie', as Neazer was called in Tralee, was from the Pallaskenry area. He was forty-three years old and had plagued the Republicans ever since the Volunteer split in 1914, when he was assigned to political duties. He had successfully investigated the shooting of Sergeant Oates at Camp the previous year and had also secured an arrest in the shooting of Michael O'Brien of Lixnaw in Ratoo on 23 March 1918. James Slattery was arrested for that attempted murder, but a jury refused to convict him, even though O'Brien identified him as the assailant. Afterwards Neazer was assigned to protect O'Brien, who had given evidence at the trial. The detective was on protection duty at the hotel when the Rathkeale company of the IRA seized the opportunity to kill him.

Ballybunion barracks was attacked in a three-hour shoot-out on 12 March 1920. Sergeant Brody and four of his constables were in Tralee for the assizes that day, leaving just six constables in the barracks. The operation was a combined effort by a number of IRA companies in north Kerry. It was their first attack on a barracks. The telegraph lines from Ballybunion were cut and trees were felled to block the roads from Tralee, Listowel and Ballylongford. The IRA then took over the houses of James Clarke, and the Costello and Beasley families opposite the barracks. The occupants were escorted to neighbouring houses, and sandbags were put in place in the three houses. The Volunteers then opened fire on the barracks.

The windows of the barracks were raked with bullets and the police responded with rapid gunfire. The attack lasted nearly three hours but no serious injury was reported on either side. The police stated that one constable had picked up a slight wound on his wrist.

As a result of such attacks, the RIC abandoned isolated barracks around the country. A couple of days later, the police moved out of the barracks at Caherdaniel, leaving their five bicycles with the caretaker of the local courthouse, Cornelius Kelly. This was to have disastrous consequences for him when the IRA decided to seize the bicycles the following week. Kelly was at home with his wife and nine-year-old daughter on 16 March when a group of armed, masked men broke into their home.

'About 9 o'clock my husband, my brother and my child were sitting at the fireside,' Bridget Kelly explained afterwards. 'My husband was sitting on a chair and I was combing my child's hair when the door slammed in suddenly and a number of men rushed into the house. There were about six of them there. They were masked and had fawn coats on them.'

'Hands up,' they shouted.

'I told them not to frighten the child,' Bridget Kelly continued. They were looking for the police bicycles.

'Take them,' Cornelius Kelly said. With that, a shot rang out and he slumped into the fire, dead.

Tom McEllistrim and his colleagues had been itching for another crack at the RIC barracks in Gortatlea since their disastrous raid on it in April 1918. As part of the preparations, McEllistrim went to Dublin to get some guns from IRA headquarters. It was later suggested that Michael Collins had provided six rifles, with the admonition that they were to make proper use of them. McEllistrim had been interned with Collins in Frongoch and would probably have remembered if the Big Fellow had given him the rifles. 'I paid cash for them,' McEllistrim recalled, 'but cannot recollect now from whom I got the rifles.'

The IRA gathered in the old hall at Ballymacelligott on the night of 25 March 1920. 'I explained the job we had on our hands,' recalled McEllistrim, who was in charge of the attack.

'We had in the hall forty men from Ballymacelligott Company, fully armed, and a few men from Cordal district who had rifles. These were Michael O'Leary, Din Prendeville and Ned McCarthy. I divided the company into sections.' There were sections for blocking roads and outpost duty, and the attacking party, which consisted of the men who were armed and fully trained.

A sergeant and six constables were stationed in the building, which was a single-storey structure. It was fortified with steel shutters on the windows; the shutters were slotted to make loopholes for guns. The walls had sandbags for protection and the building was surrounded by barbed wire. The police were heavily armed and had provisions to withstand a siege of several days. The roof was the only vulnerable part of the barracks, and it was on this that the IRA commander decided to concentrate his efforts.

'Our plan was to attack the barracks from the roof,' McEllistrim noted. The barracks was overlooked by a two-storey slate-roofed building that housed the stationmaster. They decided to use his house for the attack. McEllistrim led the attacking party from the old hall to within a hundred yards of the barracks. It was about 1.30 am. Jim Spillane, a railway porter at the station, guided McEllistrim and John Cronin by an obscure route to the door of the stationmaster's house. Then they quietly moved him and his family to a nearby house.

One section of the men took a position facing the barracks and another group went to the rear, to ensure that no police escaped in the darkness. Meanwhile, McEllistrim and about a dozen of the others began breaking through the slate roof of the stationmaster's house at the gable overlooking the barracks. As the police heard the noise of the breaking slates, they fired some Very lights, which lit up the district like day.

It was not until the men on the roof of the stationmaster's house began firing that the others opened up. 'Our fire from the roof took the garrison by surprise, as they had no protection from that quarter,' McEllistrim noted. They threw down bombs and petrol on the roof of the barracks and then dropped a lighted sod of turf. The roof went up in flames and the building quickly caught fire. The engagement had only lasted about twenty minutes when an RIC man came to the door and said they would surrender.

'I ordered my men to stay in position and with Cronin and Johnny O'Connor I came down through the trapdoor and we walked through the barracks door, which was now thrown open to us,' McEllistrim continues. The place was filled with smoke. They gathered up the guns, which consisted of six rifles, five pistols, two shotguns and some ammunition. They would have got more but the storeroom was on fire and the ammunition began exploding. The seven RIC men had to abandon the building. Three of them were wounded. Constable Hegarty had received a serious wound to the side and the thigh, while Constables Kelly and Shea each had a foot wound.

'Shoot them,' one of the volunteers shouted, but McEllistrim ordered that the prisoners should be protected and anyone who tried to harm them should be shot. Afterwards the RIC spoke about the rebel leader's chivalry. The IRA telephoned Dr John M. Murphy in Farranfore to come to tend the wounded men, who 'were mad looking for a priest,' according to Johnny O'Connor. Matt Duggan therefore cycled for the priest, in case the wounds proved fatal.

Others who took part in the attack included Moss Galvin, Johnny Duggan, Eddie McCarthy, Pa Connor, Din Prendeville, Charlie Daly and Tom Daly. As Gortatlea was near the three garrison towns of Tralee, Castleisland and Farranfore, they could not delay long. 'When all was over, a party of our men mounted the bridge crossing the railway at the station and sang "The Soldier's Song".' The men then split up, some going towards Farranfore and others towards Tralee.

Next morning at Ballyseedy Cross, Johnny O'Connor and company stopped two men cycling out from Tralee. 'Who were they but me brave sergeant in civilian clothes and another Peeler,' O'Connor noted.

'You burned us out this morning, young man,' Sergeant Walsh said. 'For God's sake don't shoot us, we're only doing our job.'

'I had my gun out and he was shivering,' O'Connor continued. The other man was so scared that he was not even able to stand. He overbalanced and fell. They had gone into Tralee to report the attack on the barracks and were on their way out again. They were let go about their business.

The British had already initiated their campaign of retaliation. On 23 March a northern gang of disguised members of the RIC killed Tomás MacCurtain at his home in front of his family. MacCurtain, who was the IRA leader in Cork, had close ties to Michael Collins, but he was also the lord mayor of the city, and Sinn Féin made propaganda capital out of the killing as an affront to democracy.

The jury at his inquest returned 'a verdict of wilful murder against David Lloyd George, Prime Minister of England; Lord French, Lieutenant of Ireland; Ian McPherson, late Chief Secretary of Ireland; Acting Inspector General Smith of the RIC; Divisional Inspector Clayton of the RIC; District Inspector Swanzy and some unknown members of the RIC.'

Collins retaliated three days later when Alan Bell, one of the three-man committee that had advised the Lord Lieutenant to infiltrate the Sinn Féin movement with spies and had assassinated selected leaders, met the fate that he had advocated for others. He was taken off a tram at Ballsbridge, Dublin, and shot dead in the street in broad daylight. Collins also tracked down the leaders of the gang that killed MacCurtain, and they were picked off one by one. The initial scheme to undermine the Republicans by infiltrating the IRA and killing its leaders had proved disastrous. All the spies had been uncovered and the RIC was utterly demoralised. The trickle of resignations of Irishmen from the force turned into a flood. Collins had essentially achieved his goal of knocking out the eyes and ears of Dublin Castle. He now expected that the British would retaliate but, without proper intelligence, would do so blindly and drive the Irish people into the arms of the Republicans.

The British had to replace the resigning policemen with ill-trained reinforcements, who were so hastily recruited that there were not enough RIC uniforms for them. They therefore wore a combination of the RIC uniform and military khaki. Some wore military khaki with just the belt and cap of the RIC, while others wore the dark pants of the police and khaki jackets, or khaki pants and dark jackets. As a result of the colour scheme, they became known as the 'Black and Tans' – which was also the name of a pack of hounds.

General Henry Tudor was brought in and put in charge of the RIC and the Black and Tans. According to one senior official at Dublin Castle, Tudor's predecessor had essentially become inactive because of the 'daily fear of one of two things, either the wholesale resignations from the force, or of his men running amok. Either, he said, would mean the end of the RIC.'

The changes meant that the British were going to adopt a more aggressive policy. Little over a week after Tudor's appointment, the divisional commander in Limerick wrote: 'I have been told the new policy and plan and I am satisfied, though I doubt its ultimate success in the main particular – the stamping out of terrorism by secret murder. I still am of the opinion that instant retaliation is the only course for this.'

In March 1920 Tim Kennedy was moved to Dublin, and he remained there until October. During that time he got a close look at how demanding Collins was and how he operated. One evening, the two of them were in a section of the city that was surrounded, as troops were conducting a house-to-house search. 'Collins took me down Henry Street and up the stairs in one of the houses,' Kennedy recalled. We went along a corridor till we reached what I took to be a bookcase. He touched a spring or something and opened up the bookcase and we went through into a darkened room, which I noticed had no windows. He closed the entrance and locked them firmly in with a contraption of levers. He told me the escape room was constructed by Batt O'Connor.

'We heard the tramping of the British soldiers along the corridor and the sound of their rifles as they touched the floor. We spent the whole night there and were not released until the following day. We slept on the floor; at least Mick did, as I heard his heavy breathing. I know I didn't sleep much and I was feeling anything but happy.'

On another occasion he had to spend the night with both Stack and Collins. 'We got into bed and I occupied the central position, but I found I could not sleep, what with the heat and the rumblings of the military and police vehicles past the house to Ballsbridge and elsewhere,' Kennedy explained. There was nothing sexual about the wanted men sleeping in the same bed. They were lucky to have a bed that they could share.

11

'Too Hot For Kerry No. 1'

News of the new British recruits intensified the efforts of the IRA. On the evening of 30 March 1920, Constable Flaherty of Cloghane was returning from Castlegregory with two colleagues – Constables Lavelle and Darlington – when they were surprised by masked men at Killiney. Lavelle and Darlington put their hands up, but Flaherty was hit by a shotgun blast that knocked him from his bicycle. Even though he eventually made a complete recovery, he received a total of 132 grains of shot from his left knee to his hip, and also some punctures on his right hand and chest. The raiders seized the guns and ammunition that the RIC men were carrying, along with their bicycles.

Next night the IRA attacked the RIC barracks in Scartaglin, which was built on rising ground. A row of houses on its east side was occupied by members of the IRA column. A fence which ran along the east of the barracks was also manned. One section of the attacking party was detailed to approach the building as closely as possible, throwing bottles of petrol and other inflammable material on the roof and against the sand-filled shell boxes which protected the walls. This operation was carried out successfully: the building was soon in flames.

The RIC garrison replied with heavy rifle fire, and fired Very flares to attract assistance. It was then about 12.30 am and the air was filled with the sound of gunfire and exploding hand grenades. Initially the attack went to plan. The barracks was aflame and subject to concentrated, harassing fire, which made the RIC's position almost untenable.

It was then that fate took a hand and came to the assistance of the besieged men. Had the attackers permitted the fire to run its course, there is no doubt that the police would have been compelled to surrender, but, impatient of delay, and anxious to hasten the end, the IRA hurled home-made grenades at the building to dislodge the protective shell boxes. One of the grenades ruptured a galvanised water tank at one corner of the barracks roof, discharging a strong flow of water on to the roof. This acted as an ideal fire extinguisher, and proved of far greater assistance to the besieged than did their rifles, hand grenades and Very lights.

While this was taking place, the Volunteers on the village side of the building maintained incessant gunfire. Further attempts to set the roof on fire had to be abandoned when the Volunteers ran out of petrol. They were further hampered when one of their number, Eddie McCarthy of Castleisland, was seriously wounded. His comrades managed to extricate him from the line of fire only with great difficulty. By 4.30 am, British reinforcements had reached the village and the attack was abandoned.

Tom McEllistrim was supported in the attack by Johnny Duggan, Mossie Galvin, Johnny O'Connor of Farmer's Bridge; Michael Cronin, Christy Cronin, T. Bowler and Moss Carmody of Ballymacelligott; Humphrey Murphy, Jeremiah O'Leary, Pat O'Connor, David O'Connor, Eddie McCarthy and David McCarthy of Castleisland; Mick Leary and Din Prendeville of Cordal; and Johnny Duggan, John Cronin, Paddy Burke, Jack Herlihy and Paddy Reidy.

The attack on Scartaglin Barracks was planned to take place exactly a month before it actually did, and on the first occasion the attackers were about to take up positions when the project was abandoned as a result of skilful and clever reconnoitring by

Thomas McEllistrim. He saved a group of men from being cut to pieces and this later led indirectly to the unmasking of a British agent who had wormed his way into the confidence of the IRA.

On the occasion on which the attack was originally planned to take place, a small group of IRA, comprising about twelve men, assembled in a field at the rear of Scartaglin police barracks. Among the group was one who presented himself as Peadar Clancy of Headquarters Staff, Dublin. In appearance he apparently resembled the Dublin Republican.

Information at the disposal of the would-be attackers was that the barracks windows would be unprotected, as the steel shutters would still be open at the time of the scheduled attack. The plan was for the twelve attackers to hurl grenades through the windows. McEllistrim, who was in charge of the operation, was uneasy about the information regarding the barracks windows. He could not understand how the RIC would be so careless as to leave their barracks windows unprotected. He therefore undertook a scouting mission of his own and learned that the windows were competently guarded by grenade-proof steel shutters that had already been fitted inside. During the urgent conference, which followed this discovery, Clancy argued strongly in favour of proceeding with the attack as planned, but McEllistrim decided to call it off. The assault party, which included Patrick Connor as captain of the local Volunteers, was disbanded.

Clancy accompanied some of the men to Ballymacelligott and later left for the Cordal area. Here he was billeted with other IRA members in a farmhouse owned by the Castleisland merchant W. H. O'Connor. One day while some of the IRA members were seated in the kitchen, Dave McCarthy, one of the Volunteers, noticed that tattoos Clancy had on one arm were like those in vogue among the British forces. The suspected spy was questioned and his answers were deemed to be unsatisfactory. He was placed under arrest and was transferred to east Limerick, where he was court-martialled, found guilty and shot as a spy. It turned out that his real name was Crowley.

Fearing that the introduction of new recruits from Britain was a prelude to the reoccupation of the abandoned RIC barracks, IRA headquarters ordered that as many deserted barracks as possible should be destroyed before they could be reoccupied. On the night of 3 April and the early hours of the following morning, the IRA in Kerry set about burning down the barracks in Anascaul, Ardea, Ardfert, Ballinskelligs, Ballyheigue, Beaufort, Camp, Castlegregory, Headford, Lauragh, Mulgrave, Keel and Templenoe. The attacks were not confined to RIC stations in Kerry. In Tralee the IRA also raided the Customs House, near the RIC barracks, and held up the caretaker, her husband and two children, while they took out the income tax registers and burned them at the back of the building. The same night, there were similar raids, in which tax books were seized and documents burned at both the Denny Street offices of William Huggard, a collector of income tax, and the home of his colleague Denis W. Clifford in Blennerville.

All the barracks had been vacated by the RIC, but the family of Sergeant Bernard O'Reilly, the man who arrested Casement, was still living in the barracks in Ardfert. They were given five minutes to get out of the building before it was torched. His wife claimed that she did not even have time to dress the children. Sergeant O'Reilly put in a claim for £620 for the loss of property and his wife for £217, much to the annoyance of the county council's lawyer.

The list of items they claimed 'would not be held in the Victoria Hotel,' according to the solicitor. 'Do you realise that it is not a barracks you would have to hold this furniture?' he asked O'Reilly.

The sergeant explained that he had been married for ten years and had served in Cahirciveen before moving to Ardfert. The judge awarded him what he claimed. Like many other RIC men, O'Reilly resigned from the force and returned to his native Clare.

The Volunteers had shown some compassion towards O'Reilly's family in Ardfert, but none was shown to two of the RIC men from the Waterville area the following fortnight. Daniel McCarthy of Waterville was shot dead while cycling through Lackmore Wood in County Tipperary on 9 April. He and two colleagues were cycling back after a court hearing in Newport when they were ambushed and two of them were killed. Part of McCarthy's head was blown away as he was shot from very close range, probably while lying wounded on the ground. A third, wounded colleague managed to escape.

Constable Martin Clifford from Derrinaden, near Waterville, was also stationed in County Tipperary, but was home on holiday when he was shot on 17 April. He was coming from Waterville when he was shot at Bradley's Cross and he died of his wounds shortly afterwards.

Constable Paddy Foley suffered a similar fate. He was a member of a large family, but he was reared by a childless aunt and uncle, presumably with a view to inheriting their farm. But Paddy was a spoiled and restless youngster. At the start of the First World War he had run away to join the Royal Munster Fusiliers. Even though he was under age, he made it to the front; he was subsequently captured by the Germans and spent four years as a prisoner of war. In January 1920 he joined the RIC and was stationed in Galway.

Then one day he turned up at Tim Kennedy's digs in Nelson Street, Tralee. Foley and Kennedy were first cousins. Foley asked about the kind of reception he was likely to get from the Volunteers at home in Anascaul. He stayed some days in Tralee and Na Fianna reported seeing him entering the RIC barracks on a number of occasions. 'I saw him go in once there myself and I advised him not to go back home,' Kennedy noted. Foley persisted, so Kennedy kept an eye on him. That weekend they went back to Anascaul together by train and had a meal at Kennedy's home. 'I again tried to persuade him to clear out but he wouldn't take any notice of my advice,' Kennedy noted.

Foley was already under suspicion, and these misgivings were heightened when he asked a lot of questions about people involved in the IRA, one of whom was his own brother, Mick Foley, who was active with the Inch Brigade. Then Tim Kennedy got an urgent message to meet RIC District Inspector Bernard O'Connor of Dingle. O'Connor had been supplying Kennedy with information. They agreed to meet at Camp Junction – one taking the train from Tralee and the other from Dingle.

O'Connor handed Kennedy some notebooks that Foley had given him at the RIC station in Dingle. Kennedy brought the notebooks to the brigade commandant, Paddy Cahill, who also happened to be one of Foley's many cousins. In these notebooks Foley had provided 'the names of every officer in the district and every prominent Sinn Féiner', including many of his own cousins. 'After my name, he had entered a big question mark,' Kennedy observed. 'It was a very painful situation for Cahill and myself.'

On 21 April Foley was kidnapped from Moriarty's Hotel in Anascaul, tried by the IRA and sentenced to death. A Franciscan priest, Edmond Walsh, gave the last rites and Foley was then shot. His bullet-ridden body was found at Deelis, near Castlegregory, about seven miles from his home, two days after he was kidnapped. He had been shot twenty-six times, with his hands bound behind his back and a handkerchief tied around his eyes.

That same weekend RIC Sergeant Cornelius Crean, 48, the older brother of Tom Crean, who had distinguished himself as a member of the Scott and Shackleton expeditions to the Antarctic, was ambushed in Ballinspittle, County Cork. He was cycling with two constables when one of the constables was shot off his bicycle.

'Oh God, run for cover!' Crean shouted. But as he and Constable William Power reached a corner, Crean changed his mind. 'Turn about and attack,' he ordered.

'I saw a man rush across the road with a rifle to his shoulder, and immediately Sergeant Crean fell,' Constable Power told the inquest afterwards. 'I picked up the sergeant and found his body trembling; his face was white and he was bleeding. I did not think at first that he was hit. I thought that he was after falling with excitement.' Crean had, in fact, been shot and fatally wounded in the left lung.

A couple of days later there was an incident in Crean's home village. Three policemen from Dingle were held up by disguised armed men while going through the village. Sergeant Howlett gave up his gun, but his two colleagues, Constables Tracy and Macpherson, made a run for it. The latter was shot in the leg.

In the aftermath of the attacks on the tax office and tax officials, as well as the burning of the vacated police barracks, the RIC rounded up the usual suspects – Thomas Clifford of the 1916 Shop in Castle Street, Eamonn O'Connor of Ashe Street, and Thomas Slattery Jr, the son of the Sinn Féin chairman of the rural district council. John and Ned Greaney of Tralee were arrested in O'Dorney, and Pádraig Ó Siochfhradha (An Seabhac) and Fionán MacCollum of Killorglin were arrested at the railway station in Tralee on their way to the Gaelic League Conference in Killarney.

The police were unable to secure convictions in the courts because no jury would dare convict any of the Republicans. Most of those arrested had to be freed after questioning, but Clifford, O'Connor and Slattery were brought to Fenit and transported to jail in a naval vessel. They were essentially interned without trial, which the British had been doing ever since the so-called 'German Plot'.

There were 145 uncharged and unconvicted IRA prisoners in Belfast Jail. They set up their own prison council, with Dan Healy as chairman. Thomas Clifford became a member after his arrival in Belfast and the council issued an ultimatum to the prison authorities. 'We demand immediate and unconditional release,' they wrote. 'Failing this, we go on hunger strike tonight, Monday 26 April 1920.' This document was signed by Healy, Clifford, Owen O'Duffy and Philip Lennon. Healy and a number of other prisoners were promptly transferred to Worm-wwood Scrubs in London.

The British began to capitulate on 8 May. Among the Kerrymen released were D. J. O'Sullivan, the chairman of Tralee Urban District Council; his fellow townsmen Billy Mullins and Dan Healy; Mortimer O'Connor of O'Dorney; and Pat O'Shea and Alexander O'Donnell of Castlegregory. The RIC was more frustrated than ever, especially as the killings continued.

On 10 May Constable William Brick, a native of Tralee, was shot dead along with two colleagues near Timoleague, County Cork. The following day Sergeant Denis Garvey, another Kerryman, was shot dead with a colleague just after leaving the RIC station at Lower Glanmire Road in Cork.

While these killings were probably taken on local initiative, they fit neatly into the broad policy conceived by Michael Collins. His people had knocked out British intelligence and the second part of his plan was to get the Crown authorities to react blindly. Indeed, they did so, playing into the hands of the Republicans. Of course, the reaction was gradual.

On 4 May the offices of solicitor J. D. O'Donnell were wrecked in Ashe Street, Tralee, and the plate-glass window of Eamonn O'Connor's shop was broken, as was a window of the public house run by Sinn Féin councillor Tom Dennehy in Bridge Street. Two nightwatchmen had seen a man acting suspiciously and when Dennehy approached, the man fled. An RIC patrol had already been informed but they made no effort to stop the suspect when he ran by them in the direction of the police barracks. They later denied that they had seen anyone. The council concluded that the police were responsible for the damage and the Volunteer commander was asked to have his men patrol the town at night to protect property.

The IRA were already patrolling Castlegregory, following the withdrawal of the RIC. This was a further blow to police morale. The people were now turning to the IRA for protection against crime – in fact, they were beginning to view the police as criminals.

People were convinced that the RIC was responsible not only for breaking the windows, but for sending letters threatening the lives of two priests who had been active in Sinn Féin and the Gaelic League. 'Beware!' read the letter to Father William Ferris, a curate at St John's Parish Church, Tralee. (Father Ferris was a second cousin of the father of Martin Ferris, a current member of the Sinn Féin Ard Comhairle.) 'For the Black Hand has come to avenge all murders, and you are a marked man. Your time may not be far off, so be prepared to meet your God.'

On 6 May 1920 a similar letter was mailed in Tralee for Father Curtayne, a curate in Ballybunion. 'We, the Black Hand, have come to avenge all murders in Ireland and to take a life for a life,' the letter read. 'We wish to give you notice to be prepared to meet your God, in whose sight all priests are murderers, who encourage and incite murder and crime in those who know no better, and those you will have to answer to before your God. Beware, you are a marked man, and your time may be short.'

In the climate in which people believed that the police were engaging in criminal activities, it was probably inevitable that opportunists would seek to exploit the situation for their own advantage. During late April, three men with revolvers visited houses in the Firies area demanding money 'in the name of the Irish Republic'. They dragged one man out of bed and ordered him to get on his knees and prepare for death. He told them he would meet his fate on his feet and dared them to shoot, but they left instead. The names of the three culprits were given to Sinn Féin and the young men were ordered to return the money to each household and 'go on their knees and crave pardon for what they had done and solemnly promise never to offend again.'

There was a similar incident in Listowel when Mrs Anne Pierce was threatened that her home would be burned down if she did not give ten shillings to a group purporting to be 'Irish Volunteers collecting for Dáil Éireann.' The *Kerry People* later reported that one John Murphy, alias Thomas Sullivan, was seized by Sinn Féiners, and two days later five others were taken in Listowel and told that they would be shot unless they made restitution. As a result, people began to look to Sinn Féin to police the community, because the British system was disintegrating.

People were warned to ignore the existing Crown courts, whose proceedings were disrupted by sheer intimidation. The courthouse in Dingle was burned down on the night of 18 April 1920, but without loss of life. On 3 May 1920, RIC Sergeant Francis J. McKenna and Constables Colgan and Rabbit were cycling back to Ballylongford from court in Listowel when they were ambushed at Galebridge, about two miles from Listowel, by volunteers from Ballydonoghue under Paddy Walsh. Those who took part in the ambush were Paddy and John Walsh, Michael Ahern, T. P. O'Shea, Patrick Corridan and John Galvin, while Thomas O'Connor acted as a scout.

McKenna, a thirty-nine-year-old married man with three

children, was from Waterford city. He had joined the RIC as a teenager and had spent some years as a sergeant in Tralee. It was later suggested that he had been involved in the arrest of Roger Casement, but this was not so. He was killed when he was hit in the face by a shotgun blast. His two colleagues were wounded – Colgan had gunshot wounds to his chest and stomach. Among the attackers, O'Shea was wounded by Colgan, but not seriously.

The same week, after the IRA warned that nobody should take part in a court session at Castlegregory, the resident magistrate, Edward M. Wynne of Tralee, was the only court officer to show up. As he was being driven to a court in Causeway on 18 May, he and his driver were stopped by a group of armed men near Young's forge at Knockbrack, about a mile and a half from Causeway.

'Hands up,' the men shouted.

The driver, one Dan Breen, was on the other side of the jaunting car. He jumped off and held the head of the horse as the shooting began. 'I pulled out my revolver and fired five shots,' Wynne explained. The nearest man to me dropped on the road, face downwards. Seeing their comrade fall, two of their comrades jumped over the fence, but the others hesitated.'

'Come on, you cowards,' Wynne taunted his attackers. He then told the driver to get back up. 'Dan jumped on the car and drove off as quickly as he could,' Wynne continued. 'As we drove off, I saw a man come up to where his comrade was lying, apparently to take him up. We drove off to Causeway, where I held the petty session, which lasted about an hour, and I returned on the police motor car.'

Wynne had been a resident magistrate for more than twenty years. 'I could have been attacked and easily shot any time within the past few years, as I walked about quite alone,' he told the petty sessions in Tralee the following week. 'Therefore I am sure that this attack on me was not planned or approved by any responsible organisation. I trusted the Kerry people, and always found them kindly and courteous. During my time here, I have tried to be just and lenient where possible, and most sincerely regret what has occurred.'

He clearly hoped that the attack had not been authorised by the IRA, but the Volunteers had indeed been involved, and Michael Nolan had been killed. Wynne realised that he would henceforth be a target for the IRA, so he moved to Britain. The IRA had to be content with burning his furniture at the railway station as it was about to be shipped to Britain. They also burned the house that he still owned in Tralee.

Paddy Cahill's brigade area extended from Glenbeigh in south Kerry all the way to Tarbert, including the whole of the Dingle peninsula. On 8 April he seemed pleased with himself that his men had burned down six empty RIC barracks in his brigade area and also destroyed the tax records in Tralee. But Michael Collins clearly wanted more action. 'Are there only six unoccupied barracks in the area?' he pointedly asked Cahill.

There was distinct disillusionment with Cahill among some of the more active men. Ballymacelligott initially came under Tralee, but Tom McEllistrim and company could not get on with Cahill. They insisted on being included within the Kerry No. 2 Brigade area, which covered south Kerry. Johnny O'Connor of Farmer's Bridge did likewise. He moved because he would not give up his rifle to Cahill. 'If you didn't do things with his authority,' O'Connor explained, 'he didn't like you to have arms.' The Ballymacelligott boys, who had gone off on their own and staged the first raid on an RIC barracks two years earlier, during the conscription crisis, were not minded to put up with Cahill. 'They were too hot for Kerry No. 1,' according to O'Connor.

Although Kerry was remote from Dublin, Collins had established a fine communications network using the railways:

he could get a message from Dublin to Kerry within thirteen hours. While McEllistrim was critical of Cahill's leadership, Cahill thought highly of McEllistrim and actually recommended him for promotion. Cahill noted, for instance, that Dan O'Mahony, the commander of the Castleisland area, was really a bit past it. 'Dan is pretty old, and his adjutant is in jail, so that it is hard for him to do work, as his area is rather large,' Cahill wrote to Collins in May 1920. 'He has a very good chap in Ballymac named Tom McEllistrim, and Dan should throw a piece of the work over on him for the present. He has two good commandants in Rathmore and Kenmare and the Firies commandant is excellent, so that the only districts that should cause him any worry are Castleisland and Killarney.' The 'excellent' commandant in Firies was Humphrey Murphy, who would eventually replace Cahill in charge of the Kerry No. 1 Brigade, little over a year later.

Even though disillusionment with Cahill started at a local level, it undoubtedly got mixed up with the growing disenchantment of the IRA headquarters staff with Austin Stack. Cahill was seen as a protégé of Stack, who was soon being dismissed as incompetent by the headquarters staff. Richard Mulcahy, the IRA chief of staff, considered Stack to be essentially useless, even though he personally got on with him. He noted that Pádraic O'Keeffe, who served with Stack as a joint national secretary of Sinn Féin, said that it was 'easy to work with' Stack. 'Of course,' O'Keeffe added, 'he did no work.'

Collins would have been quite content to let Stack alone if he had been working properly, Mulcahy argued, but Stack had never been able to get on top of his job. He then antagonised Collins by transmitting routine material through the express communications network that Collins had set up. It was a kind of 'fast track' system, using railway workers to carry sensitive IRA messages all over the country. Collins was very protective of this system: although he would not have minded if Stack had used it for something important, he resented him endangering the system just to transmit routine material.

Stack was regarded as a humble individual. Nobody ever accused Collins of humility: he was the direct opposite. He was a demanding taskmaster who drove everyone, most of all himself. He demanded results and did not suffer fools, or incompetence, gladly. He was impatient of Stack's failings and resentful of his incompetent interference. Understanding the growing rift between Collins and Stack is vital to understanding much of the confusion about what eventually happened in Kerry.

Collins had demonstrated true genius in undermining the Crown intelligence system and establishing a brilliant intelligence system of his own. While the IRA had largely undermined the existing Crown courts, Stack had not been nearly as successful in establishing Republican courts in their place. He not only fared poorly in that – which was his main task in the Dáil Cabinet – but also completely failed to operate as deputy chief of staff of the IRA. To make matters worse, Collins was annoyed at his interference in intelligence matters.

One of the police spies who subsequently proved particularly useful to Collins was David Neligan, but he would have been of no use at all if Stack had had his way. Neligan had been serving in G Division (the detective branch) of the Dublin Metropolitan Police. He wished to resign but feared that he would become a target if he returned to his native west Limerick, because local Republicans were liable to suspect him of being a British spy. His brother, Maurice – who was the transport-union organiser in Tralee and also a member of the IRB – tried to help him. Maurice Neligan sought the assistance of Tim Kennedy, the IRA's intelligence officer for north Kerry.

Kennedy, the accountant for Kerry County Council, was a small man with a cherubic face and bright eyes. He was an astute individual who worked for Michael Collins, and was trusted by him. There was some confusion about where Kennedy and David Neligan first met. Neligan thought it was in Kennedy's office in Ashe Street, Tralee, while Kennedy said it was in the street one day while Maurice and David were looking for Stack to secure a safe conduct for David.

As the officer in charge of IRA intelligence in north Kerry, Kennedy reported directly to Collins, but on that occasion he was unable to locate him, so he turned to Stack, with unfortunate consequences. 'I saw Stack and said that this fellow should not resign,' Kennedy related. Stack arranged for an aide, Paddy Sheehan, to meet the Neligan brothers. After Sheehan questioned Dave, however, Stack dismissed the idea of using Neligan as a spy.

'Get him to resign,' Stack told Kennedy. 'He's no good.'

Neligan duly resigned from the DMP on 11 May 1920, and he was provided with a note from the IRA for his own protection. Collins was furious when he learned what had happened.

'I got a flaming letter from Mick asking why the hell did I take Stack's/Sheehan's advice,' Kennedy noted. 'The result was that I went to Maurice and I told him that I had been sacked for letting Dave leave the G Division. I took Dave Neligan to P. J. Cahill in the county hall, and Dave thought of a plan. He suggested that his father's cock of hay at the back of the house should be set on fire, but he'd have to get a few threatening letters.'

Neligan burned the hay, and Kennedy arranged for the threatening letters to be sent. Kennedy also set up a meeting for Neligan with Stack at the Clarence Hotel in Dublin. 'He told me that Collins wanted to meet me and that arrangements would be made,' Neligan wrote. He was duly taken to Collins, who asked him to rejoin the police force.

Neligan reapplied and, when asked why he had changed his

mind, produced the threatening letters that Kennedy had sent him. That was good enough, and he was accepted back into G Division, the detective division of the Dublin Metropolitan Police. He went on to become one of the Big Fellow's most valuable spies within the police force.

'I thought he was the best intelligence officer I ever met in my life,' Tim Kennedy explained. 'I discussed plans with Michael Collins for the re-establishment of Neligan into favour with the Castle authorities.' Collins had stuff planted in Findlaters, a loyalist business house. When the Auxiliaries raided the place and found the planted material, they nearly wrecked the building – much to the amusement of Collins and company. 'A number of such stunts put up Dave's stock with the Castle people,' Kennedy explained, 'and when the Castle were looking for one of their G men to train and lead the military raids, they asked for volunteers and Dave came to me, and he volunteered – and, I understand, with dire consequences to the military.'

There was no doubt about the success of IRA intelligence in penetrating Crown security, but whether it really knew what was happening all the time in Kerry is another matter. Even though this was before the war with the Black and Tans had begun, there was no shortage of action in Kerry. There was a series of burnings in May 1920. Vacant barracks at Lixnaw and Lisselton were torched during the third week of May, while the coastguard station at Brandon was burned down on 23 May and the one at Ballyheigue a couple of nights later.

The Ballyheigue station, which incorporated a tower, was three storeys high and well fortified, with portholes on all sides. There was a steel roof, with steel doors and steel shutters on the windows. The IRA moved in on the station while the gunboat and its crew were out on patrol in the bay. The sentry in the watch room at the front of the tower was quietly overcome and the sleeping officers were surprised in their beds and promptly surrendered. The contents of the building included weapons, as well as rocket guns, distress rockets, flares, telescopes and field glasses. These were taken; the building was set on fire and the water tank drained so that the gunboat crew could not put out the fire when they returned.

When members of the British Cabinet discussed the Irish situation on 31 May 1920, Hamar Greenwood, the Chief Secretary for Ireland, noted that 'the people in the barracks are ostracised. They rarely get notice of attack.' He stated that 'Limerick, Kerry, Cork and Dublin are the bad areas.' Sir Nevil Macready observed that the two police forces 'are rotten'. He added that General Henry Tudor, who had just taken over as head of the police, was taking the situation in hand. 'There is no detective department in Ireland,' Macready said.

The ensuing discussion was particularly enlightening in view of subsequent events in the Black and Tan conflict. Secretary for War Winston Churchill called for legislation for a special tribunal to dispense 'summary justice' to murderers. 'It is monstrous that we have some 200 murders and no one hung,' he said. 'What strikes me is the feebleness of the local machinery. After a person is caught, he should pay the penalty within a week. Look at the tribunals which the Russian government have devised.' It was ironic that Churchill, of all people, was advocating that the British forces should behave like Bolsheviks. During the ensuing weeks, Churchill repeatedly brought his colleagues back to the necessity for executions.

'You agreed six or seven months ago that there should be hanging,' he said to Prime Minister David Lloyd George.

'I feel certain you must hang,' the prime minister replied. But he doubted that Irish juries would cooperate. 'Can you get convictions from Catholics?' he asked.

'The Cabinet decided some seven months ago on a special tribunal,' Churchill argued.

'The Irish judges were dead against it,' replied Lord French, the Lord Lieutenant of Ireland.

'Why not have three English barristers?' Churchill persisted.

'We must have Irishmen,' Lloyd George insisted. 'Decent Irishmen would object to having Englishmen sent over.'

Sir Nevil Macready, who had taken charge of British forces in March 1920, suggested that martial law might be the answer. 'The difficulty behind martial law is that you would put certain people in prison and they would hunger strike,' he added. 'What would the people in England say? Could you go through with it to the death? Imprisoned men cannot be held indefinitely. Will they return as martyrs?'

'You must assume for this argument that some will die,' Lloyd George stated.

'I do not like the uncontrolled power of a military commander,' Churchill interjected, 'because we might have incidents like we have had in India.'

'We must try to get public opinion in Ireland in favour of bringing this state of things to an end,' Lloyd George argued. 'For example, if you get at the farmers and money-loving community and find them damnified in their purses you will find public opinion in favour of ending this. There are signs of it. We must accelerate it. Increase their pecuniary burdens.'

'Why not make life intolerable in a particular area?' Churchill asked. He went on to raise the possibility of sending a new force to Ireland that would be made up of former army officers in Ireland. Some of his colleagues, however, doubted whether he would be able to get the right type of men for this force.

'I find no great alacrity among the officers to go to Ireland,' Macready explained. 'You do not want the scallywag.'

Churchill was content to suspend action on this idea of a special force, pending further information.

'Are we getting a better type of evidence?' Macready was asked.

'Quite the other way,' the commander replied. 'We are at present in very much of a fog but are building up an intelligence system.'

That discussion sheds light on the way in which the main British players were thinking on Irish affairs. Churchill wanted executions and a special force, while Lloyd George accepted that some people would have to be killed but was reluctant to take responsibility for such a policy. Before long the government tried all these approaches. A new special force, the Auxiliaries, was introduced, and they and the other police resorted to a policy of systematic arson, burning co-operative creameries in particular, and then putting the cost of this damage onto the local rates. This policy was intended to hit both farmers and business people.

The British were about to retaliate with the Black and Tan terror, but meanwhile the IRA continued as before. The RIC barracks in Fenit was attacked in the early hours of 2 June 1920. The IRA occupied the adjoining houses of Captain O'Mahony and Mrs Lynch; the Republicans began firing at 2 am and continued for two hours. One neighbour told the press afterwards that it sounded like France during the First World War. The attackers made an opening in O'Mahony's roof and poured petrol on the barracks and set it alight.

At the time, the barracks was defended by Sergeant Murphy and seven constables. While the attack was in progress, a British gunboat anchored at Fenit fired one shell, which was believed to have exploded harmlessly on Ballyheigue strand. Reinforcements from the gunboat eventually relieved the besieged police, and the IRA withdrew – although the rescuers were initially mistaken for attackers and fired on from the barracks. Sergeant Murphy was slightly wounded in the neck and one of his men, Constable O'Regan, was hit in the thigh.

The attack had been a carefully planned operation involving

extensive participation of the IRA in Tralee. The telephone and telegraph wires to Fenit had been cut, all the roads from Tralee were blocked with felled trees, and the drawbridge at Blennerville was opened and the keys thrown in the canal. An unsuccessful attempt was made to burn part of Fenit Pier, then a wooden structure, in order to prevent the sailors coming to the rescue. Finally, all the railway gates between Tralee and Fenit were spiked down in such a way that it took men with crowbars a considerable time to free the gates the next day.

That weekend six members of the IRA tried to burn down the vacated RIC barracks in Brosna, but it was a trap set by the military. The six young men were arrested. A couple of weeks later the West Limerick Column of the IRA teamed up with the Kerry No. 2 Brigade under Dan O'Mahony on 18 June 1920 for an attack on the Brosna barracks, which offered favourable possibilities for capture because of the remoteness of the village. The attacking party gathered in a large field across the river from Brosna. T. M. O'Connor and Dan McCarthy were in charge of the Kerry column, supported by Humphrey Murphy, David Griffin, Maurice O'Sullivan, Jim and Berty Mahony, Davie McCarthy, David McAuliffe, Jack Carmody, Charlie Daly, Jerry Leary, Ned and Jack Mahony, Michael Connell, Denny McCarthy, Jim Lacey, Paddy Fitzgerald, Pat and Davie Connor, David Horan, Jim McAuliffe, Jack, Jim and Denny Prendeville, Mick Leary, Mick Burke, Jerry and Tim Connor, J. Brosnan, Martin McCarthy, Philip Hartnett and Dick Rearden.

Mossie Hartnett of Tournafulla had under his command sixteen west Limerick men armed with police carbines and rifles. They included Paddy Buckley – who was subsequently killed in the Ballyseedy massacre – James Roche, Tommy Leahy, Con and Ned Cregan, Paddy Mulcahy, Jack Ahern, Paddy Aherne, J. Kiely and T. Bouchier. The men were divided into sections and marched to various positions around the barracks.

Some of the men opened fire on the barracks before all their colleagues had got into position. They had inadvertently tipped off the constabulary by making too much noise. There followed a heavy exchange of rifle fire that resounded through the village, as the barracks was at the south-eastern corner of the Square, beside the local cemetery.

A number of the west Limerick men were placed in front of the barracks, near the church, and the remainder in an old house at the back. They tried to break through the roof and gable with grenades and bombs, but to no avail. The sound of shouting and firing echoed from the hills around. Very lights were sent up by the police at intervals, rendering the scene even more weird and terrifying. Inside the barracks the police and Tans could be heard distinctly playing a melodeon and shouting 'Come on, the Rainbow Chasers!'

Because of their inadequate equipment and the expectation that British military reinforcements would arrive before long, the IRA decided to lift the siege, but some of the men had narrow escapes withdrawing from the area. The West Limerick Column was saved by members of the Abbeyfeale Company of the IRA under James Collins. On the night of the Brosna attack, seven or eight of them had been assigned to positions at Glenesrone Wood in an effort to frustrate the Abbeyfeale RIC if they tried to come to the rescue of those in Brosna.

In the early morning, the lookout at the Abbeyfeale barracks reported to his sergeant the appearance of Very lights over Brosna. As a result, nine RIC members were dispatched to Brosna by the nearest route. This was at the rear of the barracks, by the old road known as Betty's Road, which cut across the Limerick men's line of retreat from Brosna. The men in Glenesrone Wood ambushed the RIC to delay them. The brunt of this fight was borne by Jerry Sullivan of Springmount and Jim O'Connor of Mountmahon, who were armed only with double-barrel shotguns. At close range, they opened fire on the advancing police, seriously wounding Constable Martin and slightly injuring some others.

The police returned rapid rifle fire as they retreated to the barracks, where they maintained intense fire in the direction of the hill. None of the IRA suffered casualties either at Abbeyfeale or Brosna. This was all part of a calculated plan to goad the British, so that they would retaliate blindly. What happened in Kerry was a prime example of murderous intimidation provoking blind hostility, which would totally alienate the people of Kerry.

Next day Tom McEllistrim and Johnny O'Connor decided to go to Cork for the Munster final. They 'borrowed' a new Ford touring car – or what would now be called a convertible – belonging to Major Blennerhassett of Ballyseedy Castle, a local landlord. They set out with a cousin of O'Connor behind the wheel. Jim Duggan was a radio officer at home on leave, and he agreed to drive in his uniform, obviously figuring that the young men in a car would not arouse suspicion if they had a driver in a service uniform. 'We thought we weren't going fast enough, so we took down the hood. I was in front with Duggan, and Duggan spat and the wind caught it. As he turned to say, 'I'm sorry', we hit the side of the road.'

The car overturned and O'Connor injured his hand, while his cousin cracked some ribs. Shaken by the accident, they went into a bar, where they found Sergeant Walsh from Gortatlea with his wife.

'I could put the rope on that fellow's neck,' Walsh told the publican's wife. But he obviously considered discretion the better part of valour. Afterwards McEllistrim had to drive home, even though he had never driven a motor car before in his life. They left the car at the entrance gate of the Blennerhassett estate.

On the evening of 28 June, Constable Rael was home on leave from Ballyduff, County Waterford, when he was ambushed and injured as he approached his sister's house near Ardfert. He had been in the RIC for thirteen years and had taken leave to visit his sister, a nun, who was home on vacation from the United States. This incident was a measure of how dirty the conflict was becoming.

12

'WE ARE GOING TO HAVE SPORT NOW'

The British judge at the Kerry summer assizes told the grand jury that in Kerry twenty-five police barracks, three courthouses and four coastguard stations had been burned and six police patrols attacked. It was always the same as far as the police were concerned, he said: they were unable to obtain a clue about the attacks and they got no assistance from the people.

British military and police could move out from their strongly held barracks only in numbers, as they were the object of hostility and liable to attack. Some of the RIC developed a siege mentality and began to lash out. In Tralee they went in force and broke the windows of known Sinn Féin supporters. As a result, Tralee Urban District Council asked the volunteers to patrol the town in early May. But this lasted only for about six weeks, as the Volunteers on patrol were hassled by the RIC.

Two men on patrol on 26 June, for instance, were stopped in Nelson Street and searched, then stopped again minutes later in the Mall. The stick that one of the Volunteers was carrying was taken from him and one of the constables then broke it over the man's head. They were taken to the RIC barracks, where they were roughed up for not saying who had sent them on patrol. As a result, the Volunteer patrols were called off, but this only intensified the hostility towards the police.

In June the Volunteers in Ballymacelligott set up an active-service unit of men who undertook to fight full time. It consisted of Tom McEllistrim, Moss Carmody, John Brosnan, Jim Baily,

John Cronin, John Leen, Maurice Galvin, Denis O'Sullivan, Paddy Reidy, Thomas O'Connor, Pat Burke, and Johnny O'Connor of Farmer's Bridge. The struggle was entering a new phase.

The RIC, on whom the British had relied, were proving unequal to the task at hand. They were in an unenviable position, being expected to enforce repressive measures against their own people. Many of them had brothers in the IRA, but those who had long service in the RIC were not prepared to forgo their pensions. Some of the younger men who did resign found themselves despised as cowards by their former RIC colleagues and distrusted by neighbours when they returned to their homes.

The Black and Tans were introduced to bolster the RIC. Stationed throughout the country, they were guided by RIC members, who had local knowledge. The Black and Tans were confronting native rebels, who were soon backed by a generally united people. This unity was largely a result of the behaviour of the Black and Tans, who harassed people night and day, carrying out wholesale arrests and killing members of the IRA, whom they accused of terrorising the civilian population.

Lieutenant Colonel Gerald Brice Ferguson Smyth was appointed divisional commissioner for Munster on 3 June 1920 at the age of thirty-five. He had joined the British army in 1905 and served in the First World War, commanding a battalion of the King's Own Scottish Borderers. During the war, he lost an arm and was mentioned four times in dispatches.

On 16 June 1920, the RIC in Listowel was ordered to hand over its barracks to the British military. Only three of the constables were to remain in Listowel, where they were to act as guides for the soldiers in the district. The others were to be transferred, but they decided not to obey the orders. Next morning, County Inspector John M. Poer O'Shee arrived from Tralee to persuade the men to obey, but to no avail.

He asked Constable Jeremiah Mee if he was going to defy the order of the divisional commissioner.

'Yes,' Mee replied, 'I refuse to obey the order.'

'Then you had better resign,' O'Shee said.

'Accept my resignation now.'

O'Shee then asked if the others were resigning, and each stepped forward in turn and said, 'I resign.'

The military was supposed to take over the barracks at noon, so when this did not happen the whole affair was left hanging. On the morning of 19 June, the county inspector returned, this time with the divisional commissioner, Lieutenant Colonel Brice Ferguson Smyth, and the head of the police, Brigadier General Henry Hugh Tudor, along with three Crossley tenders with police and soldiers.

The assembled constables were addressed by Smyth, a tall, physically impressive man. 'Sinn Féin has had all the sport up to the present, and we are going to have sport now,' he said. 'The police are only strong enough to hold their barracks. As long as we remain on the defensive, Sinn Féin will have the whip hand. We must take the offensive and beat Sinn Féin at its own tactics. Martial law is to come into force immediately, and a scheme of amalgamation will be complete on 21 June. I am promised as many troops from England as I will require. Thousands are coming daily. I am getting 7,000 police from England.

'Police and military will patrol the country at least five nights a week. They are not to confine themselves to the main roads, but take across country, lie in ambush, and when civilians approach shout, "Hands up!" Should the order not be immediately obeyed, shoot, and shoot with effect. If persons approaching carry their hands in their pockets, or are suspicious-looking, shoot them down.

'You may make mistakes occasionally, and innocent persons may be shot, but that cannot be helped. No policeman will get into trouble for shooting any man. Hunger strikers will be allowed to died in jail. Some have died, and it is a damned bad job all of them were not allowed to die. That is nearly all I have to say to you. We want your assistance to wipe out Sinn Féin. Any man not prepared to do so had better leave the job at once.'

'By your accent I take it you are an Englishman, and in your ignorance you forget you are addressing Irishmen,' Constable Jeremiah Mee replied, appalled by the thought of such a policy. He took off his cap and belt and threw them on a table. 'These too are English,' he said. 'Take them as a present from me, and to hell with you, you murderer.'

Smyth, a native of Banbridge, County Down, denied that he was English. He ordered the arrest of Mee, who was marched out of the room by the district inspector and the head constable. Afterwards, Mee drew up an account of what had happened and thirteen of those present testified to its accuracy by signing the statement, which they gave to a local curate, Father Charles O'Sullivan, for transmission to Sinn Féin and the media. Five of the constables then quit the RIC. They were Mee, Michael Fitzgerald, John O'Donovan, Patrick Sheeran, and Thomas Hughes, who later joined the priesthood and became a Catholic bishop in Nigeria. Mee offered his services to Sinn Féin and the IRA, and he was used by Michael Collins for propaganda purposes.

On the evening of Sunday 27 June, Colonel Smyth arrived at Milltown RIC Barracks wearing full military uniform and staff cap, his breast ablaze with medal ribbons. He summoned the sergeant and six constables to the day room. Having taken his automatic weapon from his pocket and placed it on the table, he directed the men to sit down. He prefaced his remarks by stating that he was responsible to no man in Ireland and that he answered directly to the prime minister.

Henceforth, he said, RIC men would accompany Black and

Tan military raiding parties to identify Sinn Féiners. The RIC men – three of whom were middle-aged – did not immediately realise what Colonel Smyth was about, and were inclined to look on his visit as one of the 'comings and goings' of highly placed officers. The barracks orderly, one of the younger men, said that when he joined the force he did not anticipate having to shoot anybody.

Smyth said that times had changed and tactics had to change with them. Henceforth things would be different. He made light of the constable's arguments, suggesting that they were born of cowardice. Dominion Home Rule, he said, was coming, and after a few years RIC men who continued to serve would be awarded big pensions. After about an hour at the barracks, Smyth departed.

A few days later the barracks orderly received notice to transfer to Rathmore. He refused to go. On 29 June County Inspector O'Shee came to Milltown and spoke to the young policeman in a fatherly way, asking him why he would not take his transfer.

'Well, if you want to know,' he replied, 'I did not join the police to lead around Black and Tans and the scum of England which have been brought into the force.' The county inspector explained that such an attitude would create disaffection among the other men, but the young man was not persuaded. After talking to him for about two hours, O'Shee declared that he would have to suspend him.

'Take that, and that,' said the policeman, throwing his revolver, belt and jacket on the table in front of the county inspector. After spending a few days around Milltown, the suspended constable went to Killarney, where he was well known, having previously served in Beaufort. There the district inspector reasoned with him and pointed out that he was going out into a hostile people who would treat him as a spy. 'I understand well what I am doing and I'll take what is coming,' he replied.

On 14 July 1920, T. P. O'Connor, the Irish nationalist MP from Liverpool, tabled a question in the British House of Commons about the mutinous behavior in Kerry.

'The recent events presumably refer to the resignation of five constables in Listowel, County Kerry,' replied Sir Hamar Greenwood, Chief Secretary for Ireland. 'On 19 June last, the divisional commissioner, Colonel Smyth, made a speech to the members of the force, eighteen in number, stationed at Listowel. I have seen the report in the press, which, on the face of it, appears to have been supplied by the five constables already mentioned. I have myself seen Colonel Smyth, who repudiates the accuracy of the statements contained in that report. He informed me that the instructions given by him to the police in Listowel and throughout the division were those mentioned in a debate in this House on 22 June last by the Attorney-General for Ireland, and he did not exceed these instructions. The reason for the resignation of the five constables was their refusal to take up duty in barracks in certain disturbed parts of Kerry. They had taken up this attitude before the visit of the divisional commissioner. I am satisfied that the newspaper report is a distortion and a wholly misleading account of what took place.'

O'Connor tried to have a parliamentary debate on the Listowel incident on the grounds that Divisional Commissioner Smyth's words were calculated to produce serious bloodshed in Ireland, but this was blocked by the government. Next day in Dublin Michael Collins introduced Jeremiah Mee to the editor and the managing director of the *Freeman's Journal*.

For three hours Mee was questioned about the incident in Listowel. The *Freeman's Journal* covered the affair in detail. Collins was prepared to milk the controversy for all it was worth. Mee and two of his colleagues were recruited for speaking tours of the United States. In a way this was ironic, because the policy advocated by Smyth was not much different from that being pursued by the IRA in general, and Collins in particular.

Desmond Ryan recalled an incident at Cullenswood House one day when Collins picked up an old copy of *An Claidheamh Soluis* in which Pádraig Pearse had extolled the virtues of armed conflict. 'We must accustom ourselves to the thought of arms, to the sight of arms, to the use of arms,' Collins read aloud with enthusiasm. 'We may make mistakes in the beginning and shoot the wrong people, but bloodshed is a cleansing and sanctifying thing, and the nation which regards it as the final horror has lost its manhood.' With that, Collins slapped down the paper and walked out.

Collins was looking for action, not talk. His views were best represented by Ernest Blythe's article in *An t-Óglach* suggesting that anybody who assisted the British deserves 'no more consideration than a wild beast'. As was pointed out earlier, Blythe argued that those people 'should be killed without mercy or hesitation.' The Big Fellow had not only approved of those sentiments but asked Austin Stack to get Blythe to write more along the same lines. Collins wished to provoke government blunders so that the IRA would win popular backing. Smyth's speech in Listowel played right into his hands. Was there really any difference between Smyth's attitude and that exhibited by Pearse and Blythe?

While in Cork, Smyth usually stayed at the County Club, which was frequented by the landed gentry and high-ranking military officers. The Volunteer intelligence department enlisted the help of a young waiter, who furnished the names of British army and police officers who stayed at, or visited, the club. The IRA decided to shoot Smyth there on Friday evening, 16 July, but he packed his bags and went to Kerry for the weekend. He returned two days later, and the IRA mobilised a squad of six armed men to enter the County Club at 10 pm.

They held up the waiter, who was expecting them. They then passed down the hallway to the lounge, where Colonel Smyth was seated with County Inspector Craig of the RIC.

'Were not your orders to shoot on sight?' one of the IRA men remarked. 'Well, you are in sight now, so prepare.'

Smyth did not have a chance. He jumped to his feet and ran towards the door, but he was cut down by a hail of bullets. He was shot some five times and died at the scene. When the authorities sought to hold an inquest afterwards, they were unable to find enough people to serve on the jury.

The police were under terrible strain. The county inspector in Limerick warned Macready in July 1920 that half of his officers were prepared to become 'informers to Sinn Féin', while the other half were prepared to 'become assassins' due to the strain. But with the changes wrought by the introduction of the Black and Tans, he was more optimistic the following month. 'We have got rid of the majority of the old, useless men who were not pulling their weight against the rebels,' he wrote.

On 11 July 1920 members of the Kerry No. 2 Brigade attacked Rathmore RIC Barracks, firing on the barracks from a nearby railway bridge that had been fortified with sandbags. The IRA had stolen four cannons from Ross Castle and they used one of them in this attack on the Rathmore barracks, but not to any real effect. The shooting lasted through the night. At one point the IRA managed to throw a bomb through an upstairs window. It killed Constable George F. Will, 24, from Forfar, Scotland. He was the first Black and Tan fatality in the country.

A couple of days later, the IRA ambushed a police district inspector, Michael Fallon, near the Conor Pass as he was returning to Dingle from Cloghane, where he had inspected the RIC barracks. This raid for weapons was undertaken by members of the IRA flying column billeted at Fibough near the top of Slieve Mish Mountain. Those who took part in the raid included J. Dowling, Paddy Paul Fitzgerald, Dan Jeffers and Mick McMahon. Two RIC men were killed in the ambush – Constable Michael Lenihan, 34, from County Cork, and Constable George Roche, 32, from County Clare.

On the evening of 16 July, a sergeant and three constables were ambushed on the road near Curraghbeg school, about two miles from their barracks in Glencar. Constables Cleary and Cooney were both wounded in the attack.

Dr Dodd of Killorglin happened to drive on to the scene shortly afterwards and he provided medical aid. Both men had been hit by shotgun blasts. Cleary was in such a bad condition that it was considered unwise to move him to the county infirmary in Tralee. Although shotguns were outlawed as weapons of war, the IRA used them because it did not have enough rifles. The following week a daring operation at Tralee Railway Station netted eleven extra rifles.

Scouts from Na Fianna had been observing that soldiers guarding coal at the railway station would normally be having their midday meal in one of a couple of railway carriages parked at a siding around the time the train from Fenit was due. On 20 July members of D (Rock Street) Company left their employment at noon and proceeded to the Spa, where they boarded the train. Two Volunteers rode on the engine. At Mounthawk the train was halted for more IRA men to board it. The train then pulled up opposite the carriages used as a guardhouse, and the young Volunteers dashed from the train and across the platform, surprising the Englishmen at their meal and taking their rifles.

A sentry in the cabin at the Rock Street railway gates was meanwhile disarmed by two men who had whiled away the time reading a newspaper until the right moment. The whole job had been neatly planned, and the Volunteers got away with eleven rifles, which became the backbone of D Company's armoury.

That weekend the *Kerryman* made the first mention of the strange new force. 'A number of Englishmen wearing police caps and khaki uniforms arrived in Tralee on Friday, and are evidently intended to supersede the local force,' the newspaper reported on 24 July. 'A rumour is in circulation that the RIC, as it was known, is to be disbanded.'

Six RIC constables stationed at Ahabeg were ambushed in Lixnaw on 26 July as they were posting letters. Two were wounded. There was a further ambush near Camp on 18 August, as nine soldiers were returning to Tralee after delivering military supplies to Dingle. The first truck was blown off the road by a mine, and then the Volunteers opened fire with shotguns. Four of the soldiers were wounded and their colleagues surrendered.

The soldiers admitted that they were well treated by their captors. They were taken to a nearby farm and given tea, and the IRA then commandeered a passing motor car and drove the wounded men, none of whom was seriously injured, to within a mile or so of Dingle, where they were let go.

There was a great deal of military activity in the area between Anascaul and Camp in the following days. Patrick Kennedy, a brother of Tim Kennedy, the IRA's main intelligence officer in Kerry, was shot dead by troops a couple of days later near his home in Anascaul. There were different versions of what happened, but Tim Kennedy, who identified the body, believed that Paddy was saving hay when he saw the British troops approach.

Sergeant Clarke of Tralee RIC had been guiding a mixed party of soldiers and Black and Tans earlier in the day, and he pointed out Paddy Kennedy to them as the person who had ambushed Sergeant Moloney earlier that year. Later the same day, one of the soldiers, known to the IRA as 'Ginger George', and a Black and Tan nicknamed 'Japer' came upon Paddy Kennedy again. They shot and wounded him from a distance and the soldier then finished him off with a shot to the head at close range.

Two other local men, Daniel McKenna and Daniel Moriarty, were arrested at the scene and charged with having taken part in the ambush earlier in the week. McKenna refused to recognised the court and was convicted, but Moriarty stated that he had been working in a nearby field when he heard the explosion at the start of the attack.

A number of witnesses testified that they had seen Moriarty and another man working in his meadow saving hay. One of the witnesses, Tom Crean, whose brother in the RIC had been killed in Ballinspittle, was a former Royal Navy warrant officer who had distinguished himself on Antarctic expeditions. He testified that he had been saving hay himself when he heard the shooting and he could see that there were two people working in Moriarty's meadow. As a result, the court gave Moriarty the benefit of the doubt.

Volunteers in Cahirciveen staged a carefully planned operation to obtain weapons the following weekend. Between 11 pm and midnight on Saturday 28 August, they raided a number of houses, demanding shotguns that the householders were known to own. Those raided included Michael Walsh and E. O'Neill of Main Street, L. H. Dines of Westwood, Thomas C. Fitzgerald, and William Musgrave, who was relieved of his shotgun at the Cahirciveen Electric Light Company, where he worked. After leaving Walsh's house, they went next door to demand a shotgun from the widow of John A. O'Sullivan, whose family were absorbed in saying the Rosary. When the masked men entered, some of the children began screaming hysterically, and the raiders fled without the gun.

At the end of August Major William Beanney, the RIC

county inspector, reported that conditions were worse than ever in Kerry. 'The worst districts are Dingle, Tralee, and parts of Listowel, Castleisland and Killarney,' he wrote. 'In Kenmare and Cahirciveen there has not been much activity.'

'The Dingle peninsula is the worst part, being in a most lawless condition, except in the town of Dingle,' Beanney continued. 'The withdrawal of the stations at Anascaul and Camp has left the greater part of the peninsula without police or military control and, as a consequence, all the able-bodied men in the region have adopted the most aggressive attitude, and arranged, with very short notice, to attack on the return journey any police or military transport that passes which they do not deem too strong for them.

'There is everywhere a desire to boycott the police, and commandeering has to be resorted to in many places. For this reason motor transport has to be used for supplying some of the stations, especially Causeway and Brosna. There is hostility to the police everywhere through a great part of the county. I do not regard it as safe for a single police vehicle – even a Crossley tender – to travel.'

Terence MacSwiney, the Lord Mayor of Cork, had begun his hunger strike, and the county inspector warned that 'there is no doubt but that there will be grave danger of serious disturbances if he dies.' Beanney painted a very gloomy picture of the state of things in Kerry. 'Almost all local magistrates have resigned their commissions – a good number of them through fear of terrorism, which is rampant,' he wrote. 'The same terrorism prevents people from prosecuting their cases at petty sessions and drives them to the Sinn Féin courts. The local press is, of course, strongly Sinn Féin.'

'It may be taken for granted that nearly all the young people of the country are Sinn Féin and that a large proportion of the young men are Irish Volunteers,' he concluded. 'Between them, these two associations are controlling the whole life and action of the county, and every person, whether loyal or disloyal, is afraid to run counter to their wishes.'

In an effort to strike back, the RIC began circulating posters asking for 'secret information' regarding the 'innumerable murders and other outrages' allegedly committed 'by those who call themselves members of the Irish Republican Army.' The poster added: 'You will later be given the opportunity, should you wish to do so, of identifying your letter, and, should the information have proved of value, of claiming a reward.'

The IRA responded by raiding mail trains to check the kind of information that was being posted to Crown authorities. On 6 September the Mallow–Tralee train was stopped and all the mailbags were taken off the train by the IRA. Most of the mail was later returned, some of it with the notation: 'Censored by the IRA.' The following week the train was held up at Gortatlea and the mails seized, and a goods train was stopped at Ballinorig, near Tralee. Provisions destined for the military were seized. Further trains were held up and the mail was robbed at Headford Junction and Caragh Bridge.

Two policemen in plain clothes had the RIC inspector's motor car highjacked from them at Edward Street, Tralee, on 11 September 1920. The Black and Tans rounded up and searched all the men after the last Mass in Lixnaw on 12 September, and conducted similar searches in Ballybunion and Listowel. They cordoned off Convent Street and paid particular attention to D. Bunyan's forge. This kind of searching was soon to become quite vicious, but then the IRA were responding in kind.

A couple of days later, three policemen – Constables Prior, Lavelle, and Holmes – were shot and wounded as they were cycling from Tralee to their barracks in Causeway. Later the same week, the recently vacated RIC barracks at Ballyferriter was burned down.

General Sir Nevil Macready was supposed to be in charge of British forces in Ireland, but he essentially turned a blind eye as the Black and Tans took effective charge, embarking on their own campaign of revenge. 'While retaliation cannot be defended,' Macready wrote to the Chief Secretary on 27 September 1920, reprisals could only be stopped if a more effective means of punishment were devised. He therefore urged burnings as a reprisal for ambushes, because he realised that the 'obvious course' for the police would be to retaliate by shooting hostages. The police were being allowed, even encouraged, to take the law into their own hands.

In their supposed pursuit of order, the Black and Tans generated more disorder than any bandit campaign could have done, as they burned houses and businesses, disrupted local government, and abandoned the routine functions of a civic police force.

On 12 October at about 6 pm, three lorries carrying Black and Tans pulled up at Abbeydorney Cooperative Creamery. The manager, Timothy Donovan, and his staff were ordered to leave the premises. As they were going, shots were fired over their heads. They saw cheese and butter being put on a truck and what looked like petrol containers being taken from the trucks. The police then brought the manager back to open the safe, but it had already been so damaged by their own attempts to force it that his key would not work. The manager was then ordered out again. He was struck on the head with a rifle butt as he was leaving. The raiders proceeded to set fire to the creamery and left. The staff returned and put out the fire after it had caused about £2,000 worth of damage.

A few nights later, the *Cork Examiner* reported, uniformed men from the area of the county jail in Tralee, where the Black and Tans were stationed, crossed the field and broke windows in the terrace known as Urban Buildings. Although uniformed, they had masks to hide their identities. They entered Mason's house and asked for the eldest son, but he was not home, so the men roughed up his father.

Nearby, the widow McCarthy, whose sons were prominent Sinn Féiners, refused to open her door for the men. They tried to break it down, but failed, so they threw a hand grenade through the front window. The room was reportedly wrecked 'with the exception of a handsome picture of the Sacred Heart, which miraculously remained intact.' The widow also had an image of the Sacred Heart behind the front door that the men had been unable to break down. She told the press afterwards that the Sacred Heart had saved her life.

The Black and Tans repeated the process two nights later on 18 October, but this time without disguises. They raided Dowling's in Davy Lane, but the sons were out, so they destroyed a picture of the leaders of the 1916 Rising. They also raided Barry's shoemakers in Moyderwell, Vale's public house in Boherbee and E. Hogan's house in Urban Cottages, Boherbee, and they ordered Tom Clifford to take down the '1916' from the sign of his '1916 Shop' in Castle Street.

On Sunday the Black and Tans attempted to burn Lixnaw Creamery. At about 3 am they stopped at the home of Patrick McElligott, about a mile from Lixnaw. McElligott's two sons were dragged from the house into the pouring rain, dressed only in their night attire. They were then kicked around and beaten with rifle butts, before being made to stand in a deep pool of frigid water. The Tans next called at the home of Stephen O'Grady, but he escaped out a back window. They knocked his workman, named Nolan, unconscious with a rifle butt and then dragged him outside and poured a tub of water over him. They also dragged O'Grady's sister from the house and made her kneel in a channel of water while they cut her hair.

By then the Black and Tans had been making so much noise

that they woke up much of the village. They were observed breaking down the door of the creamery and bringing in petrol tins, before the place was set on fire. After leaving Lixnaw, they called at the house of Maurice Lovett, felled his son with a rifle butt and proceeded to cut his sister's hair.

The following day the national temperature was raised by the death of Terence MacSwiney, the Lord Mayor of Cork, on the seventy-fourth day of a highly publicised hunger strike in Brixton Prison. Two others also died around the same time on hunger strike in Cork. One of those, Joseph Murphy, was only seventeen years old.

On Thursday 28 October, Eamonn O'Connor was talking to a neighbour near his Tralee home – on what the residents called Ashe Street but the authorities persisted in calling Nelson Street – when he was set upon by Black and Tans. As he was being beaten, he managed to escape, but the wounds to his head required stitches. Stephen Falvey of Connolly Street also required stitches after he was beaten up in much the same manner, as were M. Horgan, T. O'Connor, Leslie Nolan and Patrick Allman.

The New York Times later reported that Patrick McDonnell, a US army veteran of the First World War, had just returned to Brooklyn with a frightening report of what had happened to him in Tralee, following a visit to his native Ballylongford. 'While I was standing on a station platform at Tralee on the return trip,' he said, 'a detachment of Black and Tans rode up and asked me my business. I told the officer I was a citizen of the United States and showed him my papers and army discharge papers.

'"You're a liar," the officer said. I protested, and one of the Black and Tans knocked me senseless with the butt of his gun after telling me that he didn't care who I was. As the officer and his men rode off, the officer shouted, "Go back to America and tell them what we did to you!"'

Terence MacSwiney was buried in Cork on Sunday 31 October, which was the eve of another traumatic event – the execution of eighteen-year-old university student Kevin Barry in Mountjoy Jail. This was the first official British execution of a rebel since 1916. The fact that a teenager was being executed was bad enough, but it seemed that the Crown authorities were determined to cause maximum offence to the people of Catholic Ireland by executing the young man on a Catholic holiday, All Saints' Day. Barry would immediately go into the pantheon of Irish saints as a martyr. He was immortalised in song:

Another martyr for old Ireland,
Another murder for the Crown,
Whose brutal laws may kill the Irish
But cannot keep her spirit down.

IRA headquarters asked for action throughout the country so that the execution would not be allowed to pass off quietly. Units were ordered to attack Crown forces. Tim Kennedy brought the order personally when he returned to Tralee in the last week in October. At the last minute, IRA headquarters called the whole thing off, but the countermanding order did not reach the Kingdom, and some of the deadliest action was in Kerry that weekend.

Five RIC men had been killed in Kerry by the Volunteers since the Easter Rising, but within twenty-four hours of Barry's execution no fewer than sixteen policemen had been shot - seven fatally - and another two kidnapped. In addition, a naval radio officer was shot and wounded.

Constable William Madden, 30, from Newcastle West, was shot dead in Abbeydorney, and a colleague, Constable Robert Gorbey, 23, was critically wounded and died later in the week. The IRA also besieged the barracks in Ballyduff, where Constable

George Morgan, 23, a native of Mayo, was killed and Constable Thomas Reidy, 42, from Clare was shot through the head. Two other colleagues were wounded less seriously. Black and Tans arrived in the village in the early hours of the morning and proceeded to torch the creamery and some of the principal business houses.

John Houlihan was taken out of his home near the village and shot by the Tans. It was suggested at the time that he was totally innocent and had merely been singled out because his brother had recently been on hunger striker in Mountjoy Jail. His parents, James and Catherine Houlihan, later testified that the military arrived at the house between 4.30 and 5.30 am. They rapped on the door and broke a window. They then dragged the teenage John from the house across the road, where one stabbed him with a bayonet in the side. He was then shot three times – in the hip, chest and side. One of the Tans finished him off with a blow of a rifle butt to the head. The young man's helpless mother looked on throughout. Catherine Houlihan pleaded with Sergeant James Allen of the RIC to intervene, but he said nothing.

This killing was clearly a reprisal for the death of Constable Morgan earlier that night – which was ironic, because Morgan was very well liked in the community. James Houlihan commented that Morgan would never have allowed the men to do what they did.

Two Black and Tan constables – Herbert Evans, 26, from Belfast and Albert Caseley, 24, from London – were killed at Hillville, near Killorglin, that night. Officially, they were on patrol, but they had actually just seen two girls home when they were attacked.

Killorglin, the stronghold and home town of Tom O'Donnell, the most enthusiastic recruiter for the British military, had been relatively quiet over the years, but the Black and Tans went on the rampage there that night. They burned down the Sinn Féin hall and an adjoining garage, as well as the Temperance Association hall. The residence of Fionán MacCollum, adjoining the school, was also torched, but the three MacCollums had gone to Cork for the MacSwiney funeral that weekend.

Shots were discharged intermittently throughout the night until about 5.30 am. The homes of other known Sinn Féiners were knocked up, but none of the 'wanted' men were found. Denis M. O'Sullivan was taken from his house in the Square and shot four times, however. He did not die of his wounds immediately, but he never recovered fully and passed away the following year.

The night of the attacks in Killorglin, Tom McEllistrim and the men from Ballymacelligott planned to ambush a police picket that regularly collected the mail each morning in Castleisland. 'We decided to take thirty men armed with rifles into Castleisland town, occupy houses at each side of the street and attack pickets the following morning,' he explained. 'I got my men into position that night at about 2.30.'

But his plans were upset by the intervention of the local parish priest, Father Patrick J. Brennan. Half an hour before the military were due to appear, Father Brennan came to McEllistrim and pleaded with him not to go through with the attack because the street would be crowded, as it was a fair day. This was intended to provide cover for the men to get away, but there was the likelihood that some innocent people would be shot.

'We insisted we would have to carry out our work,' McEllistrim wrote, 'but he said if we were determined to do so he would be compelled to go to the barracks and ask the picket not to go out that morning. We decided after a while to abandon the engagement and just walked with our rifles out of Castleisland, where we had transport waiting for us.'

On that Sunday night, two Black and Tans were wounded

in an ambush in Green Street, Dingle. Throughout the following day, there was a great deal of police activity in the town as pedestrians were held up and searched. 'Reprisals were feared and a general exodus from the town took place,' the local correspondent of the *Cork Examiner* reported. 'Some took refuge in fishing boats in the harbour; other took up quarters with their rural friends.'

The district inspector of the RIC assured the parish priest, Canon John MacDonnell, that there would be no reprisals. But on Tuesday, the premises of John Moriarty in John Street were doused with petrol and set ablaze.

Meanwhile, in Tralee, all hell was breaking loose. On Sunday evening Constable Daniel McCarthy of the RIC was shot through the knee while on patrol at Gas Terrace, and a naval radio operator, Bert Woodward, was shot in the chest at Moyderwell Corner. The Black and Tans swept through the streets in lorries and an armoured car, shooting indiscriminately, often into houses. They burned down the county hall across the road from the Dominican Church, as well as the '1916 Shop' in Castle Street.

The Black and Tans apparently did not realise that two of their police colleagues had been kidnapped after being lured into a 'honey trap' by a couple of local girls on that fateful Sunday evening. The two – Constable Patrick Waters, 23, a four-year veteran from Loughanbeg, near Spiddal, County Galway, and Constable Ernest Bright, a Londoner in his early thirties – were reportedly taken by the IRA from the Strand Street area to 'the Point' at the end of the canal, where they were shot and their bodies buried, but the IRA never acknowledged publicly that it had killed either of them. It was also rumoured that the bodies had been thrown into a furnace at the gasworks.

13

'SCENES OF THE WILDEST PANIC'

Assuming that their two colleagues, who had been kidnapped, were possibly still being held by the IRA, the Black and Tans embarked on a veritable reign of terror in Tralee for the next nine days. The worst of the terror in early November occurred in Kerry, but the national spotlight was turned on the dramatic events elsewhere, such as the execution of Kevin Barry, followed later in the month by the events of Bloody Sunday in Dublin and the Kilmichael ambush in Cork. Hence much of what actually happened in Kerry was virtually forgotten in the various histories of the period.

Most of the incidents described in this chapter were not even mentioned in Dorothy Macardle's mammoth book *The Irish Republic,* which is over 900 pages long. 'Among the operations conducted by the British forces in Ireland during November was the sacking of Granard in County Longford by men who arrived in eleven lorries with bombs and petrol and set four shops ablaze, and of Tralee in County Kerry, where uniformed men came out of the police barracks armed with crowbars and hatchets, rifles and revolvers and supplies of petrol, and attacked the homes of Republicans,' she wrote. This was the sum total of her reference to the so-called sacking of Tralee, dismissed in just part of a sentence, even though the events made front-page news on a number of days in both Canada and the United States. The sacking of the town also prompted a series of parliamentary questions at Westminster and became the subject of controversy and editorials in the British daily press. News from Tralee was reported on the front page of *The New York Times* on three separate days during the siege and on the front page of the *Montreal Gazette* on four different days.

Over a dozen of the most active members of the IRA got out of Tralee that week. Cahill left town to take control of the active-service unit. Monday 1 November was All Saints' Day, a holy day of obligation, with the result that all the churches were busy. The Black and Tans drove up and down the streets in lorries, discharging their rifles. 'Volley after volley resounded, to the terror of the people,' according to one witness. Shots were fired as people emerged from 12 o'clock Mass at St John's Parish Church. There was panic as people stampeded back into the church. For decades afterwards, bullet marks could be seen on the pillars at the church gates.

That afternoon two IRA volunteers – John Cantillon and Michael Brosnan – were killed by Black and Tans in Ardfert. A painter, John Conway, 57, a father of six, was killed in Upper Rock Street while returning from evening devotions. At the time it was said that he had no involvement with the IRA, but afterwards he was listed as one of the IRA's dead Volunteers. The Crown authorities never contended that he was a rebel. They said that he died of heart failure, and he had supposedly sustained the bullet wound to the head as he fell. Ellen Walsh, a woman in her late sixties, was shot in the leg and Simon O'Connor, an ex-soldier, was shot in the groin.

That evening two RIC Constables – James J. Coughlan and W. Muir – were jumped and overpowered by a number of young men shortly after going out on foot patrol in Ballylongford. Neither constable was armed. They were taken away in separate directions. Muir was held overnight by the local company, but word came from brigade headquarters the following morning to free the two officers immediately. The Black and Tans in

Ballylongford issued an ultimatum that Ballylongford would be razed to the ground if the two policemen were not released within forty-eight hours. After about twelve hours, Muir made it back to the barracks, shaken and badly beaten, but there was no sign of Coughlan.

A group of foreign journalists stayed at the Grand Hotel in Tralee that Monday night. They had been in Cork for Terence MacSwiney's funeral when they heard of the burning of the county hall in Tralee the previous night. They decided to see for themselves what was happening in the town. They included reporters from Associated Press of the United States, *Le Journal* (Paris), the London *Times*, the *Daily News,* the *Manchester Guardian* and the *London Evening News*. The group reached Tralee about 9 o'clock on Monday night and checked into the Grand Hotel on Denny Street.

'At half past nine, Mr MacGregor, the *Evening News* correspondent, proposed to take a walk through the town in order to see the extent of the damage and ascertain if all was then quiet,' Hugh Martin reported next day in the *Daily News*. 'Would anybody go with him? I volunteered for the reconnaissance.'

'Upon leaving the Grand Hotel, we noticed a party of from twenty to twenty-five men standing on the opposite side of the road a short distance away,' Martin continued. 'The night was very dark, but by the way in which the figures deployed in crescent formation it was plain we had been sighted. Retreat and mere evasion were equally out of the question. Mr MacGregor and I therefore crossed the road diagonally in the direction of the figures. We then saw they were police armed with rifles, and all wearing the full uniform of the RIC.'

'Good evening,' the journalists said, and asked if it was safe to walk the main streets.

'From the men's bearing, I judged at once the position was critical,' Martin noted.

'What have you come for? To spy on us, I suppose,' responded one of the men, who proceeded to ask what newspapers they represented.

MacGregor gave his own name and the name of his newspaper, as the paper had generally been favourable to the Crown forces – unlike Martin and his newspaper. 'We differed considerably in opinion as to where emphasis should be placed in giving the facts,' MacGregor explained some days later. 'I am emphatically of the opinion that there is no organised or official plan to obstruct English pressmen in Ireland.' He realised that the Black and Tans were in an unenviable position. 'The men were upset by the assassination of their colleagues and hourly expectation of their own assassination.'

Martin decided on discretion rather than valour. For more than a year, he had been denouncing what he called 'the most grotesque comedy'. He accused the Crown forces of engaging in 'the infamy of stamping on freedom in Ireland'. He had been warned by friends in official circles to be very careful, as his reports had infuriated the Black and Tans in particular.

'I decided to lie boldly, and mentioned the name of a coalition journal which both by silence and occasional comment has lent the strongest support to the government's Irish policy,' he explained. 'I also gave my name, when it was demanded, as that of an English journalist associated with the coalition.'

'Is there a Hugh Martin among you?' one of the police asked, 'because if there is, we mean to do for him. It's him we want, and we're going to get him.'

MacGregor explained that they had come to Tralee to find out about the burning of the county hall.

'Up to Saturday night we were at peace,' the sergeant in charge of the men explained, 'but they have declared war upon us.' He went on to list the names of his comrades who had been killed recently, and he then ordered the two journalists to get indoors at once.

'Just as we reached the door of the hotel, however, they changed their minds and shouted to us to come back,' Martin continued. 'I feared that they had decided to examine our papers, which must have established my real identity. As escape was impossible, we returned. I spoke in a friendly way to the men, and again succeeded in bluffing them completely, so that after a few minutes' chat we were on fairly good terms, and seemed to have gained their confidence. Finally, we were ordered to walk to the corner of the street and read a typewritten notice affixed to the wall.

'As it was too dark for reading, a policeman lit a match, which he held before the paper with fingers that trembled. To steady his nerves, I handed him a cigarette. As I took the case from my pocket, I accidentally pulled out with it a letter, which fell on the ground at my feet. By the light of the match, I was able to read my own name. A constable stooped to pick it up politely, but I was too quick for him, and breathed again.'

The Tan read out the notice, which Martin took down in shorthand on the back of the envelope. It read:

Take Notice
Warning!

Unless the two Tralee policemen in Sinn Féin custody are returned before 10 am on the 2nd inst, reprisal of a nature not yet heard of in Ireland will take place in Tralee and surroundings.

What did it mean? MacGregor asked.

'It means that after ten o'clock tomorrow it won't be safe for anybody in Tralee whose face is not known,' one of the Tans replied.

'We are all loyal men here – all true blues. We fought in the war,' another added. 'I have the military medal, and having declared war upon us, war it will be.'

On returning to the hotel, Martin had some trouble sleeping. 'As I lay in bed,' he later wrote, 'I heard the sound, then so common o' nights in Ireland, of plate-glass windows being smashed in the principal shopping street.'

The Tans broke the windows of Murtagh's tobacconist and Tom Dennehy's public house, but the army stopped further trouble by patrolling the town during the remainder of the night. Father Edward Hyacinth Collins, one of the Dominican priests and a former army chaplain, publicly complimented the local commanding officer, a Major Edwards. 'Tralee owes its safety to the protection afforded by the military, which was as effective as it was courteous and becoming of military discipline,' Father Collins declared.

The civil structure had been turned upside down. Soldiers were acting as police, while the police were acting as soldiers and behaving like terrorists.

Around 11 o'clock on Tuesday morning, Martin learned that the word was out that he was in town, and he made a hasty retreat back to Cork. 'For more than a month past,' he wrote, 'hints have been reaching me from various quarters that it would be well for me either to cease telling the truth in print or to take special precautions for my own safety.'

Next morning the *Daily News* duly printed Martin's report, along with the following editorial:

We commend to the attention of our readers the astonishing story told in our columns today by Mr Hugh Martin, our correspondent in Ireland. Sir Hamar Greenwood repeated once more in the House of Commons yesterday his statement that the government has 'no policy of reprisals' in Ireland. It is evident that the government's agents have. Mr Martin's offence is that he has told the truth about the proceedings of the government forces, regular and irregular, in Ireland. For this, his life is apparently being threatened by the presumptive defenders of law and order in that country. A few days ago we challenged the Chief Secretary to say that Mr Martin's testimony was untrue, but Sir Hamar Greenwood returned an evasive reply. We will now challenge him again. Is he aware, when he says that the government has 'no policy of reprisals', of the existence of the state of things revealed by Mr Martin's message? If so, is it the desire of the government to use police terrorism to prevent the people of this country knowing, except through official sources, what is happening in Ireland? These questions, it will be seen, are of wide interest.

When asked about this in the House of Commons that day, Sir Hamar Greenwood, the Chief Secretary for Ireland, was quite dismissive. 'There are no steps being taken against journalists in Ireland,' he told Parliament. 'Ireland is the freest country in the world – for journalists.'

Naturally, some of the press did not see things the same way. The threat to Martin, which made front-page news in the *New York Times*, was denounced as a threat to the freedom of the press in an editorial in the *Times* of London: 'An issue of importance to all independent newspapers and to the public is raised by the account published yesterday in the *Daily News* of the threatening attitude of the constabulary at Tralee towards a special correspondent and confirmed in all essentials by the special correspondent of the *Evening News* who accompanied him and heard the threats.'

'I can corroborate the verbatim accuracy of Hugh Martin's report,' MacGregor noted in the *Evening News*. 'The threats at Tralee were real. I believe Martin's life was in danger at the opening of the interview, but the threats and danger came from three or four of the party and would not have been uttered by their leaders.'

When Greenwood was confronted with the latest evidence, he refused to back down. What he had said was that 'Ireland is the freest country in the world for journalists,' he reminded the House, to cheers from the government benches. 'On reflection, I confirm that opinion.'

A French journalist who was with the group visiting Tralee depicted a frightening situation. 'I do not remember, even during the war, having seen a people so profoundly terrified as those of this little town, Tralee,' M. de Marsillac, the London correspondent of *Le Journal*, reported. 'The violence of the reprisals undertaken by representatives of authority, so to speak, everywhere, has made everybody beside himself, even before facts justified such a state of mind.'

Shopkeepers were warned by the police to close down for the funerals of their companions, who deserved as much respect as the Lord Mayor of Cork. All schools were closed and remained closed for over a week. The security forces stalked the deserted streets firing shots into the air, or shooting blindly into windows as they drove up and down the street.

Shortly after noon on Tuesday, Tommy Wall, 24, an ex-soldier who had fought in France during the First World War and returned to join the IRA, was standing at the corner of Blackpool Lane and the Mall when some Tans told him to put up his hands. Maybe as a former soldier who had fought for the Crown, he thought he would be safe. One of the men hit him in the face with a rifle butt and told him to get out of the place. As he left, they shot and fatally wounded him; they claimed later that he had been shot while trying to escape.

'All the afternoon, except for soldiers, the town was as deserted and doleful as if the angel of death had passed through it,' M. de Marsillac continued. 'Not a living soul in the streets. All the shops shut and the bolts hastily fastened. All work was suspended – even the local newspapers.'

At the time there were three newspapers in Tralee: the *Liberator*, which was published three times a week, and two weeklies – the *Kerryman* and the *Kerry People*. It was noteworthy that, when they next came out the following week, all three papers were heavily dependent on outside newspapers for accounts of what had happened in the town, as their reporters had apparently not dared to venture out much.

On Wednesday the police again warned that all businesses should remain shut. But the worst events were reserved for late that night. 'Further tumult prevailed in Tralee last night,' an *Irish Times* correspondent reported. 'It came as a great shock to the people, who had been assured that the military would, as on the previous night, take control of the peace of the town and the protection of life and property. The military remained on duty up to midnight, and left when all was quiet.'

Around two o'clock in the morning, the Tans came out in force and began firebombing the premises of Sinn Féin sympathisers. In Rock Street the grocery shop and bar owned by Thomas Slattery were broken into, doused with petrol and then ignited with incendiary bombs. The blaze promptly spread to an adjoining flour-and-meal establishment. The public house on the other side owned by Mrs Brosnan, a widow with several daughters, was also doused with petrol and put on fire, forcing the widow and her daughters to flee in their night attire. 'Some of the girls had to jump into the street to escape the flames and had marvellous escapes from injury,' according to the *Cork Examiner*. Two other adjoining businesses were also set on fire.

'Scenes of the wildest panic ensued,' the *Cork Examiner* report continued. 'The screams of the women and children were heard from the neighbourhood of the burning buildings, mingled with the ring of rifle fire and the explosion of bombs.'

An attempt was made to burn down the pub where Tom Dennehy lived (now the Castle Bar) in Upper Rock Street, but the Tans were unable to break down the shutters or the door of the building, and the straw in the thatch was too wet to burn, as it had been raining heavily that day. Eamonn O'Connor's newspaper shop was burned to the ground in Ashe Street, however, and the adjoining premises of James Murphy – a solicitor whose two sons had fought in the First World War – was seriously damaged by the fire.

'Rifle fire and explosions in different parts of the town awakened the people, who became panic-stricken,' the *Irish Times* correspondent continued. 'The flames from the burning houses lit up the sky, and the shrieks of women and children near the burning premises filled the air. The military returned to the streets from Ballymullen Barracks at about five o'clock and did their utmost to extinguish the fires.'

When a number of young men, who happened to be local Volunteers, came out to fight the fires, the Black and Tans fired shots in their direction to discourage them. 'Their escapes from the fusillades of bullets that rained were miraculous,' according to the correspondent of the *Cork Examiner*. 'In Rock Street while Slattery's was on fire, they were compelled to leave the house and line up at the opposite side of the street.' But then the military came and the lieutenant in charge ordered his men to protect the young men from the Tans with their guns at the ready. The men then turned their efforts to other places in the town.

Dunne's and O'Connor's, adjoining pubs in Upper Castle Street, were also torched by the Black and Tans, and an attempt was made to burn down O'Rourke's in Boherbee, but it was only partially destroyed, thanks to the efforts of a group of local men. The *Cork Examiner* was so impressed by the actions of 'the brave men, who at the risk of their lives tried to subdue the flames', that it named some of them. They were John Joe Sheehy, Jack Fleming, Thomas Foley, Edward Looney, Michael Connor, Bill Moriarty, Tommy Vale, Jerry Hanafin, Timothy Connor, J. Quirke, G. and William Ralph, J. Lonergan, J. Prendergast and Michael Colgan. 'There were many others whose names have not been ascertained, and who should be included in the list,' the report added, 'but they can understand the difficulties pressmen have to encounter in these times.'

John Joe Sheehy was the officer in command of the Boherbee IRA, which had stored its weapons in O'Rourke's. They managed to put out the fire before the weapons or ammunition were destroyed. They did so with the protection of the British army.

Captain Tyrell O'Malley of the Royal Munster Fusiliers at Ballymullen Barracks, who was from Mayo, despised the Black and Tans. He was sympathetic to the IRA and kept in touch with Tim Kennedy. Whenever possible, he forewarned the Republicans of plans to shoot up places.

The Tans had left a warning posted in several prominent places:

Final Notice
Take notice that all business premises, factories, shops, etc., in Tralee must be kept closed and work suspended until such time as the police in Sinn Féin custody are returned. Anyone disobeying this order will be dealt with in a drastic manner.

'So alarmed were the people that the order was rigidly obeyed,' according to the *Irish Times* correspondent. 'All business was suspended, and all shops were closed, and the streets are deserted. Hundreds are seeking safety in the country districts.'

The military patrolled Tralee on Thursday, but a deputation of the main merchants was unable to persuade Major Edwards to allow the bakeries to open, as people were going hungry. He explained that he could not usurp the civil power of the police.

When Constable James J. Coughlan finally made it back to the Ballylongford RIC station on Thursday morning, after being held by the IRA for some sixty hours, he was in a dreadful state. He had literally been beaten black and blue. He had been taken by the Newtownsands Company of the IRA. He was blindfolded, a rope was tied around his waist, and he was dragged through the countryside until dawn. He was then kept in the house of Eddie Carmody in Newtownsands, beaten for information, and again dragged across fields on the second night until dawn, when he was put in a shed near some pigs. The Ballylongford IRA had complied with the order to release Muir, but they had great difficulty in persuading their Newtownsands colleagues to release Coughlan. The third night, he was told that he was going to be taken before a Sinn Féin court. He was driven in a car for what, he said, felt like twenty miles. He was then taken out into a field, where he thought he was going to be shot, but in fact he was told that he was about a twenty-minute walk from Ballylongford.

Dr A. A. Hargrave, who saw Coughlan at Tralee Military Hospital on Friday, remarked that he had never seen a man in such a condition. He was black and blue from head to foot. He had been held for sixty hours – more than five times as long as Muir. But Muir never got over his mistreatment: he committed suicide by cutting his throat with a razor the following month.

News of the mistreatment of the kidnapped constables only hardened the determination of the RIC and the Black and Tans to secure the release of their men who were missing in Tralee. The accounts of what was happening there were still fairly sketchy on the Thursday, when T. P. O'Connor, the nationalist Member of Parliament from Liverpool, asked in the House of Commons about the deaths of John Houlihan in Ballyduff and John Conway and Tommy Wall, as well as the shooting of Simon

O'Connor in Tralee: 'I have received a report to the effect that John Houlihan was shot by masked men at Ballyduff at 6 am on Monday the first, and that Thomas Wall was fatally wounded in Tralee from gunshot wounds.'

Sir Hamar Greenwood, the Chief Secretary for Ireland, replied: 'Courts of inquiry will be held in these cases. In the case of John Conway, a court of inquiry has been held and found that he died from natural causes. I have not yet received a copy of the proceedings of this court, but I am informed by the police authorities that the deceased was found dead near his home on the first instant, and the body bore no traces of gunshot or other wounds.'

Greenwood's remarks in regard to Conway prompted a certain amount of incredulity, because the London *Times* had already reported that its correspondent had seen the body laid out with an obvious bullet wound in the temple. 'The vital fact in the tragedy is that, while the Chief Secretary is repeating his stereotyped assurances that things are getting better, it is patent to the readers of newspapers the world over that they are getting daily worse,' the *Daily News* commented. 'At the moment, the supreme need is to withdraw the troops. If the police cannot remain unprotected, let them go too. Ireland could not be worse off without them than with them. There is every reason to believe her state would be incomparably better.'

By Friday 5 November, separate stories from Tralee were front-page news in both the *Montreal Gazette* and the *New York Times*. The events in Tralee on Wednesday night were front-page news in the *Montreal Gazette*.

'A further outbreak took place in Tralee last night, which resulted in a great deal of damage to residences and business houses,' the Canadian newspaper reported. 'Some time after the military, who were in control of the town, had withdrawn shortly after midnight, forces of uniformed men broke loose and, armed with crowbars and other implements and tins of petrol, set fire to houses and shops belonging to prominent Sinn Féiners. Wild scenes of panic ensued, the residents flying for safety to country districts. The military returned about five o'clock and did their utmost to extinguish the flames and restore order.

'They remained on duty till daybreak and the civilian population expressed gratitude to them for their efforts in saving life and property during the night.' In reality the army were protecting the people of Tralee from the police force, while the British government was standing idly by, even though this disgraceful state of affairs was receiving full publicity thousands of miles away.

'When his troops left the town after midnight on Wednesday, everything was calm,' Major Edwards, the commanding officer of the British troops, reportedly stated, according to the *Toronto Globe & Mail*. 'They could not anticipate a further outbreak but when they learned of it they rushed down and gave all the assistance possible. Fearing a further outbreak last night, he kept his men on duty until morning, and promised to do the same tonight.'

Hence the *Globe & Mail* reported that 'peace and order have once more been restored in Tralee', but the report went on to observe that the people feared further outbreaks. 'A deputation of representative merchants waited on the officer commanding troops in Tralee today and represented to him the extreme hardships to which the people were subjected through lack of food, especially bread, the supply of which is exhausted,' the Toronto newspaper explained. 'Like all other establishments, the bakeries closed down, fearing that drastic measures were threatened. The officer informed the deputation that the place was not under martial law and he could not usurp the civil power.'

In short, as of that Friday morning the British commander was being portrayed as protecting the people against the police but saying that he really did not have the authority to act, because the police who were terrorising the place were the legal authority. They continued to patrol the streets of the town in lorries during the day, and they made forays into the surrounding countryside.

They shot dead a labourer named Archer, who was working in a field near Ardfert that Friday. He apparently ran when he saw them coming. Michael Maguire – who was an IRA Volunteer as well as a local shopkeeper and former councillor – was arrested by the Tans in Ardfert, and his body was later found on the village green in Causeway, with no explanation as to who had shot him, or why. The Tans reportedly killed seven civilians in Causeway that day. This again made the front page of the *New York Times*, but there were no further details, as reporters could not get to the area.

Saturday, market day, was normally the busiest day of the week in Tralee, but people were not allowed into town. The correspondent of the *Freeman's Journal* contacted his newspaper by telegraph.

'Police persist in taking measures to cut off the necessities of life from the people,' he reported. 'Black and Tans take up positions outside bakeries and provision stores where they suspect food could be secured, and at the bayonet's point send famishing women and children from the doors. Outside one baker's establishment a Black and Tan, brandishing a revolver, told women and children to clear off, adding "You wanted to starve us, but we will starve you."'

People had not been able to do any shopping for a week and there was real deprivation, especially in the poorer areas. The breadwinners had been unable to work and the poorer people could not afford to buy food, even if it had been available. The story on the front page of that day's *Montreal Gazette* carried the headline:

The report related: 'The town of Tralee, Ireland, is fast approaching starvation in consequence of a recent police order forbidding the carrying on of business – until two missing policemen are returned by the townspeople. Trade is paralyzed, the banks and bakeries even being closed, and the condition of the people is becoming desperate. An additional military order forbids the holding of fairs and markets or assemblies of any kind within a three-mile limit.'

'Each day brings the story of the murder of policemen, of the shooting of soldiers, of the killing of even those who have made themselves objectionable to their neighbours,' the *Montreal Gazette* declared in an editorial the same day. 'Each day, almost, also brings the record of "reprisals", in which men in uniform, which show that their wearers' duty is to preserve order, raid villages, fire houses, destroy property and chase the inhabitants – men, women and children – from their homes into the inclement night. Men in high places, who should understand the danger of irregular methods of lynch-law order, do not show a serious appreciation of the gravity of the situation; some give veiled excuses for the violence that almost amount to encouragement.'

That night some Tans set fire to the technical school and the Carnegie Library at Moyderwell, Tralee, but the fire was extinguished before much damage was done. Next day, Sunday, Talbot's grocery and bar on Ashe Street was bombed, because the owner refused to remove his name in Irish over the door.

'News from Tralee continues to be very disquieting,' Hugh Martin of the *Daily News* reported on Sunday night. 'During the past few days Tralee has been in the public eye more than any other town in Ireland and reprisals there have been given worldwide publicity.

'Now it is useless for the government to deny knowledge of these matters. It knows that reprisals were threatened in the most unequivocal language, and that the threat was communicated to the press for publication. It knows that in pursuance of this threat the policies are – or at any rate were until a few hours ago – forcibly preventing the baking of bread and the sale of food so that women and children, in addition to the men who may have been guilty of the kidnappings, were going hungry and may soon be faced with the prospect of starvation. How then can the government clear itself of the charge of waging war on women and children?

'Much anxiety prevails concerning conditions in the town, where the population have for the past week been living in a state of terror,' according to the *Freeman's Journal,* which carried a highly emotional editorial next day:

War on women and children!

How the cry thrilled Europe when the German jackboots trampled on Belgium!

England led the chorus of fiery protest

And Mr Lloyd George led England.

Baby-killer was the epithet that damned the Zeppelin raiders.

War on women and children!

The cry rises again today.

Not now from Belgian homes, but from the streets of a Kerry town.

Tralee is at the point of starvation.

Starvation created for political purpose.

British bayonets bar hungry children from food and threaten famishing women.

The Black and Tans will not be denied.

Their veto is final.

The military officer in command declares he is helpless even if children starve.

The British government turns a deaf ear to appeals and protests.

Tralee may perish, but the 'Black and Tans' must have their way.

That is the meaning of Greenwood's silence.

And the world is already fixing the responsibility for what the French call British 'Louvainerie'.

'There is a war on,' was the official answer made to the remonstrance of M. de Marsillac.

To which the distinguished French journalist replied, 'One does not do such things in war.'

He was thinking of honourable war.

And he did not know his Hamar Greenwood.

To whom the approving nod of Carson counts for more than the anguish of the hungry babes and the despairing mothers of Tralee.

War on women and children!

It is the essence of the plan which Greenwood is pledged to execute.

The Tralee infamy is only the beginning.

In a few days or, at most, a few weeks, the train laid and fired by Geddes will produce the desired explosion.

Irish railways will stop.

Not in one town, but in scores, will babies starve.

And Greenwood will stop his ears against their wails.

He will, no doubt, deny the starvation,

As he does the bombed creameries and pillaged downs.

It will be the Irish who make the weak and helpless suffer.

The Chief Secretary's heart, as usual, will 'bleed' for the victims.

But the starvation blockade will be maintained in its full vigour.

And the suffering heart will be cheered by Carsonite smiles.

That same day in London, T. P. O'Connor asked another series of questions in the House of Commons about what was happening in Tralee. He asked, for instance, whether it was 'true that for three or four days all business houses and factories, including bakeries, in Tralee, have been closed by the authority of the police; whether many of the poor were thereby placed in serious distress, and whether the trade of the town for the time being was destroyed?' He further asked 'by whose authority the police' were holding up 'the trade and the food of a whole community'.

'The business premises in Tralee were closed for some days following a number of assassinations of police on Sunday last, but not by order of the police,' Greenwood replied. 'I understand shops are now open and business is resuming its normal course.'

The businesses were shut down in Tralee, and if the police were not responsible, 'I would like to know on whose orders?' O'Connor asked.

Greenwood replied that he had already telegraphed Tralee for an explanation. 'As the shops were closed, admittedly, on whose authority were they closed?' he had wired. 'I am waiting a reply to that wire,' Greenwood explained.

'Is the world expected to believe that women and children went without food for days in the hope that the Chief Secretary would be blamed for reducing them to starvation?' the *Freeman's Journal* asked. 'That is the only interpretation of Sir Hamar Greenwood's so-called explanation. It gives the measure of the present Parliament that this issue of grotesque fabrications was apparently accepted by the majority, not indeed as the truth, but as a plausible substitute for the truth. Any lie, however clumsy, will serve if the object is to stifle inquiry into the Irish Terror.'

Northern nationalist Joseph Devlin asked about a statement of the *Central News* correspondent in Tralee, who reported that his house was visited on Saturday by the police, who warned that he would be put up against the wall and shot if he transmitted press messages without first submitting them to the police. Greenwood replied that he was making inquiries, and when he did respond he said that 'the police deny all knowledge of the alleged threat against the correspondent.'

Two men, named Cantillon and Brosnan, were killed near Ardfert when they ran on the approach of the Tans that Monday. In addition, a young girl named O'Connor was shot and wounded while standing in her own doorway. The *New York World* noted that the 'grim tales of shooting' in the Ardfert district were 'examples of the head-hunting game which has developed in warfare in Ireland.'

The *Irish Times* reported that Ballyduff and its surrounding district had been enduring a nightly terror since the previous Sunday: 'Night after night the sky is lighted up by the blaze of burning ricks of hay and straw – the labour of one season laid waste in a night.'

On Monday the bakeries and butcher shops and local factories were permitted to open in Tralee, but all other business were rigidly prevented from doing so. The *New York World* reported that an attempt to open others shops in Tralee on Tuesday 9 November 'was met by demonstrations by the police, who appeared on the streets shouting and discharging firearms and terrorising those who had attempted to defy the order and open their business places.'

'No coherent account of conditions in Tralee is possible,' the *New York World* correspondent explained. 'Communication is difficult, investigation dangerous, and the reports from the place are so remarkable as to be almost unbelievable. It has been suggested officially that the police are not responsible for the order, but local accounts leave no doubt that the police are enforcing it, perhaps unofficially but none the less effectively. Wholesale starvation apparently is enforced with bayonets and occasionally with bullets, as events have shown. The people cannot understand how this can be done by forces of the Crown without Crown authority.'

'A Black and Tan rule has been set up in Tralee,' the report continued. 'Many of the 10,000 inhabitants have fled, but those unable to find refuge elsewhere are the victims of this awful procedure.'

Greenwood came under further pressure in Parliament on Tuesday 9 November about the continuing state of affairs in Tralee. 'As regards the alleged closing of business houses by the police, I am informed that the police are not unduly interfering with the conduct of business in Tralee,' the Chief Secretary told the House of Commons. 'Subsequent to, and in consequence of, the recent murders of the police in this district and the kidnapping of two constables on the 31st ultimo, many young men engaged in the shops and factories have left the town, and are believed to be in the country and taking part in attacks on the forces of the Crown. These young men are members of the Irish Republican Army. It is in great measure owing to this state of affairs that business has been suspended, but my latest information is to the effect that work in the factories and business in the shops is being carried on to a considerable extent.'

The Chief Secretary's statement was patently distorted. Joe Devlin responded that the Black and Tans were enforcing a 'reign of terror' in Tralee. 'When a shopkeeper opens, his place is entered by forces of the Crown, and the proprietor is compelled to close under threats,' Devlin explained, adding that poor people were starving because they were being prevented, at the point of a revolver, from purchasing food.

'The creamery proprietors are being prevented from taking milk from the farmers, with the result that the latter have no means of disposing of it,' Devlin added. He therefore asked Greenwood what action he was 'taking to bring to an end this police despotism, which is causing such hardship and suffering to the women and children in Tralee?'

'I do not accept the suggested facts that things are so appallingly bad in Tralee as is suggested in the question,' Greenwood replied.

It was not until around 8 pm on that Tuesday night – 9 November – that the following notice was posted in Tralee:

> Business may be resumed in Tralee tomorrow (Wednesday) in view of the hardships imposed on loyal subjects. Other means will be resorted to for the recovery of the two police in Sinn Féin custody. Public houses will remain open until the usual hour.

That same night in London, Prime Minister Lloyd George made his infamous pronouncement during an address at the annual Lord Mayor's dinner at the Guildhall. He made international news when he said that the security forces 'had murder by the throat' in Ireland.

Next morning the *Daily News* carried a frightening description of conditions in Tralee by Hugh Martin:

> It is like a town with the plague. Not a shop is open and people remain behind closed doors and shuttered windows from morning to nightfall. An hour before darkness sets in, women and children leave their homes and go anywhere they can for the night.

About 280 women and children sleep in the workhouse every night. The men who remain in the town are in constant dread during the long hours of the night. When morning dawns, efforts are made to secure food some way or other, but the slightest sound on the streets, even in broad daylight, has the effect of making people run indoors again. It is quite incorrect to say that the shops were open for a couple of hours. That is not so. No merchant dares open his door even for a few moments, lest the Black and Tans should come on him unexpectedly and burn down the shop. In the house where I was staying they had a little flour, which was used for baking bread, but the majority of the people are not as well off as we were; they try to get food on the quiet, but do not always succeed. When a police lorry appears on the streets, shots are fired at street corners by its occupants, adding to the general terror. It is simply awful to witness the plight of the women and children. They are absolutely terrified. The armed police are practically always on the street . . .

It was the police who gave permission to the bakers and butchers to give supplies, and it was on the police orders that all other business is shut down.

This morning the police gave permission to two local bacon factories to work for the day in saving meat which otherwise would have gone bad. It was the acting county inspector who gave a written order to the Tralee gas manager to continue gas and water supplies.

It is, therefore, plain to everybody that police rule is the only rule in Tralee, which must be obeyed, and the police themselves so proclaim openly . . .

There is no goods traffic coming in. There is no money coming in, and no wages paid. There was not a bit of fresh meat killed in the town since Saturday week.

The whole thing is certainly a new development of the frightfulness policy. It is a deliberate attempt to starve a whole town.

Joe Devlin read the passage from the *Daily News* into the record of the House of Commons that day and then asked whether Greenwood still maintained that this holding-up of Tralee was not done by the direct order of the police. Devlin also asked to be told what steps the Secretary for Ireland 'proposes to take to put an end at once to this action by the police authorities'. By then, of course, the police had already given the order that businesses would be allowed to open as normal.

Even though notices had been posted stating that normal business could resume on 10 November, most people were afraid to venture out, and it took some hours for the residents of Tralee to realise that the siege was over. It was not until the late afternoon that normal business was resumed.

'It is impossible for any person who has not been in the town to realise the terrible plight of the people,' the *Kerry People* reported when it returned to the streets a few days later. 'The privations, particularly in the case of the poorer classes, are appalling, and starvation has by now entered many a home.'

The three local newspapers carried some reports of what happened during the ten days that Tralee was under siege, but these relied almost entirely on reports published elsewhere. Their own reporters had obviously either abandoned Tralee for the duration of the siege or else kept their heads well down.

'We do not deem it necessary to dilate on the situation which compelled us to shut down our business for two weeks,' the *Kerryman* explained in an editorial in its next edition on 20 November. 'The people of Tralee have seen for themselves all that occurred during these two dramatic weeks. The people of Kerry, of Ireland, and indeed of the world, have learned through the daily newspapers, from Irish and Continental pressmen, what we have been enduring in Tralee. It is unnecessary for us to elaborate on the press reports. They speak for themselves.'

When *Kerry's Fighting Story* was first published in 1947, it relied heavily on the contemporary reports published in the *Kerryman,* with the result that most of the material covered in this chapter was overlooked. It is ironic that these events received more coverage in the *Montreal Gazette* than in any of the local papers in Kerry. Of course, this was really a sign of the times and the level of intimidation of the press – notwithstanding the absurd protestations of Hamar Greenwood in London. While these events were going on in Kerry, the Black and Tans attacked the premises of the *Leitrim Observer* and the *Cork Examiner* and attempted to wreck their presses.

Hugh Martin of the *Daily News* later collected his reports from Ireland and published them in a book in 1921. In it he argued that what had occurred in Tralee was symptomatic of what was happening throughout Ireland.

'The police in Ireland are themselves the victims of a condition of terrorism which is only equalled by the condition of terrorism that they themselves endeavour to impose,' he wrote. 'They are, for the most part, quite young men who have gone through the experience, at once toughening and demoralising, of fighting through a long and savage war. They are splendid soldiers and abominably bad policemen. They are unsuitably and inadequately officered, quite insufficiently trained for their special duties, and expected to keep sober in nerve-racking circumstances in a country where drink is far more plentiful and potent than in England.'

'Neither the civil nor the military authorities realised till too late the depths to which the rot of indiscipline had penetrated,' he added. 'That rot was inevitable from the moment when the government determined upon the reconquest of Ireland by force.

It will be impossible to eradicate it until this government, or some other, drops the policy of reconquest and adopts the policy of negotiation.'

'I do not blame the police or soldiers for the impasse,' Martin concluded. 'I have seen and heard far too much of the dreadful conditions of boycott and slaughter under which they have to try to "carry on". But no honest man who has seen with his own eyes and heard with his own ears the fearful plight to which unhappy Ireland has been brought could fail to curse in his heart the political gamble that bred it or cease to use all the power of his pen to end it.'

14

'HE DROVE THE PEOPLE CRAZY'

Kerry No. 1 Brigade headquarters was to issue orders to all members of the IRA to dump their arms and to carry out no additional operations until they received further notice. There was considerable uneasiness in Ballylongford's Republicans circles on 23 November 1920 when Eddie Carmody, in whose house the kidnapped Constable Coughlan had initially been held, was shot dead in Ballylongford by some of the four lorryloads of Black and Tans who had descended on the village under the command of District Inspect Tobias O'Sullivan, who became a marked man himself.

Some of the local IRA members blamed brigade headquarters for the incident. This was to contribute to the growing disquiet with the leadership of Paddy Cahill, especially in comparison with the more aggressive attitude of Kerry No. 2 Brigade. At the height of the trouble in Tralee, Tom McEllistrim and his colleagues sought both to relieve the pressure and to solve a problem of their own by shooting two of the Black and Tans who had been 'giving considerable trouble and terrorising the natives' in the Farranfore area. After waiting to ambush them all day on 9 November in Ulick O'Sullivan's pub, they learned that the two men had gone to Killarney for the day and would probably be returning on the evening train.

McEllistrim and his colleagues jumped a goods train to Ballybrack, a small station between Farranfore and Killarney. O'Sullivan travelled with them to identify the two Englishmen

– Constables Archibald Turner and James Thomas Woods, who were travelling in civilian clothes.

'We got off the train at Ballybrack and waited there for the passenger train,' McEllistrim recalled. 'I instructed O'Sullivan to walk along the platform in front of us when the train arrived and to touch with his hand the door of the carriage in which the Tans were travelling.'

While O'Sullivan looked into the various carriages, he was followed by Bill Diggins and McEllistrim, with John Cronin and Moss Carmody walking behind them. Jim Reidy boarded the engine to hold the train until the job was done. O'Sullivan duly touched the door of one of the carriages.

'When we reached this carriage door, I pulled the door open and Diggins and I shot the two Tans as they attempted to draw their guns. They were alone in the carriage. We pulled them on to the platform and took their arms.' The two men, who were shot several times, were left to die on the platform as their assailants boarded the train.

Reidy then ordered the driver to leave and had him halt when the train was midway between Ballybrack and Farranfore. From there, they made good their escape.

'Following the shooting,' the *Irish Times* reported, 'several farmhouses and ricks of hay and straw were burning along the countryside from Ballybrack to Farranfore.' Readers did not have to be told that the fires were set in reprisal by the Crown forces.

'At Ballymacelligott that night, we decided to continue our pursuit of Tans,' McEllistrim wrote. 'Cronin and Moss Carmody decided to go to Castleisland the following day to shoot the Tans there.' They were joined in Castleisland by Din Prendeville and Michael O'Leary of Cordal, and the four of them shot Constable Griffin on Main Street in broad daylight. That night the Tans retaliated by burning the home of Cornelius Browne.

Twelve lorries of Black and Tans had left Tralee on 10 November to terrorise the area from Farranfore to Ballybrack. They took a number of prisoners and burned several houses, including Ulick O'Sullivan's pub. They had learned that he was involved in the Ballybrack operation and he had to go on the run.

McEllistrim and ten colleagues waited at Ballyseedy to ambush the lorries on their return to Tralee, but the Tans returned instead by Farmer's Bridge, where they stopped Frank Hoffman, an active member of the IRA, near his home.

'You are the man we want,' they told him.

'They placed him against a fence and bayoneted him and shot him dead,' the *Montreal Gazette* noted in a front-page report. There was not even the pretence of a kangaroo court: the Black and Tans were acting as judge, jury and executioners in the glare of the international press, and on the day that newspapers around the world were quoting Lloyd George as bragging that he had 'murder by the throat'. Of course, the IRA was carrying out similar attacks, but the Black and Tans, while supposedly representing the forces of law and order, were terrorising innocent people, whereas the IRA was primarily terrorising Crown forces and agents of the Crown. In the circumstances, the people were driven into the arms of the IRA – which was essentially what Michael Collins had envisaged when he set out to provoke the confrontation.

The killing of Hoffman prompted a great deal of international publicity, and Constable Edward Johnston was subsequently charged, before a military court, with the manslaughter of Frank Hoffman. Johnston contended that he had been sitting on the lorry, holding his gun a bit too tightly, because they were expecting an ambush. The truck hit a bump and the shot went off. He said he did not know whether the shot had actually hit Hoffman, but if it had, this was purely accidental. The military court accepted his explanation and found him not guilty.

Another event that received international press attention was

Jimmy Barry

Tralee IRA officers.

Back row, from left: Dan Barry, T. Lynch, T. Foley, Mick Fleming, J. Horan, Jack McGaley, E. Hogan, C. Counihan and Dan Jeffers. Seated: Nicholas Stack, Eddie Barry, Paddy J. Cahill, Mick Doyle, Willie Farmer and Paddy Barry. Front: M. Switzer and J. Fleming.

Maurice Neligan

David Neligan

Donal O'Sullivan

Thomas O'Rourke

Kathleen Fitzgerald

Johnny O'Connor

Tadgh O'Kennedy

Tim Kennedy

Kerryman

Willie McCarthy

Brian Sheehy

John Joe Sheehy

Brian Sheehy

John Joe Rice

Brian Sheehy

Constable Patrick Waters of the RIC,
who was killed on 31 October 1920

Brian Sheehy

Con Casey

Brian Sheehy

'Big Paddy' Culleton from Navan and
'the Jewman' de la Roi, a French Canadian

Auxiliaries arriving at barracks in Tralee with prisoners

Major Mackinnon's funeral leaving St John's Church of Ireland, Ashe Street, Tralee

Irish Examiner

Brian Sheehy

Éamon de Valera discussing the Sinn Féin split with, from left, John Joe Sheehy, Frank Aiken, John Joe Rice and Austin Stack

Tom McEllistrim Jr, Jack Lynch, Tom McEllistrim Sr and Tom McEllistrim III. In 1966, Tom McEllistrim Sr formally proposed Jack Lynch for the leadership of Fianna Fáil. Tom McEllistrim Jr was one of the 'Gang of Five' who led the heave against Lynch in favour of Charles Haughey in 1979.

known locally as the Battle of Ballymacelligott; abroad, it was referred to as the Battle of Tralee. This difference in names possibly helps to explain why the events in Tralee were subsequently overlooked by historians like Dorothy Macardle.

A press release from Dublin Castle stated that 'the engagement was the fiercest and probably the largest-scale of any fight between Crown forces and the Volunteers.' What was particularly sensational about the battle at the time was that it was witnessed by some journalists and recorded with a movie camera.

The whole thing began on the morning of 12 November 1920, when several lorries of Tans and RIC officers arrived at Ballydwyer Creamery, almost midway between Tralee and Castleisland. They stopped their lorries on both sides of the creamery. Some members of the Ballymacelligott active-service unit were at the creamery at the time and they made a dash to escape. The Tans immediately opened fire and four men were shot, two fatally. The two men killed were John McMahon and Paddy Herlihy, while Jack McEllistrim and Tim Walsh were wounded. The Tans set fire to the creamery and some nearby homes.

Tom McEllistrim and twelve of his men were about a mile away at the time. 'We heard the shooting and saw the lorries depart,' he explained. 'We immediately got the creamery to assist the wounded, placing a guard at the Tralee side of the creamery.'

The Volunteers summoned Dr Michael Shanahan from Tralee to attend the wounded and he came out in a car with a helper. As the wounded were being treated, a group of men assigned to keep a watch on the road were looking out for the Black and Tans from the direction of Tralee.

'We were surprised by three lorries of Auxiliaries which sailed in on us from Castleisland direction,' Tom McEllistrim explained. 'This section was not a raiding party but was, I believe, making a tour of the country. When they saw our men take cover, the lorries stopped immediately and shooting started. We had only six rifles in action but two of our party, armed with rifles, who had left the creamery yard five minutes earlier, came to our aid and opened fire from a little hill on the Auxiliaries at 300 yards' range.

'At the time, a lorry coming from the Tralee direction, seeing the ambush, pulled up immediately about 300 yards from the lorries which had been occupied by the Auxiliaries. The officer in charge of the British forces, believing that they had been surrounded, rushed to his car and ordered his men to turn their lorries, and they drove back into Castleisland. Our riflemen kept on firing at them as they retreated.'

The Auxiliaries had been escorting some press people on a tour of the country. They had been in Dungarvan, where an Armistice Day parade was staged for a cine camera, and they were moving on to Tralee, probably to show that life was normal in the aftermath of the siege of the town, which had received international publicity between 31 October and 9 November.

'Our party was contained in four cars, the first and last by tenders manned by RIC cadets, all ex-officers,' according to Clifford Hutchingson of the *Yorkshire Post*. 'Knowing of the existence of a band of between 200 and 300 members of the Republican army in this vicinity, we kept a keen lookout as we travelled over a road, not of the best.'

On seeing men rushing for the shelter of ditches as the cars approached, they stopped and the Auxiliaries opened fire and began following the men. 'Only one sentry, myself and two cinema operators remained on the roadside,' Hutchingson explained. 'The latter quickly rigged up their apparatus and coolly began taking pictures, at no small danger. The bullets were whizzing around. Three bullets ripped past me as I was getting out of the car, and two more before I had got to the side of the road.

'At the creamery a motor car stood, and a man stood near

it, who subsequently proved to be a Tralee doctor, ran forward with his hands up. Dr Shanahan, his helper and five others – J. Carmody, T. Connor, Wm Dowling, Wm Herlihy and R. McAlister – were arrested at the scene. On seeing some men alight from a vehicle coming from the Tralee direction, the Auxiliaries packed up and left hurriedly.

'The cars were turned and seven prisoners were hurled in and we left for Castleisland still under fire,' Hutchingson continued. Instead of the dozen or so men who were actually there, he estimated that the attacking party had been seventy-strong. He was, of course, mistakenly including the Tans who stopped down the road, but even then his figure was grossly exaggerated.

Questions were asked in the House of Commons the following week. Hamar Greenwood, the Chief Secretary for Ireland, told Parliament that there had been three separate ambushes at Ballymacelligott that day. A member of his own staff, G. Jones, had been traveling with the journalists. 'He was able to give me an exact description of one of these ambushes and an exact account of how one creamery was destroyed,' Greenwood told Parliament.

The confrontation was later described by the British as the Battle of Tralee. *Pathé Gazette* showed a film of the engagement, but it was doctored, with faked scenes staged elsewhere. The *Irish Independent* demonstrated from one still photograph that a segment of the film had actually been shot in Dalkey, County Dublin, as there was a distinctive lamp-post in the background. Even though there had been some skirmishes in the vicinity of Ballymacelligott that day, this incident does not merit being called a battle.

In the following days, a force of Auxiliaries were stationed at the technical school in Moyderwell in Tralee – a building the Black and Tans had tried to burn down earlier in the month. The dreaded Auxiliaries were supposed to be an elite corps of former army officers – on the lines of the later Special Air Service or the American Green Berets. The Auxiliaries were recruited, at the instigation of Winston Churchill, to bolster the Black and Tans, who were themselves recruited to reinforce the RIC.

On the whole, the Auxiliaries were much better educated and better paid than the Black and Tans. The Auxiliaries were paid £1 a day, all found, which was twice the pay of the Black and Tans. The Auxiliaries had distinctive headgear – a tam-o'-shanter, or a Scottish version of a French beret with a pompon on top. They were frequently called Black and Tans, or Auxies. Some of the Auxiliaries joined for excitement, others for the money, as jobs were very scarce in Britain at the time. Officially they were supposed to be policemen, but they acted more like soldiers out of control and bent on vengeance.

There were essentially four distinctive elements to the Crown forces in Tralee. Three of those were nominally police – the RIC and some Black and Tans were stationed together at the police barracks on High Street, and other Black and Tans were stationed at the jail in Ballymullen, while the Auxiliaries were stationed at the technical school in Moyderwell and some were also stationed in what became the County Club in Denny Street, Tralee. British soldiers from the East Lancashire Regiment were based in Ballymullen Barracks, along with some Munster Fusiliers. They 'were a different breed altogether,' according to Pat 'Belty' Williams. 'We usually had little problems with them, as they tended to mind their own business. It was the Tans and the Auxiliaries with whom we were most involved.'

Although the Auxiliaries were a completely new force, who were mainly British, they were still dependent on the RIC for their local intelligence and for people to act as guides. As the conflict got dirtier, the RIC found themselves confronted with the stark choice of supporting either the Auxiliaries and the Black and Tans or their fellow countrymen. Many preferred to supply information to the

IRA. This probably explains why comparatively few RIC men were killed in Kerry. The Listowel mutiny was symptomatic of what was happening within the RIC.

Tim Kennedy found little difficulty in securing information from the local RIC men. 'Practically all the RIC, with few exceptions, were on our side,' Kennedy told Ernie O'Malley. 'They were all contacted.'

Sergeant Thomas O'Rourke retired from the RIC in late 1920 and Kennedy was able to show the force's appreciation for his work by getting a house for him and his family in the county jail. O'Rourke's son, Micheál, later became president of the county board of the GAA and was famous among generations of schoolchildren under his nickname 'Sambo'.

Thomas O'Rourke was replaced as special crimes sergeant by Michael Costello, a native of Glin, County Limerick. Costello was moved from Cork, where he had already been furnishing information to the IRA. Florence O'Donoghue, the Kerryman who was intelligence officer of Cork No. 1 Brigade, gave Costello instructions to contact Kennedy. Costello continued to furnish the key to the codes, and he provided an invaluable service to Kennedy. At one point he warned Kennedy that the head constable, Sergeant Clarke, and a Black and Tan named Heapy from Sligo were planning to kill him at his digs on a certain night. Richard Hudson, a former schoolmate of Kennedy's who was secretary of the Freemason Lodge in Tralee, passed on a similar warning to Kennedy and told him to stay at Hudson's mother's house, which later became the Bon Secours Home in Strand Street.

Several people supposedly serving the Crown were valuable informers for the IRA. They included the county inspector of the RIC, Jimmy Duffy, who was born in Tralee, where his father had been an RIC sergeant. He had been a schoolmate of Paddy Cahill at Blackrock College and of Paddy Kennedy at Skerries

College. When he came to Tralee in the last week of October 1920, he met Kennedy in the Grand Hotel and indicated that he was anxious to meet Cahill.

The meeting took place at the Ballyard home of the mother of David Moriarty, a court clerk in Tralee. Tim Kennedy later wrote:

> Duffy and I left the town and walked to Ballyard House together and were ushered into the dining room by the housekeeper. In a short time, Paddy Cahill came in and joined us. The table was laid for tea or supper and there were some bottles of whiskey and sandwiches on the table. It was a happy reunion in turbulent times and Jim Duffy and myself enjoyed it. Paddy Cahill was an intolerant teetotaler during his life and had no drink. We discussed the pros and cons of the struggle and Jim Duffy volunteered to Paddy to go out with him and serve in any capacity they wanted him. He said he was unmarried, had nobody depending on him and that he was suffering from some form of TB as a result of gas attacks in the war. He said he saw no reason why he wouldn't fight for the freedom of his own country after going through 'hell' for the freedom of other nations, small and big. We came to the conclusion that his services would be more valuable to the IRA if he remained on in his position at the barracks, and I explained to him how important he could be to our intelligence.

Of course, there were the exceptions: people such as Sergeant Clarke, the district inspector's clerk, who were more than willing to provide information to the Black and Tans. Kennedy had good reason to want Clarke out of the way, because he was the one who had fingered his brother, Paddy, for the killing of the British soldier in Anascaul back in August.

Clarke 'went off his head when he found that we were after him,' according to Kennedy. But what Clarke did not know was that his wife was so worried about him that she was providing Kennedy with information to protect her husband for the sake of their children.

Kennedy used the same technique as Michael Collins for ingratiating himself with the enemy. He went out of his way to be friendly with the Auxiliaries and the Black and Tans. Captain Tyrell O'Malley of the Munster Fusiliers was providing information about the Tans, their threats and their plans to shoot up places. He also filed complaints about their illegal activities.

Captain O'Malley was very friendly with Colonel Berkely, who despised the Auxiliaries and the Black and Tans. Kennedy used to meet Berkely in the Grand Hotel. Although the colonel was not deliberately providing any information, it suited Kennedy's purposes to be seen as a friend of his.

Jim Duffy was terminally ill and died before the truce. While he was sick, he was replaced by County Inspector William Beanney, who was also an Irish Catholic. Duffy, who was single, stayed in the Grand Hotel under the care of the Bon Secours nuns. Kennedy visited him daily, and during one visit he met the new county inspector. 'I have reminded him,' said Duffy, 'that he is an Irishman.'

Beanney agreed to provide Kennedy with information, but he made a great blunder when Paddy Cahill came into Tralee to visit his sick father. The RIC learned that Cahill was home. Beanney was unable to contact Kennedy, so he sent Sergeant Clarke to warn Kennedy that there was going to be a raid for Cahill that evening.

Clarke told his wife that Beanney was 'a bastard' because of what he was trying to do. 'His wife had only just time to make a beeline for me,' Kennedy noted. Cahill was spirited into Bon Secours Convent on Strand Road.

Paddy Shanahan was an ex-British soldier living in the street. He had an oil painting of Lord Kitchener in his home, which afforded him a certain amount of credibility among Crown forces, but his sympathies were with Sinn Féin. His next-door neighbour, however, was a loyalist, so Paddy decided to have some fun when the Tans were unable to find Cahill.

'That fellow next door to me,' Shanahan told one of the raiding party, 'he's a Shinner.' He added that maybe the man they were looking for was hiding there.

Major John A. Mackinnon, the commander of the Auxiliaries, soon provoked the undying hostility of the IRA in Kerry. On Christmas night 1920 he raided the Ballydwyer home of the creamery manager John Byrne, who had been on the run since the so-called Battle of Ballymacelligott. Byrne was not at home when Mackinnon and three other Auxiliaries burst into the house without warning.

There were two separate versions of what happened next. The official police version was that John Leen, 24, drew his revolver and tried to fire but the gun misfired. Leen and Maurice Reidy, 25, were told to put their hands up, according to Mackinnon, but Leen cocked the gun to fire again. At that point the two of them were killed and the dying Leen fired a shot into the ceiling as he went down.

The version told by those in the house was that the two men were surprised and had no time to go for a gun. Both men had been very active in the IRA and Mackinnon shot them dead in cold blood. Had they had the opportunity, there was little doubt that they would have done the same to him. The supposed bullet hole in the ceiling might have confirmed Mackinnon's version, but he was not bothered about such niceties.

There was no dispute about what happened next. Everyone was ordered out of the house, and Mackinnon told his men to set fire to the building. He announced publicly afterwards that the same procedure would be followed in every instance in which armed men were found in a house. No matter what the provocation, Major Mackinnon had defiled Christmas in the minds of local people. Thereafter he was a marked man. 'A tall, broad-shouldered Scot, he walked with a confident swagger,' Pat Williams recalled. 'Mackinnon always carried a pistol at the ready in a holster strapped loosely to his thigh. This, together with the huge bearskin gloves that he wore, gave him an air of ruthless military efficiency. Yet he was quite suave and could be very personable when he wished.'

'Even those who despised him credited him with being incredibly brave,' Williams added. 'He was never afraid to travel alone, day or night. He would drive about in an open car, virtually daring the IRA to attack him. I often saw him walking down through the town by himself.'

'He certainly had this side of the country terrorised,' Johnny O'Connor explained. 'Mackinnon liked the bogeyman idea.' He wanted people to fear him, and he made a habit of turning up where he was least expected and of being always to the fore if there was any dirty work to be done. 'Often he came out with two men on foot, one of whom had a Lewis gun,' O'Connor said. 'He drove the people crazy.'

15

'BEST PLACE TO SHOOT O'SULLIVAN'

On New Year's Day the Black and Tans raided the Bedford area near Listowel and surprised Volunteers who had gathered together. They ran off in various directions but two of them – Patrick White and Edward Barrett – were shot and wounded trying to escape. The two young men said that they were playing cards at the time. They were luckier than Cornelius Murphy from Balydaly, near Rathmore.

Murphy had joined a flying squad formed by the nearby Millstreet Battalion towards the end of 1920. On 2 January 1921 nine members of the squad arrived in Rathmore. They were billeted near Con Murphy's home, so Con went to his own home that night. At about nine o'clock next morning, the scouts protecting the squad reported the presence of a considerable force of soldiers – and RIC raiding – in Balydaly. The little squad immediately got into a defensive position in the old rath, but word eventually came that the raiders had departed in the direction of Millstreet. When they called at the Murphy home, Con and his brother Denis had tried to flee, but they were caught and the police found a revolver and seven rounds of ammunition in a coat that Con had tried to discard. They were arrested, along with the father, Denis Murphy senior.

Con Murphy was brought before a court martial at Victoria Barracks, Cork, on 17 January and was sentenced to death for possession of a revolver. He was shot by firing squad on 1 February 1921. He became the first Volunteer to be executed in this manner since the death by firing squad at Kilmainham Jail of the leaders of the 1916 Rising.

The year 1921 would be a turning point in Irish history. Young Christy O'Grady kept a diary in which he wrote an entry for every day of the year. This provides some invaluable insights into the events of the time. Although only sixteen years old at the start of the year, he was already working for IRA intelligence. As a fully grown adult, he was only five foot five tall: the frail, bespectacled teenage photographer was unlikely to arouse the same suspicions taking pictures of the security forces as a bigger man would have done. In his diary he wrote about going for walks, which were frequently a cover for either delivering messages or scouting for the IRA. He also took photographs of local events, some of which were published in both the *Irish Independent* and the *Cork Examiner* at the time.

The O'Gradys owned the Ashbourne Hotel, which was two doors up from the courthouse in Nelson Street, Tralee. The Sinn Féin-controlled Tralee Urban District Council had renamed Nelson Street Ashe Street, though the Crown authorities refused to recognise the new name. Christy actually joined the IRA in December 1919 and was a member of C Company of the Third Battalion of Kerry No. 1 Brigade. As a result of where he lived, he was involved mainly in scouting duty, carrying dispatches and special intelligence work. On occasions, he reported directly to Michael O'Leary and John Joe Sheehy, who stayed in the hotel while he was on the run.

As the hotel was frequented by soldiers and Black and Tans, Christy got to know some of them; he helped to recruit at least four of them to work for the IRA. Sergeant Phil Roche, who was working in the wireless station at Ballymullen Barracks, Tralee, later recalled that he was approached by Christy, whose father he had known while growing up in Kerry. Roche was asked, as an Irishman and a Kerryman, to assist the local IRA.

'I stated then that I was going to desert, as I had been refused an application to be transferred out of Ireland,' Roche later recalled. 'It was pointed out to me that I could be of more assistance where I was.'

Roche therefore considered himself a member of the IRA working under cover. He supplied ammunition and grenades to O'Grady, and also 'copies of every telegraphic message that was received in the barracks affecting the IRA and the future movements of British forces. An Irish corporal under me, Corporal Perry, also gave the same assistance.'

Corporal Perry even invited O'Grady to the barracks to scout around. Christy used to carry messages from Roche and Perry to IRA intelligence. He also became friendly with a couple of Auxiliaries – a cadet named Hatfield and a driver named Porter were useful to him. For obvious reasons, O'Grady never mentioned in the diary his Republican activities prior to the truce, but afterwards he did annotate his entries with explanations.

Like every other family, the O'Gradys had their names posted inside the door of the hotel in case the Crown forces raided the establishment. Christy had finished school at Mungret College and acted as a full-time scout for the IRA, posing as a rather pampered youth. His observations on the security scene provide an insight into the reign of terror of the Black and Tans and the Auxiliaries. As a scout, he paid particular attention to the actions of the Crown forces. He noted that new Black and Tans arrived in Tralee in early January and there was 'great tramping and activity on the streets during the night'. On their first Friday night, nearly all of these Tans were drunk by the evening. 'Four of them were talking by our door when one placed his rifle on a countryman's shoulder and fired into the air,' O'Grady noted in his diary. 'The poor chap near died of fright. Mother got a shock too.'

Throughout the remainder of January, the Black and Tans

and the Auxiliaries terrorised the town. 'Got a bad fright today from a drunken Tan,' Christy noted. He was looking out of the hotel and just smiled at the Tan, who came in the hotel, waved his revolver 'and kicked up a row'. 'You might not smile at that,' the Tan remarked.

That night the Auxiliaries 'paraded streets headed by a red flag and played weird music on all kinds of instruments.' At night, they frequently did a lot of 'shouting, singing and playing drums, etc' on the streets of the town. As a result, townspeople often did not get much sleep. Any unfortunate individual the Auxiliaries or Tans happened to meet at night could be beaten up by these supposed policemen, if only for entertainment. They would also knock up a public house during the night just looking for drink, and some of them inevitably made spectacles of themselves.

On Tuesday 11 January 1921, the Auxiliaries rounded up most of the men in Tralee and compelled them to go to the Sports Field (now the Austin Stack Park), where they were all searched. The bulk of them were then let go, though a couple of lorryloads were taken to the barracks for further questioning.

Around midnight on Thursday of the following week, the Auxiliaries and Black and Tans searched all the houses in Edward Street, Tralee. The occupants were ordered out of their houses while the search was being conducted. They were taken to Denny Street, where they were personally searched outside the Grand Hotel. After about an hour, they were allowed to return to their homes. There were similar night searches in Ashe Street and McCowen's Lane in Tralee on other nights.

The following morning, around 10 am, the Auxiliaries conducted a similar search in Blennerville and later that day in Castlegregory, where the brother of Tadhg Brosnan, the local IRA leader, was arrested. This was a portent of much greater Crown activities throughout the Dingle peninsula in the following weeks.

People were not only compelled to leave their homes in the middle of the night. J. Mulvihill, a hairdresser, was compelled to move from his house, as it had been commandeered for an Auxiliary and his wife, and the Leen family had to move from Ballyheigue Castle, as it had also been commandeered.

Early in the morning, the Auxiliaries would pull up at the homes of suspected Sinn Féin supporters and seize the men as hostages. They were then compelled to accompany the Auxiliaries throughout the day as they drove through the countryside on their raiding and searching operations. The hostages would be let go in the evening.

There was some confusion as to exactly why District Inspector Tobias O'Sullivan was targeted by the IRA in Listowel on 20 January 1921. It was believed that the order originated with Michael Collins in Dublin. John Malone (alias Seán Forde), one of the more active Republicans from the Limerick area, had been arrested and was being held on Spike Island, but the authorities had not learned his true identity. They were informed, however, that they had him in custody, and it was decided that O'Sullivan should be asked to visit the prison to identify him.

O'Sullivan had already distinguished himself in County Limerick in leading the successful defence of Kilmallock RIC Station when it was attack on 29 May 1920. He was promoted to district inspector as a result, and was stationed in Listowel in the late autumn of 1920.

The immediate order to kill O'Sullivan had come from Brigade Commandant Paddy Cahill. Four men volunteered for the job – Jack Ahern (the father of Father Pat Ahern, the founder of Siamsa Tíre), Con Brosnan, Daniel O'Grady and Jack Sheehan. They thought that this was in retaliation for his role in the Kilmallock attack, in which one Kerry Volunteer, the teacher Liam Scully of Glencar, was killed. Scully had earlier been active as a Volunteer in Ballylongford.

'We discussed the details and the best time and place to carry it out with William O'Sullivan, our company captain, and member of the battalion staff,' Con Brosnan later recalled. 'It was agreed between us that the best place to shoot O'Sullivan was in the town of Listowel. We had been informed of his regular movements by a number of scouts in Listowel who had been put on his trail as soon as the order was received.'

Ahern, Brosnan and O'Grady were issued with a revolver each on the night on 18 January 1921. Sheehan did not get one, as he was to act as the scout for the other three. He was to be outside the RIC barracks. O'Sullivan usually left the barracks between 12.30 and 1 o'clock in the afternoon and he would cross the street. Sheehan's instructions were to walk parallel with him. The others were to be waiting in Stack's public house, which was next door to Sheehan's home about a hundred yards from the barracks on the opposite side of the road. Sheehan would be acting as if he was going home for his dinner.

Ahern had stayed with Brosnan in the latter's home in Newtownsands on the eve of the operation and they cycled into Listowel separately the following morning. It was early afternoon when Brosnan got to Stack's, the first to arrive, and he was soon joined by Ahern and O'Grady. They had a few drinks as they waited.

'We were behind the front window of the pub and kept a lookout for Sheehan to come to the point opposite the window,' Brosnan noted. 'This was the signal we were waiting for. As soon as Sheehan appeared at this point, we knew that O'Sullivan would be outside the window on our side.'

But when Sheehan arrived at the point opposite the window, he suddenly turned back, because in pacing himself with the district inspector, he had not noticed that O'Sullivan, who had his five-year-old son, John, by the hand, had stopped to chat with Dan Farrell, a retired RIC man. Sheehan went back, and when he came forward again O'Sullivan was outside the window in line with Sheehan.

The three inside the window immediately stood up and went into the street. 'O'Grady and I opened fire together and fired about four shots each, while Ahern fired about six,' Brosnan recalled. He did not mention that O'Sullivan, who died on the spot, was still holding young John by the hand at the time.

'Having carried out our job, we escaped through the Sports Field,' Brosnan continued. As they were crossing the Sports Field, a local loyalist, Paul Sweetman – one of Lord Listowel's stewards – called on them to halt.

'Stand your ground and take your punishment,' Sweetman shouted.

'You should get the same as O'Sullivan,' one of them replied.

'We would have shot him on the spot, only for the fact that our ammunition was very low,' Brosnan noted. The officers of the RIC and the Black and Tans were often entertained by Sweetman and his family around this period. The four men made it to Newtownsands without any further trouble.

Captain Watson, the commanding officer of the eighty British soldiers stationed in Listowel, had a meeting of prominent citizens convened at the Carnegie Hall on Sunday afternoon, 23 January. He was introduced by the parish priest, Canon O'Connor, who presided. Watson denounced the killing of District Inspector O'Sullivan, especially the circumstances in which he had his five-year-old son by the hand. Up to then, he said, his soldiers had accorded the people all the protection that he could afford them, and this would continue for the next three days, during which the shops would be allowed to open only between 10 am and noon. At the end of the three days, he could not say what would happen but, of course, he indicated that there would be official reprisals.

That evening, however, an attempt was made to burn down

the drapery premises of T. J. Walsh at the corner of Market Street and William Street. The fire was put out by the prompt action of the military, but instead of arresting the police, the military arrested Walsh, a former chairman of Listowel Urban District Council, supposedly on suspicion of trying to burn down his own place. He was lucky. He was brought to Tralee and held for three days, during which time the military protected his shop. Having accused Walsh of trying to torch it himself, they could hardly burn it down as a reprisal.

But people waited in trepidation. Many moved from Listowel to shelter with relatives living in the country. There was hectic police activity on the streets of Tralee on the night of the shooting of District Inspector O'Sullivan in Listowel.

That weekend, a new batch of Auxiliaries arrived in Tralee, along with other back-up troops. They were put up in local hotels on Saturday night, and then the next morning they began commandeering any car they could find. About 1,000 police and troops surrounded Ballymacelligott parish next morning. They rounded up all the people they could find after Mass and marched them to a field near Ballydwyer Creamery, where they were photographed and searched. Women searchers had been brought along for the occasion. The men were segregated and marched, four abreast, the five miles to the jail in Tralee, where they were further questioned. One press report put the number of men at 160, while another stated that there were 240. Afterwards, they had to make their own way home on foot.

The Ballymacelligott Company of the IRA had probably been the most active in the whole county, and the active-service unit was essentially trapped within the cordon. 'We were sleeping in a dugout right in the centre of the round-up,' Tom McEllistrim recalled. 'We heard of the activity in the morning and prepared ourselves. We were fully armed with rifles and for that day we took up positions in our dugout, which was well concealed with brushwood. British military passed close to us on either side carrying out their round-up under Major Mackinnon, bringing with them all the young men of the parish to the round-up centre.

'By a stroke of luck, they never found our dugout and we had not to fire a shot. That night we decided our active-service unit should change its position and we travelled to Ballyfinnane, a distance of ten miles, where we billeted in the early hours of the following morning, some of us in a dugout near Knockane. Four of us slept the night in the house of Cornelius W. Daly of Knockane.

Next morning they were roused by the Daly family warning that soldiers were approaching the house. 'We had not time to dress,' McEllistrim said. 'We rushed out with our clothes in a bundle in our hands. We could see the British Tommies within thirty yards of us and we rushed through the door. We were called to halt but we kept going. They could easily have shot us and we were lucky it was not Tans or Auxies entering that section.

'We joined our other comrades who had previously been with us and had slept in the dugout, moved towards a hillside and found ourselves again that day in the centre of another big round-up which was planned again by Major Mackinnon. About 800 troops were engaged in this round-up. We took up position in an old bog with British forces all around us. They passed on either side and we were left unmolested.'

A new flying column, comprising of twenty-nine men, was established in north Kerry. They assembled at Derk, near Duagh, on 30 January. Tom Kennelly, a war veteran from the British army, was elected leader, but the column was poorly armed. They had only seven rifles, four revolvers and eight shotguns, with an average of ten rounds of ammunition per man. Hence they were no match for a company of Auxiliaries, much less the kind of force that the Crown authorities had put together to search Ballymacelligott. The new column learned, however, that a force of Auxiliaries with armoured cars was heading for Derk, so the column fled into the Stack Mountains and it was essentially chased across north Kerry. In its early days, the flying column should more aptly have been called a 'fleeing column'.

There were reports of extensive searches from elsewhere in the county. 'The military made very thorough searches here during the week,' the Kenmare correspondent of the *Liberator* reported on 27 January. It was the same story around the county. 'There was considerable police activity in Cahirciveen on the twenty-fifth,' the local correspondent noted. The police commandeered the cars of W. J. Leslie of the Railway Hotel and James O'Connor of Main Street to raid houses in the countryside. The Dingle correspondent also noted 'increased activity on the part of the Crown forces. Many standing on street corners are being dispersed, and the rule against groups is being enforced. Two young men were taken during the week as hostages and compelled to accompany the RIC on the motor lorry.'

Divisional Commissioner Philip A. Holmes, who replaced Colonel Smyth of Listowel-mutiny infamy following the latter's assassination in Cork in July 1920, was shot and mortally wounded at Toureengarriv, near Castleisland, on 28 January 1921 while on his way from Tralee to Cork in a three-car convoy. A native of Cork city, Holmes had joined the RIC in 1898 and transferred to the Royal Irish Regiment during the First World War, in which he distinguished himself by attaining the military rank of brigadier general.

Toureengarriv is a wild, rocky district midway between Scartaglin and Kingwilliamstown (now Ballydesmond). It was known that officers of the British army had gone west, and the IRA waited at this place for two days to intercept them on their return. A trench had been cut across the road and the driver of the first car seemed to sense trouble ahead and tried to jump his powerful car over it, but failed.

The army officers put up a desperate resistance, but they surrendered after Constables Thomas Moyles and James Hoare were shot dead and Holmes was fatally wounded. Three others were also wounded: Sergeant Arthur E. Charman and Constable Francis D. Calder were each wounded in the arm, while Constable John H. Andrews was hit in the face, the right arm and the right leg.

Seán Moylan, who was in charge of the combined ambushing party of men from north Cork and east Kerry, ordered some of his men to search the prisoners and tend to the wounded.

'Leave me alone,' Holmes said. 'I'm finished.' But then he asked for a cigarette and thanked one of the Corkmen, Seán Kennedy, when he gave him one. Afterwards Sergeant Charman praised the IRA for the chivalrous way in which he and his men had been treated.

One of the RIC men was terrified and made rather a spectacle of himself. With a rosary beads in hand, he pleaded with Moylan. 'I'm a Catholic like yourself,' he cried. 'Don't shoot me.'

'What are you?' Moylan asked one of the man's colleagues.

'I'm a bloody Black and Tan, and you can shoot me if you want to,' the man replied defiantly.

'Shake,' Moylan said, extending his hand, 'you're a man anyway.' The Black and Tan duly shook hands with him.

A school inspector came along in his car from the direction of Cork and Moylan had him convey Holmes to the county infirmary in Tralee, where he died the following day. Meanwhile, one of the cars was so badly damaged that it could not be used; the other was driven off by the IRA in the direction of Kingwilliamstown.

Over the next few days, enraged parties of Black and Tans swept into the village, but the inhabitants had wisely fled into the hills. Three houses were bombed and burned. They included the homes of Willie McAuliffe and Timothy Vaughan – whose son, Dan, later became a member of the Dáil for Cork North.

On the following Sunday, there was a further reprisal at Knocknagree. 'A military patrol saw a body of armed civilians in a field near Knocknagree,' according to the official report. 'Fire was opened and replied to, resulting in the death of one youth and the wounding of two others.' In fact, the youths were engaged in a game of hurling. Seventeen-year-old Michael J. Kelliher was killed and the brothers Donal and Michael Herlihy were wounded. They both recovered, and later became priests. Donal ended up as the Bishop of Ferns after many years at the Vatican, while Michael became a canon and the parish priest of Castleisland.

People were not only subject to reprisals but were liable to be seized on the street and press-ganged into working for the police, clearing roads or filling trenches. On 4 February, Jeremiah Galvin, the owner of the Central Hotel, Listowel, was grabbed and compelled to march out the Tarbert road to fill trenches on a cold, wet day. He was not accustomed to such manual labour and suffered a heart attack and died on the spot.

On 9 February the Crown forces concentrated on the Dingle peninsula. They commandeered horses in Tralee and set off to scour Slieve Mish, where Kerry No. 1 Brigade had its head-quarters. The hut was on the south side of the mountain. One way to get to it was by taking the so-called 'short mountain road' towards Castlemaine and then going several miles across the top of the mountain. Afterwards they would go by Bóthar na gCloch down into Camp.

Unable to find the mountain hideout, the Crown forces cut off the Dingle peninsula by suspending all train travel and blockading the main road to the peninsula on both sides of the mountain. Sinn Féin managed to make propaganda capital out of the blockade after a stationmaster on the line telegraphed J. T. O'Farrell, the Irish secretary of the railway clerks association, on 14 February. 'District blockaded for past week,' he noted. 'Supplies exhausted. Women and children on verge of starvation.'

O'Farrell duly circulated his telegraph to the media and it was carried not only in the local and national newspapers in Ireland but in the *New York Times*. The military immediately refuted the report with a statement of their own. 'There is no truth to the statement that the inhabitants of some parts of Kerry are on the verge of starvation,' the military statement began. 'The Crown forces are not interfering with law-abiding inhabitants, and there is no embargo on the import or purchase of foodstuffs, which are plentiful in the area.'

Three-quarters of a century after the Great Famine, the charge that the Crown forces were creating starvation was likely to have a great impact in the United States, because the Dingle peninsula was one of the areas hardest hit by the famine. Nonetheless, there was no real parallel to the famine in 1921 – though the reference to law-abiding inhabitants did seem rather incongruous when the so-called Crown police were acting flagrantly outside the law. At the fair in Dingle on 21 February, for instance, they rounded up about a hundred men and marched them to the barracks. All but around thirty were released. They were then taken by train to Lispole to fill trenches cut in the main road. In effect, those young men were used as slave labour by the police, but even this was mild in the light of their trigger-happy behaviour.

Nobody was safe with the Auxiliaries and the Black and Tans on the loose. On the night of 7 February, for example, the Auxiliaries shot and seriously wounded two people near the technical school in Moyderwell, Tralee, where they had their local headquarters. On this occasion the two wounded men were an RIC sergeant and a constable. It was said that they did not halt when ordered to do so. This was only a variation on their usual excuse that they shot people trying to run away.

In Knockalough, near Duagh, four days later, Robert Browne was picked up by the Black and Tans on the roadside. He was a brother of John Browne, who was killed in the first raid on the RIC hut at Gortatlea in April 1918. He had set up a grocery business near Fealebridge before opening a business in Bally-macelligott, but he was burned out there. Shortly after he was picked up by police, his body was found discarded near the road – another captive who was supposedly shot trying to escape. In his case, he must have been trying to run backwards, because he was shot through the chest, but nobody was held responsible for that 'execution', or for a similar killing a couple of weeks later, when Joseph Taylor of Glencar was fatally wounded supposedly trying to escape after being arrested at his home. Taylor and Michael Scully, another local man arrested the same night, had both served prison terms in Belfast for illegal drilling.

The IRA planned to strike back on the night of 22 February. The North Kerry Column divided into two to engage in simultaneous attacks in Ballylongford and Ballybunion. Tom Kennelly, the column commander, went to Ballybunion with half the men, and his deputy, Denis Quill of Listowel, led the attack in Ballylongford: an ambush on two constables on a nightly patrol. 'Con Dee, Jack Ahern, Ned Joe Walsh, Dan O'Grady, Denis Quill and myself went into Ballylongford, where we ambushed the Tans,' Brosnan recalled. 'We took up positions in a side street. As the two Tans came along, we opened fire. They fell to the ground wounded, after which we disarmed them.' Constable George H. Howlett, a twenty-two-year-old from Middlesborough, was shot dead, and his colleague, Constable Wills, who was wounded badly, died later.

On reaching Ballybunion, Tom Kennelly learned that three RIC men were drinking in a local public house near the barracks, and they decided to ambush them as they returned to the RIC barracks for the nightly roll-call at 9.50 pm. Ted Houlihan, Paddy Mangan, Mick Purtill, Martin Quill, Tom Shanahan and Tomás O'Donoghue were deployed for the attack. At about 9.40, however, Constable Black headed down towards the Castle Hotel. The men had planned to target him, and O'Donoghue fired four shots at him. All missed, but the shooting forewarned the three men in the nearby bar. Police in the barracks began firing down the street, and shots were exchanged during a gun battle that lasted about half an hour, before the IRA withdrew. The Black and Tans then burned a new amusement arcade in retaliation, and some lorryloads of Black and Tans descended on Ballylongford next day and burned twenty houses there in reprisal.

16

'To Hell with Surrender!'

Kerry No. 2 Brigade set up a flying column on 2 March 1921. Tom McEllistrim and Dan Allman were put in joint control of it. A couple of days later, McEllistrim set out with twenty men to take part in the famous Clonbanin ambush in County Cork.

Word had been received from John Keogh – a porter at the International Hotel in Killarney who acted as intelligence officer for Kerry No. 2 Brigade – that a British general was in the vicinity on 2 March 1921. Keogh had been at the railway station talking casually to a British officer, who remarked, 'I must be off now, this is the general.'

Some armoured vehicles pulled up outside the Great Southern Hotel. Keogh learned that they were going to be around for three days. This information was passed to the IRA, along with the news that the general and his aides-de-camps would be travelling in a blue car.

IRA intelligence had already learned that a high-ranking military officer had left Buttevant Barracks to inspect the troops in Kerry. Brigadier General Hanway R. Cummins had become a particularly target of the IRA since the previous December, when he had announced that his men would carry prisoners as hostages on their lorries. Since then, the British army had abolished the rank of brigadier general and the general's official title had again become colonel commandant.

Since Divisional Commander Holmes, who had been a major general in the British army, had been killed in an ambush at

Toureengarriv on the Williamstown–Castleisland road, the IRA surmised that Cummins would use the Mallow–Killarney road on his return journey from Tralee on the Saturday. They therefore decided to set up an ambush at Clonbanin, about six miles from Kanturk, where a party of soldiers were stationed, and about the same distance from Millstreet, which had a very strong garrison of Black and Tans and RIC men.

'I arrived with my men at Clonbanin about 5.30 on the morning of the ambush,' McEllistrim wrote. 'The ambush was prepared by the Cork column leaders and we were in position at Clonbanin Cross in the early morning.' It was a perfect site for an ambush, with wooded hills on either side of the road. 'Three lorries of British military passed through our position going in the Kerry direction,' McEllistrim added. 'They passed through, due to the fact that the road mines which had been laid for the ambush failed to explode.'

The Tommies passed through unmolested and utterly oblivious to the fact that they had only narrowly escaped disaster. As soon as the Crown forces had passed on towards Killarney, scouts were posted on the hillsides for miles on the Kerry side, while the men were provided with breakfast, after which they again took up their positions. A section of the Millstreet men occupied the farmyard of Mark O'Shaughnessy, where they placed a Hotchkiss gun, manned by Bill Moylan and Denis Galvin. The Kerry column was on the flank. The remainder of the Millstreet men occupied a position away from the ambush, covering the roads from Kanturk in order to prevent reinforcements from arriving from that direction.

At about 3 pm, the signalers announced five military lorries coming from the Killarney direction. A few minutes afterwards, the leading lorry drove into the ambush. As it was passing, Shaughnessy's Hotchkiss gun opened fire on it. A little further on, the same lorry was engaged by the column on the northern side of the road and, having exchanged six or eight shots, was brought to a standstill. About two minutes' silence followed, until the remainder of the convoy, which consisted of another lorry about a hundred yards ahead of a touring car – which was followed at a distance of about fifteen yards by a Rolls Royce armoured car – arrived. Another lorry about a hundred yards behind brought up the rear. All the vehicles drove right into the ambush position.

Two rifle shots were fired in quick succession, and the touring car immediately swerved across the road, apparently out of control. The armoured car collided with the rear of the tourer, and the driver attempted to push on, but the armoured car got bogged in the soft dyke on the side of the road. The occupants must have been stunned, because it was some minutes before they opened up with their Vickers gun, but even then the firing was wild and they never hit anything. In the meantime, the IRA's Hotchkiss engaged the second lorry with deadly effect, and heavy rifle fire was concentrated on all vehicles from both sides of the road.

'Surrender,' one of the IRA men shouted. The response from the touring car was defiant: 'To hell with surrender! Give them the lead!'

Cummins, a tall man in uniform, leapt from the car and made a dive for cover on the north side of the road, but he never made it. He was cut down by the snipers, receiving a fatal wound to the head. That day his party was carrying a hostage – Maurice Slattery of Milltown – who managed to escape during the shooting.

'Fighting lasted for more than an hour,' McEllistrim recalled. It pitted the trained and specially picked soldiers of England against the raw and badly armed Volunteers of the IRA columns. The IRA's Hotchkiss gun went out of action early in the fight, and the Republicans' rifles had to contend with the Vickers in the armoured car as well as the Lewis gun, until the military riflemen had ceased to fire a shot – though the Vickers gun in the armoured car swept the hedge-tops with a leaden hail. It was clear that the military must have suffered heavily, and it was equally obvious that, as the armoured car, although stationary, held a position which dominated the road through the full length of the ambush position (about a quarter of a mile long), its capture was out of the question. So the IRA gradually retired, unscathed, leaving four dead and many others wounded. 'After the ambush I brought my column of twenty men back to Kerry,' McEllistrim noted.

It was later reported that thirteen soldiers were shot dead and fifteen wounded in the encounter, but the death toll was in fact two officers – Cummins and his aide-de-camp, Lieutenant H. A. Maligny – along with two unfortunate privates, whom the media did not even bother to name.

Toureengarriv and Clonbanin greatly boosted IRA morale and undermined the British contention that the Republicans were on the verge of collapse. Not prepared to admit that they were routed by a small IRA force, the British told the press that they had been attacked by a force of between 500 and 600 Republicans.

General Strickland, the general in charge of the British army in Ireland, visited Tralee as part of a tour of inspection on 1 March 1921. There was plenty of activity in the vicinity to mark his visit.

The British intelligence officer for the Kerry Command at Buttevant came to Tralee at the same time to put out some feelers for peace. Captain O'Malley of the Royal Munster Fusiliers was supposed to make contact with somebody who could get a message to the IRA, and Tim Kennedy was selected as a person who knew Cahill, as they had supposedly been at school together. Kennedy sent the following message directly to Michael Collins on 2 March under the heading 'Armistice':

General Strickland is willing to give a written guarantee of the safety of Cahill, Brown, Clifford, Jeffers and all other wanted men in Kerry, and that they can return to Tralee in safety, on condition that they, on their side, guarantee that they will not organise or take part in ambushes, and asked me if I would see Cahill and, as a neutral man, put the proposition before him. They say they want a reply within the next three or four days. I must, of course, see him, and I presume his reply will be that any negotiations for an armistice must be through Headquarters, Dublin. I would like that, for the present, this would not be made public, as it would put the tin hat on me. It is put this way that, unless this is done, the country will have to be flooded with military and they cannot guarantee to restrain the Black and Tans any longer. If you have any observations to make, send them as soon as possible, but you may rely on us to do the right thing.

Kennedy did not bother going to see Cahill; he merely waited for a reply from Collins. This came within a few days. It read:

Armistice – This sort of thing is going on a good deal. It would be very easy for General Strickland to get rid of his trouble by giving such a guarantee, after which the Black and Tans would be quite free to murder; and as for flooding the place with troops, it can be conveyed to General Strickland that we know he can do no such thing, for he is continually begging for more men from his own headquarters. The general seems to be a good propagandist, and a good bluffer. It might also be suggested to him that, if they cannot restrain the Black and Tans, they can remove them. Please report again as to what happens. I need hardly assure you that I know very well what answer Paddy and Co. will give.

IRA Headquarters was already investigating how it might increase the attacks on the British. Eamonn (Bob) Price of headquarters staff had been sent to north Kerry to suggest ways in which attacks might be stepped up. He went to Ballyheigue, where Tom Clifford had his headquarters for the Ardfert Battalion. Price suggested an attack on the RIC barracks in Causeway, where the IRA already had a man on the inside: Sergeant Buckley.

It was arranged with Buckley that the men defending the barracks would expend all the ammunition. It was further planned to drop a half-ton iron weight through the room from the roof of Roger Harty's house, which adjoined the barracks and was much taller than it. Then the IRA would pour petrol through the hole. There was a high wind on the night, however. Price and Clifford were saturated with petrol, very little of which got into the hole. That plan had to be abandoned, and the attack was called off. Sergeant Buckley quit the RIC the following week and returned home to Cork.

Even though 3 March was a particularly wet day, most of the men between the ages of sixteen and sixty were rounded up in Tralee, searched and told to watch out for an IRA flying column. The round-up lasted from noon to 3.30 pm. The same day, another attempt to kill Major Mackinnon was planned. He was to be ambushed at Ballyroe as he returned to Tralee from Ardfert, but while setting up the ambush one of the Volunteers was accidentally shot and the whole operation had to be called off. Mackinnon seemed to be living a charmed life.

Christy O'Grady was one of the scouts on the lookout for Mackinnon. Next day he watched while the Auxiliaries tried to blow up a bridge, but they did not have enough explosives and they managed only to blow off the parapets and make some holes in the road. They did succeed in destroying Farmer's Bridge that day, however. They were blowing up bridges in an attempt both to restrict the mobility of the IRA and to inconvenience the local people in order to turn them against the Republicans. Of course, the effect was always likely to be the opposite. Everybody knew that the Crown forces were blowing up the bridges, and the people held them, and not the IRA, responsible.

Some of the Black and Tans acquired infamous reputations that lived long after them in the folklore of the town; notable examples are men like 'Big Paddy' Culleton from Cavan and 'The Jewman' de la Roi, who was a French Canadian. There was also a Kerrymen – 'Dingle' Shea – who became a target for particular animosity. On 6 March a bomb was thrown at Shea, who created some excitement afterwards by wildly accusing people of trying to kill him. His head was battered and the Auxiliaries were 'very busy for a time afterwards,' O'Grady noted. There was an especially large funeral in town that day for the prominent Sinn Féiner and old Fenian Tom Slattery, who had died of natural causes. Due to his involvement with the Republican cause, there was another big round-up of the men after the funeral, but no arrests were made.

On 7 March the police imposed a curfew on Tralee from 8 pm until 5 am. About half an hour before the curfew began, the streets cleared rapidly. When the curfew bell rang, there was nobody to be seen on the streets except for Black and Tans and Auxiliaries.

There was some excitement in Blennerville on Friday 11 March, when the Auxiliaries opened fire on two young men crossing a field. More than a hundred shots were fired just outside the village. Three lorries then rushed through Blennerville at such high speed that one of them overturned, shaking up its occupants – much the amusement of the people of the village.

A train carrying Auxiliaries was ambushed between Listowel and Tralee on 12 March. When the train reached Tubrid near Ardfert, it was found that one Auxiliary – Walter Falkiner of Middlesex – had been killed and a number of people wounded, including the engine driver. Although a curfew was again imposed that night, the Auxiliaries were fired on at the top of Ashe Street on the eve of St Patrick's Day; there were no casualties. The Crown forces were expecting trouble next day. The Auxiliaries patrolled the streets in an armour-plated car throughout the day, but nothing happened.

The IRA intensified the pursuit of Mackinnon. 'We had ten fellows looking out for him,' Johnny O'Connor said. 'We knew he wore a coat of armour, but the lads had shotguns and slugs so they could get him in the face. Somehow through loose talk he found out about these lads.'

On St Patrick's Day, Mackinnon surprised some of those lads. 'He jumped out of his car and kicked the stuffing out of three or four lads,' O'Connor reported. He tied one end of a rope to Moss Hogan's legs and the other end to a colt and then drove the colt along the road. 'Poor Moss was in a devil of a way for a long time as a result of the battering he got by being dragged by the colt,' O'Connor noted.

The Kerry No. 2 Brigade Column had tried to draw the Auxiliaries or Black and Tans into an ambush at Dysert near Castleisland on 13 March. They had arranged for an attack on the RIC barracks at Farranfore, in the hope that reinforcements would be rushed from Castleisland, but the column waited for seven hours. No reinforcements were sent and the column moved off towards Scartaglin and Ballydesmond and thence through Kilquane and Barraduff.

On Sunday night the column crossed the railway line under the Paps mountains, about six miles from Headford, where a local IRA unit was already holding two British deserters and had suspicions about an itinerant called Sardy Nagle because he had been seen in the company of Captain O'Sullivan, a British intelligence officer stationed in Killarney. Sardy was in his thirties, of about average height, with a heavy build and a dark, drooping moustache. He was seized and questioned but protested that he was not a spy.

Next morning, 21 March 1921, the column was billeted about four and a half miles from Headford railway junction when its members learned that a party of some thirty British soldiers had travelled that day by train from Tralee to Kenmare and were expected to return that evening. 'We immediately decided to ambush those military troops at Headford junction,' Tom McEllistrim recalled.

Sardy was tied up with the two British deserters and left in a cowshed, while preparations were made for the Headford ambush – the biggest engagement in Kerry during the War of Independence. Dan Allman was the officer in charge and McEllistrim was his deputy. Thirty others were involved in the attack. They were John Cronin, Jack Herlihy, Paddy Burke, Moss Carmody, Moss Galvin and Jimmy Baily from the Ballymacelligott Company; Johnny O'Connor from Farmer's Bridge; Tom Fleming of Currow; Jack Shanahan, Dave McCarthy, Peter Browne and Jack Brosnan of Castleisland; Michael O'Leary of Farranfore; Dan Healy, Neilus McCarthy, Tim O'Mara and Tim O'Donoghue of Killarney; Jim Coffey of Beaufort; Patrick Cronin of Headford; John B. Lenihan, Peter O'Sullivan, Denis O'Sullivan and Denis Batt Cronin of Rathmore; Tom 'Scarteen' O'Connor, Seán Flynn, Paddy Lynch and Pat O'Shea from the Kenmare area; and Dan P. O'Sullivan of Morley's Bridge, Kilgarvan.

On arriving at the station, the men moved three open trucks and a van that would have obscured their vision. Ten were stationed on the Mallow side of the junction. 'We reached the junction about twelve minutes before the train arrived and took up positions on both sides of the railway station,' McEllistrim related. 'I was in the stationmaster's house with four men.' The stationmaster, a Mr Walsh, was about to leave the house with his wife. A guest in the building was questioned and let go, but he was not allowed to take his bicycle with him. The three of them had got about 200 yards from the station when the shooting started. By then, the rest of the staff had already fled.

The train actually arrived a little more than ten minutes early. Dan Allman, Johnny O'Connor and Dan Healy were on the middle of the main platform, so they took refuge in a lavatory. Others occupied an embankment overlooking the station.

The first off the Kenmare train were civilians. Many left the station without delay and avoided the trouble. Lieutenant C. F. Adams and the other twenty-nine soldiers were due to change trains at Headford. They were heading for Killarney and were to join the Mallow–Tralee train at Headford. That train was due to arrive about three-quarters of an hour later. The soldiers therefore took their time alighting – with the exception of one soldier, who bolted for the lavatory.

'It was our intention to allow them all to get off,' McEllistrim noted. 'Allman attempted to disarm this man without shooting him but the soldier jumped aside and attempted to use his rifle. Allman then shot him and took his rifle. The ambush started immediately and several British soldiers were shot on the platform. Three soldiers tried to take cover in front of the engine and were shot by my party from the stationmaster's house. They were only ten yards from us.'

Lieutenant Adams, who had advanced through the ranks while fighting in the First World War, was cut down almost straight away. He was standing at a carriage door when he was hit in the chest; he died on the spot. His sergeant assumed command and the entire detachment dashed towards the Rathmore side of the platform. Civilians – mostly cattle and pig buyers returning from a fair in Kenmare – were scattered about the station, some directly in the line of fire. One woman was carrying a laundry basket and had two young children with her. She dropped the basket, grabbed the children and ran the length of the bullet-swept platform. All three mercifully escaped unscathed. But three of the cattle dealers were not so lucky. John Breen of Killarney was killed on the spot, and two others – Patrick O'Donoghue of Killarney and Michael Cagney of Ballyfane, Liscarroll – were mortally wounded. Timothy McCarthy, a merchant from Loo Bridge, tried to shield his young daughter but was hit in the leg; the same bullet passed through both legs of his three-year-old daughter, doing horrific damage in the process.

The attackers advanced to within twenty yards of the Crown forces, whom they matched volley for volley. The more exposed British soldiers were coming off worst. Their dead were scattered about and firing became intermittent as the main body of the enemy was practically wiped out. It was very difficult to see the British soldiers who took cover under the train. Initially, fire was concentrated on a forward carriage where there was a Vickers gun. It was silenced when the sergeant and four men operating it were killed or wounded. One of the wounded men briefly opened fire again before succumbing to his injuries. Three separate efforts were made by the embattled men's comrades to get to the carriage, but each time they were cut down by the IRA men on the embankment.

Allman ran across to Johnny O'Connor's position. 'I think we have them now,' he said. 'There are only a few alive under the train.' Jim Coffey, an ex-British soldier with the column, joined Allman and O'Connor, and it was decided to make a dash towards the rear of the guard's van with the aim of wiping out the last of the enemy. They reached the new position and Coffey, who was in front, knelt down to take better aim but was wounded in the arm.

'I saw a soldier stand on the train coupling and I saw his rifle stick out,' Johnny O'Connor noted. 'I was at an angle but I chanced a few shots towards the carriage. I had a Mills grenade and I was anxious to see it go, so I pulled the pin and lobbed it towards him. I expect that finished him.' Allman was firing on one knee when he caught one in the chest. 'Water!' he cried.

'We knew the game was up,' O'Connor noted. 'I looked around and he pointed to his pocket and I sprinkled him with the holy-water bottle. He had a huge Sinn Féin rosette in his coat. As I watched him, the blood poured out his nose and he was grunting. The blood spattered his rosette. We tried to drag him away.'

When Bailey was killed on the embankment, Peter Browne, who was beside him, dropped his rifle and ran. Jim Coffey dashed to the stationmaster's house to tell McEllistrim that Allman and Bailey had been shot.

'We were then making arrangements to rush the military who had taken cover under the train,' McEllistrim noted. 'We called on them to surrender.'

'Never,' a sergeant replied each time.

After about fifty minutes the Mallow train approached, with an officer standing on the footboard of the engine. The men who had been placed down the line were ready. 'Jack Shanahan, Scarteen O'Connor and others saw this oncoming train with the military officer on the engine,' McEllistrim explained. 'They fired on the train immediately. The train stopped and the military got out, opening up on our section of men, who engaged them. I decided to abandon our position.' He called off the attack.

'Those in the stationmaster's house with me retreated southwards with other men at the south side of the station,' McEllistrim continued. 'Jim Coffey and I then crossed the line to the north side of the station to call off our men who were in position on the railway line there. We succeeded in crossing the line and found Johnny O'Connor and his men still in position.' They had obviously not seen the second train arrive. At that point, a tall, red-headed soldier came out, dusting off his uniform in the midst of his dead colleagues. 'I put up the rifle to have a shot at him when Mac put his hand on my shoulder,' O'Connor noted. 'The Mallow troop train had just come in.'

O'Connor, McEllistrim, Jackie Brosnan and Peter Browne – who had by then regained his composure – managed to get into a little bohereen about sixty or seventy yards long and running west towards Killarney. At the end of this, the way to safety lay across open country, mostly cut-away bog. No sooner had the little party appeared on this terrain than the British opened fire on them with a tremendous fusillade.

The party then split into two groups. McEllistrim and O'Connor paired off and succeeded in crossing the bridge over the River Flesk, which was covered by British machine-guns. 'We then retreated together along the north side of the station,' McEllistrim reported, 'crossing the railway line again at the Kenmare side of Headford. Machine-gun and rifle fire were played on us as we retreated. We joined the other section of our unit some distance from Headford Station and retreated across the hills to the south. 'We had eight rounds a man left after the scrap and it had to do us for some days until John Joe Rice was able to pick up some ammunition,' according to O'Connor.

The first official British account of the engagement was as follows:

As a train containing one officer and twenty-nine other ranks, First Royal Fusiliers, and a number of civilian passengers was nearing Headford Junction, it was heavily fired into from both sides of the cutting. The troops detrained and engaged the attackers, sustaining heavy casualties while doing so. The survivors held off the ambushers for fifty minutes, when they were reinforced by the arrival of another train, which contained a party of the First Royal Fusiliers, and the combined parties drove the rebels off. No arms or equipment were lost by the troops. The casualties were: one officer and six other ranks killed, twelve other ranks wounded, one civilian passenger killed and two civilian passengers wounded. It is believed a number of casualties were inflicted on the ambushers, and the dead body of one of them was found by the troops.

From the outset, the IRA questioned the British casualty figure. 'I think the British must have had over twenty dead,' Johnny O'Conner argued. 'Twelve coffins left Killarney later and that wasn't all. The British admitted that they had had heavy losses.' According to McEllistrim, the British later acknowledged that twenty-four soldiers had been killed at Headford and another four wounded, one of whom died later. The British Cabinet was told that seven men had been killed on the spot and that two others had died shortly afterwards.

Most of the British casualties in the conflict were classified as police officers. C. J. Street, a British intelligence officer who wrote *Ireland in 1921,* under the pseudonym I.O., provided a list of fatalities for both police officers and members of the military. Street states, for instance, that just two soldiers were killed in January 1921, four the following month, and four in April, but the death toll for March was thirty-five. The Headford ambush was not even mentioned in either Dorothy Macardle's *The Irish Republic* or Charles Townshend's *British Campaign in Ireland,* even though at the time the *Irish Times* described the battle as 'one of the fiercest that has yet taken place between Crown forces and rebels in the South of Ireland.'

Afterwards, the IRA decided that the tramp, Sardy Nagle, was indeed a spy. One man reported having heard him give information about the IRA to Captain O'Sullivan in Killarney. The man is reputed to have recognised Sardy's voice because he sang a song for which he was noted: 'Take me back to my dear old mother and there let me live and die.' That was enough to seal his fate. Tom McEllistrim shot him. His body was dumped near the Kenmare–Headford road about two and a half miles from Kenmare, at Claidy Cross, where it was found on Good Friday morning. He had been blindfolded, his hands had been tied behind his back, and tied around his neck was a card bearing the words: 'All spies beware – IRA.' He had been shot three times in the head and twice near the heart.

The Headford ambush was a dramatic start to Holy Week, as Easter was particularly early that year. The same evening in Tralee, the Black and Tans threw a grenade from a lorry as they passed down the Mall. Two young teachers at St Joseph's Industrial School, John Brosnan and Thomas Cleary, were seriously injured, along with the wife of Rock Street publican William Horgan, who owned what is now the Old Brogue Inn.

Meanwhile, the Auxiliaries undertook a big round-up in Lixnaw. On returning to Tralee the next night, they fired shots from a lorry while passing through the main street. They also beat up a man in the street. On Thursday a drunken policeman had to be disarmed in Tralee because he was pointing his revolver menacingly at people in the street.

The Tans and Auxiliaries were particularly active on Good Friday. The Auxiliaries claimed that their headquarters in the technical school at Moyderwell had come under attack from the town park. Earlier in the day the Black and Tans had arrested a Volunteer, Liam 'Sonny' McCarthy of Lixnaw. Born in Tralee on 26 March 1895, McCarthy was reared in Lixnaw, where he attended national school before going on to St Michael's

College, Listowel, and St Kieran's College, Kilkenny. In 1918 he joined the Irish Volunteers and became intelligence officer for north Kerry. He used the cover of organiser for the Kerry Farmers' Union while travelling about on intelligence operations. Among his sources were those members of the RIC who considered that their first allegiance was to their fellow countrymen in the struggle against the Crown forces. On 25 July 1920 he took part in the ambush in Lixnaw in which the two RIC constables from Ahabeg were wounded. He joined the flying column in north Kerry and became adjutant of the Third Battalion of Kerry No. 1 Brigade. On 24 March 1921 he received a message from IRA Headquarters in Dublin that had to be passed on to Battalion Headquarters in Tralee. He took the train to Tralee but was recognised at the station and arrested by the Black and Tans. After being questioned at the RIC barracks, he was taken to 'the Green' by Head Constable Francis Benson and some Black and Tans. The official version of events was that he was being transferred to the jail in Ballymullen:

> About 9 pm on Saturday he was being escorted to the jail but, as it was known that an attempt was going to be made to rescue him, he was not taken the direct route, but by a roundabout way, which passed through the Green. While crossing the green, six shots were fired at the park and in the ensuing excitement McCarthy hit a policeman over the head and bolted. He was fired on and killed.

Nobody believed that story. His body was left for others to find the following morning. It was the eve of Sonny McCarthy's twenty-sixth birthday. A monument now marks the spot in the town park where he was shot.

The Auxiliaries proceeded to rake St John's Church with machine-gun fire from the town park that evening. The church was particularly busy at the time. Five priests were hearing Confessions, and there were between 120 and 130 people, mostly women and children, in the church.

During his sermon on Easter Sunday, the Dean of Kerry, Monsignor David O'Leary, was particularly forceful in his denunciation of the attacks. 'I was in the middle of a Confession at the time and a lady who was being heard retired in the excitement of the moment,' the dean said. 'The same thing happened all round the church. The people ran the risk of their lives in order to perform their religious duties, and after about half an hour I saw the last of the people out of the church.' He added that indignation and horror at what had occurred would be felt throughout the world, not along among Catholics, but among all decent Christians.

There was a massive turnout for the removal of Sonny McCarthy's remains to St John's Church on Easter Monday. On three different occasions, Black and Tans with revolvers drawn stopped the proceedings to seize a tricolour flag from the coffin. All shops along the route of the funeral procession were closed, but the Black and Tans went from door to door insisting that they open. The following day there were further scenes at the railway station as the coffin was put on a train to Lixnaw, when the Tans seized another flag from the coffin. This time some of the women at the funeral showered them with abuse.

On the afternoon of 2 April 1921 the RIC barracks in Farranfore was attacked by the IRA. The shooting lasted about thirty minutes, but there were no injuries on either side. Shortly before midnight there was another attack on the nearby barracks in Castleisland. This shooting continued for about forty-five minutes, but again no casualties were reported. These attacks were often designed as traps to attract reinforcements, who would be ambushed on their way to the scene. The Crown forces did not respond to this particular attack, however.

17

'Up Kerry!'

The British were improving their intelligence operations. Through Serjeant Sullivan, efforts were made to organise an intelligence branch for Dublin Castle amongst Irish ex-servicemen.

'I went into the Castle with Dave Neligan to spot an ex-serviceman who was supposed to be a tout for the British,' Tim Kennedy recalled. 'I was to go in there and look around for my man, for he was supposed to be in Dublin to spot Austin Stack and others. I talked with him inside and he knew what I was there for.'

'I can't give Stack away,' he said.

As he was leaving Dublin Castle, Kennedy had a hair-raising experience. He was stopped by an Auxiliary, who checked his permit, which had been provided by Captain Tyrell O'Malley in a false name. As the Auxiliary was looking at the permit, Jimmy Murphy, an Auxiliary from Tralee, came along. He was the son of Tralee solicitor James Molyneaux Murphy. The father had got into trouble and was about to be disbarred when his two sons, Jimmy and Harry, joined the British army during the First World War in order to save the old man's career. After the war, Jimmy Murphy was tarred and feathered by the IRA. He then joined the Auxiliaries.

'When I saw him coming my knees began to wobble with fright,' Tim Kennedy explained. 'He looked at the permit and saw the name and called me by the name in the permit. I knew then that I was safe.'

Murphy told the other Auxiliary that they were friends. He asked Kennedy if he could put him in touch with Dan Brown, who was working in Austin Stack's Department of Home Affairs, over Cahill's optician shop on the Quays.

'On turning about, I was horrified to see Mick Collins just standing outside the gate where I had come out,' Kennedy continued. 'He was with a big DMP policeman, apparently in conversation with him, and, as Mick was tall, anyone would assume he was a G-man or a detective from Dublin Castle. I promised Jimmy Murphy that I would ask Dan Brown if he would meet him and he gave me a phone number at Mountjoy Jail, where he was in charge of an Auxiliary attachment. He shouted instructions to the next Auxiliary to pass me along and, just as I stepped out, Mick joined me and we were passed along from one Auxiliary to another.

One of the former servicemen recruited to spy for the British was John 'Boxer' O'Mahony, a former serviceman from Tralee. He was recruited in Belfast Jail, where he was a warder. He, in turn, is believed to have recruited other former servicemen.

Kennedy emphasised that O'Mahony and others were not targeted by the Boherbee Company because they had served in the First World War. John Joe Sheehy, who was in command of the company, had a brother, Jimmy, who was killed in September 1916, during the Battle of the Somme, while serving as a lance corporal in the British army. O'Mahony and the other former servicemen were targeted because they were acting as spies.

'Dave Neligan copied this information and it was sent to us,' Kennedy noted. 'We had evidence, for "Boxer" had money to distribute and there was a dispute about the division of money in Tralee.'

On the night of 6 April, O'Mahony was seized and taken to the Big River at the side of the Fair Field (by the current site of the primary school at Fairy Cross) in Tralee. 'He was told if he gave the names of the other men who were spies that his case might be considered,' Kennedy continued. 'We got the other names, then we shot him.' A note left on the body read: 'Shot by the IRA.' Some of those named by O'Mahony were able to get away; these included the spotter, who remained in Dublin Castle. But the IRA did kill three of the men.

The attitude towards serving and former British soldiers differed from place to place. In Tralee, where some 400 soldiers were stationed at Ballymullen Barracks, there was little Republican animosity towards the soldiers. Captain O'Malley, the commanding officer of the Royal Munster Fusiliers, continued to give information to Tim Kennedy, while Colonel Berkely obviously despised both the Auxiliaries and the Black and Tans.

Captain Watson had won the respect of many people in Listowel by keeping the Black and Tans in check following the killing of District Inspector Tobias O'Sullivan, but this did not save him when he cycled with ten soldiers to the home of Sir Arthur Vicars at Kilmorna near Listowel on 7 April 1921. On hearing of this journey, some members of the column set up an ambush on their own without even trying to inform the rest of the column to act as back-up. The ambush was set up between two bends in the road. As the first two soldiers of the advance party came around the first bend, they were ambushed. Both men were shot and fell down wounded.

Timmy Egan jumped over the fence and grabbed one of their guns. Others who took part in the ambush included Jack Carroll, Mick Galvin, Dónalín O'Grady and Mick Purtill. When the others arrived on the scene, a full-scale gun battle ensued.

One bullet struck Captain Watson on the forehead. Thinking he was seriously wounded, Mick Galvin stepped out from his cover but was shot and fatally wounded by Watson, who had only suffered a glancing flesh wound. With Crown reinforcements likely to arrive from Listowel, the already outnumbered members of the column had to withdraw after about thirty minutes, leaving the body of Galvin behind.

The Crown forces brought the body to Listowel, but nobody – not even Galvin's own mother – would identify it. She feared that Crown forces would retaliate against her other son or her neighbours. Galvin was therefore buried as an unknown person, but the body was reinterred under cover of darkness a few weeks later.

In the interim, seventeen members of the Knockanure and Duagh Companies of the IRA raided Kilmorna House, the home of Sir Arthur Vicars, on 12 April. He had become famous as the official keeper of the Irish crown jewels, which had been stolen earlier in the century. George Cunninghan, the land steward, was consulting with Vicars when the raid began, at about 10.15 in the morning. Lar Broder said that the raiders had only come to burn down the house, but three of them had been selected to shoot Vicars. While his house was being torched, he was taken outside by Jack Sheehan, Paddy Dean, and Jack Brehony, who then killed him.

The police and military had learned of the seizure of Kilmorna within minutes, and they set out in force, but they were delayed on the way when James Barrett fired on them at Shanacool Cross. Fearing a full-scale ambush, the lorries stopped and the soldiers fanned out, while Barrett fled up a hill in full sight. He raced to his own house. His father then told the Crown forces that he was hiding in the house. As they started looking for him, he made good his escape. The whole thing delayed the soldiers so long that the raiding party at Kilmorna was long gone.

The quest to kill Major Mackinnon in Tralee became even more urgent after the Auxiliaries killed sixteen-year-old Daniel O'Driscoll at Liscahane, near Ardfert, on 9 April. They surprised a group at a bridge and, as the people scattered, the Auxiliaries opened fire, killing O'Driscoll and wounding a fifteen-year-old comrade of his, John O'Sullivan. The Auxiliaries later reported that one of their men had been wounded during the incident.

Scouts were trying to watch Major Mackinnon's every move in Tralee. It was decided to ambush him at the golf course in the Oakpark area of town, where he often played. For a fortnight, an ambush party waited in vain. It was probably no coincidence that the golf-club committee decided at their meeting on 13 April to increase the fire-insurance cover on the pavilion and members' golf equipment. In fact, the amount of cover was almost quadrupled, from £786 to £2,900. The secretary was also 'given the power to take out a civil riot and commotion insurance policy on the golf pavilion for the same amount,' the committee's records state.

The ambush party got its chance on Friday 15 April 1921. That date was the start of a period that people in Tralee would never forget. 'I was a scout on duty at the top of Ashe Street that day,' Pat 'Belty' Williams recalled. 'The ambush party consisted of a sniper with a rifle, James Cornelius Healy and three colleagues – Johnny Riordan, Tommy Barrett and Jack Mason – with shotguns.' Healy, a veteran of the First World War, was a proficient marksman. He hid in a tree overlooking the third green, where he waited until Mackinnon was perfectly still while putting. Little did he realise that those with him were about to witness the most famous shots ever made on any Tralee golf course. Healy shot the major twice in the head and, in the ensuing confusion after his two colleagues opened up with their shotguns, all three managed to escape. Others involved that day included Patcheen Connor, Paddy Kelly, Tommy Sheehy, Donnchadh O'Donoghue and Tom Tangney. They were all from the Boherbee section of the column.

Willie Daly, who had taken up the job of golf professional at the club only on 24 March, was playing just ahead of Mackinnon. He rushed back and propped up the dying major's head with his jacket and said an act of contrition in his ear. Dr A. A. Hargrave of the military hospital in Ballymullen, Tralee, was called to the golf course to treat Mackinnon. He was still alive and was then hurriedly moved to the military hospital. 'I found a bullet wound on the right side of the head with a wound of exit on the left side over the left ear,' Hargrave reported. 'The bones were badly fractured and the brain protruding. There was also a bullet wound in the right side of the face under the right eye. There was no wound of exit.' Mackinnon died at about a quarter past five that afternoon without regaining consciousness. 'On examining the body after death,' Dr Hargrave noted, 'I found the buttocks, backs of legs, and hands riddled with large shot.'

Earlier that day, Judge Cusack had told the local court that he had received a letter from the county inspector informing him that the Crown forces had ordered that there could be no further hearings of any compensation cases or injury claims against them. One barrister objected that this could be interpreted as meaning that the security forces could behave as they pleased and there could be no claims for the resulting damage.

The golf-club committee held an emergency meeting that evening. There was a real danger that the British forces would burn the place down as they went on a murderous arson spree within Tralee town itself. Willie Daly was questioned by the Black and Tans and given a pretty rough time, even though he had had no involvement in the shooting. He had to go into hiding for a week as the Auxiliaries and Tans went berserk.

Although it was said that Mackinnon's last words were 'Burn Ballymac', his wounds were such that it was unlikely that he said anything. Nonetheless, the Auxiliaries went on the rampage in Ballymacelligott that evening. They set fire to Ballydwyer Creamery and more than a dozen private houses, including the Catholic Presbytery at Clogher, where Father Timothy Trant was still living. The other houses belonged to Jerry McEllistrim of Ballydwyer and Frank Hill, and to three women: the home of a Mrs O'Sullivan, the widow of a local labourer; 'Ahane', belonging to Tom McEllistrim's widowed mother; and the family home of the late Maurice Reidy, whom Mackinnon had shot dead on Christmas Day. This house was occupied by Reidy's unmarried sister, a local schoolteacher. The Auxiliaries also raided the home of an uncle of Reidy: John Reidy was shot dead as he tried to flee from the house as the lorry approached.

All shops in Tralee closed at 5.30 and remained closed over the weekend. On Sunday afternoon the IRA seized a Black and Tan, Constable Cornelius P. Meade from Sussex. He was shot dead in Ballyseedy and his body was then taken and buried in the bog at Ballyfinane, just off the road between Tralee and Castlemaine. He was subsequently listed as missing. (His body was not found until 29 September 1926.)

Major Mackinnon's funeral took place at St John's Protestant Church in Ashe Street on Tuesday morning. All the Crown forces turned out as the body was carried on his favourite car through Tralee to the railway station. There was great fear of reprisals in Tralee that evening. All the shops in town shut early, but Christy O'Grady noted that he was kept awake for most of following night by the Auxiliaries, who went on an orgy of arson and destruction.

The Auxiliaries burned down Kirby's and Brosnan's draperies in the Mall, Galvin's shop on Bridge Street, Charles Nolan's cycle shop and his home in Pembroke Street, the Railway Hotel, the offices of the *Kerryman* and the *Liberator*, and Vale's, Culloty's and Flahive's public houses in Boherbee. They pulled the Pikeman Statue off its pedestal in Denny Street and knocked off its head and arms. They then left the trunk of the statue in the middle of the Mall. O'Grady took a photograph of the decapitated statue and the empty pedestal, and these were published in both the *Irish Independent* and the *Cork Examiner*.

The IRA retaliated next day by 'executing' the second of

the ex-servicemen spies, Denny O'Loughlin. He was a local man who worked as a cook. He was shot dead in Knightly's public house in Lower Bridge Street. This led to further reprisals by the Auxiliaries. Patrick Bell, a cattle buyer from Lusk, County Dublin, was shot and fatally wounded near the Munster Warehouse, and Knightly's was bombed and burned by the Black and Tans as an official reprisal. 'It was terrible to hear the explosions, shots being discharged, etc., and to see the poor aged couple leaving,' O'Grady noted in his diary. 'Their home, all furniture, etc., was burned, biscuits, jams, tobacco, etc, being pitched into the street. A curfew was imposed at nine o'clock.'

Father E. H. Collins, OP, the former British army chaplain at the Dominican Church, was upset by the shooting of Mackinnon, and he happened to say something to this effect to the wife of Charles Nolan, who was a sister of Daniel J. Browne, the secretary of Austin Stack's department. She responded along the lines that she hoped God would bless those who had dispatched that tyrant. IRA sources in the RIC barracks reported that Father Collins complained there about Mrs Nolan's remarks and Father Collins was then blamed when the Black and Tans blew up her house and the family business as a reprisal for Mackinnon's death.

Tim Kennedy went to Dublin to discuss what to do about the priest. On instructions from Collins, he talked to Father Finbar Ryan, the superior general of the Dominican Order in Ireland. Father Ryan was greatly upset by the story. He asked what the IRA would do if Father Collins was not a priest. Of course, Kennedy replied that they would shoot him. 'You are a brave man,' Father Ryan said. 'This is no priest of God. Do your duty, boy, and you need have no fear of the future.'

'I don't know whether it was Father Ryan or I was in the greater state of fright, but I think I recovered more quickly,'

Kennedy explained. 'I said I would go back and consult again my superior officers, but he may rest assured that I would submit being put against the wall myself before I would do my "duty" on a priest, no matter how bad he was.'

Collins sent Kennedy back to the superior general with Daniel J. Browne, the aggrieved woman's brother, and they persuaded Father Ryan simply to transfer Father Collins from Tralee. It was not necessary to kill him, they decided.

Another former chaplain posed problems of a very different kind. Three curates at St John's Parish Church in Tralee – Fathers William Ferris, Jeremiah Casey and William Behan – were so outspokenly sympathetic to the Republicans that the IRA felt obliged to provide protection for them. Ferris had already been openly threatened on a couple of occasions and he found it necessary to dress in mufti in public. Those sent to protect Behan, who had served as a chaplain in the First World War, became particularly friendly with him. The friendship almost had disastrous consequences.

'He was a bit unbalanced in his mind, no doubt as a result of his service in the Great War,' Tim Kennedy related. He concluded that the priest's 'sense of valour was inclined to outrun the discretion which we had to exercise owing to our meagre resources . . . He was constantly making proposals to me to be conveyed to Paddy Cahill about operations which even I did not approve with the limited resources and personnel at our disposal. He was full of enthusiasm for helping us against the British and volunteered for some of the actions personally.'

Father Behan enlisted the support of Eamonn A. Horan, 'who suffered from the same complaint,' according to Kennedy. The outspoken priest drew up a petition protesting that Kerry No. 1 Brigade had not been active enough around Tralee. They blamed Paddy Cahill, who was described as being too old and in poor health, for this state of affairs. The petition was also signed by

Ned Horan, Joe Sugrue and Paddy Kelly. The protest was brought to Dublin by Horan's sister, Maggie May, but it was not well received there. According to Kennedy, the chief of staff, Dick Mulcahy, ordered that those who had signed it should be shot for mutiny. Cooler heads prevailed, however, and the idea of executing anybody was dropped.

Andy Cooney, a former medical student from Tipperary, had been sent by IRA Headquarters to help reorganise Kerry No. 2 Brigade. He was instructed to take a look at Kerry No. 1 Brigade, and he reported that 'Cahill has a hopeless staff.' Mulcahy wrote to Cahill, therefore, outlining reasons why the latter should resign. Cahill duly did resign, but this made matters worse. Even Cooney felt that 'he should not have been fired.' Cahill commanded the respect of most of his own men, and none of them would replace him, so Cooney had to act as brigade commander himself.

In late March the First Southern Division was set up under the command of Liam Lynch, with Florrie O'Donoghue from Rathmore as his adjutant. The new division incorporated nine brigades: the three from Kerry, three from Cork, two from Waterford and one from west Limerick. In terms of personnel, it was by far the largest division in the country, comprising more than 30,000 Volunteers.

When the various brigade representatives met near Millstreet for the first time on 26 April 1921, Cooney represented Kerry No. 1 Brigade, while Kerry No. 2 Brigade was represented by both Humphrey Murphy and John Joe Rice. However, there was no representative from Kerry No. 3, Brigade, which was having its own problems: there were difficulties between the brigade commander, J. O'Riordan, and Dinny Daly, who had strong links with the IRB.

In the aftermath of the burning of the offices of the *Kerryman* and the *Liberator,* the Crown forces did not have to cope with as much local publicity as before, because it was a few years before either newspaper reappeared. There was even more IRA activity in the following days. At 6 pm on 26 April there was another big round-up in Tralee. 'All in our neighbourhood marched to the Sports Field,' Christy O'Grady noted.

A couple of days later – more than two weeks after the killing of Sir Arthur Vicars – the Crown forces decided to carry out reprisal burnings in Listowel. They used petrol to set fire first to Daniel J. Flavin's news agency. He was chairman of the local urban district council. They then burned Breen's grocery, bakery and bar and the premises next door to J. R. Walsh, who was in jail at the time. Next, the Crown forces went to William Street, where they burned the drapery business of Jeremiah J. Foley.

'During the whole day, most of the town was enveloped in smoke from the ruined houses, and a fairly strong wind rendered it most disagreeable and almost unbearable,' according to the *Cork Examiner.* A military proclamation was issued stating that the burnings were official reprisals for the killing of Vicars, and there was a further warning that 'for any outrages in future carried out against the lives or property of loyalist officials, reprisals will be taken against selected persons known to have rebel sympathies although their implication has not been proved.'

The IRA seized eighty-year-old Thomas O'Sullivan as a suspected spy at the end of April, and they then used him to lure the RIC and Black and Tans into an ambush. Eddie Crowley, a brother of the future Fianna Fáil deputy Fred H. Crowley, who was a judge in the Republican courts at the time, reported that he had seen O'Sullivan, an itinerant, talking to the Black and Tans while he was under arrest on suspicion of involvement in the attack on the Rathmore barracks. Two British deserters, who were being held on suspicion of trying to infiltrate the IRA for British intelligence, confirmed that Old Tom was a frequent visitor to the Black and Tans.

An IRA court was constituted, consisting of Humphrey Murphy, commander of Kerry No. 2 Brigade; Jeremiah Riordan, commander of Kerry No. 3 Brigade; and four local men: Denis Reen, Con O'Leary, P. D. Moynihan and Manus Moynihan. After hearing from Eddie Crowley and the two British deserters, the court decided that O'Sullivan should be executed. The two deserters were subsequently shot after they were handed over to the IRA in Cork, with the result that the evidence against O'Sullivan amounted to little more than that he had been seen talking to a Black and Tan.

'The prisoner was left in my custody and I was given discretion as to when and where he would be shot,' Manus Moynihan, the officer commanding the Rathmore company, recalled. 'After thinking things over, I decided that when I executed Old Tom, I would use his body as bait in an attempt to draw some of the garrison out of Rathmore Barracks.'

Moynihan decided to shoot Old Tom at the Bog Road just outside Rathmore. The road was clear of fences on both sides and the surrounding countryside was flat, boggy land crossed by drains. A bohereen intersected the road and curved slightly towards the road.

'This was a Rathmore Company job and I, as captain of the Rathmore company, was the officer responsible for carrying out the job,' Manus recalled. He sought help from both his own battalion headquarters and the IRA in north Cork. Members of the Rathmore company who took part in the operation were Dee Reen, Denis J. Reen, Dan Courtney, John Lenihan, John Cronin, Mick Rahilly, Pat Cronin, John Moynihan and Din Batt Cronin. The battalion sent David McCarthy, Pat (Ned) O'Connor, Denis Prendeville, Mick Leary, Jack O'Connor and Jack Prendeville, and the north Cork IRA provided four men to help out: Con Morley, Denis

Galvin, John Vaughan and Mick Sullivan.

'I had all my plans completed on 1 May 1921,' Moynihan noted. 'Old Tom was held about half a mile from the spot selected for the job. On the night of 3 May 1921, I sent one of my men, P. D. Moynihan, to the presbytery at Rathmore for a priest to come out and give Old Tom spiritual consolation. Old Tom was brought to the spot on the Bog Road selected for his execution and three separate shots were fired. His body was labelled as a spy and left on the roadside.'

The first people to come along the following morning were two men going to the bog on a donkey cart around 8 am. The older man insisted on reporting the body to the RIC, while the ambush party looked on in hiding. The police responded about two hours later by sending out a nine-man party comprising both RIC officers and Black and Tans. As they approached the area, one RIC man lagged behind.

'We saw them from the time they entered the Bog Road but held our fire,' Moynihan recalled. 'When they approached the body, four of them moved to the side of the road and bent over. I gave the order to fire. It was a fine clear volley. It sounded like one shot. Whether they were hit or not, the whole party dropped to the ground. We continued firing. Only one or two of the Tans returned the fire.

'Three of the Tans rolled off the road to our right and were dead when we found them; three lay on the road dead and two (the only ones who fired) lay just off the road to the left behind a couple of stunted bushes.' The two who lay behind the bushes were mortally wounded and died the following day. The one who had been lagging behind was Constable Steve Hickey, who obviously sensed trouble. He had in fact been spying for the IRA, and he took off for Rathmore as soon as the first shot was fired, dropping his gun as he fled.

Those killed outright were Sergeant Thomas McCormack

from Roscommon and five Black and Tans: Constables William Clapp, Robert Dyne, Samuel Clapp and Hedley Woodcock – who were all in their twenties – and Constable Alfred Hillyer, a teenager who had joined the force only eight months earlier. The two mortally wounded men were Constable James Phelan, a native of County Limerick in his early thirties, and Constable Walter T. Brown, twenty-nine, from Middlesex.

'We collected eight rifles and 200 rounds of .303 off each body,' Moynihan noted. We also collected the rifle of the one who got away. Our party dispersed to their own areas and all got safely back.'

Next day a force of Black and Tans arrived by train and burned down the four houses near the scene of the ambush. These were the homes of Garret Nagle, Timothy Moynihan and Patrick O'Donoghue, which was the family home of Florrie O'Donoghue, the intelligence officer for Cork No. 1 Brigade. The other house was that of Thomas O'Connor, the father of Patrick O'Connor, who had been killed in Moore Street with The O'Rahilly in 1916.

Head Constable William K. Storey, a native of County Limerick, was shot dead coming from Sunday Mass in Castleisland on 8 May. He was survived by his wife and nine children. A colleague of his, Sergeant Butler, was shot with him at the time. Butler was shot in the spine, but his wife protected him by throwing herself on top of him. He was thus spared any further injury, but he died of his wounds anyway.

After these shootings, the Black and Tans went out on the streets in Tralee, firing at random. They literally 'kicked people off the street,' Christy O'Grady noted. Porter and Hatfield, the Black and Tans recruited by O'Grady, were anxious to desert. Hatfield asked for a safe-conduct pass from the IRA next day, but the IRA suspected a trap. O'Grady was therefore told to bring Hatfield out to Ballyseedy for a supposed meeting with the IRA, who were anxious to see if there would be any activity by the Crown forces in the area that afternoon.

'I walked him out to Ballyseedy Wood to meet the IRA,' O'Grady noted. 'Nobody [was] there of course, but he passed the test, suggested to me by our lot.' O'Grady secured a safe-conduct pass from the IRA before he deserted.

In early May, members of the North Kerry Flying Column, who were frequently compelled to live in unhygienic conditions, had to break up temporarily due to an outbreak of scabies, which was often called 'the Republican itch'. On 12 May 1921 four members of the column – Con Dee, Paddy Dalton, Paddy Walsh and Jerry Lyons – happened to meet at Gortaglanna Bridge, Listowel. They had chatted there for about half an hour, when they were surprised by a Black and Tan patrol of three lorries. They were searched for arms, but they were all unarmed. Dee was accused of having shot Sir Arthur Vicars.

'Now it is our turn to shoot,' one of the Tans said.

'Where are the rest of the column?' they asked. 'What are the names of the other members?'

'When the Tans got no answer, we got a stroke of a rifle,' Dee noted. 'When they found they could get no information, they marched us into the lorries. Paddy Walsh and Paddy Dalton were put on the first lorry. I was put on the second and Jerry Lyons on their third.' They drove a short distance and then the lorries turned around and Walsh and Dalton were transferred to the lorry with Dee. They then drove for about a mile.

'We were then ordered out of them,' according to Dee. 'I saw blood on Jerry Lyons' face and on Paddy Walsh's mouth. Paddy Dalton was bleeding from the nose. We were then asked to run but we refused. We were again beaten with rifles and ordered into a field by the roadside. We refused but were forced into the field. We asked for a trial but the Black and Tans laughed and jeered and called us murderers. We were put standing in a line facing a fence about forty yards from the road.

'Then a Black and Tan with a rifle resting on the fence was put in front of each of us,' he continued. 'We then realised we were to be shot. We shook hands and said goodbye, each giving a promise that the first one to get to heaven would pray for the others. We stood with clasped hands in the field beyond the fence facing the road. In unison, we shouted at the top of our voices, "God grant freedom to Ireland!"

'I looked straight into the face of the man in front of me. He delayed about twenty seconds, as if he would like one of his companions to fire first. The second Black and Tan fired. Jerry Lyons flung up his arms, moaned and fell backwards. I glanced at the blood coming on his waistcoat. I turned and ran.'

Although he was shot in the thigh, Dee managed to keep running and eventually threw himself into a drain in a state of exhaustion. He was later helped to a house. Dee had survived but his three colleagues were dead. He was able to identify a couple of the assailants. 'I recognised Head Constable Smith, Listowel,' he said. 'Also Constable Raymond, and there was one in the uniform of a district inspector of the Royal Irish Constabulary.'

The Black and Tans later claimed that they had been attacked that day. In a report, dated 17 May, General E. P. Strickland wrote that 'a small patrol' of police from Listowel 'encountered a gang of about eighty rebels and put them to flight after killing their leader and two others and wounding several more. The operation was doubly successful in that the dead rebel leader has been recognised as Jeremiah Lyons of Duagh, the commander of the flying column which has been active in north-east Kerry for some time.' The report was, of course, a tissue of lies. There was no ambush, and the Black and Tans encountered only four men, who were unarmed. They shot them in cold blood. Fortunately, Con Dee was able to tell the true story. He would not be the last such witness to live to tell the tale of an atrocity in Kerry.

On 14 May there was trouble in Tralee, Cahirciveen and Rathmore. Head Constable Francis Benson from Sligo was shot dead in Pembroke Street, Tralee, on a busy Saturday afternoon. He was shot by two members of the IRA in revenge for his role in the killing of Liam 'Sonny' McCarthy on Easter Saturday in the Green. The IRA men alighted from a field in what is now Austin Stack Villas. Benson, who was the father of five children, was returning to the barracks after dinner at his residence in Pembroke Street. He was shot in the temple, and then the two men stood over his prostrate body and fired further shots at point-blank range.

After the shooting, there were a lot of whistles blowing. The crowd of country people who normally came to Tralee to shop on a Saturday fled the town. It was only a month since Mackinnon had been killed. The Black and Tans were 'kicking chaps and beating them with rifle butts,' according to O'Grady, who stayed in a friend's house for a time and then hurried home. The Black and Tans were driving around in 'lorries out firing volley after volley, shouting, etc,' he wrote. 'Many chaps have been beaten. Auxies out in the evening shouting and firing, not a soul out since four and all shops shut. Stray shots fired during the night. Thus ends a terrifying day both for myself and many others.'

Benson's death sparked another round of the usual excesses by the Black and Tans. Everybody was ordered to stay indoors after Mass the next day. There was a big turnout as Benson's body was taken to the railway station on Monday morning. The Black and Tans then burned the four houses nearest the scene of the killing. They were the homes of Charles Nolan, William Hurley, Patrick Slattery and James Sugrue. It was assumed that they must have known of the plans to kill Benson. All were given an hour to remove their valuables, but they had to leave their furniture. Coffey's, next to Nolan's, was destroyed by accident in the ensuing explosion.

'The explosion was terrific, smashing nearly every window in the street,' O'Grady noted in his diary. 'The crowd in the street were scattered by revolver fire, and whilst they were being chased I got a good photo of the wreckage.' He sent the photographs to the *Irish Independent*, which duly published them the next day.

On the same day that Benson was shot in Tralee, a police patrol was fired on in Cahirciveen and one constable was slightly wounded, while nobody was hurt in an attack on the RIC barracks in Rathmore, or when shots were fired at sentries outside the military barracks in Kenmare.

But the following day a sergeant in the Royal Fusiliers was shot off his bicycle and seriously wounded as he was going through Kenmare. The Crown forces responded by surrounding the town and rounding up all the male inhabitants. Those rounded up were marched with 'hands up' to the military barracks, where all were searched and identified before being released.

There had been 'a long period of inactivity' in the Kerry No. 3 Brigade area in the Iveragh peninsula. But on 16 May a party of off-duty RIC men were fired on in Cahirciveen. They reported that they had been shot at by about half a dozen men from each end of the town. Constable Kilgannon was hit three times and seriously wounded, as was a little girl, Bridie Connell, who had been playing in the street when the shooting started.

A curfew was proclaimed in Cahirciveen extending from 9 pm to 6 am, and large reinforcements of Auxiliaries and soldiers were brought into the town the following week. The Auxiliaries commandeered the Carnegie Hall and other premises, trenches were dug across roads and all trains and mail were suspended. 'The town is practically isolated,' the *Cork Examiner* reported.

Many people, fearing reprisals, moved out of town. Official reprisals were carried out on four houses: the houses, which were owned by Bartholomew Sheehan, Jeremiah O'Connell, Joseph Brennan and Jeremiah O'Riordan, were destroyed by bombs. At the same time, an airplane flew over the town dropping anti-Republican leaflets.

Christy O'Grady was on scouting duty in Tralee on Saturday 21 May when he got caught in a round-up. By then, people were taking such incidents in their stride. Those involved were ordered to go up to Stand Street. O'Grady provided a graphic description of being lined up in a field. 'A lot of ex-soldiers, Evans, etc, were there, drunk,' he wrote. 'Had great sport with them as they were giving cheek continuously to the Auxiliaries, who took it good-naturedly. All of us were then searched and allowed go home.'

There was a general election in the last week of May for the new Southern Parliament to be established in Dublin under the Partition Act, but the campaign in the south-west never amounted to anything, because all eight Sinn Féin candidates were returned unopposed in the constituency, which covered all Kerry and west Limerick. Those elected were Austin Stack and Paddy J. Cahill of Tralee, Fionán Lynch of Cahirciveen, James Crowley and Thomas O'Donoghue of Listowel, and Piaras Beaslaí, Edmond Roche and Con Collins. There was no public interest in the campaign. The plethora of local newspapers had been virtually wiped out in the previous year: only the *Kerry People* remained. 'There was not a particle of public interest taken in the elections in Tralee,' the *Kerry People* noted.

Five RIC men were fatally shot while on bicycle patrol between Killorglin and Castlemaine on 1 June 1921, when their twelve-man patrol was ambushed on the Milltown side of Castlemaine by a twenty-strong flying column of Kerry No. 1 Brigade under the command of Tadhg Brosnan of Castlegregory. The Volunteers were spread behind the ditch on one side of the road at about ten-yard intervals. Seven of them had rifles: Paddy

Paul Fitzgerald, 'Big' Dan O'Sullivan, Mike O'Leary, Jerry 'Unkey' O'Connor, Donnchadha O'Donoghue, Jerry Myles and Eugene Hogan. The others, who had shotguns, were Billy Myles, John L. O'Sullivan, Jerry Cronin, Michael Fleming, Tom O'Connor, Michael McMahon, Dan Jeffers, Dan Mulvihill, Joe Sugrue, John O'Sullivan and the future Dáil deputy for Kerry South, Jack 'the Fiddler' Flynn.

District Inspector Michael F. McCaughey, a thirty-two-year-old native of County Monaghan, was killed almost immediately, in the first volley of shots, as were Sergeant James Collery, forty-five, from Sligo, who was the father of nine children, and Constable John Quirk, thirty-three, from Cork. Constable Joseph Cooney, twenty-five, from Leitrim, also died at the scene and five others were wounded. One of them – Constable Joseph S. McCormack, twenty, from Dublin – died the following week. Two of the RIC men managed to escape uninjured – much to the irritation of the members of the flying column, who were particularly anxious to get one Constable Foley. They considered Foley to be a very dangerous character, according to Michael Fleming, one of those who took part in the attack. He noted that they were particularly proud of their haul of arms, which included eight rifles and six revolvers, as well as 800 rounds of ammunition.

The only casualty on the IRA side was Jerry Myles, who received a serious bullet wound in the neck and back. He was treated in safe houses in Beaufort and Glencar, where he made a complete recovery. He later served as secretary of the Kerry County Board of the GAA for many years.

On 3 June 1921 Tom McEllistrim learned that thirty British soldiers and six RIC men had gone to Tralee for the day by train, and arrangements were made to ambush them on their way back to Castleisland that night. The IRA removed one of the tracks on a curve in the line on the Castleisland side of Gortatlea and waited there for the train.

'The position we occupied was ideal for an ambush,' McEllistrim noted. The loose rail was left on the line with a strong wire attached, so that they could pull the rail away once the train came within a hundred yards of them.

'As we lay crouched on either side of the railway ready for action, the trainload of military sailed into our position at good speed,' he wrote. 'The railway track was pulled out of place but, to our amazement, that train travelled along that railway line on one track. It travelled a distance of thirty feet in that way and jumped onto the railway track at the other end, where the railway line had been disconnected by us.

'We had only time to fire a few volleys as the train tore past us. We could scarcely believe that it was possible for a train to travel a distance of thirty feet without an iron rail at one side and jump on the track at the other end.' They later learned that they had made the mistake of removing the inside rail while all the pressure was on the outside rail on the curve.

The following weekend, the IRA shot the third ex-serviceman who was believed to be spying against the Republicans. John 'Cousy' Fitzgerald was shot through both eyes near Ballybeggan Racecourse. He had been prominent in Redmond's National Volunteers after the split in the Irish Volunteers. He was the one whom Tom O'Donnell and the other Redmondites had given a great public send-off at the railway station in Tralee on 6 February 1915. This was big news at the time, but Fitzgerald's demise on the night of 5 June 1921 was barely reported. All fairs in Tralee were banned for a month in retaliation.

James Kane, a fisheries inspector, was shot dead near Listowel on 11 June because he had reportedly furnished the police with details of those responsible for the death of District Inspector Tobias O'Sullivan back in January. He had a message attached to his body: 'Convicted spy. Let others beware. IRA.' But more than a few local people were convinced that Kane was really shot because he was due to prosecute a number of poachers at the next petty session.

On 22 June a police convoy from Farranfore claimed that they had been ambushed about two miles from Castleisland by some fifty members of the IRA, but none of the patrol was injured in that attack. They returned fire with a machine-gun. It was not yet a year since RIC Divisional Commissioner Gerald Brice Ferguson Smyth had indicated that the police would retaliate against the Republicans. Since then, the police had been going around with machine-guns and hand grenades, but murder was more prevalent than before and the country was in a more lawless state than ever.

In May 1921 the British forces suffered their heaviest casualties since the Easter Rising. This made a mockery of the Lloyd George government's assertion that they were defeating the IRA. Pressure on the prime minister to change his policy became intolerable. South African Prime Minister Jan Christian Smuts warned that the existing policy would destroy the British Empire. Even Winston Churchill, the Secretary for War, feared the reaction of American public opinion. Lloyd George and his colleagues therefore decided to try to secure a negotiated settlement.

As arrangements were being made to contact Éamon de Valera, however, de Valera was suddenly arrested by troops who apparently did not realise that the government had issued instructions the previous December that the Long Fellow should not be apprehended. De Valera, the president, had designated Austin Stack to take over in the event of his arrest. This was indicative of serious strains within the Republican movement. Stack, who had considered himself out of his depth as Minister for Home Affairs, was being given charge of the whole movement. This situation undoubtedly reflected the developing rift between de Valera and Michael Collins, who had been ridiculing the president for some time.

When de Valera went to the United States in June 1919, he nominated Arthur Griffith as his replacement, and Griffith had nominated Collins to take over from him, following his arrest in November 1920. Collins had then acted as president during most of December 1920, but de Valera's first act upon his return was to criticise the way the military campaign was being run. He said that the ambushes were creating a bad impression on public opinion in America. He then advocated major monthly battles involving around 500 men on each side.

Aware of the real strength of the IRA, Collins knew that it would be quickly wiped out in such confrontations. He ridiculed de Valera over such proposals. The president, who was aware of Collins's behaviour, retaliated by selecting Stack as his deputy.

But Stack's tenure as acting president did not last even a full day. De Valera was released the next day and was told to make himself available for a message, which turned out to be an invitation from Lloyd George to talks in London. The president demanded that there should be a ceasefire first, and the terms of a truce were agreed on 8 July 1921. The truce was to come into effect at 11 am three days later.

On the eve of the truce, O'Grady noted that there was an air of 'subdued excitement'. That night during curfew, he was out putting up IRA notices on lamp-posts listing RIC men 'Wanted for Murder'. He noted that the list included 'Big Paddy', 'the Jewman' and others 'who were sure to be shot. This ends what I hope is the last day of the war.'

Others were determined to get a last crack at the enemy on the eve of the truce. The IRA in Castleisland was determined to settle some old scores. The biggest shoot-out of the whole war in Castleisland took place that night near the local library. Four British soldiers were killed and three were wounded, while the IRA suffered five fatalities, one of whom was John Flynn, who had taken part in the first ambush at Gortatlea, only to be killed on the last full day of the war.

Tom McEllistrim was in Killorglin that evening. There were plans to attack the Black and Tans there, but the whole thing was called off at the last minute.

Members of the North Kerry Flying Column went to Tarbert in the hope of killing Constable Farmolie, who had bragged that he shot Jack Sheehan near Listowel, from a distance of more than a quarter of a mile, a little over a month earlier. When they learned that Farmolie and two colleagues were in a certain public house, Jack Ahern stayed to keep an eye on the bar, while a couple of his colleagues went to round up the others. But the three policemen came out before the others returned. As the police officers reached the doorway of the RIC barracks, Ahern fired on them, wounding Constables Farmolie and Dent. Both later recovered from their injuries.

Two Royal Fusiliers were shot, one fatally, in Killarney outside the Imperial Hotel, in which a maid, Hannah Carey, was killed by a stray bullet the following morning. But all the shooting stopped by 11 o'clock, and the celebrations began.

'People were elated at the starting of the truce,' a reporter wrote from Tralee. 'The discharged soldiers' band played through the streets shortly after eleven o'clock, when enthusiastic scenes were witnessed, the populace cheering wildly.' Men on the run came out in the open and engaged the Black and Tans in some good-natured banter.

'Truce heralded by firing of rockets and the ex-soldiers' band playing national airs,' Christy O'Grady noted in his diary. 'Sinn Féin colours prominently worn and by people whom I never saw very fond of it. Tans ironically cheered.' He noted that a number of wanted men were moving about the town freely, and there was no trouble.

'Bonfires lit in evening, free fights in lane,' O'Grady added. 'Mrs Wall and Bodley prominent. The body of chap killed in ambush at Castleisland brought to mortuary. Strong Tan picket out but soon disappeared. Walked past barracks at 12 o'clock. What a change! Tans take the abuse they get in very good part.'

Next day O'Grady cycled to Castleisland to see what had happened there for himself. He arrived in the town at about 11 am. Lorries full of soldiers arrived shortly after him. A shot was fired on the street, and someone shouted, 'Up Kerry!'

18

'The Last Man in the World I'd Suspect'

At the start of the truce, Tim Kennedy was appointed liaison officer for the IRA in relation to the British armed forces. He went to Ballymullen Barracks wondering about his reception, because he had played the part of a friend of the military for so long. 'When I saw O'Malley inside,' Kennedy said, 'he laughed with glee.' Kennedy then entered the room and Captain O'Malley became quite formal and saluted him as a soldier. 'Then I presented my documents.'

'Good Christ!' the colonel exclaimed. 'I hand it to you people – you're the last man in the world I'd suspect.' He then held out his hand and the two men shook hands.

During the truce, Christy O'Grady mentioned many mobilisations and training sessions in his diary. There was a great influx into the IRA in the following weeks. These new recruits were somewhat derisively known as 'Trucileers' by those who had been involved in the IRA when it was dangerous to do so.

Although the War of Independence had begun as series of sporadic local incidents, in early 1921 moves were made to formulate the IRA brigades into divisional units. The benefits of cooperation between units of different brigades from adjoining counties became apparent with the Toureengarriv and Clonbanin ambushes. While Kerry No. 2 Brigade had no problem in cooperating with the Cork IRA, there was little cooperation with Kerry No. 1 Brigade, because the members of No. 2 Brigade did not get on with the brigade commander, Paddy Cahill, who was replaced in April by Andy Cooney from Nenagh, County Tipperary. With his athletic build, Cooney commanded respect even by his appearance. He was a serious man, not given to wisecracks or jokes, who had been a medical student and eventually became a doctor. Cooney was a good organiser and a strict disciplinarian, but his appointment as commander of Kerry No. 1 Brigade was never intended to be more than temporary. He was unable to make much headway because of the local hostility to the way in which headquarters had interfered with the brigade.

Cooney got little local help. 'Con Casey was given over to me as an adjutant because they thought he was just a schoolboy and would have been of no use to me,' Cooney explained. Casey, who was later the editor of the *Kerryman* for many years, turned out to be a 'grand adjutant', according to Cooney. Indeed, Cooney would later invite him to be his adjutant when he was moved to Drogheda as commandant of the First Eastern Division of the IRA. While with Kerry No. 1 Brigade, however, Cooney 'was in splendid isolation,' according to Casey. Tim Kennedy, the brigade intelligence officer, was friendly, but Cooney felt – probably rightly – that Kennedy was acting in Cahill's interest in order to learn Cooney's views and ideas about what was happening.

At a council meeting of Kerry No. 1 Brigade in Derrymore, Tadgh Brosnan of Castlegregory refused to take Cahill's place, as did Tom Clifford. 'No one would take the command,' Cooney noted. As Cahill had been asked to resign before the First Southern Division was formed, Liam Lynch insisted that headquarters should clean up its own mess.

Dan Jeffers, one of the bravest gunmen in the flying column, told Cooney that he would not carry out any of his orders. 'This is not a personal refusal, nor has it anything to do with you,' Jeffers explained. The problem was the way headquarters had treated Cahill. On explaining this, Jeffers burst into tears – much to Cooney's astonishment.

For the young men, the summer of 1921 was a particularly memorable one, not just because the weather was especially good, but also because of the feeling of relief that existed after so much tension. Yet some tension remained. On the night of 20 August, an Auxiliary officer ordered soldiers out of the Ashbourne Hotel at about eleven o'clock. 'They stuck into him in the shop and gave him a terrific mauling,' O'Grady noted. The Munster Fusiliers had no more love for the Black and Tans than most other Irishmen, but O'Grady noted the following weekend that there was a bust-up at the Forester's Hall in Tralee when the Black and Tans 'quite rightly' batoned some people who had been 'blackguarding them'.

The initial enthusiasm of some the Trucileers soon waned. On Saturday 10 September 1921, few of them attended a mobilisation. An officer and five Volunteers were sent to round them up. 'Most of the crowd refused to go,' Christy O'Grady noted. 'Had to drag a few. One drew a jackknife.' Eventually they managed to get most of the reluctant ones together, but these men then made an attempt to get away. It was therefore decided to court-martial some of them. All were fined, two were ordered to be at home by nine o'clock every night for a week, two for every night for two weeks, and the fifth man for three weeks. 'As one gave cheek, we pretended we were going to shoot him and carried him over the fields,' O'Grady wrote. 'He was in a blue funk when we finished.'

The following Saturday there was another mobilisation and they 'drilled, route-marched, etc, for five solid hours.' On the evening of Wednesday 5 October, there was a full turnout of some 120 men and they trained, practised and marched until 5.30 the following morning.

The negotiations with the British were conducted behind

closed doors. De Valera initially chose Austin Stack to accompany him to London for the opening meetings with Lloyd George in July. This was significant in that the president pointedly refused to bring Michael Collins, who was bitterly disappointed at being excluded. Although de Valera brought a number of Cabinet colleagues and some friends with him, he did all the talking for the Irish side himself.

'We remained in London for about eleven days. During that time the president and Lloyd George met,' Stack recalled. 'None of the rest of us were present on these occasions.' Following each meeting, the president used to tell them what had been said.

'After the second interview, we had reason to believe they were not going beyond Dominion Home Rule,' Stack wrote. 'I was anxious to go home at once but was asked to stay on.'

He recalled walking with Griffith around London one evening. 'Passing through Whitehall, Griffith turned to me and then, looking up at a building, said, "Would you like to take that to Dublin with you, Austin?"'

'It is a fine place,' Stack replied. 'What is it?'

'That's the Home Office.'

'Surely you do not regard it as possible that we should accept the British terms?'

'I think they are pretty good,' Griffith insisted.

'How could we conscientiously accept the British king? Look at the dead who have given their life for the Republic!' Stack exclaimed.

'Oh, I see that it is your conscience that is the matter,' Griffith said.

De Valera received the British proposals on 20 July and read them to his colleagues. 'I demurred at one,' Stack wrote.

The following Sunday the proposals were discussed with the rest of the Cabinet at de Valera's house in Blackrock. 'I got the impression strongly forced upon me that Griffith and Collins and Mulcahy were inclined to view the proposals favourably,' Stack noted. 'Michael Collins described the offer as a great "step forward".'

When it came to the selection of a team to negotiate with the British, de Valera proposed Arthur Griffith and Michael Collins. 'I entered a weak kind of objection and said that my reason was that both gentlemen had been in favour of the July proposals,' Stack explained. Griffith objected to this complaint.

'I understand from him he only wanted some modifications,' Stack said.

'Yes,' replied Griffith, 'some modifications.'

Collins also denied that he would accept the British offer.

'I reminded him what he had said at Blackrock,' Stack related, but Collins protested that he had said nothing of the kind. Brugha and de Valera supported Collins. 'Cathal and the president then assured me that I had misunderstood Mick at Blackrock,' Stack continued. 'I accepted this and said no more.'

Although he clearly resented Stack's objection to him as one of the plenipotentiaries who were selected to go to London to negotiate a treaty with the British, Collins was reluctant to go, because he was suspicious of de Valera. In addition to the five plenipotentiaries, four secretaries were selected to assist the delegation. One of them was Fionán Lynch of Cahirciveen. Another Kerryman, included as one of the aides to deal with the press, was Mike Knightly, a Dublin-based newspaperman from Tralee.

Collins brought several of his own aides with him. He stayed with them, separate from the main part of the delegation. Collins invited Tim Kennedy to be part of his team, 'but I refused, as I was worried about the situation [in Kerry No. 1 Brigade],' Kennedy noted. Collins therefore brought Dinny Daly of Cahirciveen instead. Kennedy had declined to go to London because he was unhappy about the removal of Paddy

Cahill, and he thought that going with Collins to London would, in some way, constitute disloyalty to Cahill.

Kennedy gave a rather different reason to Collins. He said that feelings were running so high in Kerry that it would be better if he stayed at home to keep an eye on things, as he could keep in touch with headquarters and maybe even smooth things over. 'I persuaded him that it was more important that I should be in Kerry than with him in London,' Kennedy explained.

On 15 September, the Republican leadership decided to put the IRA on a regular basis, subject to the Dáil through the Minister for Defence. Brugha's idea was to have Stack take an active role as deputy chief of staff. Although he had been appointed as deputy chief of staff in 1919, he had never carried out any responsibilities in that position. Now the headquarters staff baulked at his appointment. As Cahill was seen as Stack's man, the removal of Cahill inevitably got mixed up with the reorganisation of the IRA.

While the negotiations were going on in London, an inquiry was held at IRA Headquarters into the Cahill affair. Cathal Brugha chaired it, and Collins came over from London for a meeting. All the headquarters staff were there, along with Tadhg Brosnan, Tom Clifford, Tim Kennedy and Andy Cooney. Kennedy felt that he had divided loyalties. He had been close to Cahill as an intelligence officer, but he was reporting to Collins. 'I faithfully reported to Michael Collins what was happening,' he insisted. Kennedy and Brosnan discussed the situation while travelling to Dublin together on the train.

'I knew of the rift between Cathal Brugha and Michael Collins,' Kennedy explained. 'Surrounding Michael Collins was a gang of fellows who rightly or wrongly regarded him as chief of the army and believed that nobody else counted.' In Kennedy's mind, the problem was basically that headquarters was reporting to Collins, rather than the other way around. Moreover, a rift had developed between Collins and Stack, because the Big Fellow had been ridiculing him.

'Collins used to pass remarks in fun about Stack's department to me, and other fellows to whom perhaps similar remarks were made would convey them back to Stack's men, or to Stack,' Kennedy noted. He told Brosnan 'all about this rift on the way up and we decided that, rather than have any further trouble, we would resign and go back as privates to the ranks. Stack would, we knew, be in favour of Paddy Cahill.'

At the meeting, Brugha made some remarks, and Dick Mulcahy, the official chief of staff, contradicted him. Kennedy then spoke in favour of Cahill, but Mulcahy was dismissive.

'He was too old,' the chief of staff said.

But that argument did not wash because both of Mulcahy's alternatives – Humphrey Murphy and Tadhg Brosnan – were the same age as Cahill.

'I said, we'll make things very easy for this inquiry, for I have tendered my resignation to Thomas O'Donoghue,' Kennedy noted.

'How dare Tomás O'Donoghue poke his nose into my department,' Collins snapped. 'You belong to my department . . . Nobody has any right except me to receive your resignation.' This was typical of the Big Fellow: nobody had a right to interfere in his department, but he involved himself in other people's business at will.

Tadgh Brosnan made it clear that he would not accept an appointment as Cahill's successor. He said that he would rather go back to Castlegregory as a private. At that point, the inquiry adjourned. Afterwards, Collins asked Kennedy to bring Brosnan with him to the Bailey, so the three of them could discuss the whole thing.

At this meeting, Kennedy and Brosnan continued to support Cahill. 'I told M.C. [Collins] that I couldn't carry on, in view of my sympathies with Paddy Cahill,' Kennedy noted. Collins tried to persuade Brosnan to take over Cahill's old position as commander of Kerry No. 1 Brigade, but Brosnan was adamant in his refusal.

'Very well,' said Collins to the two of them, 'you can give me your resignations.'

'I did give him my resignation, then he gave me an appointment on his staff with my base at Tralee,' Kennedy explained.

The Cahill affair was eventually resolved at a divisional meeting in Castleisland. Liam Lynch, the commander of the Southern Division of the IRA, and his deputy, Liam Deasy, fixed up the situation. With none of Cahill's men prepared to take on the job, Humphrey Murphy was moved from Kerry No. 2 to take command of Kerry No. 1, and John Joe Rice took over Kerry No. 2. Paddy Cahill was appointed commander of a separate entity within Kerry No. 1 Brigade; this unit was not called a brigade, however. Whatever orders were sent to Humphrey Murphy were duplicated to Cahill. 'That was the foundation of what was called "The Ninth Battalion", which was really a farce,' Kennedy admitted.

On 4 November, the IRA was recommissioned, with all the headquarters and other senior officers being reappointed, which meant that Stack was again officially appointed deputy chief of staff. But again the headquarters staff unanimously refused to accept him. Mulcahy demanded the appointment of Eoin O'Duffy instead of Stack, but Brugha insisted that 'the whole General Staff will be appointed by the Cabinet on the recommendations of the Minister for Defence.'

Mulcahy stated that his acceptance of the post of chief of staff was contingent on the Cabinet's acceptance of all of his recommendations. 'If the ministry decides to make an appointment to such an important staff position against my judgement,' he warned, 'I cannot accept the responsibility attaching to any position on the staff.'

It was obvious that Stack was being included in order to undermine the influence of Collins. Hence the headquarters staff resolutely resisted all efforts to impose Stack. People like Liam Lynch and Seán Russell, who would later break with Collins and Mulcahy, supported them strongly in this controversy. The whole business reached boiling point at a meeting on 25 November 1921. De Valera suggested a compromise in which Stack and O'Duffy would each be appointed joint deputy chief of staff. O'Duffy would act on Mulcahy's behalf, while Stack would be 'Cathal's ghost on the staff,' according to de Valera. It was like Cahill's phantom 'Ninth Battalion' all over again.

O'Duffy, who was prone to hysterics, reacted indignantly to de Valera's unwillingness to accept Mulcahy's appointment of him as sole deputy chief of staff. 'After a very short time,' Mulcahy noted, 'Dev rose excitedly in his chair, pushed the small table in front of him and declared in a half-scream, half-shout: "Ye may mutiny if ye like, but Ireland will give me another army," and he dismissed the whole lot of us from his sight.'

It was against the backdrop of this kind of infighting at home that the Treaty negotiations were concluded in London. The agreement was signed in the early hours of 6 December 1921.

On the evening of 6 December, after reading the terms of the Anglo-Irish Treaty, which had been signed in the early hours of that morning, President Éamon de Valera summoned a meeting of the available members of the Cabinet. 'I am going to pronounce against the Treaty,' he declared, adding that he intended to demand the resignations of Arthur Griffith, Michael Collins and Robert Barton from his Cabinet upon their return from London.

Austin Stack and Cathal Brugha agreed with him, but W. T. Cosgrave objected. He insisted that those ministers should have an opportunity to explain what had happened before any pronouncement was made.

A full Cabinet meeting was therefore called for 8 December 1921, and a press release was prepared. 'In view of the nature of the proposed treaty with Great Britain,' it read, 'President de Valera has sent an urgent summons to members of the Cabinet in London to report at once so that a full Cabinet decision may be taken.'

Minister for Publicity Desmond Fitzgerald, who had just returned from London, where he had been helping the Irish delegation, was surprised at the tone of the release. 'This might be altered, Mr President,' he said. 'It reads as if you were opposed to the settlement.'

'And that is the way I intended it to read,' replied de Valera. 'Publish it as it is.'

Fitzgerald was amazed. 'I did not think he was against this kind of settlement before we went over to London,' he whispered to Stack.

'He is dead against it now, anyway,' replied Stack. 'That's enough.'

It was like a cry of triumph. Fitzgerald thought Stack was gloating that he and Brugha had persuaded the president to abandon his more moderate views while the delegation was in London.

'Terms of peace in papers today,' Christy O'Grady wrote next day. 'They are very bad, in my humble opinion.'

The Cabinet met in the drawing room of the Mansion House. De Valera was depressed, while Stack was in a blazing mood, and Brugha was 'the personification of venom,' according to Collins. The Treaty itself was not examined in any great detail, according to Stack. The main topic of discussion was the circumstances under which it had been signed.

The Cabinet eventually voted to endorse the Treaty by the

narrowest margin. Griffith, Collins and Cosgrave voted in favour, while de Valera, Brugha and Stack were opposed. It was therefore Robert Barton's vote which made the difference. Even though he was personally opposed to the agreement, he felt bound to vote for it, because he had signed it in London and agreed to recommend it to the Dáil.

After the vote, de Valera was urged to go along with the majority, but he refused. Stack appealed to Collins, on the other hand, not to use his influence in favour of the Treaty.

'You have signed and undertaken to recommend the document to the Dáil,' Stack said. 'Well, recommend it. Your duty stops there. You are not supposed to throw all your influence into the scale.' If the Dáil rejected the agreement, Stack argued, the Republicans would be in an even stronger position than before. 'Will you do it?' Stack asked.

'Where would I be then?' Collins snapped.

The Cabinet was irrevocably split. De Valera announced that he would resign if the Dáil accepted the Treaty, while Griffith and Collins said that they would do the same if it was rejected. In the interim, all agreed to carry on until the Dáil voted on the agreement.

'The greatest test of our people has come,' de Valera declared in a public statement afterwards. 'Let us face it worthily, without bitterness and above all without recriminations. There is a definite constitutional way of resolving our political differences – let us not depart from it, and let the conduct of the Cabinet in this matter be an example to the whole nation.'

One of the controversies over the Treaty was the failure of the plenipotentiaries to refer it back to Dublin before signing it. In fact, they had discussed it on the previous Saturday and the plenipotentiaries felt that they had thereby fulfilled their obligations. But Griffith had promised that he would not sign the document. He maintained that he secured significant changes, but if that was so it was a different document and should have been referred to the Cabinet under the terms of the agreed instructions.

'Why did you not come back to Ireland?' Tim Kennedy asked Collins.

'God blast you!' Collins replied. 'Why didn't you go across with me?'

Kennedy personally agreed with the Treaty, but he sided with those who opposed it, because '99 per cent of the people in the brigade [Kerry No. 1] were anti-Treaty and my friendship with Austin Stack also helped my opinion.' The people of Tralee 'might have favoured' the Treaty, according to John Joe Sheehy, 'but the followers of Stack managed to secure the town, so that it stayed anti-Treaty.'

Later, anti-Treaty people would blame the IRB for having somehow schemed to get the Treaty accepted, but the main IRB people in Kerry were opposed to the Treaty, as was the divisional commander, Liam Lynch, who was a member of its Supreme Council. 'Stack showed me the IRB Supreme Council's recommendation of the Treaty,' Tim Kennedy noted. This stipulated that the Supreme Council advocate that the Treaty should be ratified. 'Members of the organisation, however, who have to take public action as representatives are given freedom of action in the matter.'

'I stood alone at the meeting,' Lynch wrote to his brother. But he was by no means unhappy with the fact that Collins was running the Supreme Council. 'I admire Mick as a soldier and a man,' he added. 'Thank God all parties can agree to differ.'

In order to generate support for the Treaty, the British began releasing Republican prisoners. On 10 December the Tralee prisoners arrived home to a massive reception at the railway station. But the signs of unrest soon became apparent. Three days later, Captain Tyrell O'Malley of the Royal Munster

Fusiliers was shot in the leg at Ballyheigue. This was a flagrant breach of the Truce, but it was also evidence of the lack of discipline on the Republican side, because O'Malley had been spying for the IRA and supplying valuable information to Tim Kennedy.

Next day there was an even more serious breach of the Truce when four members of the IRA from Ballylongford killed RIC Sergeant John Maher, 24, from County Carlow, and seriously wounded his colleague Constable Gallagher on the Castle Green in Ballybunion. This was in retaliation for the part Maher had played in killing Eddie Carmody in Ballylongford the previous November.

The Dáil had begun debating the Treaty on 14 December 1921 in what is now the National Concert Hall at Earlsfort Terrace, Dublin. For a time it went into private session, from which the press and public were excluded.

In response to a challenge from Collins that he say exactly what terms he was looking for, de Valera produced his own alternative, which became known as 'Document No. 2'. De Valera made the startling admission that it was 'right to say that there will be very little difference in practice between what I may call the proposals received and what you will have under what I propose. There is very little in practice but there is that big thing that you are consistent and that you recognise yourself as a separate independent state and you associate in an honourable manner with another group.'

De Valera argued that, if the Dáil stood by his counter-proposals, the British would not go to war for the difference. 'I felt the distance between the two was so small that the British would not wage war on account of it,' de Valera explained. 'You may say, if it is so small, why not take it? But I say, that small difference makes all the difference. This fight has lasted through the centuries and I would be willing to win that little sentimental thing that would satisfy the aspirations of the country.'

According to Document No 2, the Irish Free State would assume the same de facto status as any of the Dominions without being a member of the British Commonwealth, whereas the Treaty accorded the country de facto status as a member of the Commonwealth. No oath was prescribed for members of Dáil Éireann in the new document, but there was a stipulation that 'for the purposes of the Association, Ireland shall recognise His Britannic Majesty as head of the Association.'

Britain would, for at least five years, be accorded the same defence concessions as had prevailed before. The partition clauses were included verbatim in de Valera's alternative, with the addition of a declaration to the effect that 'the right of any part of Ireland to be excluded from the supreme authority of the National Parliament and Government' was not being recognised.

In other words, de Valera explained, the alternative would not 'recognise the right of any part of Ireland to secede', but for the sake of internal peace and in order to divorce the Ulster question from the overall Anglo-Irish dispute, he was ready to accept the partition clauses of the Treaty. Nonetheless, he found these clauses objectionable because they provided 'an explicit recognition of the right on the part of Irishmen to secede from Ireland,' he said. 'We will take the same things as agreed on there,' the president declared. 'Let us not start to fight with Ulster.'

In later years, the mistaken notion would take root that the Treaty controversy had somehow revolved around the partition issue. Never once during the fourteen days of public and private debate did Austin Stack even allude to the partition question. Stack based his objection to the Treaty on Ireland's membership of the British Commonwealth and on the wording of the Treaty oath to be taken by members of the Dáil. He seconded de Valera's opposition to the Treaty. At the outset, Stack had promised 'to be very brief', and he was true to his word. His speech was over in less than fifteen minutes.

While Stack was in London, de Valera had argued with Lloyd George that Canada's real status was that of an independent state and, if Ireland was accorded the same de facto status as Canada, then Ireland would be completely independent and he would be satisfied with that. The Treaty stipulated that Ireland had the same status as Canada in 'law, practice and constitutional usage.' That was taken to mean that Ireland would have the same de facto status as Canada. Stack could not be sure if those words did indeed assure Ireland the de facto status of Canada, but he said that he would not be satisfied with Canada's status anyway. Nevertheless, he spoke in the Dáil in terms of total support for de Valera's position.

'There are men in this assembly who have been comrades of mine in various places, who have been fighting the same fight as I have been fighting, the same fight which we have all been fighting, and which I sincerely hope we will be fighting together again ere long,' Stack said. 'There are men with whom I was associated in this fight whose fathers had worn England's uniform and taken oaths of allegiance, and these men were as good men and took their places as well in the fight for Irish independence as any man I ever met. But what I wish to say is this: I was nurtured in the traditions of Fenianism. My father wore England's uniform as a comrade of Charles Kickham and O'Donovan Rossa when, as a '67 man, he was sentenced to ten years for being a rebel, but he wore it minus the oath of allegiance.

'Now I ask you, has any man here the idea in his head, has any man here the hardihood to stand up and say that it was for this our fathers have suffered, that it was for this our comrades have died on the field and in the barrack yard? If you really believe in your hearts that it was, vote for it. If you don't believe it in your hearts, vote against it.'

Of course, Stack had no way of knowing that his father had in reality offered his services to the Crown while in prison and had sung like a canary. If he had known, maybe he would not have been as quick to justify his own attitude on the stand supposedly taken by his father.

Even though de Valera pressed for his own alternative proposals, he knew that they would be unacceptable to the British. 'No politician in England would stand by them,' he admitted. 'Because they would have the same difficulty in legally ratifying this proposed Treaty that I hold our delegates have in ratifying it here constitutionally. It would not be a politician's peace but a people's peace.'

Fionán Lynch from south Kerry spoke in favour of the Treaty the next day. But just as Stack had personalised his opposition to the agreement by backing de Valera's stand, Lynch supported the Treaty by backing Collins. Lynch complained that it had been suggested 'that Lloyd George, shaking a paper in front of the face of Michael Collins, was able to put the wind up Michael Collins. Let the people of Ireland judge whether it is so easy to put the wind up Michael Collins. That kind of eyewash is not going to go down with me or with any man who has soldiered with Collins, or with any person in Ireland who knows what he has done.' For many in the Dáil, the Treaty issue was decided by whether they supported de Valera or Collins.

'The bones of the dead have been rattled indecently in the face of this assembly,' Lynch added. 'I stand for this Treaty on four grounds, and the one I mention last is the one that will mean the most to me. I stand for it because it gives us an army, because it gives us evacuation, because it gives us control over the finances of the country, and lastly, and greatest of all to me, because it gives us control over our education.'

'I know that I can speak for my own people – for the people of south Kerry, where I was bred and born.'

'No!' a woman shouted from the public gallery.

'With one exception. Yes, a minority of one against – an Englishwoman,' Lynch continued.

J. J. O'Kelly, who was better known by his pen-name, 'Sceilg', was another Kerryman in the Dáil. Although he was elected to represent Counties Louth and Meath, he said that he knew he was speaking for the people of east Kerry when he opposed the Treaty.

One of the bitterest speeches was the last one made on the anti-Treaty side, delivered by Cathal Brugha, who made some withering criticisms of Michael Collins. He also took a swipe at Fionán Lynch for saying 'that he spoke for the people of south Kerry.'

'And I still maintain it,' Lynch interjected.

'I had in my pocket a document signed by people who are entitled to speak for the young men, the fighting men, the men who count and who are ready to make sacrifices in his constituency, and that is the brigade commandant in his area – the two brigade commandants who cover the area which his constituency is in,' Brugha continued. 'In this they say very respectfully to the government that they are absolutely against the Treaty. Since Deputy Lynch has made that statement, he has been repudiated in the papers.' The leaders of all three Kerry brigades of the IRA came out publicly against the Treaty.

The other Kerrymen in the Dáil, Paddy J. Cahill and Thomas O'Donoghue, made no contribution at all to the debate. They simply voted against the Treaty without making any speech, while James Crowley of Listowel voted for the Treaty without making any other contribution.

19

'WADE THROUGH IRISH BLOOD'

When the Dáil reconvened the following week, de Valera resigned as president of the Dáil. He then ran again for the office but was defeated by Arthur Griffith. In accordance with the Treaty, a Provisional Government was set up with Collins as chairman. In effect, Griffith was president and Michael Collins was prime minister. There were two Cabinets, but nearly all the ministries were filled by the same people, with the result that there was effectively only one government.

During the ensuing days, there were a number of truce violations around the country. One of the worst in Kerry occurred in Tralee, on Friday 20 January 1922. It went down in local folklore as another atrocity carried out by the Black and Tans, but in reality the violation was precipitated by three members of the local Fianna.

Percy Hanafin, Mick Mullaly and Pat 'Belty' Williams had decided to hijack a truck to supply their training-camp needs. On that Friday afternoon at about five o'clock, they thought they could hijack a Black and Tan truck that called at Benner's Garage in Edward Street. 'The three of us decided to act on the spur of the moment,' Williams explained. 'We had seen one of the Tans go into the garage, leaving the driver alone at the wheel. Thinking there was only the two of them, we decided to seize the truck. Our plan was to take the driver as a hostage and drive out of town, where we would release him. The driver seemed submissive enough and turned to get out of the cab but there was a sudden burst of fire from inside the garage, where there were actually two Tans. My two comrades were wounded.

'Percy was shot in the head and the left arm, while Mike had a remarkable escape. When the firing started, we all dropped to the ground and he was hit in the face by what must have been a "spent" bullet, which went up his nose and into his mouth, from whence, he "spat it out," as he told in his own racy style sometime later.'

During the exchange of fire, the driver was mortally wounded. 'We were sure that none of us fired at the driver, so he must have been hit by his own men shooting at us,' Williams explained. 'Mick and I managed to escape and the Tans raced off to their barracks in the vehicle. We took Percy to the Bon Secours Nursing Home in Strand Street, while the Black and Tans went on the rampage.

'In a few minutes, lorries with police dashed through the town, discharging intermittent shots,' according to the *Kerry People*. 'People in a state of terror took shelter where it could be found, and pandemonium prevailed for some time.

'Early next morning before dawn, Percy's two brothers – Michael and Jerry – and I helped to move him to the Mercy Hospital in Cork. Our driver was Tim Leahy, a Castleisland man who was in charge of transport for the brigade. A lorry driver for Slattery's bacon factory in Tralee, he knew the Cork road well.' Dr Mikey Shanahan made arrangements with the Mercy Hospital, and they left before dawn in order to avoid a possible hold-up by the Tans.'

The Killarney road was quiet and they went on from there through Macroom and on to Cork. 'I knew the Mercy Hospital well, as it was only about a hundred yards from the wireless college,' Williams wrote. 'After leaving Percy at the hospital, we went down to Mrs Carbury's on Sheares Street, where I had boarded while attending the college. She agreed to put the

Henafins and me up until Percy was out of danger.

The Cork No. 1 Brigade of the IRA had been informed about what had happened and told the three boys that their expenses would be taken care of locally. But the real action that night was taking place in Tralee. What happened there was even worse than the aftermath of the Mackinnon shooting. According to the *Kerry People*, 'Not in the worst of the reign of terror was such a night of horror experienced.'

Although the *Irish Times* was generally frowned on locally at the time as little more than a unionist propaganda organ, even it described what happened as an 'outbreak of the police'. The paper's report gives a flavour of the events:

> Tralee was in a state of siege for over three hours on Saturday night. Fighting began at about nine o'clock, when some members of the RIC appeared in the street, shouting and discharging firearms. People in the Roman Catholic churches awaiting Confessions remained there all night.
>
> The Republican forces quickly mobilised in Nelson Street, where a pitched battle was fought. The RIC retreated to Dominic Street, and for a half an hour volley after volley were exchanged. At about 12.30, military appeared in the streets and peace was restored.
>
> The outbreak of the police is attributed to the attempt made on the previous evening to capture a motor car during which one sergeant and one civilian were wounded.

Unlike on previous occasions, when the Black and Tans had been able to run amok without local resistance, the Republicans responded forcefully. The IRA had recently secured German rifles, which were being stored in O'Rourke's premises in Boherbee. These were now issued to the men. Although they were handicapped by the fact that they were unfamiliar with this type of weapon, they knew enough to make their presence felt as they fought back.

Very lights lit the sky on the Clash side of Boherbee and in the centre of the town. In local folklore, the Tans were put to flight that night: they were driven down Denny Street and retreated across the Green to the safety of their barracks. The IRA suffered no losses.

Tensions mounted and mobilisation orders were issued to the town companies and to all units from the surrounding districts. Next night, the IRA was ready for action, but the Crown forces remained within the comparative safety of their barrack walls. They had learned a lesson, as far as the local IRA was concerned.

Percy Hanafin rallied for a few days and was quite lucid for a time but then lapsed into unconsciousness and never came out of it again. He died following an operation, a week to the day after he had been shot. 'I was with him when he died, along with his two brothers,' Belty Williams recalled. 'They had lost a brother. I had lost a good comrade. We had joined Fianna Éireann together after growing up as next-door neighbours, living almost in one another's houses. I missed him sorely.'

'The funeral, which left for Rath Cemetery at three o'clock [on Sunday 29 January] was the largest and most impressive ever witnessed in Tralee,' according to the *Kerry People*. 'Upwards of 800 Volunteers and Fianna Boys marched in processional order after the remains, while many thousands of people from town and country, on foot, on horseback and in cars, joined in the procession.'

During the spring of 1922, Éamon de Valera and Michael Collins travelled around the country speaking on the Treaty. De Valera's visit to Kerry in late March was fairly uneventful in comparison with the visit by Collins the following month. Nevertheless, de Valera made more news: this was his most controversial speaking tour ever in Ireland. It was in Killarney that he uttered the controversial aphorism that 'The people have never a right to do wrong.' He blamed the press for distorting what he said, but people can make up their own minds.

On first learning of the terms of the 1921 Treaty, he initially announced that it was a matter for the Dáil Cabinet, which approved the Treaty by four votes to three, but the majority was really opposed to it. Robert Barton, the Minister for Agriculture, admitted that he personally disliked the Treaty, but he felt honour-bound to support it because he had signed the agreement in order that the people's representatives would have a say in the matter. De Valera therefore announced that it was a matter for Dáil Éireann.

When the Dáil approved the Treaty, however, de Valera announced that only the Irish people had the power to ratify the agreement. And in the following weeks, when it became apparent that the Irish people supported it, he seemed to question even the people's right.

On 15 March 1922, de Valera launched Cumann na Poblachta, which was essentially an anti-Treaty breakaway from Sinn Féin. He set out on a short speaking tour that took him to Dungarvan, Carrick-on-Suir, Thurles, Killarney and Tralee over the next five days. They were five days that shook the nation. and left an indelible imprint on de Valera's own reputation. It was during this swing through the country that he was accused of threatening Civil War, if the people ratified the Treaty.

'If the Treaty was accepted the fight for freedom would still go on,' he declared on St Patrick's Day in Carrick-on-Suir, according to the *Irish Independent*. 'The Irish people, instead of fighting foreign soldiers, would have to fight Irish soldiers of an Irish government, set up by Irishmen.'

De Valera always maintained that his words were taken out of context by the press. He tended to qualify his statements so much that his spoken sentences often became rather tortuous.

His line of argument was much easier to follow while listening to him, rather than trying to understand his words in cold print.

Reporters therefore tended to summarise what he said in order to make it more easily intelligible to readers, but in view of the importance of the issues at stake he is worth quoting at length. Here is what he actually said on the subject of the Treaty in Killarney on 19 March 1922:

In future, in order to achieve freedom if our Volunteers continue − and I hope they will continue until the goal is reached − if we continue on that movement which was begun when the Volunteers were started, and we suppose that this Treaty is ratified by your votes, then these men, in order to achieve freedom, would have to, as I said yesterday, march over the dead bodies of their own brothers. They will have to wade through Irish blood.

If you do not want that, do not put up that barrier, because, to use a phrase of the late Dr O' Dwyer [the Catholic Bishop of Limerick], so long as grass grows and water runs, so long as Irish children are born into this world, so long as Ireland remains unfree, they will be born with the spirit to achieve complete freedom.

It is not peculiar in our time to have Volunteers and men who are willing to give up their lives for the freedom of their country. Their aspirations will continue, and the next generation will strive to do it, and the road will be barred by their own fellow countrymen and, feeling that they have a right to complete freedom, they will not allow that to stand in the way. Therefore, they will oppose even the troops of an Irish government set up in accordance with that, because it will be felt that, even if the Treaty were ratified, it would not be ratified with your free will, but under the threat of war.

'Mr de Valera's wild speeches, with their threats of civil war, have been read everywhere with amazement,' the *Irish Times* observed. 'Our Dublin correspondent telegraphs that Mr de Valera has shocked the whole country,' the London *Times* reported. 'He has actually declared that, if the electors support the Treaty, his followers will wade through Irish blood to defeat it.'

De Valera indignantly denied that he was trying to incite civil war. He contended that he was merely assessing the situation realistically by refuting the argument that the Treaty contained the freedom to achieve freedom. He accused his critics of using his words to do the very thing of which they were accusing him. 'You cannot be unaware,' he wrote to the editor of the *Irish Independent*, 'that your representing me as inciting the civil war has on your readers precisely the same effects as if the inciting words were really mine.'

From a careful reading of his actual words in Killarney, it is clear that de Valera was not personally threatening civil war. He was saying that such a conflict would almost inevitably ensue if the Treaty was ratified. The press argued that, whether he was foretelling or threatening civil war, it was essentially the same thing, but de Valera disputed this. On the Sunday afternoon, he denounced the press at a rally of some 7,000 people in Market Square in Tralee. He complained that newspaper owners had an influence that was disproportionate to their value to society.

De Valera told the people of Tralee that, in making up their minds on the Treaty, they should not allow themselves to be hypnotised into thinking that something was true simple because they read it in a newspaper. In fact, he suggested, if they read it in the paper it was more likely to be untrue.

Although de Valera had no trouble in Kerry, things did not go as smoothly for Collins the following month, because the IRA's three Kerry brigades were all strongly anti-Treaty. The only split was strictly on the anti-Treaty side, as a result of the ongoing bitterness over the way Brigadier Paddy J. Cahill had been ousted. Humphrey Murphy, Liam Lynch and Andy Cooney had all been essentially hand in glove with the IRB element that had ousted Cahill, but the three of them were strongly anti-Treaty themselves. Murphy and Brigadier John Joe Rice of the No. 2 Brigade both proscribed the pro-Treaty rallies planned by Collins for Killarney on Saturday 22 April 1922 and for Tralee on the following day.

Collins arrived by train in Killarney on the Saturday morning, together with Seán MacEoin, Kevin O'Higgins and Fionán Lynch, as well as a twelve-man guard under Joe Dolan. They were met at the railway station by an anti-Treaty officer who told them that the meeting would not be allowed. Posters had already been put up around the town banning the gathering, and the platform built for the occasion had already been burned down.

The heavily armed contingent of anti-Treaty people had a Thompson sub-machine gun, but their threats were withdrawn following the intervention of a Franciscan priest. Collins was allowed to hold his rally in front of the Franciscan church, where the sloping ground formed a natural platform.

'"Maintain the Republic," Mr de Valera and his followers exhort us,' Collins exclaimed. 'What Republic? Do they mean the Republic we have had during the last few years with the British here – a Republic functioning incompletely, with British laws, British taxation, British stamps affixed to our cheques and agreements, paying our revenue to the British? Is that the Republic we are to maintain? A Republic during which ·the enemy was here hunting, imprisoning, torturing, shooting and hanging our people?'

Next day the Big Fellow and company went on to Tralee, where they again met with strong opposition. Special trains had been put on for the Sunday meeting, but only the Dingle train reached Tralee. Others from Killarney, Kenmare and Newcastle

West were stopped because rail lines had been taken up.

Virtually every road leading to the town was heavily obstructed; this was in marked contrast to de Valera's visit, when no effort was made by opponents to disrupt his rallies. Collins and his colleagues were at morning Mass when the Dean of Kerry, Monsignor O'Leary, denounced the attempts to prevent the meeting.

The military escort under Dolan had been strengthened with the addition of about two dozen men under Commandant Dinny Galvin of Knocknagoshel. Humphrey Murphy, the commandant of Kerry No. 1 Brigade, was less truculent than Rice had been in Killarney. As a member of the Supreme Council of the IRB, he had a better understanding and appreciation of Collins, even if he disagreed with him strongly over the Treaty. Murphy warned that there would be bloodshed if the rally went ahead.

'I said there would, but we were going to uphold the right of free speech, whatever the consequences,' MacEoin later explained. Some of those who were advocating free speech had seen nothing wrong with breaking up a meeting of Redmond's followers only a few years earlier, but now, when the shoe was on the other foot, they were highly critical of tactics they had previously used themselves. The anti-Treaty people could at least claim that they were consistent, even if their methods made a mockery of their supposed commitment to democracy.

Murphy suggested that both sides should confine their troops to barracks during the rally, and this was agreed. After 1 pm, the pro-Treaty volunteers were confined to their headquarters at the Central Technical School and the Central Hotel in Denny Street, while Murphy's men went to Ballymullen Barracks.

Some 4,000 people showed up for the rally in Denny Street, despite all the intimidation. Two or three shots were heard on the outskirts of the crowd, but they were not allowed to disrupt the proceedings.

Since publication of the *Kerryman* was still suspended after the burning of the newspaper's offices by the Auxiliaries, the *Kerry Leader* was trying to fill the local void. It came out on the Friday with a series of questions posed by Robert Barton, the one man who had signed the Treaty and later withdrawn his support for the document. The *Leader* suggested that Collins should answer those questions in Tralee. They were the kind of questions that would be asked again and again for the next fifty years.

Had the pro-Treaty men signed without fulfilling their commitment to the Cabinet, Barton asked. In a way, it was ironic that he should ask this question, because he actually believed that they had fulfilled all their obligations to consult the Cabinet before signing. It was only later that Barton came to the conclusion that, by promising not to sign the draft Treaty, Arthur Griffith had put the delegation under a further obligation.

Collins skilfully ducked the question with his reply in Tralee. 'Not one of the plenipotentiaries when they gathered together in their own house in London that night ever raised this question,' he said. That was quite true, but Barton was asking it now and it was being ignored.

Barton's second question was whether Collins and Eamonn Duggan had flatly refused to present counter-proposals following their return to London on the Sunday before the Treaty was signed. They certainly had, but Collins responded with a disingenuous distortion in which he sought to brush aside the question by appealing to the emotions of the crowd.

'No,' Collins lied, 'we did not definitely refuse. We put it like this, and there are members of the Dáil Cabinet who will bear me out on this.' Cathal Brugha had complained at the Cabinet meeting about the exclusion of Barton from the talks and Collins said that he just adopted the attitude that Barton could try for himself. 'Go ahead and see what you can do,' Collins had told him at the time, according to himself.

'That is the reason that I did not go, and my staying away

got better proposals than we would get otherwise, because they thought that I was going to take the field against them again.' The crowd cheered loudly. This was a time when emotion had more influence than reason. Collins continued: 'We ourselves are now responsible for the charging and collection of all tax – income tax, customs and excise, death duties, stamp duties, excess profits duty, corporation profits tax, etc, and all the moneys received now from the taxes are paid over to the Provisional Government and will be available for the Irish Parliament about to be elected to us for the benefit of the country.' This was the essence of independence as far as he was concerned.

After the rally, there was a celebratory meal, during which Galvin arrived to say that ten of his men had been disarmed by anti-Treaty people. MacEoin told him to take the arms of ten opponents, but when MacEoin retired to his room later he found Galvin there with ten prisoners. 'I didn't tell you to take prisoners,' MacEoin snapped. 'I told you to take rifles.'

Murphy arrived to secure the release of his men and a scene ensued as MacEoin grappled with him. 'I grabbed hold of him,' MacEoin recalled. 'He was at a disadvantage and I knocked him on my bed. That shook him – he was a fairly weighty man. Then I whipped him up, ran him through the door and shoved him down the stairs. I was vexed with myself, vexed with Galvin, vexed with everyone I could take it out on.'

'Unfortunately,' MacEoin continued, 'I jumped on him at the bottom of the stairs and I gave him a few pucks when Collins caught me by the collar, hauled me up, slammed me into a little room near the front of the stairs and locked the door.' After letting him cool off for what seemed like twenty minutes, Collins let MacEoin out and ordered him to shake hands with Murphy, which he did, grudgingly.

That Collins could get the two men to shake hands was a

measure of the bonds that still existed among members of the IRB, and he was determined to try to bring the two sides together. A number of pro- and anti-Treaty IRA officers were brought together in Dublin in early May. They included Humphrey Murphy, Eoin O'Duffy and Dan Breen. The officers realised that 'a conflict of comrades is inevitable', Kennedy recalled, unless the existing drift was stopped. To ensure this, they decided to recognise that the majority of the people were willing to accept the Treaty and they would then hold an agreed election with a view to forming a government that would have the 'confidence of the whole country,' Kennedy noted.

Some of the more active Kerry people were in Dublin during those talks. 'I was in the Clarence [Hotel] with Cathal Brugha the night the Military Pact was signed,' Tim Kennedy explained. Humphrey Murphy, Paddy Cahill, and Tom McEllistrim were also there. Murphy was actually one of the signatories of the pact that was agreed by the two sides, but Rory O'Connor and his more hardline colleagues, occupying the Four Courts, promptly denounced it. Nevertheless, the document became the basis for further discussions and ultimately led to the ill-fated election pact between de Valera and Collins on 20 May 1922.

In accordance with the pact, Sinn Féin set aside its differences over the Treaty and put forward candidates for the general election of 16 June 1922 in proportion to the existing Treaty divide within the party. Assuming that the party would win the ensuing election, they would form a coalition government, with the ministries being apportioned in relation to their existing strength – four anti-Treaty ministers for every five pro-Treaty ones. Other parties and independents were to be allowed to stand in the election.

Two days before the poll, Tim Kennedy was travelling from Dublin to Tralee when he met Michael Collins on the train. 'He persuaded me to go to Cork with him instead of going on to Tralee,'

Kennedy recalled. 'I did, and before arrival at Cork Station, we made arrangements to meet at the hotel where I was to stay with him. There was a tremendous crowd to meet him and I stayed in the door of the railway carriage until the platform had cleared.'

Tadhg Brosnan was working in Cork at the time and he was at the station. He noticed Kennedy and waited for him. 'We went to the meeting together,' Kennedy noted. 'To my astonishment, Michael Collins repudiated the pact. But he had never said a word to me that he would do so.'

Whether Collins actually repudiated the letter of the pact is open to question, but there is no doubt that he flouted the spirit of it when he called on the people at a rally in Cork to vote for the candidates who represented their views. This amounted to telling them to give their second-preference votes to independents or the pro-Treaty Labour Party instead of to any anti-Treaty Sinn Féin candidate. Even though many seats were uncontested, there was no doubt that, in contested seats, the overwhelming majority of people favoured giving the Treaty a chance. The Labour Party had put up eighteen candidates and seventeen of them were elected, in a development that clearly reflected growing public disillusionment with the squabbling in Sinn Féin.

Rory O'Connor and those occupying the Four Courts refused to accept the results of the election and announced that they were going to invade the Six Counties to restart the war. At that point, the British ordered their army in Dublin to clear out the Four Courts, but General Nevil Macready delayed. Those in the Four Courts seized a number of cars from a Dublin garage and took General J. J. O'Connell, the deputy chief of the Provisional Government army, prisoner. Infuriated by this move, Collins gave the order to attack the Four Courts in the early hours of 28 June 1922. British artillery was borrowed for the purpose. This was the start of the Civil War.

20

'The Ordinary Citizen Did Not Count'

The majority of Irish people clearly welcomed the Anglo-Irish Treaty, but the great majority of Republican activists in Kerry were opposed to it. 'To me in those days, the ordinary citizen did not count,' the late Pat 'Belty' Williams recalled shortly before his death. 'It was an attitude born of continued associations and indoctrination as a member of the guerrilla force. In later years, I saw the error of such thinking.'

Once the Civil War erupted, with the Free State attack on the Four Courts, the overwhelming majority of those who had been active in the IRA sided with the Republicans in Kerry. The No. 1 and No. 2 Kerry brigades joined forces to attack the Provisional Government's soldiers billeted at the workhouse in Listowel on 29 June. Johnny O'Connor of Kerry No. 1 Brigade noted that the government troops there had no stomach for a fight. 'We just fired and they surrendered,' O'Connor explained.

The Kerry IRA went to areas of County Limerick to defend a mythical defence line that they set up from Limerick to Waterford in what Éamon de Valera privately called 'the Republic of Munster'. John Joe Rice, the officer in charge of Kerry No. 2 Brigade, led his men to seize Rathkeale. 'There was no fight, for there was no one to fight,' Rice explained. The pro-Treaty forces had withdrawn to Limerick city.

The IRA, on the other hand, abandoned Limerick city – much to the disgust of Tom McEllistrim and his men. 'What's the use of carrying on a fight when we ran away in Limerick?'

McEllistrim's men asked him, he recalled. 'I knew the war was over when we left Limerick,' he commented.

'Our assignment was to hold a line based on towns like Bruree, Bruff, Kilmallock and Effen Bridge,' Pat Williams explained. 'The fighting was quite severe. We were fighting to prevent the Free State forces from advancing towards Kerry, but then we got word that they had encircled us by sea and landed a strong force at Fenit, and had taken Tralee without much difficulty, as the town was largely undefended.'

In the Tralee area, the squabbling over the Cahill affair continued. 'The division does not approve of the formation of a new battalion in the Tralee district,' Humphrey Murphy wrote to Cahill on 13 July. The post of deputy commander was again offered to Tadhg Brosnan, but he declined it. He was still not prepared to cooperate with what he considered to be the unfair way in which the whole matter had been handled.

While the others were off defending the front in Limerick, Cahill warned Murphy of 'the danger of coast landings' by Free State troops. 'Fenit, Dingle and Tarbert are likely places,' Cahill wrote. The Free State forces duly slipped behind IRA lines by sending a series of invasion parties in by sea, the first of which was at Fenit on 2 August 1922. That episode is well covered in Niall C. Harrington's book *Kerry Landing*, which provides an excellent first-hand account of Free State army's operations at Fenit and subsequent capture of Tralee within a matter of hours.

The whole operation had tremendous significance from a psychological standpoint. It was a daring manoeuvre that succeeded to a degree that the invading forces had had no right to expect. If the IRA could not hold Tralee for even a day, this was just another indication that they could never win the Civil War.

On 31 July 1922, some 450 troops boarded the ship *Lady Wicklow*. Brigadier Paddy O'Daly, who had been a senior member of Michael Collins's famous Squad, was in charge of the invasion force. With him were some of the Big Fellow's most trusted men; these included Jim McNamara and David Neligan, who had been the two most important spies in Dublin Castle during the Black and Tan period. The inclusion of such people in the invasion force was a testament to the importance that Collins attached to the whole operation.

The bulk of the men in this force were from Dublin. Although Niall Harrington was born in Dublin, he had been reared in Tralee, where his uncle had been the publisher of the *Kerry Sentinel*. O'Daly got advice from Harrington on the best route to take to Tralee from Fenit.

The *Lady Wicklow* docked at Fenit Pier without arousing the suspicions of the defenders. The troops were already disembarking before any shooting started. Efforts were made to warn the IRA in Tralee, but this was before the age of direct dialling. Nobody could get a telephone call in or out of Fenit without going through the local postmistress, who went into a frenzy of praying once the shooting started.

The Free State troops were already on their way to Tralee before word reached the town of the landing. Paddy Paul Fitzgerald, the officer in charge of the newly formed Ninth Battalion of the IRA's Kerry No. 1 Brigade, had been assigned the task of defending Fenit. On hearing of the landing, Fitzgerald telephoned Ballymullen military barracks, only to be greeted with incredulity at the news.

Captain Mike McGlynn dismissed the report as a false alarm, as there had been no such news from Fenit. Efforts to contact the postmistress in Fenit were futile. She was still intently beseeching divine protection – to the exclusion of all earthly considerations.

Most of the IRA's best men were away defending the mythical front line stretching from Limerick to Waterford, and there were no real plans to defend Tralee. John Joe Sheehy got a car and raced out in the direction of Fenit to see for himself, as did Captain Mike McGlynn.

On learning that the landing had indeed taken place, Sheehy raced back and gave the order to burn down Ballymullen Barracks, as the IRA had no chance of defending it. Panic obviously ensued, as the defenders sprinkled petrol around the ground floor and then ignited it, only to learn that a couple of men were asleep upstairs. The soldiers had to rescue them with a ladder – after prying the bars from a window of the second-floor dormitory.

'It was a near thing and it cost us valuable time,' Sheehy admitted years later. Johnny O'Connor arrived at Ballymullen 'to find our men there in the greatest state of funk and disorganisation I ever saw high-ranking officers,' he recalled. To make matters worse, their Model T Ford then refused to start, so they had to run back into town to set up a defensive position at Moyderwell Cross. By then it was too late to organise any kind of effective resistance. 'There was no plan,' O'Connor added, 'just firing of ammunition.'

The Kerrymen on the front line in County Limerick raced home, and next day the Free State forces had little difficulty in exploiting the situation. They seized Kilmallock, which had been left virtually defenceless. At the same time another Free State force, of 240 men, landed in Tarbert. They quickly took Ballylongford and then Listowel. Most of the members of this force were from the Western Division, but they included the famous contingent from Tralee who were known as 'the Dandy Six': Billy Clifford, Jack Flavin, Stephen Scannell, Jimmy Lyons, Tom Slattery and Harold Reid.

The loss of Tralee was a severe blow to the Republicans. In the following days the Free State forces captured Killarney, Castleisland and Killorglin with little difficulty. The IRA was in disarray and division headquarters was unable to find out what was happening on the ground. 'For God's sake give yer typewriter and index finger a rest for a few weeks,' Humphrey Murphy wrote. He was under acute pressure as commandant of the fractious Kerry No. 1 Brigade. Ballymacelligott and Castleisland Companies had been returned to the brigade after the removal of Cahill, but Tom McEllistrim and the Ballymacelligott men had little stomach for the Civil War after the Limerick fiasco.

'We have to keep shifting our HQ, owing to the poverty of the people in the most suitable places, and want of finance and proper supplies, etc,' Murphy noted. The brigade had already lost three of its four Lewis guns: two had been left in Tipperary and Kilmallock, and a third was captured in Castlemaine.

In the initial days of the Civil War, eleven Free State soldiers were killed. On 7 August Michael Collins attended a Requiem Mass in the library of Portobello Barracks for nine of the soldiers who had been killed in Kerry in recent days. 'The scenes at the Mass were really heartbreaking,' he wrote to his fiancée, Kitty Kiernan, afterwards. 'The poor women weeping and almost shrieking (some of them) for their dead sons. Sisters and one wife were there too, and a few small children. It makes one feel, I tell you.'

Up to this point, Collins had been stressing the necessity for moderation, but it was significant that next day he wrote to Joe McGrath, the director of intelligence, that 'Any man caught looting or destroying should be shot on sight.'

The IRA evacuated and burned the military barracks in Fermoy on 11 August 1922. It was the last post held by the Republicans. 'The first phase of the civil war was ended,' Florrie O'Donoghue wrote in his book *No Other Law*. O'Donoghue and many others recognised at this point that the IRA could not win the war. Michael Collins went south searching for peace.

Next day, 12 August, Collins was in Tralee. He sent David

Neligan to the county jail to see Tim Kennedy, who had been arrested by Eamonn A. Horan on 3 August 1922. Kennedy was just one of more than a hundred Republicans who had been arrested. Others included Paddy Paul Fitzgerald and Billy Mullins. All the prisoners were held in the county jail in Ballymullen.

Neligan said that Collins would visit Kennedy at the jail that evening, but this did not happen because, in the interim, Collins received word that President Arthur Griffith had died of a brain haemorrhage in Dublin. 'There seems to be a malignant fate dogging the fortune of Ireland, for at every critical period in her story the man whom the country trusts and follows is taken from her,' Collins moaned. 'Only those who have worked with him know what Arthur Griffith has done for Ireland; only they can realise how he has spent himself in his country's cause.'

'Is it possible that the death of Mr Arthur Griffith may unite the nation?' a reporter asked.

'At the moment I am a soldier,' Collins replied, 'but I think I can promise that if those who are against us will, even now, come forward and accept the terms offered by the government, our differences can be composed. I must not be misunderstood on this point.

'Militarily, our position warrants us in our belief that our opponents are in a hopeless position,' he continued. 'Look at the map: See where our troops are, what they have achieved and where the armed forces of the other side have been driven. But even so, it is not too late for de Valera and those who are with him to honour the passing of a great patriot by now achieving what that patriot has given his life for – a united Ireland and an Irish nation.'

The previous day, a further 200-strong invasion force under Commandant Tom 'Scarteen' O'Connor had landed in Kenmare. This force went on to take Rathmore and Millstreet before doubling back to capture Cahirciveen. By mid-August the Free State forces had taken the main centres of population in Kerry.

'Beyond the occupation of some of the more important towns, the national forces have been able to do very little,' the *Irish Times* reported. The Republicans ambushed government troops regularly on the roads of Kerry. The conflict turned particularly bitter. 'Nobody asked me to take my kid gloves to Kerry and I didn't take them,' General Paddy O'Daly explained.

One of the early defining moments of the Civil War occurred on 22 August, when Michael Collins was shot dead at Béal na mBláth, not far from his childhood home in west Cork. Who fired the fatal shot has long been a matter of controversy, but there can be little doubt that the killing was a tragedy. Some would later suggest that the Republicans had not meant to kill Collins, but they were involved in a Civil War, and there can be no doubt that the carefully planned ambush was not just a greeting party.

The Republicans lay in wait for Collins throughout most of the day but then concluded that he must have returned to Cork city by another route. Collins and his party had stopped for drinks at a number of places, and by the time they arrived at Béal na mBláth they were 'pissed,' according to Emmet Dalton. The ambush had already been called off and there were few more than half a dozen men left clearing up the site. They had already dismantled their road mine when the convoy of vehicles including Collins approached them. The first shots were fired into the air to warn the men on the road that troops were approaching. The Republicans did not realise that Collins was in the convoy, as they still assumed that he had returned to Cork by another route.

In the following years, accounts would be given of those who arrived on the scene in the midst of the shooting. One story – told by Father Patrick Twohig in his book *The Dark Secret of Bealnablath* – concerned a group of Kerrymen who were heading home through the fields after their defeat in Cork. The shooting at Béal na mBláth attracted them. 'We saw an army column stopped on the road below,' Michael O'Donoghue of Glenflesk recalled. 'Of course we threw ourselves down. The shooting had stopped now. There was a Whippet armoured car at the end of the line and there was a big man like he was standing on top of it looking around. The fellow next to me put up his gun and fired a shot and we saw the big man fall. I hit down the gun. "What did you do that for?" O'Donoghue asked. "Do you want to draw them on us!"'

The Kerrymen then got out of the place and did not learn until the following day that the big man was the Big Fellow himself. Father Twohig supports this story with a somewhat contradictory piece of evidence. There was a dance that night in Ballingeary. Pádraig Greene, a teacher from Ballinalee, County Longford, was in the area to attend an Irish course. He was standing with Liam Twomey, a local Republican, when O'Donoghue and the other Kerrymen arrived in the hall.

'What the hell is Mike O'Donoghue doing here!' exclaimed Twomey, who went over to talk to him, while Greene stayed put.

Moments later, Twomey returned with tears in his eyes. 'Michael Collins was shot this evening at Béal na mBláth,' Twomey said. 'My mother isn't going to like this!'

Father Twohig further boosts the story with an account by another Kerryman, Robert 'Bobs' Doherty from Glenflesk. He and James Sheehan, from near Killarney, were making their way home together. They were not part of O'Donoghue's party. They heard the firing over a nearby hill; each of them had a rifle and they raced over the hill.

'We dived for cover,' Doherty said, recalling that the grass was still wet from the recent shower. 'There were some men already in position near us, and a little distance away. I didn't know who they were. There was an armed column below us on the road and a big man started to walk away from it. Someone near us fired just then and I saw the big man fall. I heard him say: "I put two into him!" That's all I know.'

Austin Stack's reaction to the death of his former friend was poignant. 'He did great work for Ireland up to the truce – no man more,' he said.

Prior to Collins's death, the Civil War had been a virtual procession of victories for the Free State forces. On 26 August, however, a Free State convoy was ambushed between Tralee and Killorglin, and its commanding office, a Captain Burke, was killed. Two weeks later, the Free State forces suffered their biggest reverse when an eighty-four-strong IRA contingent under the command of Seán Hyde retook Kenmare. This contingent was a mixed force containing Republicans from throughout Munster.

David Robinson, a veteran of the First World War from Tipperary who was involved in this attack, complained that there was little planning for it. The Republicans had poor intelligence information and insufficient forces, as some men from Cork did not turn up. Robinson also suggested that there seemed to be 'a lack of assistance or enthusiasm on the part of the brigade staff.' The IRA lost a lot of time in looping, which was the practice of breaking a way through the walls of adjoining houses. They made their way to the post office, only to find that it was unoccupied. The Free State forces were concentrated mainly in the National Bank, the library and the workhouse. Robinson noted that, when they took the National Bank, the Republican troops were more interested in the contents of the bank than in moving on to take the library.

If the IRA was poorly prepared for the attack, the Free State forces were utterly disorganised. Tom 'Scarteen' O'Connor, the local Free State commander, was shot dead at his home, along with his brother, at the start of the attack. Some thirty Free State troops deserted, and their colleagues were never able to organise themselves properly. After the fall of the forces at the National Bank, their comrades at the library and workhouse surrendered: they walked down the main street carrying a white flag. In all, 120 Free State troops, including a younger brother of Kevin O'Higgins, the Minister for Justice, were taken prisoner. They were all promptly released, because the Republicans had no place to hold them. The IRA was content with the haul of arms. John Joe Rice reported that 110 rifles were seized, along with two Lewis guns and 20,000 rounds of .303 ammunition.

Although Rice was prepared to share some of the ammunition, he refused a request for rifles by the IRA in Cork. 'No day passes without a fight of some description,' he wrote, 'and I cannot spare a single rifle out of the brigade, unless I want to have a fearful row, which I do not wish, now that everything is working smoothly.'

The success of the Kenmare operation provided a tremendous boost to IRA morale. 'Kenmare kept us going,' Rice later told Ernie O'Malley.

Next day, seven IRA men retook Tarbert, and Free State troopers were killed when a convoy under Colonel J. McGuinness was ambushed between Killarney and Rathmore. 'The development of the campaign has been more rapid and satisfactory in Kerry than in any other area,' Liam Lynch, the IRA chief of staff, wrote on 17 September 1922. 'Enemy columns several hundred strong can move along the hills in full view and complete impunity,' the *Irish Times* reported on 27 September.

But this was the high-water mark of the Republican campaign. That same day the IRA launched its own attack: an attempt to take the town of Killorglin with a force of some 500 men. This assault was led by Seán Hyde and Humphrey Murphy, but the attack 'was a total failure,' according to David Robinson, who reported that two Republicans were killed, fifteen were wounded and fourteen captured. He was again highly critical of the organisation and planning of the assault. He was a veteran of the First World War whose idea of 'planning was based on the fact that you could always afford to lose thirty or forty men,' according to John Joe Rice. Of course, Rice added that Robinson 'would reserve the most dangerous part of an operation for himself.'

'I had a section specially picked for the workhouse, which was a mile outside the town,' Rice recalled. He had a local farmer, Mike O'Brien, scout the place for him. As they were overlooking Killorglin, Robinson was standing on a railway trolley with a pair of field glasses and a blackthorn stick.

'Who is that man over there on the trolley?' Mike asked.

'That's General Robinson,' Rice replied.

'He's a quare general indeed,' said Mike, 'if he thinks this town is going to be taken with a blackthorn stick and a pair of field glasses.'

Part of the IRA's plan was to blow up the military barracks. They tried to worm their way from one house to the next. Sometimes they went by the backyards, other times by knocking a hole in the wall between adjoining houses.

'Our plans were upset, however, when we learned that there was a machine-gun post located in the Belfry, or Square Tower,' Pat 'Belty' Williams recalled. 'We had reached our objective by noon, but the machine-gunner in the tower made it impossible for the engineers to furnish us with the mine that was to be used to destroy the barracks. As a result, our party was trapped until after nightfall. By then, word was received of a large relief force of Free State troops on their way from Tralee. Believing that discretion was the better part of valour, we retreated got away under the cover of darkness.'

One of those involved in this operation was Jack Galvin of Killorglin, who admitted under interrogation that he had killed a pro-Treaty officer during an attack on a bridge in Castlemaine the previous week. Galvin was found dead near Ballyseedy the following day. 'I cannot believe that Mulcahy would tolerate it for a minute,' David Robinson wrote, 'but I wonder would he take enough trouble to find out the real truth?' Galvin was just one of at least forty Republicans who died in Free State custody in Kerry.

A month earlier, Sean Moriarty of Tralee had been taken by pro-Treaty troops to the grounds of Balloonagh Convent, where he was shot and left for dead, but he survived to tell the tale. Jeremiah Casey of Beaufort, Thomas Prendeville of Castleisland, John Lawlor of Ballyheigue, and Herbert Murphy were not so fortunate. Casey had been with Republican forces in the west but had quit the fight and returned to Beaufort. He offered to surrender, but when he did he was shot dead. John Lawlor was arrested on October 30. No explanation was given as to how he died. His body was unceremoniously dumped on the street outside the church gate.

General Richard Mulcahy, the commander-in-chief of the Free State army, asked the Dáil to authorise the army to execute people who were found to be in possession of arms. He warned that, otherwise, the men would take it upon themselves 'to execute people in an unauthorised way.' Of course, they were already doing this in Kerry.

The unauthorised possession of a gun was made a capital offence. By November 1922, the struggle had taken on a regular pattern. 'All members of the IRA had gone back to their own districts and were on the run there,' Seamus O'Connor of Knocknagoshel wrote. 'Though we did not know it then, our side had lost and, in reality, the war was over.' But the Republican leadership refused to recognise this for another six months and the struggle plumbed the depths of a depravity worse than anything that had been witnessed in Black and Tan times.

On 19 December 1922, the Free State army issued posters stating that Matthew Moroney of Boherbee, Tralee, Thomas Devane of Dingle, Dermot O'Connor of Moyderwell, Tralee, and Con Casey of Bridge Street, Tralee, had been found guilty of possessing a weapon. But the military indicated that the sentences would not be carried out, on condition that all attacks on Free State troops be stopped and that interference with railways, roads and private property cease. Otherwise, the military warned that 'the stay on the execution of the sentences will be removed and the sentences of death on each of the above-named will be forthwith carried out.'

The four men were effectively being held as hostages over the Christmas period. On Saturday 23 December, Daniel J. Browne was arrested as he alighted from a train in Tralee. That evening, Free State troops took over a number of farmhouses at Curaheen, about three miles from Tralee. The following morning they surrounded the local church during Mass and afterwards arrested twenty-two members of Paddy Cahill's column. Seven of these men were found hiding under the altar. Fortunately for all, none was armed. The death sentences of the four men held over Christmas were subsequently commuted.

21

'DIFFICULT TO SURPRISE OR SHOCK US'

Although it was apparent to most Republicans that they could not win the Civil War, Liam Lynch still held out, telling himself that the IRA would somehow get hold of heavy artillery that would turn the tide of the war. The Free States forces had control of all the towns in Kerry, but the hinterland was so hostile that it was necessary to close the more isolated posts, just as the British had abandoned their isolated barracks during the War of Independence. The Free State troops had to move in convoys between the towns and there were frequent IRA ambushes on the main Tralee–Castleisland, Tralee–Killorglin and Tralee–Killarney roads.

The war was made all the more bitter because the Free State troops were like an occupying force in Kerry. In many areas, the Republicans could move about freely, as even pro-Treaty families helped them. Although the Free State forces were on the brink of victory, they were unable to seal it, and, in their frustration, they became all the more ruthless.

Seventy-seven IRA prisoners were officially executed for possession of arms. Seven of these were executed in Tralee: James J. Daly of Knockeenduff, Killarney; John Clifford of Mountlake, Cahirciveen; Michael Brosnan of Ballyfedora, Rathany, Tralee; and James Hanlon of Causeway were officially executed at Ballymullen Barracks on 20 January 1923.

The situation became so bad that the many IRA members felt that they could no longer stay in their safe houses. They had to sleep in dugouts or in the open. Some of the better dugouts were in turf sheds under piles of turf or, in at least one instance, hidden under a pile of manure.

Most of the Free State troops were from outside Kerry, but there were a few local men in their midst who used their local knowledge to capture men on the run. Special animosity was reserved for men like 'the Dandy Six' and Lieutenant Paddy 'Pats' O'Connor in Castleisland, where the Free State garrison was 'alarmingly successful in picking up members of the Castleisland Company in night raids on the houses in which they had been sleeping,' according to Seamus O'Connor of Knocknagoshel.

Some months earlier, Paddy Pats O'Connor's father, Pats O'Connor of Glounsharoon, near Castleisland, had got into an argument with IRA men Patrick Buckley and John Daly. When Free State troops visited the locality shortly afterwards, Buckley and Daly suspected that Pats O'Connor had called them. He was seized, held prisoner for three days and ordered to pay the Republicans a hundred pounds, which he and his family refused to do. The IRA then seized his ten cows, wrecked his home and stole what money he had – thirty-six pounds and five shillings – on 16 December 1922. His son was so incensed that he joined the Free State troops in Castleisland the next day, and wreaked havoc on the local IRA.

On 4 February 1923, O'Connor helped the Free State troops to capture John Daly and Patrick Buckley – the men who had initially got into the argument with his father. Buckley was something of a hero among Republicans because, as an RIC constable, he had persuaded his colleagues to hand over their barracks in Newmarket-on-Fergus to the IRA; this was the only time the IRA ever captured a barracks intact.

Humphrey Murphy ordered the IRA to kill Lieutenant Paddy Pats O'Connor. Initially, the plan was to blow him up in the barracks in Castleisland, but that proved impractical, so they decided to lure him to a bomb. A trap mine was prepared and placed in Ballanarig Wood near Knocknagoshal, just off the main road. The trigger mine was attached to a weapon which was left lying at the scene so that it would go off if anyone picked up the gun. A letter to O'Connor from a local informer had been intercepted some time earlier and a young woman who was an IRA sympathiser forged a letter in similar handwriting to lure O'Connor to the mine.

O'Connor duly took the bait: he walked into the trap around two o'clock the following morning, 6 March 1923. The explosion decapitated him and killed four others who were with him: Captains Michael Dunne and Joseph Stapelton, both of the Dublin Brigade, and Privates Michael Galvin of Killarney and Laurence O'Connor of Causeway. Another soldier was so badly injured that he lost both legs as a result of the explosion.

The men who had set the mine were sleeping in a dugout covered by a turf shed about a mile away. They woke to the sound of an explosion.

'The mine,' somebody said.

'The Lord have mercy on their souls,' Seamus O'Connor remarked.

'I struck a match and looked at the watch,' O'Connor recalled. 'It was two o'clock. Then we all turned over and fell asleep. Our falling asleep immediately may now look dreadfully callous, but by this time it would be difficult to surprise or shock us. We were living from day to day, fatalistically untroubled, and not thinking of what the next hour might hold, though the instinct for survival was, perhaps, as strong as ever.'

The Free State troops retaliated with a vengeance, killing no fewer than nineteen Republican prisoners in Kerry in the next two weeks. Dunne and Stapelton had served in the Squad with Paddy O'Daly. He promptly issued orders to all officers in the

Kerry Command that 'in the event of encountering any obstacles, such as stone barricades, and also dugouts or dumps, they are not to interfere with same. The officer or NCO in charge should immediately proceed to the nearest detention barracks and bring with him a sufficient number of Irregular prisoners to remove same. The tragedy of Knocknagoshel must not be repeated and serious disciplinary action will be taken against any officer who endangers the lives of his men in the removal of such barricades.'

But O'Daly and his men were not prepared to wait for IRA prisoners to be killed by moving booby-trapped barricades. A mine was constructed by Captains Ed Flood and Jim Clarke in Tralee and, with the full knowledge and approval of Major General O'Daly, this was placed in a pile of stones in the middle of the road at Ballyseedy Cross, a little over three miles outside Tralee.

Nine prisoners, who had been mistreated over a number of days, were taken from Ballymullen Barracks in Tralee. The men were not selected for having done anything in particular, but because they were on the Republican side. One of the main criteria in their selection was that they were not closely related to any priests or nuns, so as not to antagonise unduly the clergy or, to be more specific, the hierarchy, which tended to be supportive of the Free State side. The prisoners were selected by Colonel David Neligan, who picked John Daly, Michael O'Connell and Patrick Buckley of Castleisland; Stephen Fuller, George O'Shea and Tim Twomey of Kilflynn; Patrick Hartnett of Finuge; James Walsh of Churchill; and John O'Connor from Waterford.

The Republicans were taken from Ballymullen Barracks in an army truck and brought to Ballyseedy. On the way, Commandant Ned Breslin of Donegal offered them a cigarette each, saying it would be 'the last you'll have.' He told them they were going to be blown up with a mine, just like the Free State soldiers had been killed at Knocknagoshel. On several occasions in recent days, they had been taken out and told they were going to be shot, so they would not have known what was in store for them – at least not initially. They may have thought that the soldiers really wanted them to make a break for it so that they could be shot while trying to escape.

The men were ordered to stand around a pile of rocks in which a mine had been placed earlier. 'They then came round the front of us and tied our ankles and knees. One fellow asked to be let say his prayers and the fellow who was tying him hit him on the top of the head with the rope and said, "No prayers",' Stephen Fuller recalled. 'Just like children, we did as we were told and no more,' he said.

'Some of you fellows might go to heaven. If you do, you can say hello to our boys,' the soldier added. Escape was out of the question. The soldiers moved away about 150 yards. An officer stayed behind. 'You can be praying away as long as you like,' he said.

'I kept my eyes on him all the time,' Fuller added, 'and it wasn't until the fellow beside me started saying his prayers that I thought of saying mine. I said, "Goodbye", and George O'Shea said, "Goodbye, goodbye, lads." Then the mine went off.'

By some freak, Fuller was blown clear and found himself beside the road. 'I made for the ditch,' he said. He slipped across a shallow river. At that point, the soldiers opened rapid fire with a machine-gun to kill the wounded. 'I thought they were firing at me and I ran until I met another fence and met the gable of a house,' he recalled. The house was Curran's at Hanlon's Cross. Its occupants were the first of many families – not all of them Republican sympathisers – who sheltered Stephen Fuller. In the darkness, the soldiers did not realise that they had not killed all the men.

The Free State Army issue the following statement in relation to the incident:

A party of troops proceeding from Tralee to Killorglin last night came across a barricade of stones build on the roadway at Ballyseedy Bridge.

The troops returned to Tralee and brought out a number of prisoners to remove the obstruction.

While engaged in this work, a trigger mine (which was concealed in the structure) exploded, wounding Captain Edward Breslin, Lieutenant Joseph Murragh and Sergeant Ennis, and killing eight of the prisoners.

Johnny O'Connor and Johnny Duggan of Farmer's Bridge collected Fuller in a pony and trap and took him to a dugout, where Dr Shanahan of Farranfore treated him. 'All the skin was burnt off my hands and the skin was burnt off the back of my legs,' Fuller recalled. 'My hands were tied behind my back and met the full force of the explosion.'

The same day as the Ballyseedy massacre, a similar incident took place at Countess Bridge, Killarney. Jer Donoghue, Stephen Buckley, Daniel Donoghue, Tim Murphy and Tadhg Coffey had been taken from jail to the bridge. There was a low barricade of stones across the road and the men were ordered to move them out of the way. They saw a soldier at the far side of the fence bending down and the rest of the soldiers draw the bolts of their guns. The prisoners thought they were to be shot while moving the stones. Then the mine went off. When Coffey looked up, he could see Murphy, Buckley and Dan Donoghue, covered with blood, moaning and moving feebly on the ground. They were not dead, but grenade after grenade was thrown among them and shots were fired. Amid the confusion, Coffey made it to a wood and escaped.

Five days later, in Cahirciveen, the Free State troops made sure that nobody would escape, by shooting five men in the legs before laying them over a landmine and blowing them up. On this occasion, one of the Free State soldiers, a Lieutenant

McCarthy, was so revolted by what had occurred that he publicised the story.

'There were six or eight in the lot that murdered them,' McCarthy said. 'It was a murder gang that is going around trying to keep on the war. We ourselves will support the Free State government and fight for it, but we will not fight for murder.'

Two other prisoners – Bertie Murphy of Castleisland and Jeremiah Casey of Beaufort – were also killed while in Free State custody that week, and James Walsh of Currow was killed in similar circumstances the following week. Richard Mulcahy had persuaded the Dáil to make the possession of a firearm a capital offence, in order to prevent the soldiers taking the law into their own hands, but they were doing it anyway and the government was turning a blind eye to it. Niall Harrington was so disgusted with the conduct of the Free State troops that he prepared his own report for Kevin O'Higgins, the Minister for Justice. Based in south Kerry, he feared for his own life once his colleagues learned that he had reported their barbarous activities. He therefore asked to be transferred out of Kerry.

When he was moved to Tralee, Harrington feared the worst and spent a night in Benner's Hotel in an armchair facing the door, with two loaded pistols at the ready. But it transpired that his move to Tralee had been the result of a clerical error and word of his transfer up the country came through the following day.

With the publication of Fuller's story, Richard Mulcahy, the Minister for Defence, ordered an army inquiry, but this was always going to be a whitewash, because he selected Major General Paddy O'Daly – the man who was essentially behind the whole thing – to preside at the inquiry, along with two of his own officers: Colonel J. McGuinness and Major General Eamonn 'Bob' Price from headquarters.

The inquiry was a monumental charade. One officer testified

that he had been bringing a message to Killorglin when he came across the barricade, so he returned to Ballymullen Barracks to get some prisoners to clear the road, in line with O'Daly's orders. Commandant Breslin then testified that he delivered nine prisoners to Ballyseedy. 'I got the prisoners out of the truck, lined them up, told them what I had brought them there for, and instructed them to remove the barricade, which they proceeded to do,' Breslin testified. 'I inspected the barricade myself. I became suspicious and asked my men to move back. The prisoners were at work on the barricade for a couple of minutes when I heard a very loud explosion. For a few minutes after that, I was knocked to the ground. When I got up, I found that the bodies had been scattered on the road.'

This was a tissue of lies. There was no mention of the machine-gun being used, to ensure that all the men were killed. If the government had been remotely interested in the truth, it would only have had to examine the mutilated bodies to find the bullet wounds.

So many people were being killed while in military custody in Kerry that the army issued orders on 21 March that henceforth 'Prisoners who die while in military custody in the Kerry Command shall be interred by the troops in the area in which the death has taken place.' This was tantamount to approving the barbarities that were being perpetrated and merely telling the soldiers to cover up their vile acts properly.

The previous autumn, General Paddy O'Daly and David Neligan had had a secret meeting in Ballymacelligott with John Joe Rice and Tom McEllistrim at the home of a well-known imperialist. Although none of them were supposed to be armed, Neligan threw open his coat at one point to reveal two guns. Rice had taken the precaution of coming to the gathering armed as well. Nothing came of the meeting.

'I suppose it's safe to stay in Ballymacelligot?' MacEllistrim asked before the other two departed.

'Oh yes, for a few days,' replied O'Daly. But the area was searched within a couple of hours.

Further efforts were being made to persuade the IRA to abandon the Civil War. Most of the Republican prisoners in Kerry County Jail were transferred to the internment camp at the Curragh, but three were retained in Tralee, with a view to them making contact with their Republican colleagues. These three were Paddy Paul Fitzgerald, Billy Mullins and Tim Kennedy. The men were approached by James McNamara, who was the intelligence officer in charge of the Kerry Command of the Free State forces and had been one of the two most important spies that Collins had had within Dublin Castle. McNamara had worked with Tim Kennedy before, and he was asked by the chief of staff, General Eoin O'Duffy, to get in touch with Paddy Cahill in order to arrange a meeting with O'Daly and McNamara.

The meeting duly took place, in a hotel, but adjourned, at Cahill's request, so that he could consult with colleagues. That night, however, some former British soldiers in the Free State army, led by Jimmy Wall, raided Cahill's father's house. They did not find Cahill there, as he had taken the precaution of staying at T. J. Liston's house in Ballyard that night. Cahill promptly broke off the negotiations the following day, accusing the others of reneging on their guarantee of safe conduct. For their part, O'Daly and McNamara asserted that the peace initiative was so secret that the men who had carried out the raid had not known about it and had merely searched Cahill's father's house by chance.

McNamara left Tralee under strange circumstances. Tim Kennedy stated that McNamara came to him to say that he was being sent back because he would not comply with orders instructing him to mistreat Republican prisoners. 'Dave Neligan told me afterwards that MacNamara was admitted to hospital with a bullet wound in his head, from which he died,' Kennedy noted. 'The bullet, he alleged, was fired by some National Army lad who belonged to what was known as "the Dublin murder gang".'

Kennedy was in fact released and went to Dublin to contact Austin Stack to try to arrange an end to hostilities. 'Though I didn't succeed, I am sure I made a strong impression,' Kennedy wrote afterwards.

'I attended brigade meetings at Daly's of Knockancoulteen and at other places where the question of carrying on the war and other matters were discussed. I drafted what I thought should be the "conditions", if I might put it that way, of unconditional surrender, and that document was found on Stack when he was captured.'

When the IRA executive convened on 24 March 1923, de Valera wanted it to call off the fighting. Among the Kerrymen present at this meeting were Austin Stack, Humphrey Murphy and John Joe Rice. Stack supported de Valera – much to the irritation of Liam Lynch, the IRA chief of staff.

'You have the wind up!' Lynch said to Stack.

Tom Barry of Cork said the war was lost, but Bill Quirke challenged that assessment.

'When was the last fighting in Kilkenny?' Barry asked.

'Eighteen sixty-seven,' replied Quirke, and those assembled collapsed into laughter, according to Rice.

The meeting adjourned for a couple of weeks. Stack, who was extremely upset by Lynch's remark about him being windy, produced the document drawn up by Kennedy and asked the executive to sign it. This document called on de Valera 'to order an immediate cessation of hostilities.' But the others refused to sign. Three days later, Stack was captured with that document in his pocket. It probably saved his life.

Meanwhile, the fighting continued in Kerry. On the morning of 6 April 1923, there were exchanges near Glencar in Derry na Feena, a gray, barren valley under the shadow of the Macgillicuddy Reeks, which looms over Loch Acoose, one of the most desolate lakes in Kerry. The Free Staters tried to surround members of the IRA in a pre-dawn operation.

The Free State soldiers were seen by sentries Bill Landers and Dan O'Shea, both from Tralee. 'They [the Free Staters] opened fire on a party of troops moving along the foot of the mountain in a pincer movement,' Pat Williams wrote later. 'Awakened by the gunfire, we were not long getting out of the cottages of the mountainy men.'

As George Nagle emerged from one cottage, he was hit in the leg; this ruined his chances of escaping. 'Our retreat was almost vertical – virtually straight up the mountain,' Williams recalled. 'But for the persistent fire of Landers – keeping the Free State forces from making too fast an advance – we would have lost more than the two men who were killed.'

Having heard of what had happened to so many prisoners, the Republicans were not prepared to risk capture. 'It was almost a certainty at that stage of the Civil War that "captured" meant "summary execution" – in many cases without any kind of trial,' Williams said.

'The Republicans retreated up a nearby ravine until we were more or less out of range of the rifle fire,' Williams continued. 'When the fighting died down, Nagle asked Molly O'Brien, the woman of the house where he had been staying, for a glass of water. As she was fetching it, the Free State troops arrived. She heard the shot outside and found Nagle shot through the heart. The soldiers then took a cart from a nearby shed and put the body on it and took it away.'

The Free State soldiers also captured Conway O'Connor, who had been shot in the shoulder. From the hill above, his companions could see him being led away by the Free Staters. It was the last time they saw him alive. A little later, some people met the troops with the cart carrying the bodies of Nagle and O'Connor.

In mid-April, there was one last, epic struggle in Kerry, when Free State troops trapped Timothy 'Aero' Lyons and five comrades in Clashmealcon Caves near Kerry Head. Lyons had got his nickname from his reputation for escaping from the tightest corners, as he seemed to vanish into thin air. This time there was no escape, however. For three days and two nights, the Republicans held out as the Free State soldiers tried to smoke them out. The Free Staters mistakenly believed that de Valera and Humphrey Murphy were in the cave. Two soldiers who tried to go down to the cave were shot dead, and two of the IRA men – Tommy McGrath and Patrick O'Shea – fell to their deaths while trying to scale the cliff in the darkness.

Finally, on 18 April 1923, Lyons decided to give himself up. The soldiers dropped a rope to him, but as he neared the top of the cliff the rope gave way and he fell a hundred feet to the rocks below. He was then riddled with bullets where he lay. He was, as the Black and Tans used to say, 'Shot while trying to escape.'

Lyons's three remaining comrades – Jim McEnery, Edward Greaney and Reginald Hathaway – were taken to Tralee and executed on 25 April 1923. It just two days before Frank Aiken – who replaced Liam Lynch as IRA chief of staff – ordered 'the suspension of all offensive operations' from noon on the last day of the month. The Civil War was over, but the bitterness lasted for generations, as the memories of Ballyseedy and the other atrocities were regularly aired, especially at election time. Nobody was ever charged, or even disciplined, for those atrocities.

Stephen Fuller recognised that there had been wrong on both sides, and he refused to talk about the events, because he felt that would only perpetuate the bitterness. In 1980, while he was in a nursing home, shortly before his death, he finally gave an interview on the atrocities of the time to Robert Kee, a British historian who was compiling a television history of the period.

Over the years, much of the talking was left to those who had only a peripheral involvement in the Civil War, with the result that the actual record became distorted. But the war had been so traumatic that those who had been most active in it wished to put the events behind them. Soon few would know what the Civil War had been about. Many thought it was about the partition issue, but neither the debates nor the documents of the time sustain that belief.

The worst of the atrocities of the Civil War occurred in Kerry, with the result that the conflict left a bitter legacy, but J. J. Barrett argued persuasively in his book *In the Name of the Game* that Gaelic football played a major role in binding up the old wounds. In 1923, Kerry won the Munster Championship, while some of the best players were still in jail, so a game was arranged between the team and the internees. Then the following year the two sides got together, with people like Con Brosnan, a Free State army officer, and John Joe Sheehy, the commandant of Kerry No. 1 Brigade, playing on the same team. This team, with Sheehy as captain, went on to win the all-Ireland title. The football field became the place where even the most bitter differences could be resolved.

Ned Breslin, the officer who had been in charge of the Free State troops at Ballyseedy on the night of the massacre, later married a sister-in-law of George O'Shea, one of the men he had helped kill. He frequently visited Kerry and one night entered a bar in which Stephen Fuller was drinking. Fuller did not say a word. He just finished his drink, got up and walked out.

BIBLIOGRAPHY

ARCHIVE SOURCES

Ernie O'Malley papers, UCD Archives, Dublin; Todd Andrews papers, UCD Archives, Dublin; Michael Collins papers, National Library of Ireland, Dublin; Austin Stack papers, private sources; minute-book of Irish Volunteers, Kerry County Museum, Tralee; diary of Christy O'Gray, Kerry County Museum, Tralee; Christy O'Grady papers, private source; transcript of Thomas McEllistrim's interview with the Bureau of Military History, Tom McEllistrim Jr; transcript of Con Brosnan's interview with the Bureau of Military History, private source; Ernie O'Malley's notebooks, UCD Archives, include interviews with Con Casey, Andy Cooney, Tim Kennedy, John Joe Rice, Michael Fleming, Johnny O'Connor, Dennis Quill

NEWSPAPERS

Éire, the *Evening Mail* (Dublin), the *Freeman's Journal,* the *Irish Independent,* the *Kerry Advocate,* the *Kerry Evening Post,* the *Kerry Sentinel,* the *Montreal Gazette,* the *Toronto Globe,* the *Manchester Guardian, The Irish Times,* the *Liberator* (Tralee), the *Kerry Champion,* the *Kerry People,* the *Kerry Weekly Reporter,* the *Kerryman,* the *Killarney Echo, The New York Times, The Times* (London)

BOOKS AND JOURNALS

Abbott, Richard. *Police Casualties in Ireland, 1919-1922.* Dublin and Cork: Mercier Press, 2000.

Allen, Gregory. *The Garda Síochána: Policing Independent Ireland, 1922–82.* Dublin: Gill & Macmillan, 1999.

Andrews, C. S. *Dublin Made Me: An Autobiography.* Cork: Mercier Press, 1979.

Barrett, J. J. *In the Name of the Game.* Dublin: Privately printed, 1997.

Comyn, James. *Irish at Law: A Selection of Famous and Unusual Cases.* London: Martin Secker & Warburg, 1981.

Cronin, Sean. *The McGarrity Papers.* Tralee: Anvil Books, 1972.

Deasy, Liam. *Brother Against Brother.* Cork: Mercier Press, 1982.

_____. *Towards Ireland Free.* Cork: Mercier Press, 1973.

Dee, Con. 'The Valley of Knockanure,' *Shannonside Annual, 1958.*

Fitzpatrick, David. *Politics and Irish Life, 1913–1921: Provincial Experience of War and Revolution.* Cork: Cork University Press, 1998.

Gaughan, J. Anthony. *A Political Odyssey: Thomas O'Donnell (MP for West Kerry 1900–1918).* Dublin: Kingdom Books, 1983.

_____. *Austin Stack: Portrait of a Separatist.* Dublin: Kingdom Books, 1977.

_____. *Listowel and its Vicinity.* Dublin: Kingdom Books, 1973.

_____. *Memoirs of Constable Jeremiah Mee, RIC.* Dublin: Kingdom Books, 1975.

Gwynn, Denis. *Traitor or Patriot? The Life and Death of Roger Casement.* New York: 1931.

Harrington, Niall C. *Kerry Landing.* Dublin: Anvil Books, 1992.

Herlihy, Jim. *The Royal Irish Constabulary: A Short History and Genealogical Guide.* Dublin: Four Courts Press, 1997.

Hopkinson, Michael. *Green Against Green: The Irish Civil War.* Dublin: Gill & Macmillan, 1988.

Hyde, H. Montgomery. *Famous Trials 9: Roger Casement.* London: Penguin Books, 1964.

Inglis, Brian. *Roger Casement.* London: Hodder and Stoughton, 1973.

Kerryman, The. *Kerry's Fighting Story.* Tralee: The Kerryman, 1947.

_____. *Sworn to be Free: The Complete Book of IRA Jailbreaks 1918-1921.* Tralee: Anvil Books, 1971.

Lynch, Denis. 'The Years of Ambushes and Round-Ups', *Journal of Cumann Luachra,* June 1989.

Lynch, Florence Monteith. *The Mystery Man of Banna Strand: Irish Brigade, 1915-16.* New York: Vantage Press, 1959.

Macardle, Dorothy. *The Irish Republic: A Documented Chronicle of the Anglo-Irish Conflict and the Partitioning of Ireland, with a Detailed Account of the Period 1916-23.* London: Corgi, 1968.

_____. *Tragedies of Kerry.* Dublin: Irish Freedom Press, 1924.

MacColl, René. *Roger Casement.* London: Hamish Hamilton, 1956.

MacEoin, Uinseann. *Survivors: The Story of Ireland's Struggle as Told through Some of Her Outstanding Living People Recalling Events from the Days of Davitt, through James Connolly, Brugha, Collins, Liam Mellows and Rory O'Connor, to the Present Time.* Dublin: Argenta Publications, 1980.

Martin, Hugh. *Ireland in Insurrection.* London: Daniel O'Connor, 1921.

Moynihan, Manus. 'Troubled Times . . . A First-Hand Account of the Bog Road Ambush,' *Journal of Cumann Luachra,* 1982.

Neeson, Eoin. *The Civil War in Ireland 1922-23.* Cork: Mercier Press, 1966.

Ó Céilleachair, Seán. 'Tureengarriv Ambush', *Journal of Cumann Luachra,* 1983.

O'Connor, Seamus. *Tomorrow Was Another Day.* Tralee: Anvil Books, 1970.

O'Donoghue, Florence. *No Other Law.* Dublin: Anvil Books, 1986.

O'Farrell, Padraic. *Who's Who in the Irish War of Independence and Civil War, 1916-1923.* Dublin: Lilliput Press, 1997.

O'Grady, Brian. 'Where Eddie Carmody Died', *The Shannonside Annual*, 1960.

Ó Luing, Seán. *I Die in a Good Cause*. Tralee: Anvil Books, 1970.

O'Malley, Ernie. *The Singing Flame*. Dublin: Anvil Books, 1978.

Ó Riordáin, J. J. *Kiskeam Versus the Empire*. Tralee: The Kerryman, 1985.

O'Sullivan, Donal J. *The Irish Constabularies, 1822-1922: A Century of Policing in Ireland*. Dingle: Brandon Books, 1999.

Spillane, Denis. 'Rathmore: E Company, 5th Battalion: Kerry No. 2 Brigade,' *Journal of Cumann Luachra*, 1983.

Spindler, Captain Karl. *The Mystery of the Casement Ship*. Tralee: Anvil Books, 1965.

Stack, Austin. 'Landing of Casement,' the *Kerry Champion*, 31 August–21 September 1929.

_____. 'Thomas Ághas: The Story of a Noble Life and Heroic Death,' the *Kerry Champion*, 29 September 1928.

Younger, Calton. *Ireland's Civil War*. London: Frederick Muller, 1968.

INDEX

1916 (Easter) Rising, 8, 15, 60, 84-5, 91-2, 114, 115, 121, 145-6
  plans for Rising in Kerry, 61-4
  Rising aborted in Kerry, 92-3
  aftermath of Rising in Kerry, 95-8
Adams, Lieutenant C. F., 290
Ahern, Jack, 204, 270, 271, 279, 321
Ahern, Michael, 194
Aherne, Paddy, 204
Aiken, Frank, 377
Allen, Sergeant James, 225
Allman, Dan, 281, 289-93
Allman, Patrick, 223
Andrews, Constable John H., 276
Anglo-Irish Treaty negotiations, 325-8, 331
Anglo-Irish Treaty, 331-4
Ashe, Nora, 121
Ashe, Thomas, 8-9, 15, 16, 114-5, 116, 118, 125, 143, 144
  commander in 1916 Rising, 91-2
  arrest, hunger strike and death, 120-122, 123
Asquith, Herbert J., 15, 41, 64-5, 97, 100
Associated Press, 230
Aud, the, 14, 65, 66, 67, 68, 69, 70-2, 84, 99
  scuttled, 85
Auxiliaries, 259-60, 269, 270, 273, 274-5, 278-9, 286-7, 295-6, 196-7, 298-9, 301-2, 303, 316, 325
  on the rampage after killing of Mackinnon, 303-4
  impose curfew on Cahirciveen, 315-6

Bailey, Daniel (Sergeant Julian Beverley), 66, 69, 73, 74, 75, 85, 86-7, 98
Bailey, James, 46
Bailey, Timothy, 173
Baily, Jim, 208-9, 289, 292
Baily, John, 94, 95
Balfour, Arthur J., 57
Ballymacelligott creamery controversy, 170-5
Ballymacelligott, Battle of, 257-9, 264
Ballyseedy massacre, 369-71
Barrett, Edward, 266
Barrett, J. J., 378
Barrett, James, 301
Barrett, Tommy, 302
Barry, Ed., 96, 101, 108
Barry, Kevin, execution of, 224, 228
Barry, Paddy, 157
Barry, Tom, 10, 375
Barton Robert, 331, 344, 349
Barton, Detective Sergeant Johnny, 167
Beanney, County Inspector William, 218-20, 263
Beaslaí, Piaras, 145, 150, 153, 165, 166, 316
Beasley, Maurice, 119, 123
Behan, Father William, 306-7
Bell, Alan, 169, 182
Bell, Patrick, 305
Benson, Head Constable Francis, 296, 314, 315
Benson, Sergeant, 170-1

Berkely, Colonel, 263, 300
Black and Tans, 183, 203, 209, 215, 217, 267, 268-9, 276-7, 278-9, 285, 287, 288, 295-6, 297, 303, 304, 310-11, 312-3, 321-2, 340, 342-3
  burn property in reprisal, 221, 288-90, 308
  on the rampage, 221-3, 225-7, 311, 314-5, 341
  impose reign of terror in Tralee, 228-48
Bloody Sunday (Dublin), 228
Blythe, Ernest, 36, 40, 48, 51, 54, 123, 147, 214
Boland, Gerry, 105
Boland, Harry, 120, 150, 163
Boland, John Pius, MP, 43, 152
Bouchier, T., 204
Bowler, T., 186
Boyle, Sergeant Martin, 128-30, 137-40
Breen, Dan (Tipperary), 10, 126, 351
Breen, Dan, 195
Breen, Father Joe, 38, 43, 44, 46, 60
Breen, James, 119
Breen, John, 291
Breen, Professor P., 37
Brehony, Jack, 301
Brennan, Father Charlie, 34, 35, 37, 38, 46
Brennan, Father Patrick J., 226
Brennan, Joseph, 48, 316
Brennan, Tadhg, 68
Breslin, Commandant Edward (Ned), 369, 371, 373, 378
Brick, Constable William, 192
Bright, Constable Ernest, 227
British Campaign in Ireland, The (Townshend), 294
Britten, District Inspector Frederick, 52, 87, 99
Broder, Lar, 301
Brophy, Constable Michael, 124
Brosnan, Con, 270, 271-2, 378

Brosnan, J. (Jack), 204, 208-9, 289, 293
Brosnan, John, 295
Brosnan, Michael, 229, 366
Brosnan, Tadhg (Thady, Timothy), 96, 97, 123, 124, 151, 157, 269, 316-7, 328, 329-30, 352
Brown, Constable Walter T., 310
Brown, Dan, 299
Browne, Bishop Robert, 133
Browne, Con, 117
Browne, Daniel J., 105, 153, 305, 306, 365
Browne, John, 127, 129-30, 279
Browne, Peter, 289, 292, 293
Browne, Robert, 140, 279
Brugha, Cathal, 34, 116, 124, 145, 161, 165, 328, 329, 330, 331, 332, 349
Buckley, Patrick (Paddy), 204, 367, 369
Buckley, Sergeant, 286
Buckley, Stephen, 371
Burke, Captain, 361
Burke, Mick, 204
Burke, Paddy, 186, 289
Burke, Pat, 209
Butler, John, 165
Butler, Sergeant James, 85
Butler, Sergeant, 311
Byrne, Alfie, 110
Byrne, John Charles (alias Jameson), 175-6
Byrne, John, 96, 101, 108, 264
Byrne, Lieutenant John, 90. 93

Cagney, Michael, 291
Cahill, Paddy J., 45, 67, 78, 80, 81, 87, 90, 96, 101, 103, 106, 107, 108, 123, 124, 157, 190, 196-7, 199, 229, 254, 261-2, 270, 284, 285, 306, 316, 323-4, 327-30, 339, 347, 351, 354, 357, 374
  forced to resign, 307
  inquiry into Cahill affair, 328-30

Cahirciveen massacre, 371-2
Calder, Constable Francis D., 276
Cantillon, John, 229
Caomhánach, Seaghán Óg Mac Murch-
    adha, 40
Carey, Hannah, 321
Carmody, Eddie, 239, 254, 335
Carmody, Jack, 204, 259
Carmody, Maurice (Moss), 127, 139-
    40, 174, 186, 208-9, 256, 289
Carroll, Jack, 300
Caseley, Albert, 225
Casement, Roger, 8, 14, 63, 72, 75,
    86, 145
    career in consular service, 57
    involved in nationalist movement,
        57-8
    seeks German help, 58-9, 63-4
    tries to stop 1916 Rising, 64-5
    travels to Ireland by submarine, 66
    arrives at Banna beach, 69-70
    under arrest, 76-81, 85
    trial, 99-101
Casement's Last Adventure (Monteith),
    75, 87, 90
Casey, Con, 324, 365
Casey, Father Jeremiah, 306
Casey, Jeremiah, 364, 372
'Cat and Mouse Act', the,124
Central News, the 243
Charman, Sergeant Arthur E., 276
Childers, Erskine, 39
Churchill, Winston, 201-2, 319
Civil War, beginning of, 352
Civil War, the, 7, 8, 10, 11, 352-78
Claidheamh Soluis, An, 213
Clann na nGael, 58, 59
Clapp, Constable Samuel, 310
Clapp, Constable William, 310
Clarke, Captain Jim, 369
Clarke, Constable, 170
Clarke, Sergeant, 217, 262, 263
Clarke, Tom, 59
Cleary, Constable, 98, 216
Cleary, Thomas, 295

Clifford, Billy, 256
Clifford, Constable Martin, 189
Clifford, Denis W., 188
Clifford, John, 366
Clifford, Thomas (Tom), 157, 191-2,
    222, 285, 286, 328
Clonbanin ambush, the, 281-4, 323
Coffey, Dr Bryan McMahon, 47
Coffey, Jim, 158, 289, 291, 292
Colgan, Constable, 194, 195
Colgan, Michael, 238
Colivet, Con, 63
Collery, Sergeant James, 317
Collins, Con, 69, 75-6, 80, 84, 94,
    98, 115, 145
Collins, James, 204
Collins, Martin, 99
Collins, Michael, 9, 79, 91, 102, 109,
    120-1, 123, 125, 134-5, 158, 159,
    160, 179, 182-3, 192, 196-200,
    213-4, 256, 270, 284-5, 299, 305-
    6, 319-20, 326-30, 331-4, 335, 338-
    9, 343, 346-50, 351-2, 357-61
    reorganises IRB and nominates
        prisoners for election, 114-5
    view of Austin Stack,143-4, 147
    assumes control over Sinn Féin and
        the Volunteers, 144-150
    masterminds 1918 general election,
        150-1
    develops counter-intelligence net-
        work, 160-1
    policy disagreements with de Valera,
        161
    frustrated by moderates in Sinn
        Féin, 162-3
    profits by de Valera's absence in
        America, 164, 166
    arranges escape of Austin Stack
        form jail, 166
    a wanted man, 167-8, 169, 175-6,
        183-4
    military tactics, 214
    pro-Treaty speeches disrupted in
        Kerry, 347-8

questioned on Treaty, 349-50
Collins, Father Edward Hyacinth, OP, 233, 305-6
Connell, Bridie, 315
Connell, Michael, 204
Connolly, James, 81, 82, 91
Connolly, Seán, 145
Connor, Michael, 238
Connor, Patcheen, 302
Connor, T., 259
Connor, Timothy (Tim), 204, 238
Conroy, J., 151
Conscription Act, the, 125
   opposition to, 126-35
Considine, Constable John, 128-9
Conway, John, 229, 239, 240
Cooney, Andy, 307, 324, 328, 347
Cooney, Constable Joseph, 216, 17
Cork Examiner, the, 221-2, 227, 236-8, 267, 304, 308, 315
Corkery, Dermot, 101
Corridan, Patrick, 194
Cosgrave, William T., 119, 134, 331-2, 333
Costello, Special Crimes Sergeant Michael, 261
Cotton, Alfred W., 60, 96
Coughlan, Constable James J., 229-30, 239
Counihan, James, 97
Counihan, Jim, 33
Countess Bridge massacre, 371
Courtney, Dan, 309
Courtney, P., 33
Crane, Charles P., 163-4, 176-7
Crean, Diarmuid, 34, 35, 36, 38, 151
Crean, Sergeant Cornelius, 190-1
Crean, Tom, 165, 190, 218
Cregan, Con, 204
Cregan, Ned, 204
Cronin, Christy, 186
Cronin, Denis (Din) Batt, 289, 309
Cronin, Jerry, 317
Cronin, John, 127, 137-40, 180, 181, 186, 209, 255, 289, 309

Cronin, Michael, 186
Cronin, Pat, 309
Cronin, Patrick, 289
Crosbie, Captain Talbot, 37
Crowley, Eddie, 308
Crowley, Fred H., 308
Crowley, James, 150, 153, 316, 339
Crowley, Sergeant Daniel, 76
Culleton, 'Big' Paddy, 287
Cumann na mBan, 89, 90, 118
Cumann na Poblachta, 344
Cummins, Brigadier General (Colonel Commandant), Hanway R., 281-4
Cunningham, George, 301
Curragh Mutiny, the, 36
Curran, John, 37
Curtayne, Father, 193

Dáil Éireann (First Dáil), 159
Dáil Éireann, 16
Daily Chronicle, the, 147-8
Daily News, the, 230, 233, 234, 240, 243, 249, 251, 252
Dalton, Paddy, 312-3
Daly, Charlie, 181, 204
Daly, Cornelius W., 274
Daly, Denis (Dinny), 82-3, 84, 101, 103, 118, 158, 307, 327
Daly, James J., 366
Daly, James, 173
Daly, John, 367, 369
Daly, Tom, 181
Daly, Willie, 302-3
Danaher, R. M., 136
Dark Secret of Bealnablath, The (Twohig), 359-60
Darlington, Constable, 185
De Marsillac, M. de, 235-6
de Valera, Éamon, 8-9, 16, 45, 92, 114-5, 116, 118-9, 131, 133, 134, 160-162, 319-20, 326-7, 331-3, 335-7, 343-6, 353, 375
   elected President of Sinn Féin, 123
   seeks international recognition for Ireland, 161

Dean, Paddy, 301
Deasy, Liam, 330
Dee, Con, 279, 312-3
Defence of Ireland Fund, the, 38-9
Defence of the Realm Act, 50, 53, 55, 62, 77, 78, 109, 120, 137
Dennehy, Denis, 157
Dennehy, Tom, 46, 95, 151, 193, 237
Denning, Constable Michael, 128
Dent, Constable, 321
Derrig, Tom, 105
Devane, R., 157
Devane, Thomas, 365
Devlin, Joseph (Joe), 131, 247, 248-9, 251
Devoy, John, 58, 59, 63
Diggins, Bill, 255
Dillon, John, 40-1, 46, 131
Dillon, Tom, 158
Dines, L. H., 218
Document No. 2, 335-6
Dodd, Dr, 216
Doherty, Robert 'Bobs', 360-1
Dolan, Joe, 347, 348
Donoghue, Daniel, 371
Donoghue, Jer, 371
Donovan, Timothy, 221
Doran, John, 1511
Dowling, J., 216
Dowling, William, 258
Doyle, Michael (Mick), 78, 96, 101, 157
Drummy, William, 48, 96
Duffy, County Inspector Jimmy, 261-2, 263
Duggan, Eamonn, 349
Duggan, Jim, 206
Duggan, Johnny, 181, 186, 371
Duggan, Matt, 181
Duhig, Michael, 97
Duke, Henry E., 119
Dunne, Captin Michael, 368
Dunne, Joe, 96
Dyne, Constable Robert, 310

Easter Rising, see 1916 Rising
Edwards, Major, 233, 238-9, 241-2
Egan, Constable, 170
Egan, Michael, 132
Egan, Timmy, 300
Ennis, Sergeant, 371
Evans, Herbert, 225
Evening Mail, the, 86

Falkiner, Walter, 288
Fallon, Constable Patrick, 128-30, 137-40
Fallon, District Inspector Michael, 215-6
Falvey, Stephen, 223
Farmer, William, 96, 101, 108
Farmolie, Constable, 321
Farrell, Dan, 271
Farrell, John, 165
Fenton, Thomas, 171
Ferris, Father William, 193, 306
Figgis, Darrell, 39, 123, 148
Finn, Dan, 45, 96
Finucane, Father, 153
First Southern Division established, 307
Fisher, Sir Warren, 166
Fitzgerald, Constable Michael, 211
Fitzgerald, Desmond, 36, 37, 48, 51, 117, 332
Fitzgerald, Dick, 51, 97, 101, 103, 108, 109, 153
Fitzgerald, John 'Cousy', 318
Fitzgerald, John, 49
Fitzgerald, Maurice, 171
Fitzgerald, Paddy Paul, 216, 316-7, 355, 358, 374
Fitzgerald, Paddy, 204
Fitzgerald, Thomas (Castleisland), 96
Fitzgerald, Thomas (Dingle), 101
Fitzgerald, Thomas C., 218
Fitzgibbon, Seán, 63
Flaherty, Constable, 185
Flavin Daniel J., 136, 308
Flavin, Jack, 356

Flavin, Michael J., MP, 43, 46, 104, 106, 107, 110-12, 119, 152
Fleming, C., 33
Fleming, Jack, 238
Fleming, Michael, 157, 317
Fleming, Tom, 289
Flood, Captain Ed, 369
Flynn, Jack 'the Fiddler', 317
Flynn, John, 127, 320-1
Flynn, Maurice, 67
Flynn, Michael, 165
Flynn, Seán, 289
Foley, Bishop Patrick, 133
Foley, Constable Paddy, 189-90
Foley, Constable, 317
Foley, Jeremiah J., 308
Foley, John, 123, 124
Foley, Thomas, 123-4, 238
Four Courts occupation, the, 352
Free State army captures Tralee, 356-7
Free State coastal landing at Fenit, 354-6
Free State coastal landing at Kenmare, 358-9
Freedom Club, the, 60
Freeman's Journal, the, 111, 113, 242, 244-6, 246-7
French, Lord, 134, 169
Frobes Redmond, Detective Inspector W. C., 5-6
Frongoch internment camp, 101-13, 127
Fuller, Stephen, 11, 369, 370, 377-8

Gaelic Athletic Association (GAA), the, 34, 104, 108, 143
Gaelic League, the, 33, 46, 60, 91-2, 144
Gaelic-American, the, 109
Gallagher, Constable, 335
Galvin, Denis (Dinny), 287, 309-10, 348, 349
Galvin, Jack, 363-4
Galvin, Jeremiah,, 277

Galvin, Maurice (Moss), 181, 186, 209, 289
Galvin, Mick, 300-1
Galvin, Patrick, 194
Galvin, Private Michael, 368
Garvey, Sergeant Denis, 192
Gaughan, Father J. Anthony, 35, 80
Geaney, John, 36
general election (Southern Parliament), May 1921, 316
German Plot, the, 134-5
Gleeson, Edward J., 35-6, 54, 136
Goodwin J., 97
Goodwin, Frank, 97
Gorbey, Constable Robert, 224
Gorman, Mary, 69, 99
Gortatlea Barracks, first attack, 9, 11, 16, 126-30, 279, 320
Gortatlea Barracks, second attack, 17, 179-81
Greaney John, 191
Greaney, Edward (Ned), 191, 377
Greene, Pádraig, 360
Greenwood, Sir Hamar, 200, 213, 233-4, 235, 239, 242, 248-9, 259
Grey, Sir Edward, 65
Griffin, Constable, 255
Griffin, David, 204
Griffin, David. J., 48, 96
Griffin, Martin, 165
Griffin, Maurice, 96, 104
Griffin, Michael, 165
Griffith, Arthur, 114-5, 123, 131, 134, 320, 326-7, 331, 333-4, 358
Guiney, D., 49
Gwynn, Stephen, 49

Hamilton, Constable,170-1
Hanafin, Jerry, 238, 341, 343
Hanafin, Michael, 341
Hanafin, Percy, 340-2, 343
Hanlon, James, 366
Hargrave, Dr A. A., 239, 302-3
Harrington, Niall C., 354, 372
Hartnett, Mossie, 204

Hartnett, Patrick, 369
Hartnett, Philip, 204
Harty, Roger, 286
Hatfield, Constable, 311-2
Hathaway, Reginald, 377
Hayes, Canon, 36
Headford ambush, the, 289-95
Healy, Captain Michael J., 48
Healy, Daniel, 78, 96, 101, 107-8, 111, 112,123, 124, 157, 192, 289, 290
Healy, James Cornelius, 302
Healy, T. M., 122
Healy, Tim,. MP, 110, 132
Heard, County Inspector, 136
Hearn, Sergeant John Thomas, 76-8, 99
Hegarty, Constable, 181
Herlihy, Donal, 277
Herlihy, Jack, 186, 289
Herlihy, Michael, 277
Herlihy, Paddy, 257
Herlihy, William, 258
Heygate-Lambert, Colonel F. A., 103
Hickey, Constable Steve, 310
Hill, Frank, 303
Hill, J., 33
Hill, William, 173
Hillyer, Constablel Alfred, 310
Hoare, Constable James, 275
Hobson, Bulmer, 81
Hogan, Eugene, 317
Hogan, Moss, 288
Hogan, P. J., 96, 101, 108
Holland, Constable, 170
Holmes, Constable, 220
Holmes, Divisional Commissioner Philip A., 275-6, 281-2
Home Rule Bill, 42
Horan, David, 204
Horan, Eamonn, A., 306-7, 358
Horan, John, 101
Horan, Ned, 124, 307
Horgan, M., 223
Horgan, Pat, 33

Horgan, Tadhg, 33
Horgan, William (Willie), 97, 101, 108, 295
Houlihan, Catherine, 225
Houlihan, James, 225
Houlihan, John, 225, 239, 240
Howlett, Constable George H., 279
Howlett, Sergeant, 191
Howth gun-running, 13, 39, 50
Hudson, Richard, 261
Huggard, William, 188
Hughes, Constable Thomas, 211
Hunter, Thomas, 116
Hurley, William, 314
Hutchingson, Clifford, 258-9
Hyde, Douglas
Hyde, Seán, 361, 362

In the Name of the Game (Barrett), 378
IRA (Irish Republican Army), 193, 200, 203, 204, 205, 206, 216, 217, 227, 267, 280, 284, 287, 296, 311-2
   raids mail trains, 220
   flying columns, 216, 274, 281, 288-9, 296
   attempts to consolidate brigades, 323-4
   recommissioned, 330
Ireland in 1921 (Street), 294
Irish Independent, the, 105-6, 149-50, 259, 267, 304, 315, 344, 346
Irish Parliamentary Party, the, 36, 38, 42, 43, 46, 47, 95, 125, 126, 131-2, 134, 153, 154
Irish Republic, The (Macardle), 10, 228
Irish Republican Brotherhood (IRB), the, 34, 38, 56, 58, 60, 84, 114, 118, 307, 334, 347, 348, 351
Irish Times, The, 236, 238, 247, 294, 342, 346, 359
Irish Volunteer, the, 73
Irish Volunteers, 8, 13-14, 49-51, 56, 59, 60, 62-3, 73, 81, 84, 88, 91, 92, 114, 117, 118, 121, 124, 127, 146, 157, 196, 216, 219-20

established in Kerry, 33-41
split in 1914, 41, 43, 44-5, 49
Irish Volunteers Dependants' Fund,
104-5

Jeffers, Dan, 216, 285, 317, 324-5
Johnson, Tom, 132
Johnston, Constable Edward, 256
Jones, Servelus, 96
Journal, Le, 230, 235-6

Kalem Film Company, 39
Kane, James, 318-9
Keane, John, 136
Keane, Laurence, 173
Keane, Thomas, 37
Kearney, Head Constable John, 49,
78-9, 86, 95
Keating, Con, 82, 83, 84, 145
Kee, Robert, 378
Kelliher, Jeremiah, 36
Kelliher, Maurice, 47
Kelliher, Michael J., 277
Kelly, Constable, 181
Kelly, Paddy, 302, 307
Kenmare recaptured by IRA forces
361-2
Kennedy, James, 97
Kennedy, John J., 155
Kennedy, Paddy, 154, 155, 217-8,
261, 262
Kennedy, Patrick J., 154
Kennedy, Patrick T., 154
Kennedy, Patrick, 155
Kennedy, Timothy P. (Tim)., 11, 105,
154, 155, 158-9, 168-9, 183-4, 189-
90, 198-200, 217, 224, 238, 261-3,
284-5, 298-300, 305-7, 324, 327-
30, 334, 351-2, 374-5
develops intelligence network in
Kerry
liaison officer with British during
Truce, 323
Kennelly, Tom, 274, 279-80
Kenny, Constable, 170-1

Kenny, James, 136
Keogh, Constable Maurice, 169-70
Keogh, John, 281
Kerry Advocate, the, 48
Kerry Evening Post, the, 49, 86, 100
Kerry Landing (Harrington), 354
Kerry Leader, the, 349
Kerry People, the, 48, 194, 236, 251-
2, 316, 341, 342, 343
Kerry Sentinel, the, 47
Kerry's Fighting Story (The *Kerryman*),
11, 252
Kerryman, the, 11, 44, 47, 53, 54-5,
96, 103, 104-5, 106, 108, 118, 153,
217, 236, 304, 308, 324, 348-9
Kiely, J., 204
Kiernan, Helen, 120
Kiernan, Kitty, 120
Kiernan, Maud, 120
Kilgannon, Constable, 315
Killarney Echo, the, 108
Kilmichael ambush, the, 228
Kilmorna House, 301
Kitchener, Lord, 43
Knightly. Michael (Mike), 101, 103,
327
Knocknagoshel ambush, the, 368

Lacey, Jim, 204
Lady Wicklow, the, 354-5
Laide, Richard, 127, 129-30
Landers, Bill, 376
Landers, Patrick, 135, 157
Lavelle, Constable, 185, 220
Lawlor, D Michael,, 117
Lawlor, Edward, 136
Lawlor, Jack, 117
Lawlor, John, 364
Leahy, Tommy,204
Leary, Jerry, 204
Leary, Mick, 186, 204, 309
Leen, Edward, 35, 37
Leen, John, 173, 175, 209, 264
Leen, Michael, 173
Lenihan, Arthur, 93

Lenihan, John B., 289, 309
Lennon, Philip, 192
Leslie,W. J., 275
Lewes Jail, 114, 115
Libau, the, *see Aud*
Liberator, the, 136, 275, 304, 308
Liston, T. J., 47, 374
Lloyd George, David, 116, 117, 125, 132, 150, 182, 201-2, 256, 319
Logue, Cardinal Michael, 133
London Evening News, the, 230, 235-6
Lonergan, J., 238
Looney, Edward, 238
Lord Listowel's land, 135-7
Lovett, Maurice, 223
Lynch, Father John, 145
Lynch, Fionán, 117, 118, 123, 145, 146, 150, 153, 316, 327, 338-9, 347
Lynch, James, 136
Lynch, Liam, 307, 330, 331, 334, 347, 362, 366, 375
Lynch, Paddy, 289
Lyne, Father, 131
Lyne, T., 33
Lyons, Constable James F., 119-20
Lyons, Jerry, 312-3
Lyons, Jimmy, 356
Lyons, Tomothy 'Aero', 377

McAlister, R., 258
Macardle, Dorothy, 10, 228, 294
McAuliffe, David, 204
McAuliffe, Jim, 204
McAuliffe, Willie, 277
McCarthy, Constable Daniel, 189, 227
McCarthy, Dan, 147, 204
McCarthy, David (Dave) (Castle-island), 186, 187, 289
McCarthy, David (Rathmore), 309
McCarthy, Davie, 204
McCarthy, Denny, 204
McCarthy, Eddie, 181, 186
McCarthy, John, 69, 76, 99
McCarthy, Liam 'Sonny', 295-6, 297, 314

McCarthy, Lieutenant, 372
McCarthy, Martin, 204
McCarthy, Myra T., 144, 168
McCarthy, Ned, 180
McCarthy, Neilus, 289
McCarthy, Thomas. J., 96, 101, 104, 106, 108
McCarthy, Timothy, 291
McCaughey, District Inspector Michael F,, 317
MacCollum, Fionán, 144, 191, 226
MacCollum, Miss, 118
MacCollum, Una, 42
McCormack, Constable Joseph S., 317
McCormack, Sergeant Thomas, 310
MacCurtain, Tomás, 182
MacDermott, Seán, 38, 62, 63, 67, 145, 146
MacDonagh, Sergeant, 176
McDonnell, Canon John, 227
McDonnell, Dr, 151
McDonnell, Patrick, 223
McElligott, Garret, 173
McElligott, M. P., 36
McElligott, Patrick, 222
McElligott, Thomas J., 175
McEllistrim, Jack, 257
McEllistrim, Jerry, 303
McEllistrim, Tom, 10-11, 90, 92-3, 96, 101, 108, 127-30, 137-9, 179-81, 186, 187, 196, 197, 206, 208-9, 226, 254-6, 257-8, 273-42, 281-4, 289-90, 292-3, 295, 304, 317-8, 321, 351, 354, 356, 373-4
McEnery, Jim, 377
MacEoin, Seán, 147, 148, 150-1
McGaley, Jack, 53, 123, 124
McGarry, Seán, 115
McGlynn, Captain Mike, 355-6
McGrath, Joe, 357
McGrath, Tommy, 377
MacGregor, Mr, 230, 231, 234-5
McGuinness, Colonel J., 362, 372
McGuinness, Joe, 114-6
McInerney, Tom, 82, 83, 96

McKenna, Daniel, 218

McKenna, Jack, 36, 117, 135, 137

McKenna, Michael, 97

McKenna, Sergeant Francis J., 124, 194-5

Mackinnon, Major John A., 264-5, 286, 288, 301-2, 304, 314

McLoughlin, Constable, 98

McMahon, John, 257

McMahon, Matthew, 33-4, 45

McMahon, Michael (Mick), 216, 317

McMahon, Thomas, 96

McNamara, James (Jim), 176, 355, 374-5

MacNeill, Eoin, 13, 14, 41, 43, 45, 46, 48, 51, 81, 84-5, 87, 91, 118

Macpherson, Constable, 191

Macready, Sir Nevil, 200, 201-2, 352
    encourages burnings as reprisals, 221

MacRory, Bishop Joseph, 156

McSweeney, William, 96

MacSweeney, Marquis, 54

MacSwiney, Terence, 219, 235
    death on hunger strike, 223, 224, 230

Madden Tom, 76

Madden, Constable William, 224

Maguire, Michael, 242

Maguire, Sam, 158

Maher, John, 335

Mahony, Abel, 97

Mahony, Berty, 204

Mahony, Jack, 204

Mahony, Jim, 204

Mahony, Ned, 204

Maligny, Lieutenant H. A,, 284

Malone, John, 270

Manchester Guardian, the, 230

Manchester Martyrs, the, 50

Mangan, Bishop John, 95

Mangan, J., 33

Mangan, M. E., 151

Mangan, Paddy, 280

Martin, Constable, 206

Martin, Hugh, 230-4, 243-4, 249-51, 252-3

Mason, Jack, 302

Maunsell, Michael, 165

Meade, Constable Cornelius P., 304

Mee, Constable Jeremiah, 210, 211, 213-4

Melinn, Joe, 45, 78, 96, 101, 157

Military Pact, the, 351

Mills, Inspector John (DMP), 116

Molloy, District Inspector, 136

Moloney, Sergeant Patrick J., 154, 217

Monahan, Charles, 82, 83

Monteith, Capain Robert, 59-60, 63, 66, 69, 73-6, 85-6, 87-90, 92-4, 98

Montreal Gazette, the, 10, 22, 229, 239-40, 242-3, 252, 256

Moore, Thomas, 50

Moran, John, 36

Morgan, Constable George, 225

Moriarty, Bill, 238

Moriarty, Daniel, 218

Moriarty, David, 262

Moriarty, Dr Paddy, 154

Moriarty, Edward, 48

Moriarty, James, 97, 101, 108

Moriarty, Michael, 97, 101, 108, 109, 157

Moriarty, Mossy, 75

Moriarty, Sean, 364

Morley, Con, 309

Moroney, Matthew, 365

Moylan, Bill, 282

Moylan, Seán, 276

Moyles, Constable Thomas, 276

Moyniham, Manus, 309-11

Moynihan, John, 309

Moynihan, P. D., 309, 310

Moynihan, Timothy, 310

Muir, Constable W., 229-30

Mulally, Michael (Mick), 136, 340

Mulcahy, Paddy, 204

Mulcahy, Richard (Dick), 7, 92, 105, 165, 175, 307, 327, 329, 330-1, 364, 372 elected chief of staff of the Volunteers, 124-5

Mulcahy, Risteárd, 7-8

Mullins, William (Billy), 82, 84, 88, 96, 101, 106-7, 108, 123, 124, 157, 192, 358, 374

Mulvihill, Dan, 317

Mulvihill, Patrick, 119

Mulvihill, Roger, 36

Munster Hotel (Dublin), 144, 168

Muphy, Canon Arthur, 37

Murphy, Bertie, 372

Murphy, Con, 101

Murphy, Cornelius (Con), 101, 266-7

Murphy, Denis, 266

Murphy, Dr John M., 181

Murphy, Edward, 136

Murphy, Fintan, 112

Murphy, Herbert, 364

Murphy, Humphrey (Free), 108, 157, 186, 197, 204, 307, 309, 329, 330, 347, 348, 349, 351, 354, 357, 362, 367, 375

Murphy, James Molyneaux, 298

Murphy, Jimmy, 298-9

Murphy, Joseph, 223

Murphy, Michael, 112

Murphy, Sergeant, 203

Murphy, Thomas, 136

Murphy, Tim, 371

Murragh, Lieutenant Joseph, 371

Musgrave, William, 218

My Fight for Irish Freedom (Breen), 126

Myles, Billy, 317

Myles, Jerry, 317, 317

Nagle, Garret, 310

Nagle, George, 376

Nagle, Sardy, 289, 195

National (Irish National) Volunteers, the, 14, 42, 47-8, 49-50, 52-3, 54

foundation of, 41

Neazer, Constable George, 124, 178

Neligan, David (later Colonel David), 198-200, 298, 299, 365, 357-8, 369, 373

Neligan, Maurice, 198

New York Times, The, 10, 22, 229, 234, 239, 242, 278

New York World, the, 247-8

No Other Law (O'Donoghue), 357

Nolan, Charles, 314

Nolan, Leslie, 223

Nolan, Michael, 196

Nolan, Mrs Charles, 305

Nolan, Tom, 104

North Kerry Flying Column, 312, 321

Oates, Sergeant Bernard, 164-5, 178

O'Brien, Joseph, 96

O'Brien, Michael, 178

O'Brien, Mike, 363

O'Brien, William, 40-1, 132

Ó Cadhlaigh, Cormac, 144-5

O'Callaghan, J., 101

O'Casey, Sean, 33, 51

O'Connell, Constable J. J., 164, 165

O'Connell, Denis J., 48

O'Connell, General J. J., 352

O'Connell, J. D, 151

O'Connell, Jeremiah, 316

O'Connell, Michael, 369

O'Connell, Mortimer, 101, 118, 146

O'Connell, Mrs Jeremiah, 118

O'Connell, Sir Morgan, 51-2, 55, 56

O'Connor, Eamonn, 38, 45, 191-2, 223, 237

O'Connor, Batt, 101, 102, 103, 105, 144, 175, 184

O'Connor, Brian (Gortglass), 96

O'Connor, Brian (Scartaglin), 96-7

O'Connor, Chief Justice James, 147

O'Connor, Conway, 376-7

O'Connor, David, 186

O'Connor, Davie, 204

O'Connor, Dermot, 365

O'Connor, District Inspector Bernard, 180

O'Connor, Dr Michael, 136

O'Connor, J. T, 94

O'Connor, Jack, 309

O'Connor, James, 275

O'Connor, Jerry 'Unkey', 317

O'Connor, Jim, 205

O'Connor, John (Waterford), 369

O'Connor, John 'The Hawk', 154

O'Connor, Johnny, 11, 181, 182, 186, 196, 206, 209, 265, 288, 289, 290, 291, 292-3, 294, 353, 356, 371

O'Connor, Lieutenant Paddy 'Pats', 367-8

O'Connor, Michael, 97

O'Connor, Michael. J., 44, 45, 51, 78, 95-6, 97, 101, 107, 108, 111, 112

O'Connor, Mortimer, 97, 101, 192

O'Connor, Pat (Ned), 309

O'Connor, Pat, 186

O'Connor, Patrick (Pa, Pat), 181, 87, 204

O'Connor, Patrick, 187

O'Connor, Patrick, 310

O'Connor, Pats, 367

O'Connor, Private Laurence, 368

O'Connor, Rory, 166, 351

O'Connor, Seamus, 364, 367, 368

O'Connor, Simon, 229, 239-40

O'Connor, T., 223

O'Connor, T. M., 204,

O'Connor, T. P., MP, 212, 239-40, 246

O'Connor, T. T., 36, 96

O'Connor, Thomas (Ballymacelligott), 96, 101, 209

O'Connor, Thomas, 194

O'Connor, Thomas, 310

O'Connor, Tom 'Scarteen', 289, 292, 358-9, 361

O'Connor, Tom, 157

O'Connor, Tom, 317

O'Connor, W. H., 36, 48, 117

O'Daly, Brigadier (Major) Paddy, 354, 359, 368-9, 372, 373-4

O'Doherty (Doherty), Floss, 118, 146, 157

O'Donnell, Alexander, 192

O'Donnell, J. D., 105, 192

O'Donnell, J. P., 96, 151

O'Donnell, J., 96

O'Donnell, John, 69

O'Donnell, Tom (MP), 36, 38, 41, 42-4, 46-7, 49, 51, 52, 54, 106-7, 225

withdraws from 1918 election contest, 152-3

O'Donoghue, Donnchadh. 302, 317

O'Donoghue, Florence (Florrie), 261, 307, 310, 357

O'Donoghue, Michael, 360

O'Donoghue, N. F., 51

O'Donoghue, Paddy, 159

O'Donoghue, Patrick (missing)

O'Donoghue, Patrick, 291

O'Donoghue, Thomas, 97, 101, 316

O'Donoghue, Tim, 289

O'Donoghue, Tomás, 280, 329, 339

O'Donovan, Constable John, 211

O'Driscoll, Daniel, 301

O'Driscoll, Pat, 76

O'Duffy, Owen (Eoin), 7, 192, 330, 331, 374

speech in Bandon, 7

O'Farrell, J. T., 278

Offman, Frank, 256

O'Flaherty, Father, 93-4

Ó h-Annrachán, Peadar, 144

Óglach, An t-, 147, 214

O'Grady, B., 157

O'Grady, Christy, 267-9, 286-7, 304, 305, 308, 311-2, 314-5, 317, 320, 321-2, 323, 325

O'Grady, Daniel (Dan), 270, 271, 279

O'Grady, Dónalín, 300

O'Grady, Stephen, 222

O'Hegarty, Diarmuid, 146, 150

O'Higgins, Kevin, 347, 372
O'Keeffe, Pádraic, 197
O'Kelly, Seán T., 105
O'Leary, Con, 309
O'Leary, Jeremiah, 186
O'Leary, Michael, 180, 255
O'Leary, Michael, 289
O'Leary, Michael (Mike), 317, 267
O'Leary, Monsignor David, 174, 297, 348
O'Leary, Mort, 67, 68
O'Loughlin, Colm, 82, 83
O'Loughlin, Denny, 305
O'Mahony, Dan, 49, 78, 96, 101, 111, 157, 197, 204
O'Mahony, John 'Boxer', 299-300
O'Malley, Captin Tyrell, 238, 243, 284, 298, 300, 334-5
O'Malley, Ernie, 362
O'Mara, Tim, 289
O'Neill, E., 218
O'Neill, Lawrence, 131
O'Rahilly, The, 15, 35, 56, 89, 311
killed in 1916 Rising
O'Regan, Constable, 203
O'Reilly, Constable John Bernard, 76-7, 188-9
O'Reilly, Jack, 101
O'Riordan, Jeremiah (Cahirciveen), 316
O'Riordan, Jeremiah, 158, 307, 309
O'Rourke, J., 46
O'Rourke, Mícheál, 261
O'Rourke, Sergeant Thomas, 124, 158, 159, 261
O'Shaughnessy, Mark, 282
O'Shea, Dan, 376
O'Shea, Daniel, 97
O'Shea, George, 369, 370, 378
O'Shea, J. E., 151
O'Shea, J., 33
O'Shea, James J., 48
O'Shea, John Francis, 97, 101, 109
O'Shea, Michael, 170
O'Shea, Pat (Catlegregory), 67-8, 192

O'Shea, Pat (Kenmare), 289
O'Shea, Patrick (Pat) (Killarney), 97, 101, 108, 157-8
O'Shea, Patrick, 377
O'Shea, Tim, 152
O'Shea, T. P., 194, 195
O'Shee, John M. Poer, County Inspector, 209-10, 212
Ó Siochfhradha, Pádraig ('An Seabhac'), 33, 144, 151, 157, 191
O'Sullivan, 'Big' Dan, 317
O'Sullivan, Bishop Charles, 131
O'Sullivan, Captain, 289, 295
O'Sullivan, Dan P., 289
O'Sullivan, Denis, 157, 209, 289
O'Sullivan, District Inspector Tobias, 254, 270-2, 273, 300, 318
O'Sullivan, Father Charles, 211
O'Sullivan, Gearóid, 145, 14
O'Sullivan, James, 119
O'Sullivan, John A., 218
O'Sullivan, John L., 317
O'Sullivan, John, 301
O'Sullivan, John, 317
O'Sullivan, Maurice, 204
O'Sullivan, Michael J., 51, 101
O'Sullivan, Morty, 117
O'Sullivan, Peter, 289
O'Sullivan, T. D., 136
O'Sullivan, T., 107
O'Sullivan, Thomas (Old Tom), 308-10
O'Sullivan, Tim, 96
O'Sullivan, Timothy M., MP, 43, 152
O'Sullivan, Ulick, 254-5, 256
O'Sullivan, William D. F, 33
O'Sullivan, William, 36, 37, 271

Partridge, William T., 52, 82, 84
Pearse, Mrs Margaret, 118
Pearse, Pádraig, 13, 14, 37, 50, 60, 80, 81, 84, 85, 118, 214
Pearse, Willie, 118
Pendy, Margaret, 159
Perry, Corporal, 268

Phelan, Constable James, 310
Pierce, Mrs Anne, 194
Plunkett, Count, 123
Plunkett, Joseph Mary, 64, 69
Plunkett, Philomena, 68
Porter, Constable 311-2
Portland Prison, 111
Prendergast, J., 238
Prendeville, Denis (Din/Denny), 180,
    181, 186, 204, 255, 309
Prendeville, Jack, 204, 309
Prendeville, Jim, 204
Prendeville, Thomas, 364
Prevention of Crimes Act, 164
Price, Eamonn (Bob), 286, 372
Prior, Constable, 220
Purtill, John, 35
Purtill, Mick, 280, 300

Quill, Denis, 279
Quill, Martin,
Quinlan, Constable Michael, 124
Quinlan, P. J., 117
Quinlisk, Timothy A., 167-8, 176
Quirk, Constable John, 317
Quirke, Bill, 375
Quirke, J., 238

Rabbit, Constable, 194
Rael, Constable, 206-7
Rahilly, Mick, 309
Ralph, G., 238
Ralph, William, 238
Rathmore Barracks, attack on, 215
Raymond, Constable, 313
Rearden, Dick, 204
Redmond, John, 13, 36, 40-1, 42, 43,
    44-5, 48, 51, 52, 53, 56, 148, 348
    Woodenbridge speech, 1914, 41, 42,
    43
Redmond, Willie, 49, 118
Reen, Denis J., 309
Reen, Denis, 309
Regan, Sergeant James, 124
Reid, Harold, 356

Reidy, Constable Thomas, 225
Reidy, Jim, 255
Reidy, John, 48
Reidy, Martin, 173
Reidy, Maurice, 127, 264, 304
Reidy, Michael, 96
Reidy, Paddy, 186, 209
Reilly, Constable, 76-8, 99
'Republic of Munster', the, 353
Restrick, Sergeant, 86-7
Rice, John Joe, 158, 293, 307, 330,
    347, 353, 362, 363, 373, 375
Ring, Eugene J., 48
Ring, Timothy, 97, 101, 109
Riordan, Detective Inspector, 169
Riordan, Jerome, 118
Riordan, Jim, 98
Riordan, Johnny, 301
Riordan, P., 157
Robinson, David, 361, 362-3, 364
Roche, Captain James, 165
Roche, David, 153
Roche, James, 204
Roche, Sergeant Phil, 267-8
abandon isolated barracks, 179
Royal Irish Constabulary (RIC), 53,
    79, 119, 123, 156, 164, 176, 177,
    217, 220, 227, 229, 315
demoralised, 183
social ostracisation, 161, 201, 219
attacks on barracks and personnel,
    185-6, 216-7, 218-9, 220-1, 297
mass resignations, 183, 209
burning of evacuated barracks, 188-
    9. 220
viewed as criminals by people, 193
develop siege mentality, 208
Listowel mutiny, 209-214
under severe strain, 215
attacks on RIC after execution of
    Kevin Berry, 224-7
have to choose between Tans and
    IRA, 260-2
Russell, Seán, 331
Russell, Tom, 124

Ruttle, Sam, 96
Ryan, Constable Michael, 152
Ryan, Desmond, 214
Ryan, Father Finbar, 305
Ryan, Father Frank, 81, 85
Ryan, Jim, 105
Ryle, Maurice P., 35, 47-8, 49

Scanlon, Dan, 119
Scannell, Stephen, 356
Scully, Liam, 270
Scully, Michael, 279
Shanahan, Dr Mikey, 78-9, 105, 257, 341, 371
Shanahan, Jack, 289, 292
Shanahan, Paddy, 264
Shanahan, Tom, 280
Sharry, Patrick, 136
Shea, 'Dingle', 287
Shea, Constable, 181
Sheehan, Bartholomew, 316
Sheehan, Donal, 82, 83
Sheehan, Jack, 270, 271-2, 301, 321
Sheehan, James, 360
Sheehy, John Joe, 238, 267, 299, 356, 378
Sheehy, Morgan, 136
Sheehy, Tommy, 302
Sheehy-Skeffington, Hannah, 163
Sheeran, Constable Patrick, 211
Shortis, Patrick, 91
Sinn Féin, 46, 47, 55, 114, 115, 123, 125, 131, 134, 146, 147-8, 162, 174, 219-20, 222, 226, 277-8, 287, 344
    Food Committee, 135-6, 137
    contests November 1918 general election, 150-3
    victorious in 1918 election, 153-4
    banned, 166
Slattery, Edmond B., 173-4
Slattery, F. B., 47
Slattery, James, 178
Slattery, Jeremiah M., 46, 172
Slattery, Maurice, 283
Slattery, Patrick, 314

Slattery, Thomas, 34, 48, 96, 101, 104, 106, 108, 151, 191-2, 236, 287, 356
Slattery, Timothy, 94-5
Slieve Bloom, the, 97
Smith, Head Constable, 313
Smith, Sergeant Patrick, 165-6
Smuts, Jan Christian, 319
Smyth, Lieutenant Colonel Gerald Brice Ferguson, 209, 210-12, 213, 214-5, 275, 319
Soloheadbeg ambush, the, 10, 11, 16, 126, 158-9
Spicer, George, 73-5
Spicer, Hanna, 74-5, 76
Spillane, Jim, 180
Spillane, Michael (Mick), 33, 51, 56, 97, 101, 157, 165
Spillane, Timothy, 165
Spindler, Captain Karl, 65-6, 69, 70-2, 85
Spring, Henry, 97, 101, 108, 153
Stack, Austin, 9, 34-5, 39, 45, 48, 49, 51, 60, 67, 74-6, 82, 87, 94, 96, 104, 111, 117, 118, 121, 125, 148, 149, 150-1, 160, 162, 184, 214, 298, 299, 316, 319-20, 326-7, 328-9, 330-2, 333, 334, 361, 375
    decides not to rescue Casement, 80
    arrested 80-1
    tried and sentenced to life imprisonment, 98
    leads campaign in Belfast Prison for political status, 141-3, 151-2, 155-6
    relationship with Michael Collins, 143-4, 197-8
    elected MP, 153
    escapes from jail, 166
    becomes Minister for Home Affairs, 168-9
    incompetence, 197-9
    opposes Treaty in the Dáil, 336-8
Stack, Dan, 138-9
Stack, John, 119

Stack, Moore, 34
Stack, Nicholas, 111, 141
Stafford Military Detention Centre, 98
Stapleton, Captain Joseph, 368
Storey, Head Constable William K., 311
Strangeways Jail, 166
Street, C. J., 294
Strickland, General, 284, 313
Sugrue, Denis, 165
Sugrue, James, 97, 135, 314
Sugrue, Joe, 307, 317
Sullivan, Cornelius, 174
Sullivan, H., 158
Sullivan, Jack, 159
Sullivan, Jeremiah, 50
Sullivan, Jerry, 205
Sullivan, Michael John, 33, 97, 108, 157
Sullivan, Mick, 310
Sullivan, Serjeant Alexander. M., 16, 17, 79, 120, 172-4, 298
Summers, J., 37
Sunday Independent, the, 87
Sweetman, Paul, 271

Tangney, Tom, 302
Taylor, Joseph, 279
Thornton, Hugh, 109
Times, The, 55, 130, 234, 239
Toronto Globe and Mail, the, 241
Townshend, Charles, 294
Tracy, Constable, 191
Tralee, Battle of *see* Battle of Bally-macelligott
Tralee, Black and Tan terror in, 228-53
Trant, Father Timothy, 172, 174, 303
Traynor, Oscar, 105
Truce (Anglo-Irish) of July 1921, 7, 319-20, 321
    eve of Truce violence, 320-1
    violations, 334-5, 340-3

Trucileers, 7, 323, 325
Tudor, General Henry, 183, 201
Turner, Constable Archibald, 255
Toureengarriv ambush, the, 275-6, 282 284, 323
Twohig, Father Patrick, 359
Twomey, Liam, 360
Twomey, Tim, 369

Ulster Volunteer Force, The, 33, 38

Vale, Joseph, 96
Vale, Tommy, 238
Vaughan, John, 310
Vaughan, Timothy, 277
Vicars, Sir Arthur, 300, 301, 308, 312
Von Papen, Franz, 58

Wakefield Prison, 97-8, 104, 127
Wall, James (Jimmy), 101, 108, 374
Wall, Tommy, 235, 239, 240
Walsh, District Inspector Tom, 154, 155
Walsh, Ellen, 229
Walsh, Father Edmond, 190
Walsh, Florence, 96
Walsh, J. R., 308
Walsh, James (Currow), 372
Walsh, James, 369
Walsh, John, 152, 154
Walsh, John, 194
Walsh, M., 46
Walsh, Michael, 218
Walsh, Ned Joe, 279
Walsh, Paddy, 194
Walsh, Paddy, 312-3
Walsh, Thomas (T. J.), 136, 137, 273,
Walsh, Tim, 257
Walsh, Tomás, 152, 154, 155
Waters, Constable Patrick, 227
Watson, Captain, 272, 300-1
Wharton, Sergeant, 166-7
Whelan, Lieutenant Patrick, 89
White, Patrick, 266

Will, Constable George F., 215

Williams, Pat 'Belty', 260, 265, 302, 340, 343, 353, 354, 363, 376

Wilson, President Woodrow, 99-100, 117, 161

Wimbourne, Lord, 134

Windrim, Sam, 82, 83

Woodcock, Constable Hedley, 310

Woods, Constable James Thomas, 255

Woodward, Bert, 227

Wormwood Scrubs, 106, 127

Wynne, Edward M., 165, 195-6

Yorkshire Post, the, 258